COSTUME

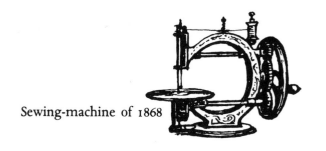

Sewing-machine of 1868

written and illustrated by

IN DETAIL

Women's dress 1730–1930

NANCY BRADFIELD
A.R.C.A., O.B.E.

NEW EDITION

ERIC DOBBY PUBLISHING

First published in Great Britain 1968

© Nancy Sayer 1968 1981 1997 2001 2003 2005

All rights reserved.
No part of this publication may be reproduced
in any form or by any means without the
permission of
Eric Dobby Publishing Limited
4 The Old School
South Street
Barming
Kent ME 16 9EY
England

ISBN: 1-85882-038-3

Printed by Sino Publishing House in Hong Kong

INTRODUCTION

Some of the most fascinating garments which have survived in England are those on the wax effigies preserved in the Undercroft of Westminster Abbey.

For hundreds of years it was customary for these life-sized, fully robed figures of wood or wax to be borne through the streets, on the coffin, at the funeral of kings or queens or other great persons. The faces were either a carefully modelled likeness or a death-mask, and they were dressed, in most cases, entirely in the robes and underwear of the person they represented.

This custom was still observed into the 18th c., and the last effigy to be actually so carried was that of Catherine, Duchess of Buckingham, in 1743.

The outer robes on these amazingly lifelike figures can be seen and studied, but not so the undergarments; these were last seen in 1933, when the effigies were cleaned, and for anyone interested in the subject the photographs taken then are rather remarkable.

Throughout the country there are many items of dress still preserved, hidden away and seldom seen, although rare examples, in time, usually do find their way to museums, where they can be viewed and enjoyed by the public. Few 16th and 17th c. materials survive to the present day, but from the 18th c. onwards quite a number of men's and women's garments exist.

Usually it is a woman's garments that are kept, a wedding or an evening dress, because of the beauty of the material, or for sentimental reasons. But these, by themselves, are not sufficient to give a true picture of the fashion of the period; a simple morning or afternoon dress can often play as important a role as the most elaborate bridal gown.

Women's dress presents a greater variety, both in cut and cloth; the changes in fashion are more rapid and their underwear intriguing. The inside of a dress is often as interesting as the outside, and at times more complicated, and to understand a period dress fully, a knowledge of the inside, with the correct foundation and underwear, is essential.

These studies, then, are entirely from private collections; only a mere handful have ever been exhibited or seen by the general public. Several are too frail or too soiled ever to be put on view, and for that reason I have studied them in detail before their delicate charm is rotted away and lost to us for all time.

At first I had intended to include men's wear, but found that either the book would be too large or that many women's pages would have to be omitted.

In order to appreciate the fluctuation in fashion a period of two hundred years at least seems to be necessary; even then what I have shown is only a selection; much has had to be left out, and many important and interesting accessories only touched on.

The Charles Wade Collection at Snowshill Manor, now a property of the National Trust, proved a valuable starting-point for local research, and from there the circle widened.

One day, when examining dresses stored at Chastleton House, some ten miles distant from

Snowshill, I experienced one of those exciting moments that do occasionally occur in such a study as this. Folded away at the bottom of a drawer containing examples of lace, was a dark purple-black gauze with a delicate leaf pattern. Thinking it was perhaps a shawl, I shook it out, and, to my surprise, found it was a complete gauze over-dress, with the huge sleeves of the 1830's. It was carried with delight to the room where I was working. While making my study of it something seemed vaguely familiar; then I noticed the very narrow piping in purple-black satin, strangely speckled in pale brown, which I knew I had seen before. Some two years earlier I had drawn a satin under-dress with large puffed sleeves, and with it a matching embroidered reticule; both were of exactly this same material. The speckled appearance had intrigued me. Was it a faulty dye, as seemed most likely, or was it by design? The gauze must surely pair with the under-dress in the Snowshill Collection. This proved to be true, and Chastleton House generously relinquished, on an indefinite loan, this elegant and charming gauze, so that the dress might once more be complete.

Thinking it over afterwards, we decided that the lady of the house of over a century ago must have kept the gauze with her other examples of lace, but had perhaps given away to her favourite maid the plain satin under-dress; years later, by some strange chance, this had found its way into Charles Wade's Collection.

During all these years of research one thing has been quite outstanding: I have met such charming people, who have welcomed me into their homes with warmth and kindness at every turn. I cannot thank them sufficiently for all their interest and help; without it this study would never have been completed. But even more I want to thank my husband Harold Sayer and my daughter Wendy, who have given me unfailing support always, and who have endured 'costume' for 'breakfast, dinner, tea—and supper.'

NANCY BRADFIELD

ACKNOWLEDGMENTS

My sincere thanks are due to the following, for dresses, accessories, advice, and help in various forms: Gordon Bennett, T. Stanley Brown, Mrs A. Cartwright, Miss A. Chatwin, Mr and Mrs A. Clutton-Brock, Paul Crosfield, Curator of Snowshill Manor, Miss A. Eccles, Mrs J. Fison, Lady Caroline Baroness Friesen, Donald Hall, the late Mrs V. Hands, Miss N. Hawker, Commander Hart, Mrs J. B. Hooton, Mrs M. J. King, Miss P. Lewis, Librarian of Gloucestershire College of Art, Mrs M. Macbeth, Mrs M. S. Mallam, Mrs M. Martin, H. W. Maxwell, previously Curator of Snowshill Manor, John E. Nelmes, F. Norris, Miss J. Proctor, Miss Ursula Radford, Richard Radway, Gordon Ramsden, Mrs Wickham Steed, the late Captain E. G. Spencer-Churchill, Lawrence E. Tanner, C.V.O., F.S.A., Librarian, Westminster Abbey, Miss Freda Wills, Mrs Gwen White, the Dean and Chapter of Westminster Abbey, and the Victoria and Albert Museum.

NANCY BRADFIELD

CONTENTS

1735–36 From part of the painting *The Marriage Contract*, by Hogarth. The white sack-backed gown of the future bride has richly embroidered cuffs and robings. Squanderfield wears a blue coat, the huge cuffs of brocade, matching his long and full-skirted waistcoat.

1775 Family group by Zoffany. The young girl is dressed in pink with a plumed headdress, the elder lady is in grey and white, the man in grey, his coat lined in red silk. The painting of this unknown family was exhibited 1891 by Lady Sarah Spencer at the R.A., but later sold.

c. 1796 From two large separate paintings at Stackpole Court, of John, 1st Baron Cawdor, by Joshua Reynolds, and of Caroline, Baroness Cawdor, daughter of the 5th Earl of Carlisle, by Sir W. Beechey. She wears white muslin; his red coat has fur cuffs and is fur-lined.

1

1730–1800

For seventy years the hooped petticoat supports, yet dominates, women's dress; in various forms it determines the spread of the skirts, in much the same way as did the farthingale of the mid-16th c. and the crinoline of the 19th c. During the first ten years of the 18th c. a small bustle pad is tied under the dress, emphasizing the looped-back draperies of the over-skirt, and it remains in use under Court dress for many years, as can be seen by the Coronation robes on the effigy of the Duchess of Buckingham, made in 1735, although the hooped petticoat has appeared in 1710.

This early foundation of cane or whalebone distends the petticoat into a dome shape, which by 1740–'50's flattens front and back, spreading out fan-wise towards the hem. An oval-shaped hoop with the width on each hip is fashionable in 1740's–'60's, surviving for Court wear as late as 1820. A bell-shaped hoop is found throughout this period until c. 1780, when bustle pads again became popular for some years, diminishing in size during the '80's.

Materials play a great part in the cut and style of the dress. The rich silks and stiff brocades of the first half of the century show to fine advantage over the wide spreading hooped foundations, but with thinner silks, and later the printed cottons, dresses are looped up in various ways, giving the popular polonaise of the 1770's to early '80's.

One dress which gives full display to these lovely silks is the sack-backed gown, fashionable for over fifty years until 1780. Although worn from c. 1720, it was, in fact, known much earlier than this. It originated in France, and Pepys' comment in his Diary on March 2nd, 1669, is now well known.

Finally, by the turn of the century, with printed cottons and plain white muslins, women's dress is transformed into figure-clinging draperies.

Many accessories are needed to give a complete picture of the period; some survive, others do not. Such tiny items as patches on the face were once important to some women's toilet. First used early in the 17th c., mentioned by Pepys in the 1660's, they become most fashionable in the 1770's, and are apparently still used late in the 18th c. In *The Lady's Monthly Museum*, Dec. 1st, 1799, there is a letter 'informing all the Fair Ladies in Great Britain, that I have formed a selection of Characteristic and Secret Patches, which I design for their service . . . and I shall with pleasure show them where to place them with effect, if they will apply at my Miroir Salle in Bond Street.' This is signed 'THE FLAPPER,' a word that takes the mind immediately to the 20th c. But many things happen in the world of dress between 1799 and 1920.

1730-40

Green and pink silk striped floral brocade, open robe with wide, loose sleeves and deep cuffs below the elbow. Front folds on bodice are missing. Bodice is linen-lined, sleeves half lined in green silk. A rich, heavy brocade, coarsely sewn together. Separate 18th-c. boned stomacher, with steel band across front and pocket in lining. *Snowshill Collection*

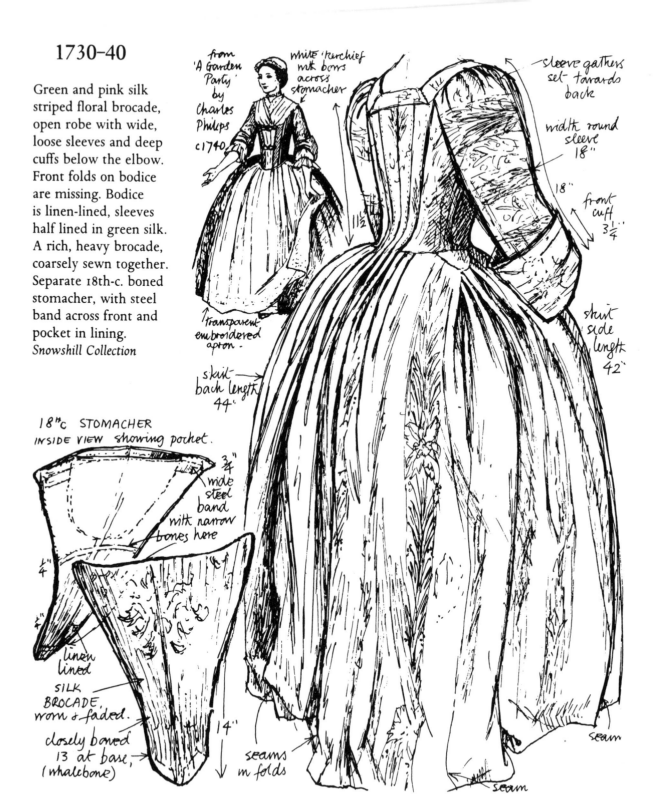

from 'A Garden Party' by Charles Philips c1740

white 'kerchief with bows across stomacher

transparent embroidered apron.

sleeve gathers set towards back

width round sleeve 18"

18"

front cuff 3¼"

1½"

skirt back length 44"

skirt side length 42"

18ᵗʰc STOMACHER INSIDE VIEW showing pocket.

3¾" wide steel band with narrow bones here

4¼"

linen lined

SILK BROCADE, worn & faded.

closely boned 13 at base, (whalebone)

14"

seams in folds

seam

seam

During the 1730's dresses are plain and untrimmed, with long fitting bodice sewn to a wide fully gathered or pleated skirt, worn over a dome-shaped hooped petticoat. By the '40's the skirt widens and opens in front to show the petticoat. The bodice usually has folded back edges

3

from
'The Governess'
by Chardin
1739

white cap & kerchief

white apron with bib front over a blue & lilac striped gown

Bodice lined white linen with fold at front edge A–B

brocade front folded edges are missing

sleeves lined green silk top half only

one seam in sleeve 6" long

back cuff 6¼"

A

B

skirt front length 44"

back skirt

front skirt

seams

INSIDE!
pleats sewn to LINEN LINING

silk

5"

5"

alteration to bodice

CENTRE BACK

pleating to centre.

selvedge

seams →

3¼"

2¾"

dark green foliage & pink flowers

2¾"

2"

pale green foliage & pink flowers

width of brocade 22"; mustard yellow threads in selvedge

with a separate stomacher. The example shown here does not match this dress, but it has an interesting feature, the pocket in the lining; this would be for herbs, giving the wearer a pleasant fragrance. Deep cuffs are typical of this date.

4

1735-45

Green silk open robe with deep pleated cuffs and a wide spreading skirt, both of which are characteristic of the early '40's. The silk has a speckled effect, with blue and bright yellow threads and a rectangular pattern of both blue and tiny yellow dots. This dress is neatly sewn; the stomacher is missing.
Snowshill Collection

the English hoop 1748

length back 12"

width round sleeve 15"

centre-back bodice & skirt cut in one

front cuff 1¼

hoops, large but flexible, with handles for lifting -

pleats face towards centre back -

SILK
green ground & yellow dots

yellow

blue

SHOES green silk damask

2¼

Buckled here

8¾ rounded

white kid

leather sole

width of silk 16"

Hogarth's paintings show many dresses of this period. This would have been worn over a hooped petticoat similar to the one shown above, which spreads out sideways. A white neckerchief would have covered the throat and stomacher. A small 'round-eared' cap might have

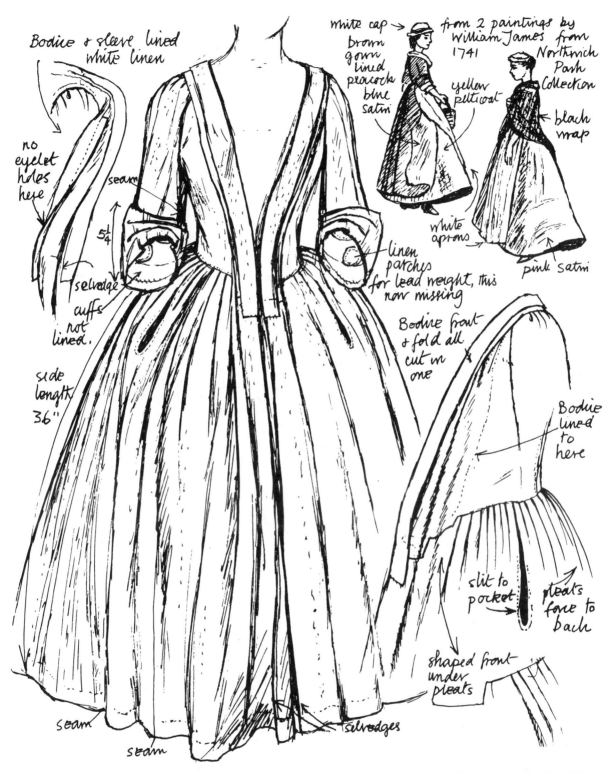

Bodice & sleeve lined white linen

no eyelet holes here

seam

$5\frac{1}{4}$

selvedge
cuffs not lined.

side length 36"

white cap → brown gown lined peacock blue satin

from 2 paintings by William James 1741 from Northwich Park Collection

yellow petticoat

black wrap

white aprons

pink satin

linen patches for lead weight, this now missing

Bodice front & fold all cut in one

Bodice lined to here

slit to pocket

pleats face to back

shaped front under pleats

seam

seam

selvedges

been worn tied with pink ribbon, as in the tiny figure details from William James' *The Old Stocks Market, London*, also an apron, as in his other miniature-like painting of *Fountain Court of the Inner Temple*.

1st half 18th c.

Faded blue damask stays, lacing back and front, 6 seams. Red silk stays, laced back & front, 10 seams, stomacher missing. Green linen stays, back lacing, 6 seams. All narrow-boned and linen-lined. Stockings, knitted, of blue silk, embroidered clocks, sewn seams. Black satin shoes, low heels, black buckles.
Snowshill Collection

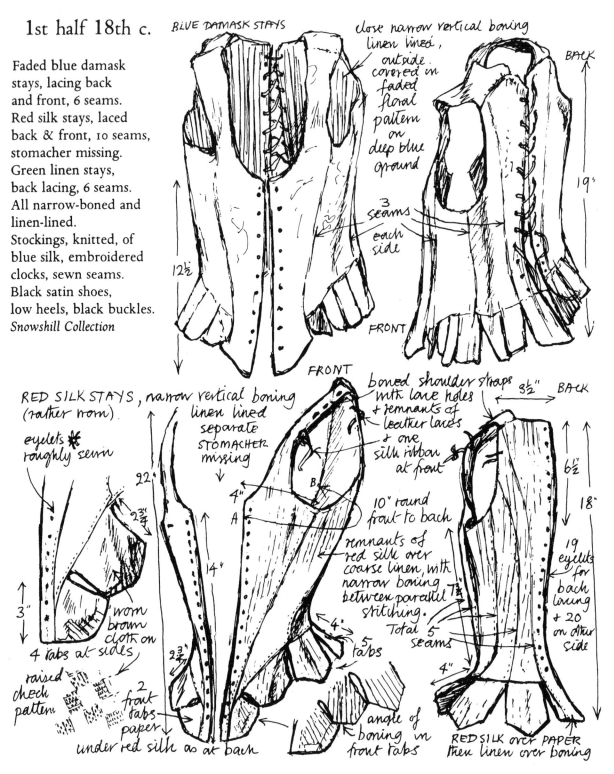

BLUE DAMASK STAYS

close narrow vertical boning linen lined, outside covered in faded floral pattern on deep blue ground

BACK

3 seams each side

19"

12½

FRONT

FRONT

BACK

RED SILK STAYS, narrow vertical boning (rather worn).

eyelets roughly sewn

worn brown cloth on 4 tabs at sides

raised check pattern

3"

2 front tabs

paper under red silk as at back

22"

2¾"

14"

2¾"

linen lined separate STOMACHER missing

4"

A

B

boned shoulder straps with lace holes + remnants of leather laces + one silk ribbon at front

3½"

10" round front to back

remnants of red silk over coarse linen, with narrow boning between parallel stitching.

Total 5 seams

7½"

4"

5 tabs

angle of boning in front tabs

6½"

18"

19 eyelets for back lacing + 20 on other side

4"

RED SILK over PAPER then linen over boning

Few painters have shown underwear as candidly as Hogarth; here we see the chemise, stays, gartered stockings, and shoes. Stays were fairly long but shortened to a higher waistline as the century progressed. They were very closely boned & beautifully sewn, with hardly space for

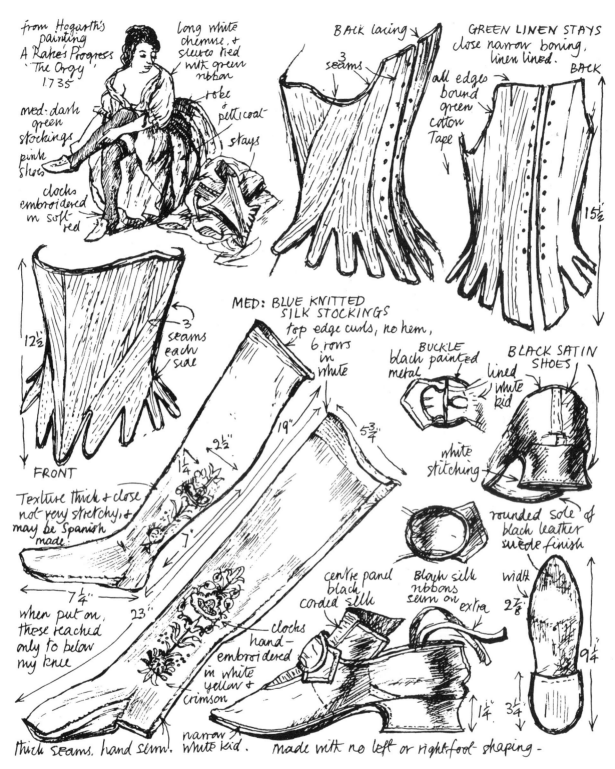

from Hogarth's painting 'A Rake's Progress 'The Orgy', 1735

long white chemise, & sleeves tied with green ribbon

robe & petticoat

stays

med: dark green stockings

pink shoes

clocks embroidered in soft red

BACK lacing

3 seams

GREEN LINEN STAYS close narrow boning, linen lined.

all edges bound green cotton tape

BACK

15½

12½

3 seams each side

FRONT

MED: BLUE KNITTED SILK STOCKINGS top edge curls, no hem, 6 rows in white

Texture thick & close not very stretchy, & may be Spanish made

when put on, these reached only to below my knee

2½"

1¼"

19"

5¾"

7"

7¼"

23"

clocks hand-embroidered in white, yellow & crimson

thick seams. hand sewn.

narrow white kid.

BUCKLE black painted metal

BLACK SATIN SHOES

lined white kid

white stitching

rounded sole of black leather suede finish

centre panel black corded silk

Black silk ribbons sewn on extra

width 2⅞

9¼

made with no left or right foot shaping —

1¼

3¾

the needle between the bones, making them stiff and rigid. Stockings were gartered above or below the knee. The unbending black shoes with wide heavy heels make it obvious why their wearer added the ribbons!

1740-50

Mustard-yellow dress of figured silk, this is a closed robe. Extending wing cuffs with horizontal front pleating, self-faced, lead-weighted. Bodice and sleeves linen-lined, skirt is unlined. Décolletage wide, to tip of the shoulders. Stomacher missing. Ruffles from chemise would show below cuffs.
Snowshill Collection

from Hogarth's painting of the Strode family c. 1745

round eared cap

pink dress & white apron

Bodice back length
12½"

2½"

10"

back cuff 5"

3¾"

8"

pleats face to inverted pleat at side

back skirt 38½"

"petal" pattern of spotted background in yellow & white

hem faced mustard yellow band of woollen cloth ¾"

seam

seam

seam

seam

This figured silk is similar in colour to the rare woollen dress of 1755-75 of mustard-yellow, very fashionable in the 18th c., and worn by men and women. The winged cuffs are of the same shape as the pair in the set of silver lace robings and stomacher shown later;

9

bodice front

$13\frac{1}{2}$

$16\frac{1}{2}''$ front folded edge

linen lined.

width, 1" lead weight covered in silk.

cuffs faced in same yellow figured silk

pleat

Seam

13"

centre front

S

S

S

from the painting by Joseph Highmore 1744 a scene from 'Pamela'

black gauze neckerchief and embroidered robings & winged cuffs

sack-back gown

younger women wear round-eared caps in the '40s.

seam

$7\frac{1}{2}''$

from Hogarth's engraving The Harlot's Progress C1733

she wears long mittens & carries bag & scissors.

length of skirt front 39"

S

seam

seam

embroidered cuffs and robings, occasionally seen in paintings prior to the '50's, are really more usual after this date. As in the two previous dresses, the bodice back pleats and skirt are cut in one length.

1720–50

Riding-jacket, fawn worsted woollen cloth, matching velvet collar and cuffs, buttonholes of silver thread with silver buttons. Bodice and sleeves are lined white linen. Bodice front and skirt faced with pink silk. 1720–50 jacket in yellow patterned silk of 1715–20, but cut later than this and afterwards altered. *Snowshill Collection*

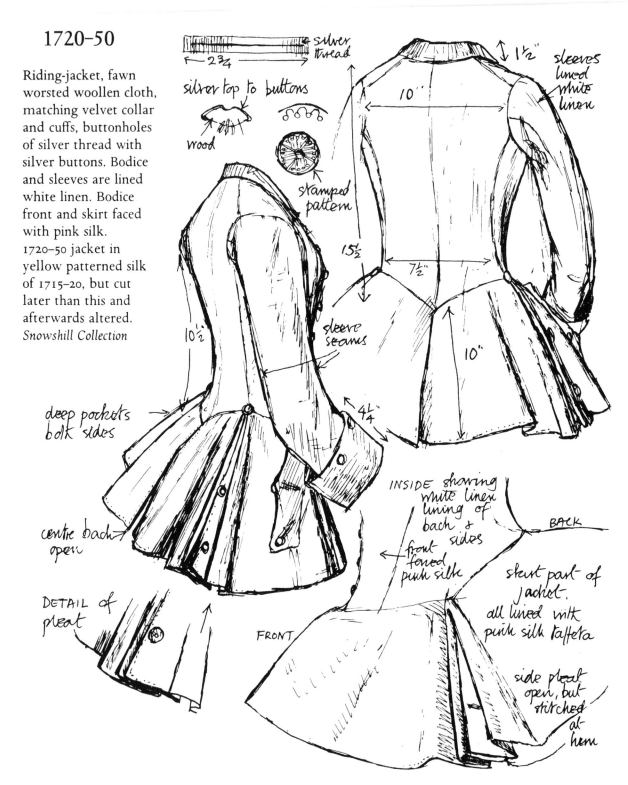

silver thread

silver top to buttons

wood

stamped pattern

↑ 1½" sleeves lined white linen

10"

15½"

7½"

10"

sleeve seams

4¼"

10½"

deep pockets both sides

centre back open

DETAIL of pleat

FRONT

INSIDE showing white linen lining of back & sides

front faced pink silk

BACK

skirt part of jacket, all lined with pink silk taffeta

side pleat open, but stitched at hem

The riding-jacket, long-waisted and slender, followed the masculine fashion, with a deeply pleated skirt, and would probably have been worn with a matching petticoat supported over a hooped petticoat. A three-cornered hat would complete the outfit. Of similar cut is

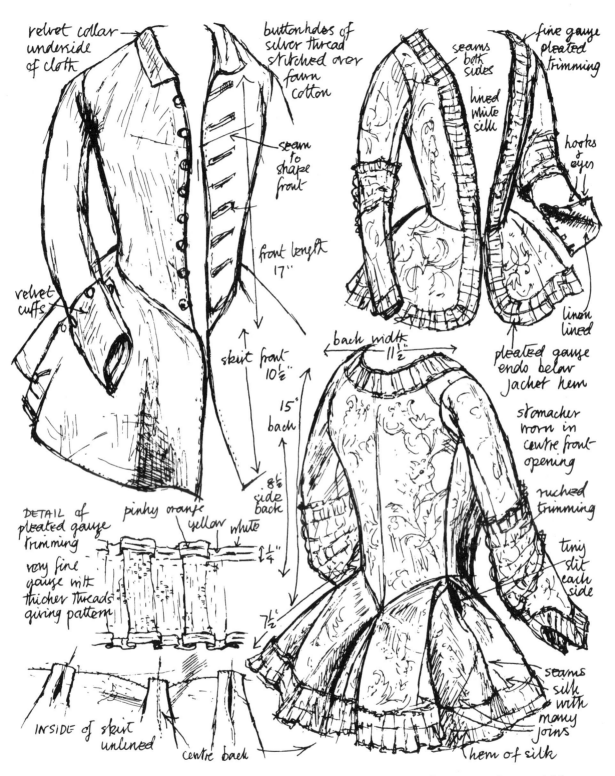

velvet collar
underside
of cloth

buttonholes of
silver thread
stitched over
fawn
cotton

seam
to
shape
front

front length
17"

velvet
cuffs

skirt front
10½"

seams
both
sides

lined
white
silk

fine gauze
pleated
trimming

hooks &
eyes

linen
lined

pleated gauze
ends below
jacket hem

back width
11½"

stomacher
worn in
centre front
opening

ruched
trimming

tiny
slit
each
side

15"
back

8½
side
back

DETAIL of
pleated gauze
trimming

very fine
gauze with
thicker threads
giving pattern

pinky orange
yellow   white

1¼"

7½"

seams
silk
with
many
joins

hem of silk

INSIDE of skirt
unlined

centre back

the richly woven patterned silk of mustard-yellow with pinks, jade-green, white and blue,
made in the style of about 1730–50. The ruched silk gauze trimming and sleeve style suggest
alteration 1770–80.

12

1742-52

Sack-backed gown, 'robe à la française,' blue silk damask, pattern in paler blue and silver-grey, and trimmed with blue ribbon. Décolletage very wide and deep. Bodice front closed, skirt open, with deep pocket slits at sides. All back of gown in full lengths of silk, shoulder to hem. Dress is fully lined. *Snowshill Collection*

from an anon! engraving

published by Robert Sayer c1730

2½"

7½"

1½"

lined white linen

seam 9"

10½" slit to pocket

seam

sleeve trimmed with ruched ribbon

1½"

blue silk ribbon

60"

2½"

satin edge
2 rows of fine threads

s

seam

seam

This richly graceful dress must have been a favourite, as the silk shows considerable signs of wear. The large floral pattern is similar to several other examples found in paintings of the first half of the 18th c. The inside back lacing and deep, wide neckline also point to this

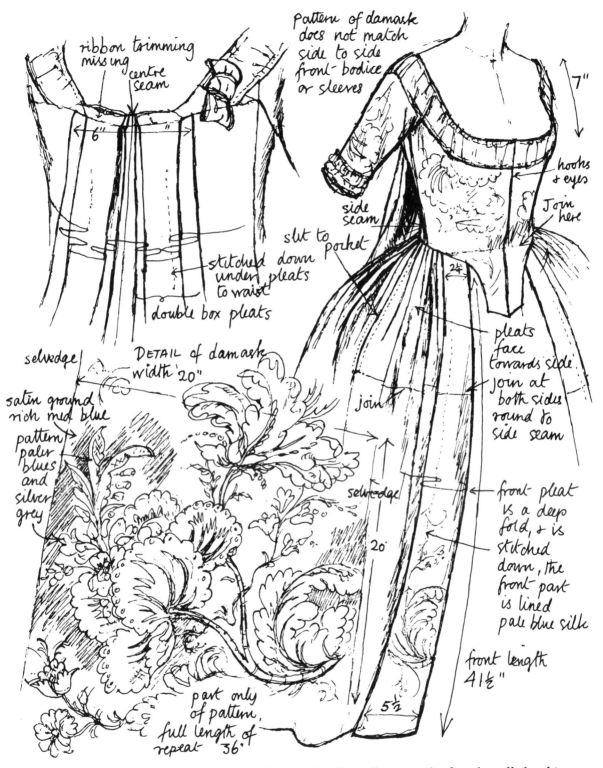

ribbon trimming missing

centre seam

pattern of damask does not match side to side front bodice or sleeves

7"

hooks & eyes

Join here

side seam

slit to pocket

24

stitched down under pleats to waist

double box pleats

pleats face towards side join at both sides round to side seam

selvedge

DETAIL of damask width 20"

satin ground rich mid blue

pattern paler blues and silver grey

join

selvedge

20"

front pleat is a deep fold, & is stitched down, the front part is lined pale blue silk

front length 41½"

part only of pattern, full length of repeat 36"

5½"

sack-backed gown as being the earliest of several in this collection. The fact that all the skirt, as well as the bodice, is lined, obviously has helped in its preservation, and the dull red colour gives warmth to the silk.

14

1742–52

Sack-backed gown of blue silk damask, fitting sleeves, elbow-length, trimmed with blue silk ribbon as on neck opening. Sleeves and bodice lined in white linen, pleats at back lined pink cotton, skirt all fully lined in dull red medium-thick cotton, side-fronts faced thin blue silk. Centre back lining of bodice laced across. *Snowshill Collection*

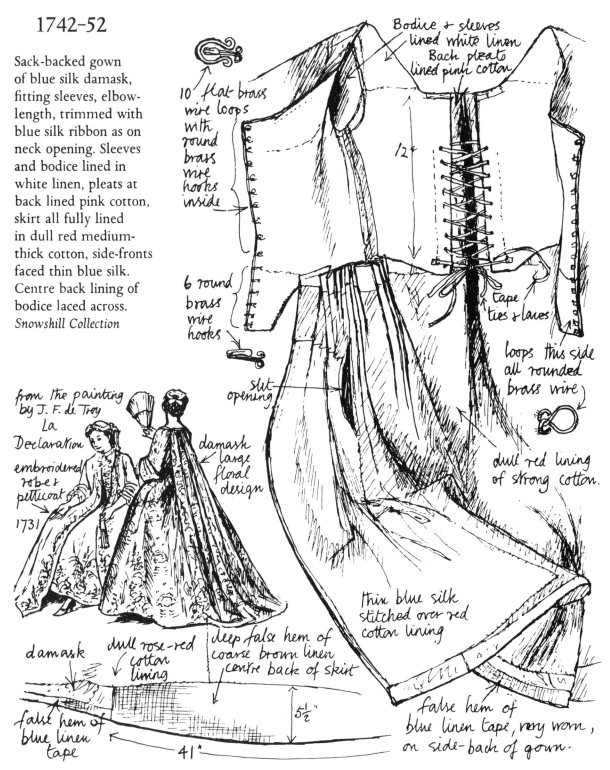

Bodice + sleeves lined white linen
Back pleats lined pink cotton

10 flat brass wire loops with round brass wire hooks inside

12"

6 round brass wire hooks

slit opening

tape ties + laces

loops this side all rounded brass wire

dull red lining of strong cotton.

from the painting by J. F. de Troy La Declaration

embroidered robe + petticoat 1731

damask large floral design

thin blue silk stitched over red cotton lining

damask

dull rose-red cotton lining

deep false hem of coarse brown linen centre back of skirt

false hem of blue linen tape

$5\frac{1}{2}$"

41"

false hem of blue linen tape, very worn, on side-back of gown.

The small figure studies of the women show that a dress of this style would have been worn over side-hoops, similar to those of *c.* 1760 found on the effigy of Queen Elizabeth (see back endpapers) or those on p. 43. The width thus obtained gives full value to the long sweeping

seam

patches here

ruched ribbon.

underside of pleats stitched down

back stitched under pleat

bodice front very worn

2½"

8"

6"

double inverted pleat

seam

pleats face to side seam

stitched bar

seam

seam

1742 child age 10 to 12.

from the painting by Philip Mercier of the Fauconberg Sisters showing similarity of material & style of dress particularly the bodice.

seam

front only lined pale blue silk.

the up-+-down frills are usual on girl's sleeves.

seam

seam

folds from neck to hem, displaying the lovely silk to its full advantage. The number and arrangement of the hooks and eyes on the bodice are interesting, again indicating that this dress must have been worn for some years.

c. 1750

Mustard-yellow robe, figured silk, delicate floral sprays with a tiny spot pattern. The bodice is lined and has stitched eyelets for lacing hidden under the front folds; these have been sewn separately to bodice lining. There are several joins in this rather frail silk; the sleeves have been altered. Yellow satin shoes.
Snowshill Collection

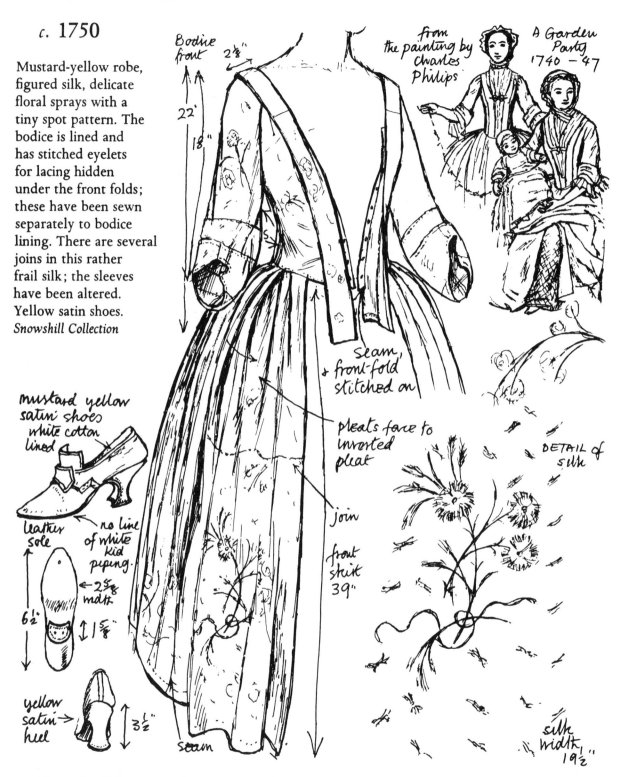

Bodice front

2⅛"

22"

18"

from the painting by Charles Philips

A Garden Party 1740 – 47

seam, + front-fold stitched on

pleats face to inverted pleat

join

front skirt 39"

mustard yellow satin shoes white cotton lined

leather sole

no line of white kid piping

2⅝" width

6½"

↕ 1⅝"

yellow satin heel

3½"

seam

DETAIL of silk

silk width 19½"

The style of this open robe is very simple, with as yet no sign of elaboration and trimmings. It would have been worn over the smaller dome-shaped hoop which became more usual during the '50's. A long apron would have covered the front opening and petticoat, which

The front of this dress would have been laced across a stomacher.

armholes set high & small

bodice & sleeves lined white linen

WAIST 20"

sleeves lined to here

joining seam

no slit to pocket in this dress

yellow silk

strip of linen facing

11" width round sleeve

10"

3"

14½"

3"

5"

seam

seam

seam

seam

The sleeves show signs of alteration, & this dress, like the sack-back is considerably worn.

is now revealed as part of the dress. The bodice here is still long with a low waistline, which rises slightly during the later '50's. Shoes become a little more dainty, with the heels higher and less broad, and the toes more rounded.

1745–55

Pet-en-l'air, or a French jacket; ivory silk brocaded with open flowing flower sprays, in pink, green, dull yellow, white, and pale blue. The lining, which laces inside the centre back, is white linen; the top half of the back pleats is not lined. Fastening with hooks and eyes sewn to tabs forming a stomacher.
Snowshill Collection

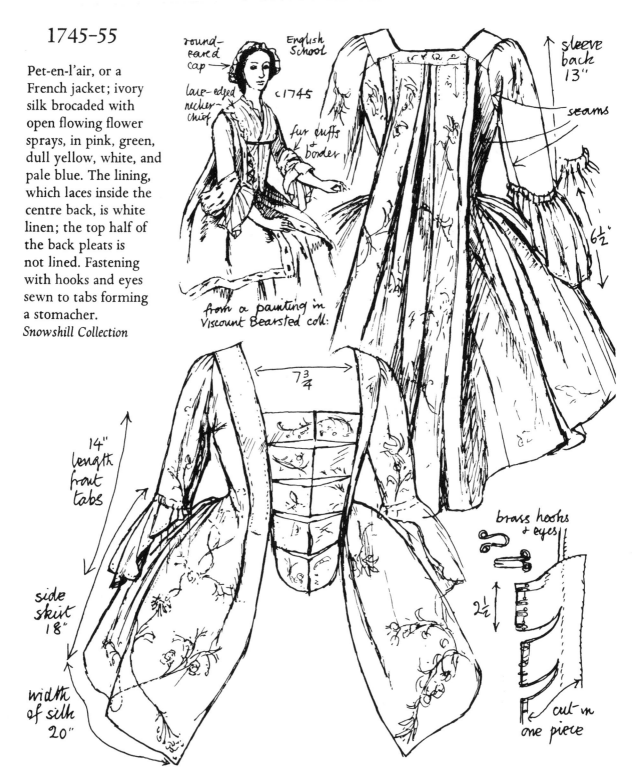

round-eared cap

English School c 1745

lace-edged necker-chief

fur cuffs + border

sleeve back 13"

seams

6½"

from a painting in Viscount Bearsted coll:

7¾

14" length front tabs

side skirt 18"

width of silk 20"

brass hooks + eyes

2½

cut in one piece

The sack-backed jacket, worn over a petticoat and with a kerchief at the neck, was worn in England from about 1745 to 1780, although in France it was in use for some time earlier than this. Such jackets could have sleeves with plain winged cuffs (in the small drawing they

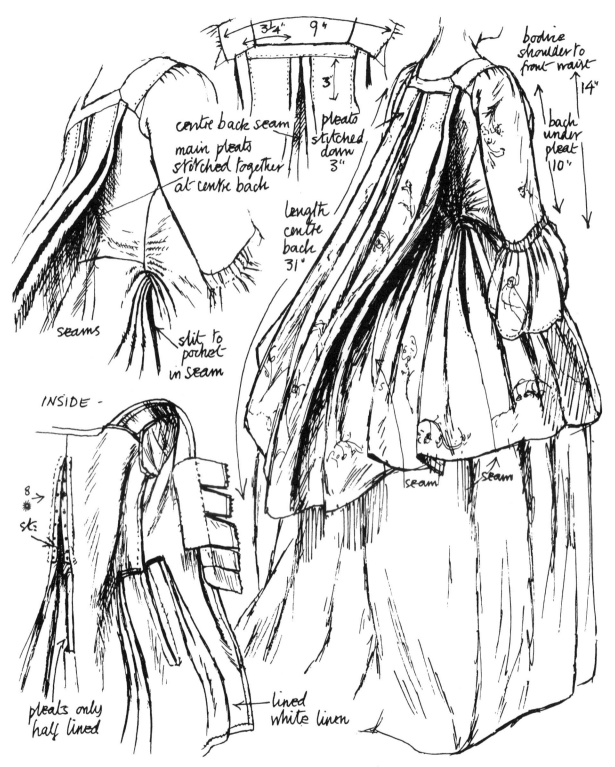

3¼" 9"

3"

centre back seam
main pleats
stitched together
at centre back

pleats
stitched
down
3"

bodice
shoulder to
front waist

14"

back
under
pleat
10"

length
centre
back
31"

seams

slit to
pocket
in seam

INSIDE —

8

sts

seam   seam

pleats only
half lined

lined
white linen

are of fur) or the fan-shaped cuff as here, or, later, bands of frilled or ruched ribbon finished the sleeve. At this date a rounded hoop could have supported the petticoat, and side-hoops would also have been fashionable.

1745-55

White quilted satin hooded jacket with matching petticoat. It is backed with white silk, with a layer of fine wool in between. The jacket and sleeves are lined with white linen, and the bodice is boned, six at the back, two in the front. Fastening at front with hooks and eyes of rounded tin wire. All in a very fragile state. *Snowshill Collection*

quilted flowers at top & side

6"

shaped end to sleeve

1¼"

¾"

DETAIL of quilting

slit to pocket in seam

waist to hem 40½"

seam

seam

seam

This rather rare and very beautiful example of a quilted garment is now quite well known, but owing to its very delicate condition, particularly the petticoat, it is difficult to exhibit. It was made for a stout woman of medium height. The bosom would have been covered with

21

hooks & eyes of rounded tin wire

10 — front & back boned

2 bones

10

2½

15"

sleeve end

linen lining loose at waist with pleats of jacket skirt only, stitched to it.

Tape bound top & ties,

pleats face to opening in centre back petticoat seam

average depth floral motif 18"

narrow hem

seam

seam

seam

centre back 14"

waist

13"

seam

seam

hem to here faced with linen

width round hem 160"

seam

seam

seam

seam

silk width 20"

a kerchief, and ruffles would have shown below the sleeve. The quilting of the floral pattern appears nearly the same, side to side, but the back of the jacket is not symmetrical. A hooped petticoat would have been worn.

22

18th century

An early example of a woman's quilted waistcoat; white linen sewn to a coarse linen with cream silk thread, with fine cording in the quilting.

Blue satin petticoat, quilted in lozenge-shape pattern; two quilted petticoats of blue silk later in date with an elaborate pattern at the hem. Interlinings, cotton and lamb's wool.

Snowshill Collection

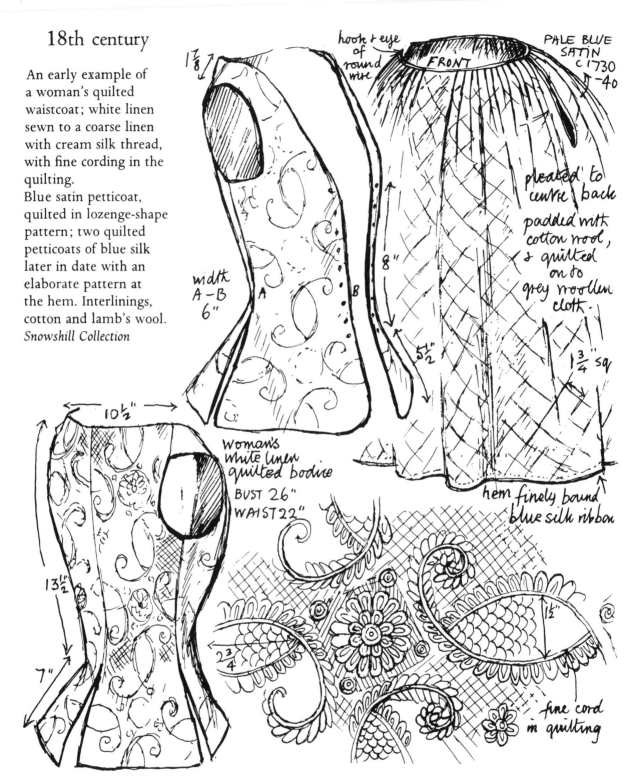

hook + eye of round wire

FRONT

PALE BLUE SATIN c 1730 -40

$1\frac{7}{8}$

width A – B 6"

8"

$5\frac{1}{2}$"

pleated to centre back

padded with cotton wool, & quilted on to grey woollen cloth.

$1\frac{3}{4}$" sq

hem finely bound blue silk ribbon

woman's white linen quilted bodice

BUST 26"

WAIST 22"

$10\frac{1}{2}$"

$13\frac{1}{2}$"

7"

$2\frac{3}{4}$

$1\frac{1}{2}$"

fine cord in quilting

The fine white linen bodice or waistcoat, with its delicate quilting, appears never to have been worn and is in excellent condition. Plain quilted petticoats *c.* 1710 were at first used as an under-garment for warmth. During the '40's, when skirts opened in front to display

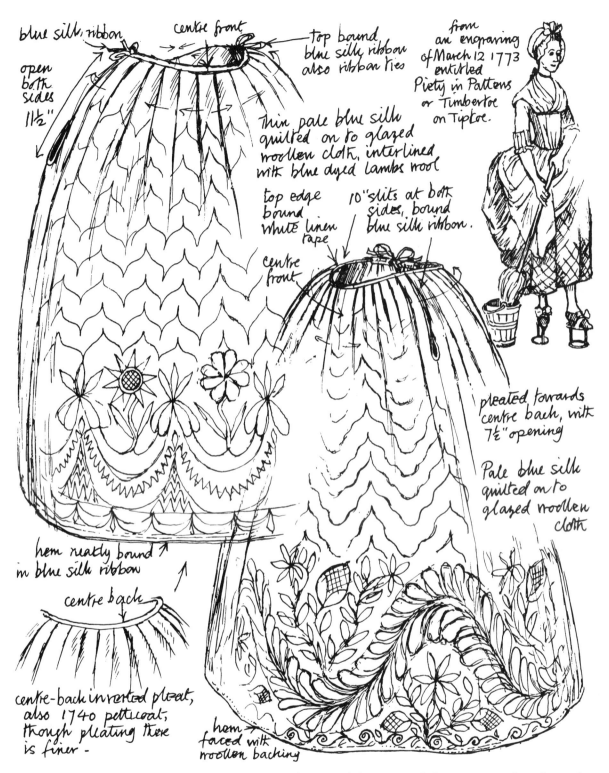

blue silk ribbon

centre front

top bound
blue silk ribbon
also ribbon ties

open
both
sides
11½"

Thin pale blue silk
quilted on to glazed
woollen cloth, interlined
with blue dyed lambs wool

from
an engraving
of March 12 1773
entitled
Piety in Pattens
or Timbertoe
on Tiptoe.

top edge
bound
white linen
tape

10" slits at both
sides, bound
blue silk ribbon.

centre
front

pleated towards
centre back, with
7½" opening

Pale blue silk
quilted on to
glazed woollen
cloth

hem neatly bound
in blue silk ribbon

centre back

centre-back inverted pleat,
also 1740 petticoat,
though pleating there
is finer -

hem
faced with
woollen backing

the petticoat, the quilting became more and more elaborate, and this garment then formed
an important part of the dress, although still called a 'petticoat.' Simple quilting remained
in use for many years, as shown in the print 1773.

1740's–'70's

Elaborate quilted petticoats, in white silk, pink satin, pale blue satin, and a pale fawn satin, with 3 different methods of fastening. Quilted mostly on to a glazed woollen lining (callamanca) and interlined with a layer of fine wool or blue-dyed lamb's wool. One sewn on to a waistband, with fine gathers, at later date. *Snowshill Collection*

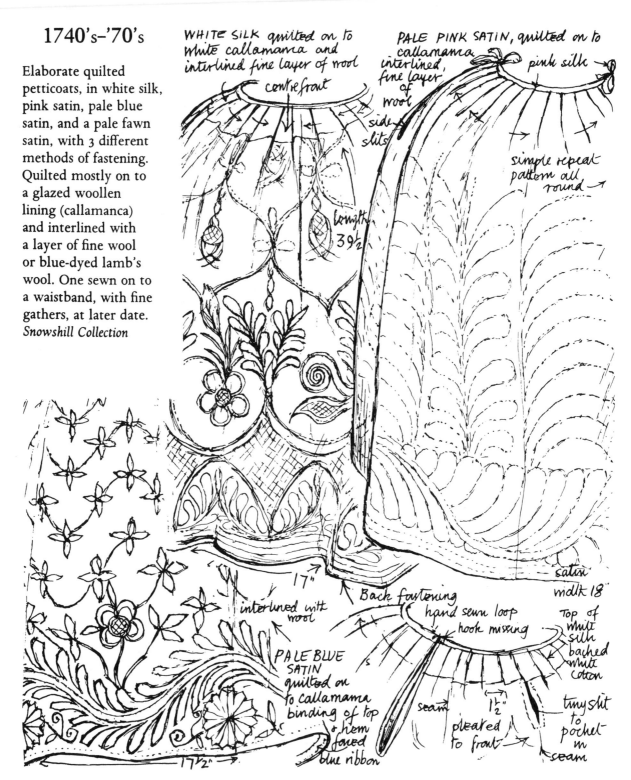

WHITE SILK quilted on to white callamanca and interlined fine layer of wool

centre front

PALE PINK SATIN, quilted on to callamanca interlined, fine layer of wool

pink silk

side slits

simple repeat pattern all round →

length 39½

interlined with wool

Back fastening
hand sewn loop
hook missing

satin width 18

Top of white silk backed white cotton

17"

PALE BLUE SATIN quilted on to callamanca binding of top & hem faced blue ribbon

seam

1½"

pleated to front →

tiny slit to pocket in seam

17½" →

Quilting varies in quality, some sewn finer than others, the designs being either rounded or 'squared' in effect. Although the examples in this collection are all in pale colours, blue predominating, other bright colours were used. The Grandmother from the Zoffany painting

blue silk binding & ties

centre front

BLUE SATIN quilted on to glazed woollen lining (CALLAMANCA) & padded with blue dyed lambs wool.

slit

CREAMY-FAWN SATIN quilted to coarse woollen cloth

Top of fine, stiff cream wool - double

very fine gathers

front

seam

S

from the painting by Zoffany of the Bradshaw family.

green silk
red bows & stomacher
calash
red satin

1770's

satin spread flat

bone & linen buttons

BACK opening

inside blue silk tape

thin, very coarse woollen cloth lined, like blanketing

seam

17½ width of satin

wears a bright red satin one, under a rich green robe. She appears to have pulled her apron aside to show the petticoat. She wears long white mittens and carries a white-lined, black silk calash hanging over her arm.

c. 1750

Stiff pale blue silk sack-backed gown, matching petticoat; floral pattern in silver thread. White linen lining to bodice and sleeves. Treble falling cuff; one flounce is missing. Front bodice laced, original front or stomacher missing. Pink satin shoes, with embroidery in silver, lined with white kid, Pompadour heels.
Snowshill Collection

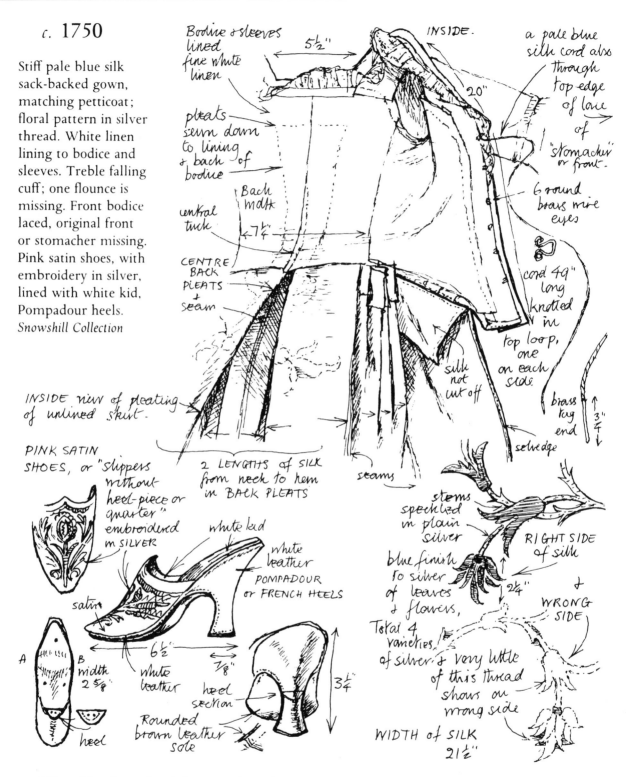

Bodice & sleeves lined fine white linen

5½"

INSIDE.

a pale blue silk cord also through top edge of lace of "stomacher" or front.

20"

pleats sewn down to lining & back of bodice

Back width

central tuck

7¼"

CENTRE BACK PLEATS + seam

6 round brass wire eyes

cord 49" long knotted in top loop, one on each side

silk not cut off

brass tag end

3¾"

selvedge

INSIDE view of pleating of unlined skirt.

PINK SATIN SHOES, or "slippers without heel-piece or quarter" embroidered in SILVER

2 LENGTHS of SILK from neck to hem in BACK PLEATS

seams

stems speckled in plain silver

RIGHT SIDE of silk

white kid

white leather

POMPADOUR or FRENCH HEELS

satin

blue finish to silver of leaves & flowers,

2¼"

WRONG SIDE

A   B width 2⅝"

6½"

⅞"

white leather

heel section

3¼"

Total 4 varieties of silver & very little of this thread shows on wrong side

Rounded brown leather sole

heel

WIDTH of SILK 21½"

Silks with a large floral design such as this are found about 1740 to the '50's; this elegant yet simple pattern is a rich example, although the stiff silk shows signs of splitting. French influence on dress increases, and there is a growing use of elaborate trimming, as the bows on

silk cord

FRONT ADDED LATER
gathered net
over white satin

silver lace
once here?

1⅝
⅝
lace
4"

hem
outside
with
raw
edge

front
skirt
length
36"

seam

lace

14"

from the painting of
Madame de
Pompadour,
by
Q. de la Tour
1755
at the
Louvre

wearing a
sack-back
gown
with lace &
ribbons.

stiff silk
with
large
floral
pattern

note
shoes
with
french
heels

lace sewn
to sleeve
flounce

great
variety
of pattern
in lace

seams

waist
to hem
length of
petticoat
39"

the stomacher of the dress in the small study show. The original front of this robe may have been similar. The pink satin shoes were not called mules; that was a 16th c. term which was revived in the 19th c.

c. 1750

Sack-backed gown of stiff pale blue silk, floral pattern in silver. Back view showing pleats in full length of silk, neck to hem.
Snowshill Collection

Early 18th-century fan. Leaf of painted skin, sticks and guards of carved ivory.
Later, decorated fan, painted cream silk leaf, ivory sticks and painted carved guards.
Richard Radway

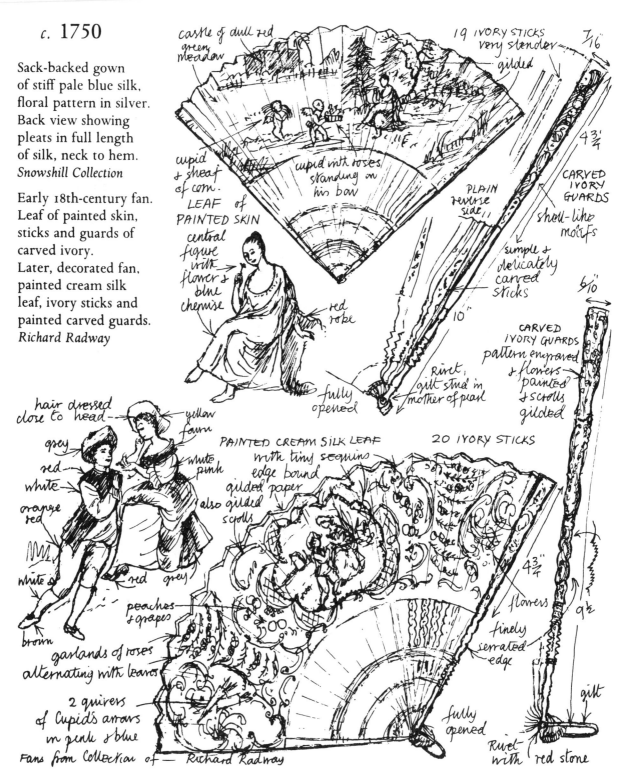

castle of dull red green meadow

19 IVORY STICKS very slender — 7/16

gilded

4 3/4

cupid & sheaf of corn.
LEAF of PAINTED SKIN

cupid with roses standing on his bow

central figure with flower & blue chemise

red robe

PLAIN reverse side

CARVED IVORY GUARDS shell-like motifs

simple & delicately carved sticks

5/10

10"

CARVED IVORY GUARDS pattern engraved & flowers painted & scrolls gilded

Rivet, gilt stud in mother of pearl

fully opened

hair dressed close to head —
grey
red
white
orange red
white
brown
red grey
garlands of roses alternating with leaves
2 quivers of cupid's arrows in pink & blue

yellow fawn
white pink

PAINTED CREAM SILK LEAF with tiny sequins edge bound gilded paper also gilded scrolls

peaches & grapes

20 IVORY STICKS

4 3/4

flowers

finely serrated edge

9 1/2

gilt

fully opened

Rivet with red stone

Fans from Collection of — Richard Radway

The earlier fan is particularly light and slender to hold; it is beautifully painted and has the quality of Chinese work. The central figure wears a low-necked chemise. The second fan shows the increased decoration and French influence of 1750–90. Both the guards and leaf

29

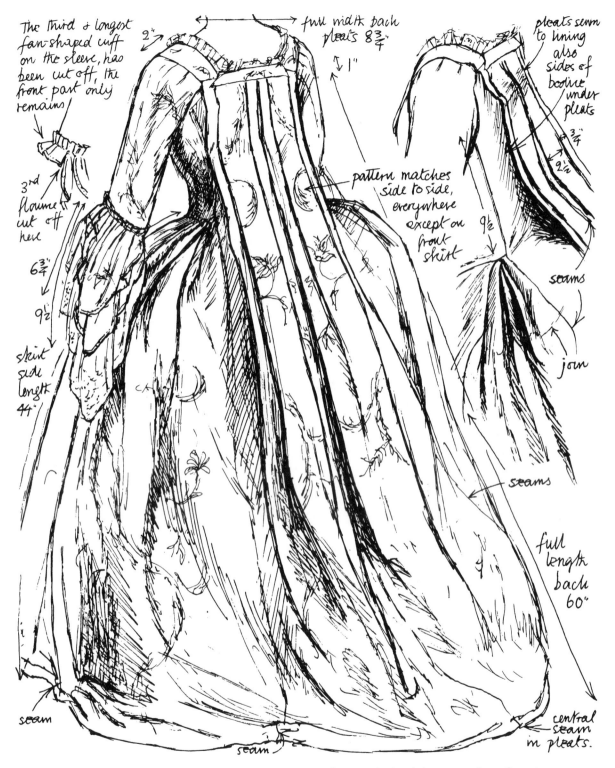

The third & longest fan-shaped cuff on the sleeve, has been cut off, the front part only remains

2"

full width back pleats 8¾"

↓ 1"

pleats sewn to lining also sides of bodice under pleats

¾"

2½"

3rd flounce cut off here

6¾"

pattern matches side to side, everywhere except on front skirt

9½"

9½"

skirt side length 44"

seams

join

seams

full length back 60"

seam

seam

central seam in pleats.

on the later fan are more elaborate; the painting is fine, with the delicate quality of a miniature. The blue and silver sack-backed robe, with its rich pleating and wide skirt, would have been worn over a hooped petticoat.

1755-65

Mustard-yellow, crisp watered silk, an open robe, long folded back edges sewn to bodice, which is linen-lined. Skirt is lined, white silk. Sleeves have two falling fan-shaped frills, edges scalloped. Double lace ruffles of finest white silk net. Stomacher, of white satin, embroidered. Mustard-yellow silk shoes, green pattens.
Snowshill Collection

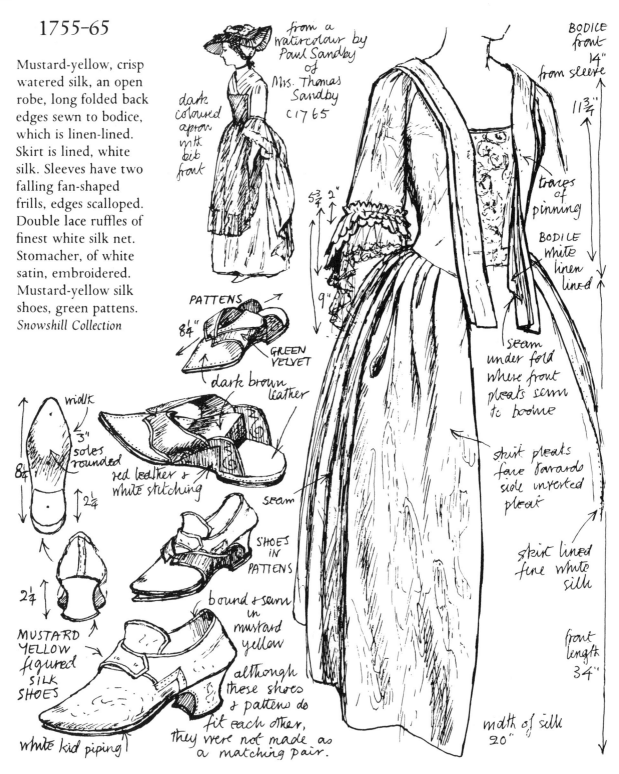

from a watercolour by Paul Sandby of Mrs. Thomas Sandby c1765

dark coloured apron with bib front

BODICE front 14" from sleeve

11¾"

traces of pinning

BODICE white linen lined

5¾ 2"

9"

PATTENS

8¼"

GREEN VELVET

dark brown leather

width

3" soles rounded

8¼"

2¼"

red leather & white stitching

seam

2¼"

SHOES IN PATTENS

MUSTARD YELLOW figured SILK SHOES

bound & sewn in mustard yellow

although these shoes & pattens do fit each other, they were not made as a matching pair.

white kid piping

seam under fold where front pleats sewn to bodice

skirt pleats face forwards side inverted pleat

skirt lined fine white silk

front length 34"

width of silk 20"

It is rather unusual to find a dress of this date with a lined skirt, but this silk does not appear to have been added later. The embroidered stomacher is of much earlier date than the dress, probably early 17th c. The lace ruffles are exactly the same as on another dress in this collec-

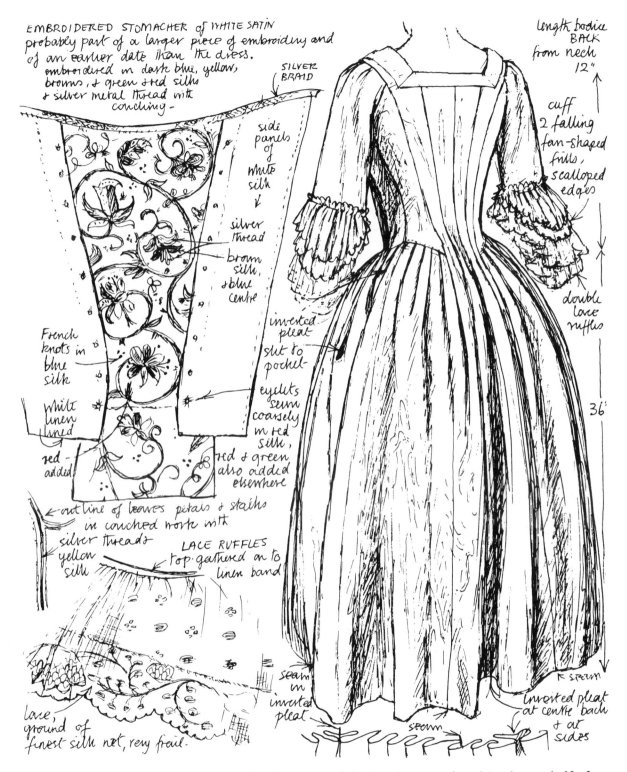

EMBROIDERED STOMACHER of WHITE SATIN probably part of a larger piece of embroidery and of an earlier date than the dress. embroidered in dark blue, yellow, browns, & green & red silks & silver metal thread with couching -

SILVER BRAID

length bodice BACK from neck 12"

cuff 2 falling fan-shaped frills, scalloped edges

double lace ruffles

side panels of white silk

silver thread

brown silk, & blue centre

French knots in blue silk

white linen lined

red - added

outline of leaves petals & stalks in couched work with silver threads & yellow silk

inverted pleat

slit to pocket

eyelets sewn coarsely in red silk, red & green also added elsewhere

LACE RUFFLES top gathered on to linen band

lace, ground of finest silk net, very frail.

seam in inverted pleat

36"

seam

inverted pleat at centre back & at sides

tion, also with a silk-lined skirt. The shoes are of the heavier type found in the 1st half of 18th c. The pattens are worn out of doors as a protective over-shoe, a form of galosh; they probably matched green shoes.

1755-75

Bright mustard-yellow fine woollen cloth, an open robe with two matching stomachers. Double falling flounce on sleeve, matching pleated trimming. Bodice and sleeves lined in white linen. Tiny guinea purse of pink and silver. Cream netted long purse, silver decorated. c. 1724-50 white cotton-embroidered pocket. *Snowshill Collection*

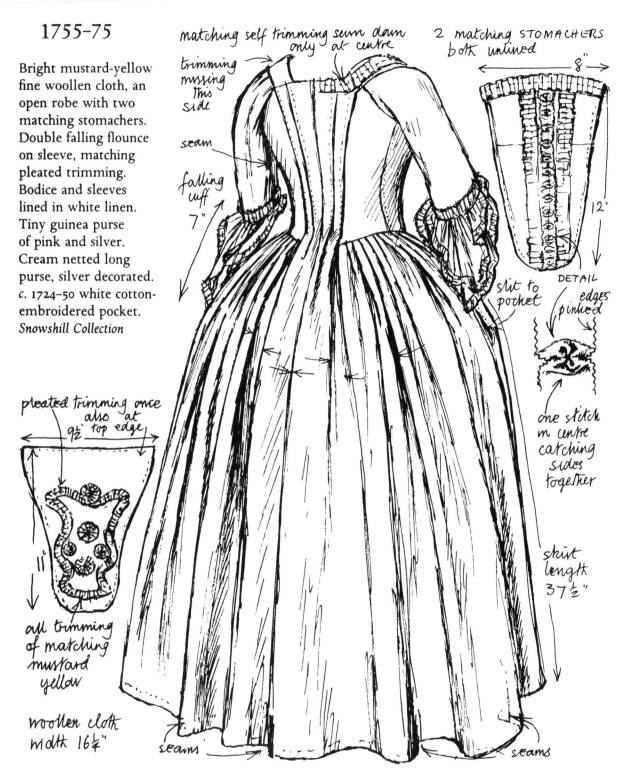

matching self trimming seam down only at centre

trimming missing this side

seam

falling cuff 7"

2 matching STOMACHERS both unlined

8"

12"

DETAIL

slit to pocket

edges pinked

one stitch in centre catching sides together

skirt length 37½"

pleated trimming once also at top edge 9½"

11"

all trimming of matching mustard yellow

woollen cloth width 16¼"

seams

seams

This rare example of a fine woollen cloth open robe is in good condition, and has been exhibited for some years at the Victoria and Albert Museum. To have two matching stomachers to one dress is rather unusual. This is a good example of a plain but fashionable dress of this

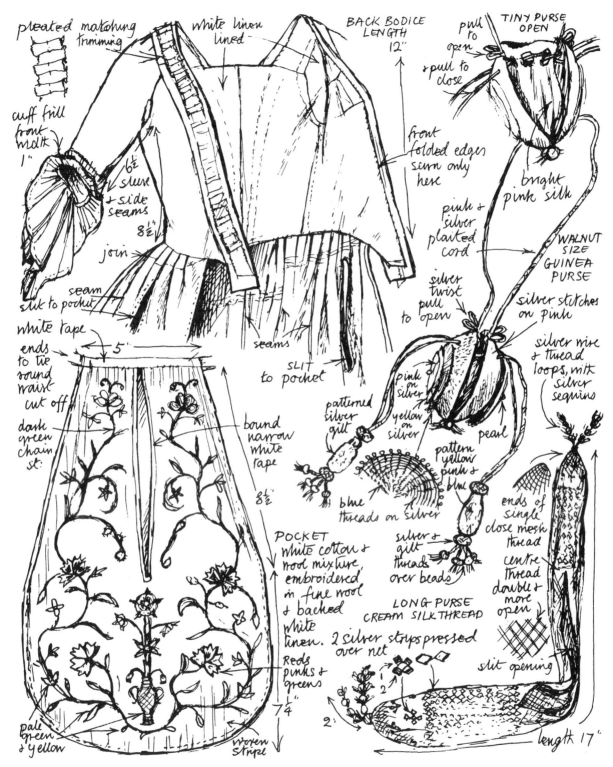

pleated matching trimming

white linen lined

BACK BODICE LENGTH 12"

TINY PURSE OPEN

pull to open

pull to close

cuff frill front width 1"

6½ sleeve + side seams

8½

join

seam silk to pocket

white tape

ends to tie round waist cut off

dark green chain st:

5

bound narrow white tape

8½

front folded edges sewn only here

pink & silver plaited cord

bright pink silk

WALNUT SIZE GUINEA PURSE

silver stitches on pink

silver twist pull to open

silver wire & thread loops, with silver sequins

seams

SLIT to pocket

patterned silver gilt

pink on silver

yellow on silver

pearl

pattern yellow pink & blue

POCKET white cotton & wool mixture, embroidered in fine wool & backed white linen.

Reds pinks & greens

blue threads on silver

silver & gilt threads over beads

LONG PURSE CREAM SILK THREAD

ends of single close mesh thread

centre thread double & more open

2 silver strips pressed over net

slit opening

pale green & yellow

woven stripe

¼"

7¼

2"

2"

length 17"

time. The embroidered hanging pocket would have been one of a pair. The tiny pink and silver guinea purse is exquisite, and beautifully made; so too is the long netted purse of cream silk with silver foil strip.

c. 1766–75

Cherry-red and white striped silk brocade, sack-backed gown, matching petticoat and stomacher with button fastening front. Gown and petticoat are flounced and trimmed with furbelows edged with red silk braid. Bodice and sleeves are lined in white linen. Red leather shoes, slender heels, traces of buckle fastening. *Snowshill Collection*

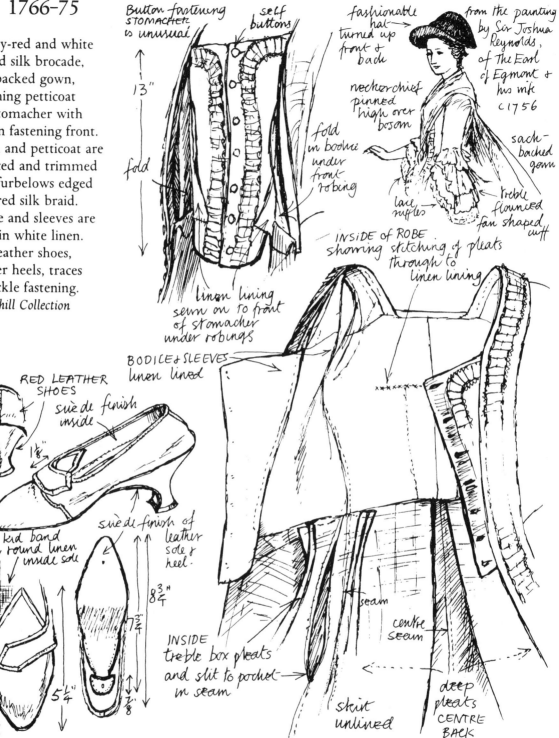

Button fastening STOMACHER is unusual
self buttons

13"

fold

linen lining sewn on to front of stomacher under robings

fashionable hat turned up front & back

neckerchief pinned high over bosom

fold in bodice under front robing

from the painting by Sir Joshua Reynolds, of the Earl of Egmont & his wife c1756

sack-backed gown

treble flounced fan shaped cuff

lace ruffles

INSIDE of ROBE showing stitching of pleats through to linen lining

BODICE & SLEEVES linen lined

RED LEATHER SHOES
2"
suède finish inside
2½"
1⅛"

white kid band round linen inside sole

suède finish of leather sole & heel.

red silk bound

5¼"

8¾"

7¾"

⅞"

INSIDE treble box pleats and slit to pocket in seam

skirt unlined

seam

centre seam

deep pleats CENTRE BACK

The sack-backed gown remained in fashion a remarkably long time, but the pattern and type of silks used changed over the years. By this time the back pleats were sewn in position, where previously they had hung loose, thus giving the bodice a closer fit. During the 2nd

DETAIL of
red silk
BRAID

wire
covered
in
red
silk

on all
edges
of flounces
& furbelows

ruched or pleated
trimming or
"furbelows"

edged
with
red silk
braid

robe
skirt
40½"
front
length

8¾"
flounce

36"

seam A

seam to seam 19.
B

2"

DETAIL from
the linen & cotton fabric
plate printed design
in blue,
from scenes in
Garrick's play
LETHE,
possibly
commemorating
Command
Performance
Drury
Lane
1766

hat with brim
turned up

'peten'lair'
& stomacher,
muslin
& lace
ruffles

treble sleeve flounces
& slit to pocket

side hoops or
"panniers"
supporting
robe, as in
figure above.

seams

this trimming
widens towards hem

half of this century shoe heels became less broad and far more slender in shape, with a deep
curve under the instep. The soles are less heavy, no longer being rounded underneath. Heels
grow smaller as the century progresses.

c. 1766–75

Cherry-red and white striped silk brocade, floral pattern in pink and green on white stripe. Sack-backed gown and petticoat, worn over side-hoops. Sleeves with treble falling fan-shaped cuff, trimmed with a narrow red silk braid, as on all pleated trimmings. Matching petticoat. Detail of gold knotting shuttle. *Snowshill Collection*

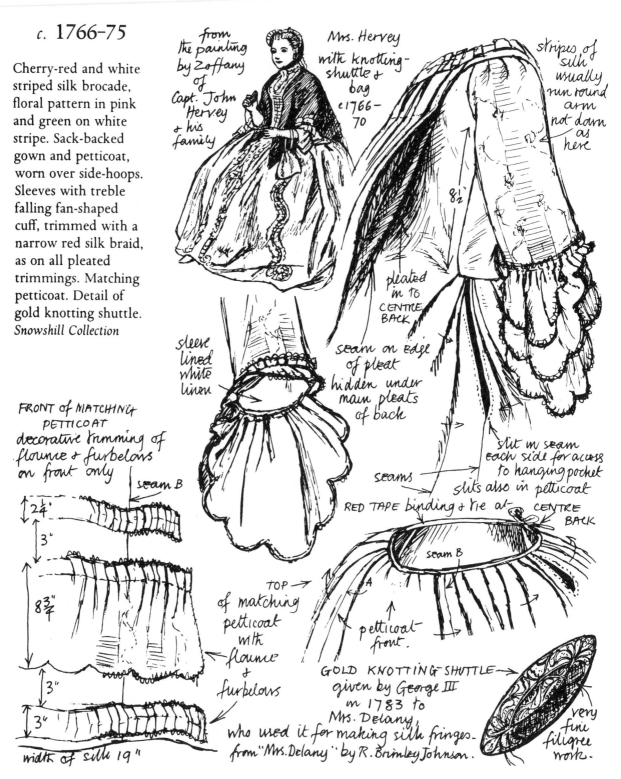

from the painting by Zoffany of Capt. John Hervey & his family

Mrs. Hervey with knotting-shuttle & bag c1766–70

stripes of silk usually run round arm not down as here

8½

pleated in to CENTRE BACK

seam on edge of pleat hidden under main pleats of back

sleeve lined white linen

slit in seam each side for access to hanging pocket

seams

slits also in petticoat

RED TAPE binding & tie at CENTRE BACK

seam B

A

petticoat front.

FRONT of MATCHING PETTICOAT
decorative trimming of flounce & furbelows on front only

seam B

2¼"

3"

8¾"

3"

3"

width of silk 19"

TOP → of matching petticoat with flounce & furbelows

GOLD KNOTTING SHUTTLE given by George III in 1783 to Mrs. Delany who used it for making silk fringes. from "Mrs. Delany" by R. Brimley Johnson.

very fine filigree work.

There are two interesting points about this dress which are rather unusual: the button fastening stomacher, shown on previous page, and method of cutting the silk so that the stripes run down the arm, instead of round it as is usual. The flounced cuff continued in

ribbed" white red white red
← red → plain ← → ←

4½"

flowers "embroidered" in pink & green

WRONG SIDE
no pink or green
silks show, only
weft threads of
pink over
warp stripes
of red &
white.

length
need
to hem
60"

centre
seam

seam

pleats at back
held in place
by stitching
4½" down

12"

central
flounce
continues
round as
frill to
front
sleeve

skirt
side
length
47"

seam

fashion from c. 1750 to 1775. Knotting became popular in England at the end of the 17th c.,
when Queen Mary II took it up as a hobby, and it continued throughout most of the 18th c.
The lady in Zoffany's group on p. 1 has a shuttle.

38

1765–75

Delicate pink silk taffeta sack-backed gown, with matching petticoat. Striped silk in shades of pink, greeny-grey, orange dots and narrow white horizontal lines. Robe with furbelows, edges scalloped, petticoat with deep flounce. Triple falling cuffs on sleeve, fine white silk braid trimming. Lace ruffles added later. *Snowshill Collection*

DETAIL of RIGHT sleeve showing hanging lead weight covered in white linen, & about size of penny weighing 2 to 2½ oz

white lace & folded net added later

weight stitched at top only, to sleeve lining

white silk braid

slit to pocket

20"

trimming of fine white silk braid, has a flower-like effect

16"

deep flounce at front only, finishing at sides below pocket slits.

hem of petticoat

A lovely example of a typical sack-back of this period; the softly rustling silks are usually now lighter in colour as well as in texture, and of striped patterns such as this, the stripes running round the arm as here, and horizontally on the flounce of the petticoat. The white

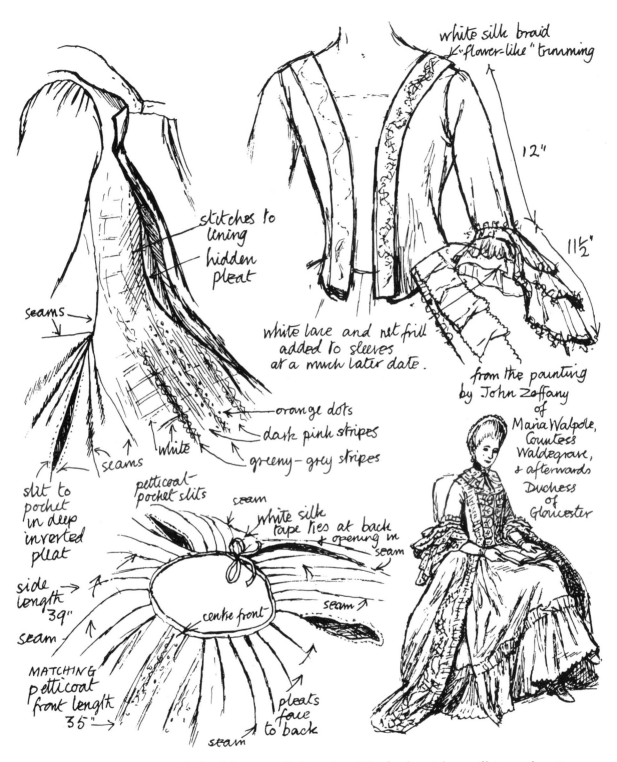

stitches to lining
hidden pleat

seams

white silk braid
"flower-like" trimming

12"

11½"

white lace and net frill
added to sleeves
at a much later date.

orange dots
dark pink stripes
greeny-grey stripes

white

seams

slit to pocket in deep inverted pleat

side length 39"

seam

MATCHING petticoat front length 35"

petticoat pocket slits

seam

white silk tape ties at back opening in seam

seam

centre front

seam

seam

pleats face to back

seam

from the painting by John Zoffany of Maria Walpole, Countess Waldegrave, & afterwards Duchess of Gloucester

braid trimming is particularly delicate and charming. The lead weights, still intact hanging at the sleeve elbow, are interesting, ensuring that the silk hangs straight and smooth. Lace ruffles would have been worn.

1765–75

Delicate pink silk taffeta sack-backed gown with matching petticoat. Silk striped in pinks and greeny-grey with orange dots and narrow white line. Flounced, furbelowed, and braid-trimmed. Sleeves with small lead weight hidden under fan-shaped cuff. Linen lining to bodice and sleeves. Stomacher is missing.
Snowshill Collection

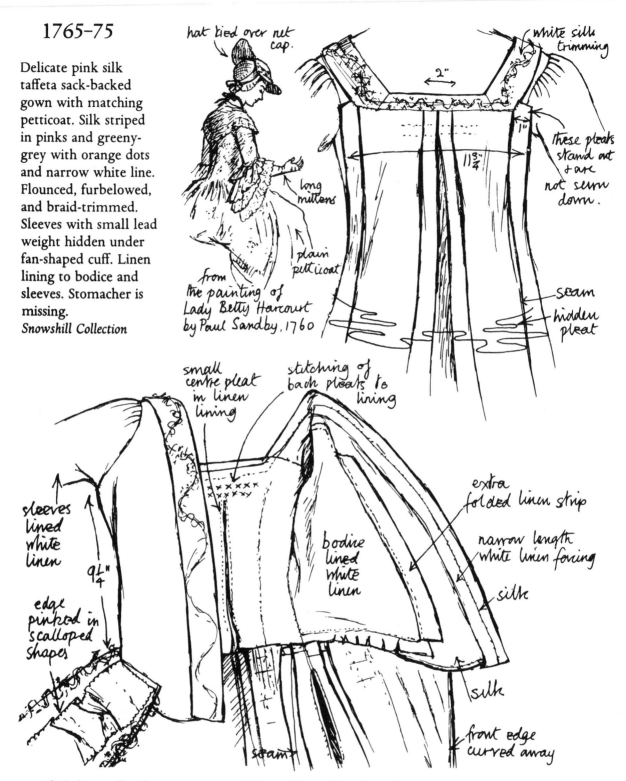

hat tied over net cap.

long mittens

plain petticoat

from the painting of Lady Betty Harcourt by Paul Sandby, 1760

white silk trimming

2"

1"

11¾"

these pleats stand out & are not sewn down.

seam

hidden pleat

small centre pleat in linen lining

stitching of back pleats to lining

sleeves lined white linen

9¼"

edge pinked in scalloped shapes

bodice lined white linen

extra folded linen strip

narrow length white linen facing

silk

silk

front edge curved away

seam

Slightly smaller hoops are more fashionable under these dresses, which can hang straight, sweeping the floor, or the skirt can be gathered up, with the front ends pulled through the pocket slits, as shown in the small figures. It is most likely that the missing stomacher matched

41

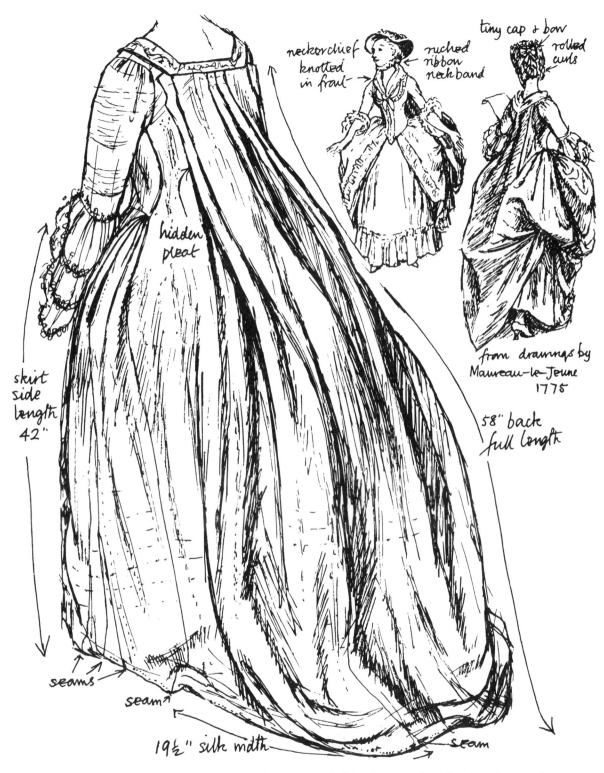

neckerchief knotted in front

ruched ribbon neckband

tiny cap & bow

rolled curls

from drawings by Moreau-le-Jeune 1775

hidden pleat

skirt side length 42"

58" back full length

seams

seam

19½" silk width

seam

the dress; this is usually so 1750–70; and it was probably decorated with trimmings or bows, as shown in study on previous page of Maria Walpole. Hair styles increase in height and elaboration during the 1770's.

Mid-18th c.

Pair of 'false hips' or 'panniers,' of brown and black striped horsehair, over four pairs of metal hoops, with tape ties.

2nd half 18th c.

Linen stays, close narrow boning, of dark grey whalebone; front with stiffened centre panel.
Fawn cotton stays, half-boned, wide and narrow whalebone.
Snowshill Collection

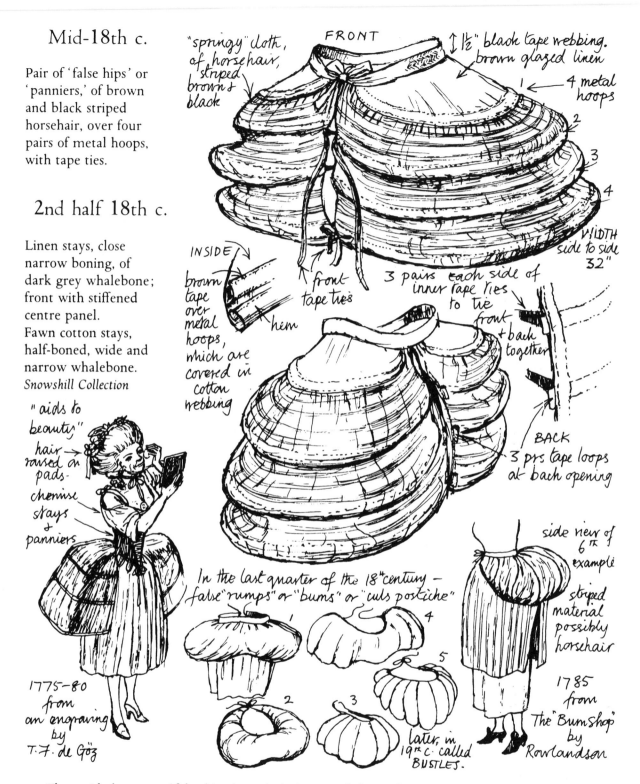

"springy" cloth, of horsehair, striped brown & black

FRONT

↕ 1½" black tape webbing. brown glazed linen

4 metal hoops

1
2
3
4

WIDTH side to side 32"

INSIDE

brown tape over metal hoops, which are covered in cotton webbing

hem

front tape ties

3 pairs each side of inner tape ties to tie front + back together

BACK 3 prs tape loops at back opening

"aids to beauty"
hair raised on pads
chemise
stays
+ panniers

1775–80 from an engraving by T. F. de Göz

In the last quarter of the 18th century – false "rumps" or "bums" or "culs postiche"

1
2
3
4
5

later, in 19th c. called BUSTLES.

side view of 6th example
striped material possibly horsehair
1785 from The "Bum Shop" by Rowlandson

These side-hoops or 'false hips,' 1740's–'60's, are of the earlier style; improved hinged ones appeared *c.* 1750. They continued to be worn under Court dresses long after they went out of use for day wear; but the 'false rumps,' fashionable during the '80's, do in some examples

43

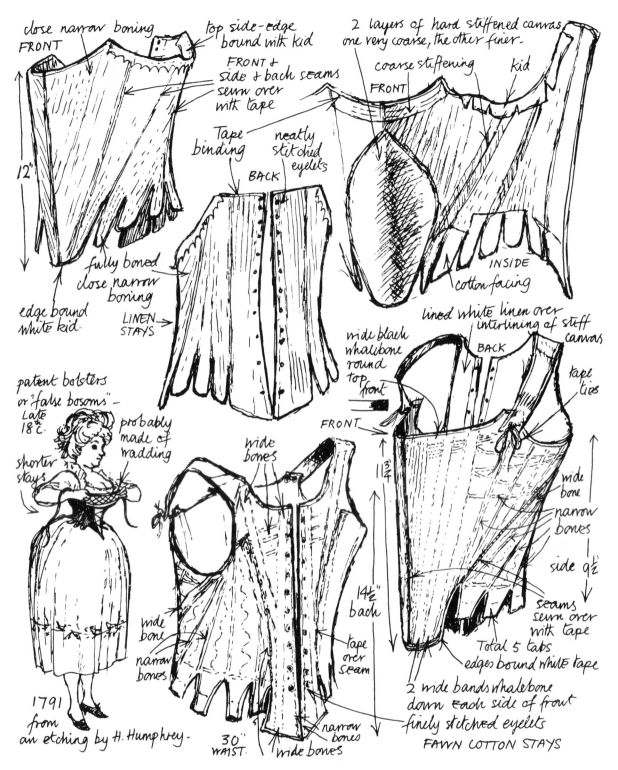

close narrow boning
FRONT

top side-edge
bound with kid

2 layers of hard stiffened canvas
one very coarse, the other finer.

coarse stiffening

kid

FRONT

FRONT &
side & back seams
sewn over
with tape

Tape
binding

neatly
stitched
eyelets

BACK

INSIDE

cotton facing

12"

fully boned
close narrow
boning

edge bound
white kid.

LINEN
STAYS

lined white linen over
interlining of stiff
canvas

wide black
whalebone
round
top
front

BACK

tape
ties

FRONT

patent bolsters
or "false bosoms" -
Late
18th c.

probably
made of
wadding

shorter
stays

wide
bones

11¾

wide
bone
narrow
bones

side 9½

seams
sewn over
with tape

14½
back

tape
over
seam

Total 5 tabs
edges bound white tape

wide
bone
narrow
bones

1791
from
an etching by H. Humphrey.

30"
WAIST

narrow
bones
wide bones

2 wide bands whalebone
down each side of front
finely stitched eyelets
FAWN COTTON STAYS

have width at the side as well as at the back. The terms 'pannier' and 'bustle' were not actually used during the 18th century. Both the pairs of stays show the rising waistline; they are extremely finely stitched.

44

1770-75

Striped floral silk jacket, pale rose-pink and silver-grey. Rose and dot pattern in pink with stripes of blue and green. Lined cream cotton. Cuffs of earlier style than date of silk. Fine stiff cream silk jacket, with floral sprays exquisitely hand-embroidered, earlier in date than style of jacket. *Snowshill Collection*

floral pattern of roses with stripes of blue alternating with thin green stripe (A).

seams

INSIDE CENTRE BACK

join

A

A

lined thin cream cotton

seams

seams

seam

seam

2 blue stripes

SILK of pale rose pink striped blue & green with pink roses & dots

seam

2 bands of blue behind pattern of roses

joining seam

10"

9¾"

8¼"

2½

16"

5"

seams

gusset at sides

2 blue stripes

On closer inspection, each of these jackets is extremely interesting. The first, the silk dating c. 1770–75, must have been made for an older woman, as its size suggests, and one who preferred the cuffs that were in fashion during her youth. But the adjustable front of the

45

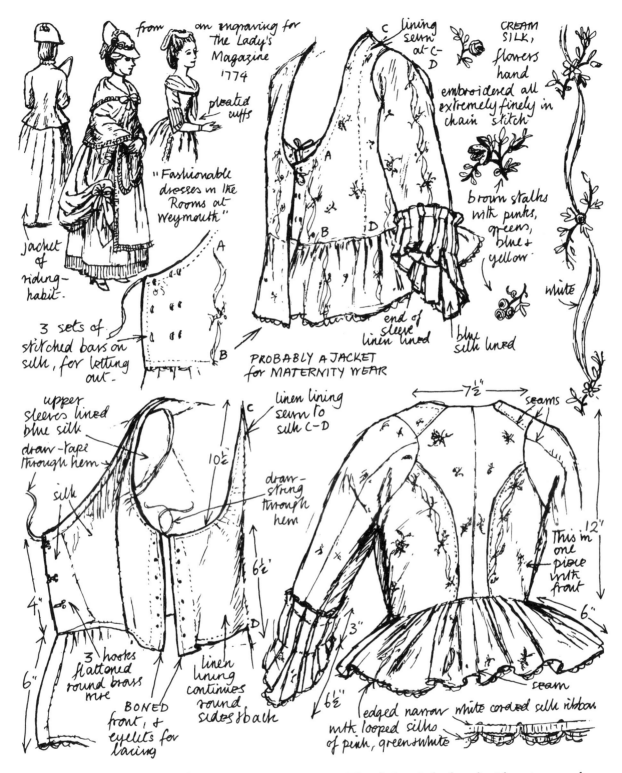

from an engraving for The Lady's Magazine 1774

jacket of riding-habit.

"Fashionable dresses in the Rooms at Weymouth"

pleated cuffs

3 sets of stitched bars on silk, for letting out.

C lining sewn at C-D

A

B D

end of sleeve linen lined

blue silk lined

CREAM SILK, flowers hand embroidered all extremely finely in chain stitch

brown stalks with pinks, greens, blue & yellow.

white

PROBABLY A JACKET for MATERNITY WEAR

upper sleeves lined blue silk
draw-tape through hem

silk

linen lining sewn to silk C-D

C

10½

draw-string through hem

6½'

D

4"

6"

3 hooks flattened round brass wire

BONED front, & eyelets for lacing

linen lining continues round sides & back

7½"

seams

This in one piece with front

12'

6"

3"

6½

6½

edged narrow white corded silk ribbon with looped silks of pink, green & white

seam

cream silk jacket can only suggest maternity wear. The chain-stitched embroidery is remarkably fine and of great variety, and was done before the jacket was made up. The front and sides are cut in one, round to back seam.

1766–70

Soft yellow and white striped figured silk, trailing floral pattern. Bodice closes centre front, sewn on bands. Trimmed white silk braid. Very fine silk net, double ruffles, lace-edged, fine net ground, in very frail condition, same as on yellow silk dress, also with white silk lined skirt. Neatly made, patterns matching.
Snowshill Collection

white silk braid trimming

front cuff 1" Z

lead weight sewn inside cuff

double ruffles

full dress

from an engraving in The Lady's Magazine 1775

38"

seam

seam

seam

seam

centre back inverted pleat

DETAIL of figured silk

dots & sprays white on white

white sprays on wide yellow stripe

white

yellow

With the skirt lined with the same quality fine white silk, and the ruffles made of the same delicate net and lace, this charming gown must have belonged to the owner of the yellow watered silk, slightly earlier in date than this. The shape of the lead weight in the sleeve

yellow stripe

bodice from
sleeve seam

yellow &
white
stripes
round
arm

12"

cuff

to waist
front length

5"

pleats
face
to
back

35"

width
of silk 23¼"

white
& yellow
stripes

centre only
sewn to
bodice

white
linen
lined

side
back
13"

skirt lined
thin white silk

probable method
of fastening
with laces
no
trace
of other
fastening
used

tape tie

FRONT of
LEFT SLEEVE

lead
weight
inside
cuff

both
sides
are
covered in
white linen
& sewn to cuff

1½"

LACE RUFFLES
very fine silk
net
edged
with
lace

lace
on fine net
ground

these
ruffles,
very frail.

is also interesting. The stomacher now usually matches the dress, and by about 1770 the bodice closes in front, meeting edge to edge, as this does, although the applied folded band follows the earlier style.

c. 1775

Plain bright yellow silk taffeta polonaise. Back pleats on bodice sewn down, tapering to waist, silk still in one length, neck to hem. Bodice and sleeve lined white linen. Pleated trimming at neck, bodice closing centre front. Inside skirt eight silk cord loops, sewn each side for looping up the gown. Finely sewn. *Snowshill Collection*

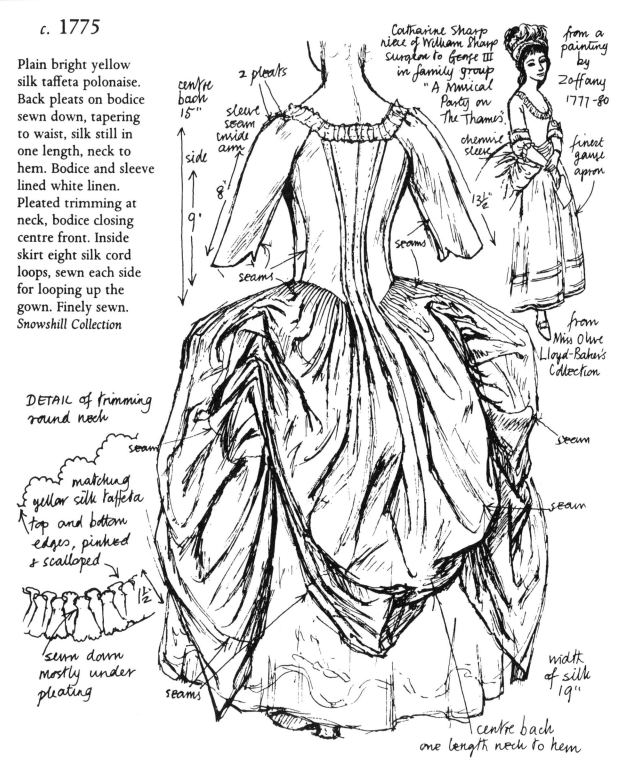

centre back 15"

2 pleats

sleeve seam inside arm

side

8"

9"

seams

seams

Catharine Sharp niece of William Sharp surgeon to George III in family group "A Musical Party on The Thames"

chemise sleeve

13½"

from a painting by Zoffany 1777-80

finest gauze apron

from Miss Olive Lloyd-Baker's Collection

DETAIL of trimming round neck

seam

matching yellow silk taffeta top and bottom edges, pinked & scalloped

1½"

sewn down mostly under pleating

seams

seam

seam

width of silk 19"

centre back one length neck to hem

The finely tapering pleats on this bodice give an illusion of a tiny waist, which from the side view is not so. The pleating of the skirt on to the bodice is very fine and regular, and the method of looping up is dainty. A gown suitable for a young girl, and one that could be

49

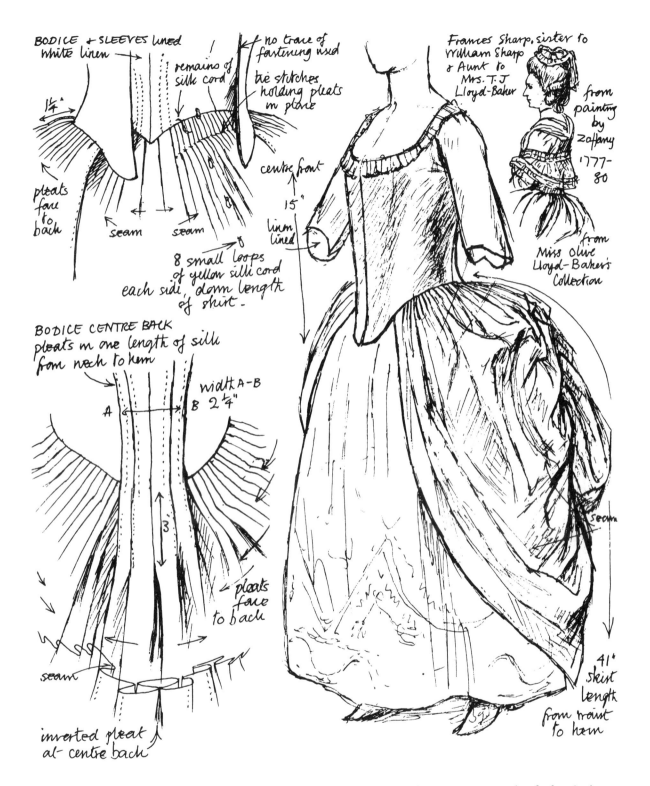

BODICE + SLEEVES lined
white linen

no trace of
fastening used

remains of
silk cord

tie stitches
holding pleats
in place

1¼"

pleats
face
to
back

seam   seam

centre front

15"

linen
lined

8 small loops
of yellow silk cord
each side, down length
of skirt.

Frances Sharp, sister to
William Sharp
& Aunt to
Mrs. T.J
Lloyd-Baker

from
painting
by
Zoffany
1777-
80

from
Miss Olive
Lloyd-Baker's
Collection

BODICE CENTRE BACK
pleats in one length of silk
from neck to hem

width A-B
B 2¼"

A

3

pleats
face
to back

seam

inverted pleat
at centre back

seam

41"
skirt
length

from waist
to hem

worn on any but the most formal of occasions. The polonaise is typical of the '70's. The closed bodice lengthens a little as here 1770-75, and the falling fan-shaped cuff goes out of fashion.

1770-80

White taffeta gown, bodice closed centre front, two long bones in centre back. Sleeves and bodice lined in white linen. Two lead weights originally sewn at elbow of each sleeve; cuffs are missing. Extremely fine pleating of skirt to bodice, tapering, very narrow pleats at bodice back. Finely pleated trimming. *Snowshill Collection*

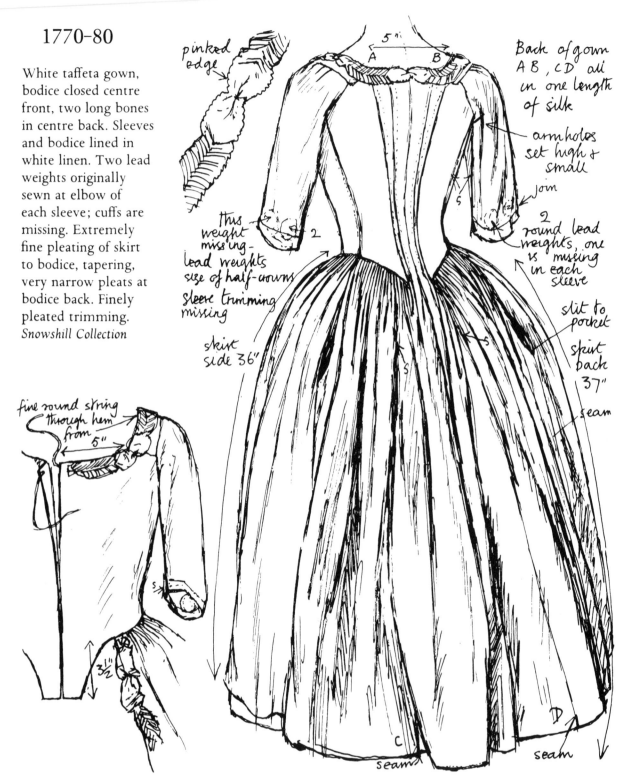

pinked edge

5"
A   B

Back of gown AB, CD all in one length of silk

armholes set high & small

join

2 round lead weights, one is missing in each sleeve

this weight missing — lead weights size of half-crowns sleeve trimming missing

2

slit to pocket

skirt back 37"

skirt side 36"

5

seam

fine round string through hem from 5"

3½"

s

C
seam

D
seam

The pleating, trimming, and sewing on this dress are again very fine, and the silk is in good condition. The bodice back pleats, although so narrow, are still cut in one length of silk, neck to hem. The bodice back is boned, an interesting detail in this dress. Others of about

51

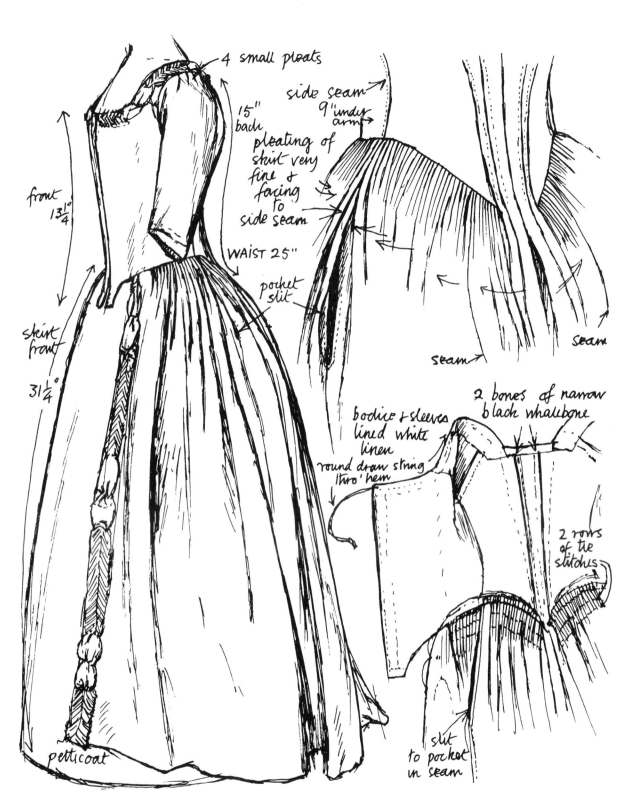

4 small pleats

side seam
9" under arm

15" back

pleating of skirt very fine & facing to side seam

front 13¼"

WAIST 25"

pocket slit

seam

seam

skirt front

31¼"

2 bones of narrow black whalebone

bodice & sleeves lined white linen

round draw string thro' hem

2 rows of tie stitches

petticoat

slit to pocket in seam

this date in the collection also have boned bodices. Two, each with 6 bones, and another with 12. There is no trace at all in this bodice of the method of fastening, and the dress shows no sign of wear.

1770-80

Cream figured silk open robe. Two narrow pinky-red satin stripes with central pin-stripe in black, and narrow cream satin stripes outlined in black dots. Bodice, very narrow tapering sewn-down pleats, facing in to centre back. Bodice and sleeves lined in white linen. Striped silk shoes, triangular high French heel. *Snowshill Collection*

from the painting by J. F. Rigaud 1779 The Locker Family.

hair not powdered

seam

sleeve shape altered, with narrow bound edge added

9½

length elbow to cuff 3"

Bodice front meets edge to edge

seams & joins on both sleeves

Transparent apron over petticoat with open robe.

cream figured silk, striped with narrow pink satin and centre pin-stripe black with black dots each side cream satin stripe

1"

2¾"

deep false hem of different striped silk

skirt length side back 40½"

¼"

seam

bound cream satin

3½

cream, yellow & silver thread

cream satin section

Buckle missing ⅛"

A

B width A-B 2⅝"

7¼"

STRIPED SILK SHOES

seam

A simple, beautifully made dress, with a most interesting back; for this type of construction is not found so frequently as the outward-facing pleats. There is no sign of fastening on the front bodice, which meets edge to edge; concealed lacing or hook and eye would probably

53

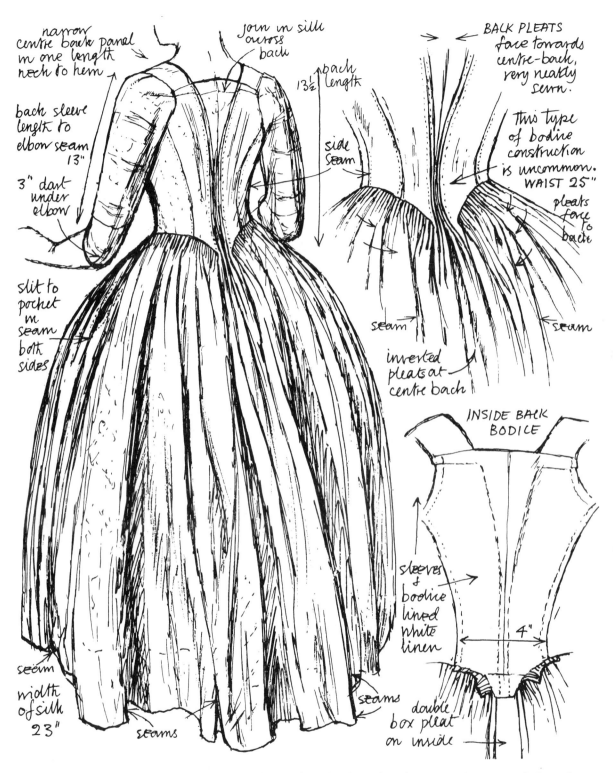

narrow centre back panel in one length neck to hem

join in silk across back

BACK PLEATS face towards centre-back, very neatly sewn.

back sleeve length to elbow seam 13"

13½ back length

This type of bodice construction is uncommon. WAIST 25"

3" dart under elbow

side seam

pleats face to back

slit to pocket in seam both sides

seam

inverted pleats at centre back

seam

INSIDE BACK BODICE

sleeves & bodice lined white linen

4"

seam width of silk 23"

seams

seams

double box pleat on inside

have been used. The sleeve-ends have been slightly altered and are now longer, to below the elbow. The earlier fan-shaped cuff is sometimes replaced by a ruched or pleated band, as shown in the small study.

1770–90

Black glazed cotton calash, lined pink cotton, black ribbons. Two tiny straw hats, one of fir-cone scales. Small cream satin muff, late '70's–'80's, probably French, with sequin decoration, and finely printed miniatures on satin. Early umbrella, grey-blue silk, handle of wood. *from Barnard Collection and now in Snowshill Collection*

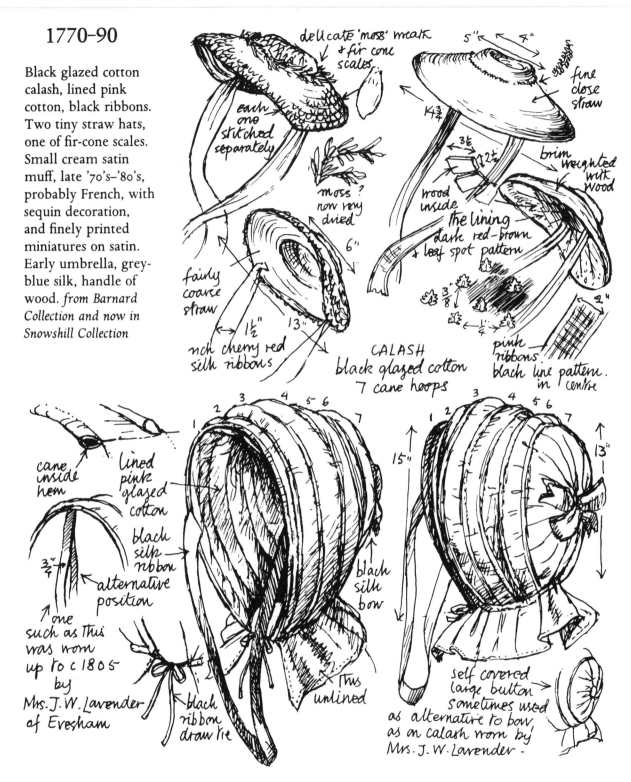

delicate 'moss' wreath & fir cone scales

each one stitched separately

moss? now very dried

6"

fairly coarse straw

rich cherry red silk ribbons

1½" 13"

5" 4"

fine close straw

K 3¾

3½   2½

brim weighted with wood

wood inside

the lining dark red-brown & leaf spot pattern

3/8   1/4   13

2"

pink ribbons black line pattern in centre

CALASH
black glazed cotton
7 cane hoops

cane inside hem

lined pink glazed cotton

black silk ribbon

alternative position

3/4

one such as this was worn up to c 1805 by Mrs. J. W. Lavender of Evesham

black ribbon draw tie

black silk bow

this unlined

15"   13"

self covered large button sometimes used as alternative to bow, as on calash worn by Mrs. J. W. Lavender.

Tiny hats such as these were fashionable in the 18th c., with ribbons tied under the chin or at the back of the head as shown on p. 41, and in the contemporary prints from wood blocks of *c.* 1770 printed in *Forgotten Children's Books*, showing the hat, calash, and muff in use, with

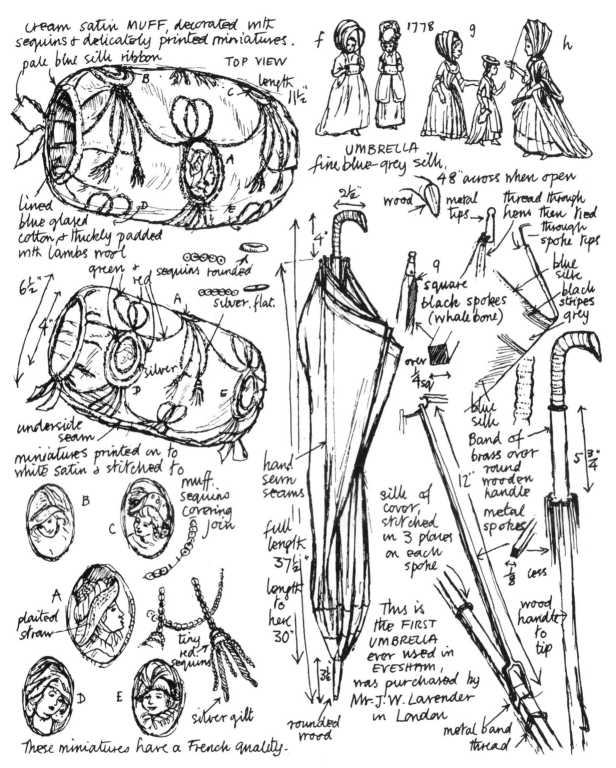

cream satin MUFF, decorated with
sequins & delicately printed miniatures.
pale blue silk ribbon

TOP VIEW

length 11½"

1778

f   g   h

lined
blue glazed
cotton & thickly padded
with lambs wool

6½"

green & red sequins rounded
silver. flat.

4"

silver

underside
seam

miniatures printed on to
white satin & stitched to

B

C

A
plaited
straw

D   E

tiny
red
sequins

silver gilt

These miniatures have a French quality.

muff.
sequins
covering
join

UMBRELLA
fine blue-grey silk,
48" across when open

2½"

wood   metal
tips

thread through
hem then tied
through
spoke tips

4"

9
square
black spokes
(whalebone)

blue
silk
black
stripes
grey

over
¼ sq.

blue
silk
Band of
brass over
round
12" wooden
handle
metal
spokes

5¾"

hand
sewn
seams

silk of
cover,
stitched
in 3 places
on each
spoke

full
length
37½"

length
to
her
30"

This is
the FIRST
UMBRELLA
ever used in
EVESHAM,
was purchased by
Mr. J. W. Lavender
in London

3½"

rounded
wood

⅛ less

wood
handle
to
tip

metal band
thread

the ribbon holding the calash erect. The large dome-shaped umbrella is very heavy. Jonas
Hanway was the first man, in c. 1750, who ventured to walk in London holding up an umbrella;
he died in 1786.

1770-80

Cream silk polonaise, fine thread stripe with tiny yellow dot pattern, woven flower motif in coloured silks. Pleated bands of self silk on skirt front and round neckline, with fine silk braid edging. Bodice and sleeves lined in white linen. Back and front bones in bodice. *worn by Miss Massey of Llanorald, County of Limerick, Ireland. Snowshill Collection*

long thin bone bodice front A - B

red
pink
brown
green
brown

peach tan

brown

or flowers mauve & red

enlarged

slit

small pleat

neck 9"

side seam 10"

front 15"

skirt front 44"

sleeve 14" 11"

8½"

10"

linen lined

A

2 bones

B
boned

thin silk tapes stitched through to buttons hang on inside.

no marching petticoat

Bodice and skirt are here cut separately, no longer having the back pleats in one length of silk neck to hem. This bodice has 8 long bones. The waist is not small but appears quite slender from all but the side view. The thin silk tapes on the inside, for looping up the skirt,

57

1½" 10"

E E

17" centre back

13" side back E-F

2¾"

F

F

V F

V

2 long thin bones at each side of seam

buttons self covered

boned this side of seam

S

S

Bodice front has no indication of any fastening

WAIST 30"

slit to pocket in seam

S

pleated towards centre-back

S

There are No tapes on outside, but this could be an alternative method for looping up the skirt.

centre seam

silk loops tied with green silk

DETAIL of pleated trimming button padded with cotton wool.

hem

seam

silk 19½" width

are quite short, although they may have been cut; there are no traces of loops or other ties, so it is probable that the skirt was caught up by fastening the silk ties round the buttons on the bodice back.

1770-80

Rich plum-coloured shot-silk taffeta robe. A polonaise, petticoat matching, trimmed all round with deep flounce. Trimmings or 'furbelows' with applied serpentine bands and 'buttons' on skirt. Bodice with 6 bones at back. Bodice and sleeves lined white linen. Trimmings on sleeve missing.
Snowshill Collection

trimming DETAIL
tiny box pleats

1½"

edges pinked & scallop shaped

14"

WAIST 28"

petticoat front 35"

14½"

Box pleats

fold here stitched down

length of back skirt 52"

MATCHING PETTICOAT has pleats facing to sides, smaller, & unlike box pleats on gown.
    Applied serpentine pleated band has flat, self-covered buttons, larger towards hem width 1¾"

top button 1"

petticoat side length 40"

fold stitched

flounce on petticoat, all round.

This crisp silk dress is looped up with three ties inside the skirt. A 'bustle' pad or 'false rump' under the petticoat would give the extra fullness to the skirt, which is cut separately and sewn to the bodice in flat box pleating. The petticoat is not pleated in the same way. The

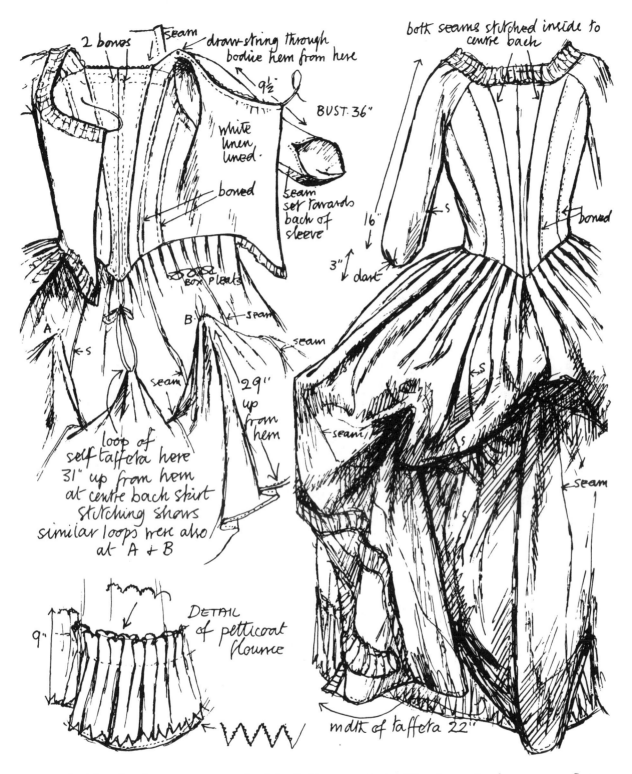

2 bones

seam

draw-string through
bodice hem from here

9½"

BUST 36"

white
linen
lined.

boned

seam
set towards
back of
sleeve

both seams stitched inside to
centre back

16"

3" dart

s

boned

box pleats

A

B

s

seam

seam

seam

29"
up
from
hem

seam

s

s

s

seam

loop of
self taffeta here
31" up from hem
at centre back skirt
stitching shows
similar loops were also
at A + B

9"

DETAIL
of petticoat
flounce

width of taffeta 22"

applied bands of trimming remained in fashion c. 1760–80. The decorative buttons are flat card covered in self silk; on some dresses they are padded with cotton-wool. The bodice has no trace of fastenings.

1775-80

Stiff cream silk, with wide ribbed satin stripe brocaded with flower sprays in coloured silk. Polonaise, with bodice fully boned, total 12. Three pairs tape ties inside, bodice to skirt. White linen lining to bodice and sleeves. Embroidered muslin ruffles, sewn to sleeve. Matching petticoat, with flounce of deep scallop shapes.
Snowshill Collection

These seams face in towards centre back which is boned.

pleats from side seam only - all face to centre back

S →

Total, 12 bones in this bodice

seams

30" WAIST.

slit to pocket in seam, This side only, corresponding one also in matching petticoat.

S.

two fine muslin ruffles

DETAIL of embroidered muslin ruffles

leaf

detail of stem, in outline stitch.

the leaves are over-stitched on wrong side giving a raised effect

very fine patterns of drawn thread work

seam

seam

seam   C.   B   A   B

C

width of silk 19"

The popularity of these looped-up skirts declined during the early '80's, and the use of elaborate trimming went out of fashion. The cut of the bodice changed, but the number of seams and bones here is rather uncommon. The pleating of the skirt too altered, the fullness moving

Bodice & sleeves lined white linen

Traces of stitching probably cuff alteration

detail of these embroidered muslin ruffles on facing page

waist to hem 38"

centre back

14"

7⅜"

This motif repeated but reversed

all pinky-red

A ↑ B

large & small flower sprays alternating

pink
red
black
green

2⅜"

1"

plain silk trailing pattern

C

wide ribbed satin panels 7⅜ full width

ostrich feather & roses on head-dress

striped silk polonaise over quilted petticoat with flounce

from the painting by John Zoffany of John Wilkes & his daughter 1779

apron of striped gauze also flounce of gauze

Zoffany included his dog in many of his paintings

towards the back, shown well in this dress, which has the side-front skirt quite plain. The small study of John Wilkes' daughter well shows the accessories, ribbon trimmings, and hair style worn by the fashionable lady of the late '70's.

1775–80

Inside and front view, stiff cream silk dress, ribbed satin stripe with flower sprays. Polonaise. Matching petticoat, with one flounce of deep scallop shapes, 2nd flounce missing. Bodice front and back boned, stitched eyelets for front lacing. Sleeve shows alteration, sewn on muslin ruffles. Separate pair, double embroidered ruffles. *Snowshill Collection*

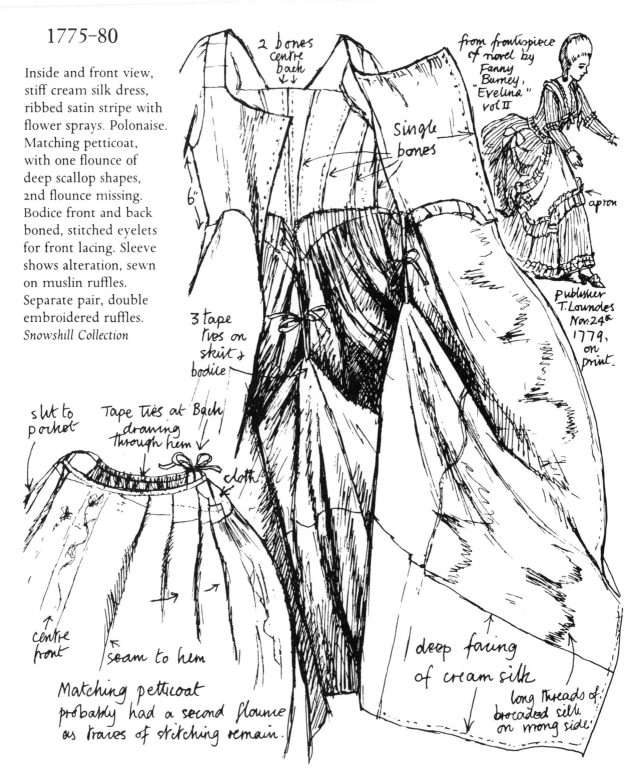

2 bones centre back

Single bones

from frontispiece of novel by Fanny Burney, "Evelina" vol II

apron

Publisher T. Lowndes Nov. 24th 1779, on print.

6"

3 tape ties on skirt & bodice

slit to pocket

Tape ties at Back drawing through hem

cloth

centre front

seam to hem

Matching petticoat probably had a second flounce as traces of stitching remain.

I deep facing of cream silk

long threads of brocaded silk on wrong side.

Front and side-front of this petticoat are of the matching silk, also a band at the back, 12" up from the hem, which is made from odd pieces sewn together. The rest of the petticoat is made of a cream woollen cloth. A false rump or bustle pad would have been worn under-

63

draw-string across front in hem

front boned

front 12"

ALSO in SNOWSHILL COLLECTION
a pair of double Embroidered muslin ruffles

seams 1½"

1"

2"

6"

8"

for Left arm + one of the pair for Right arm

wrong side

13"

right side

Detail

traces of stitching

10

1

2

4   3

neath. Longer sleeves to below the elbow were now becoming fashionable. These show signs of lengthening. The long sleeves in the study could be detached, and are similar to those on the patterned yellow silk jacket (p. 12).

c. 1780

Printed cotton robe, a polonaise. Stripes of pale pink and white with trailing floral sprays in pinky-red, blue and green leaves, blue and mauve for other flowers. This is printed in madder colours with pencilled blue added. Bodice and sleeves lined in white linen. Skirt is sewn to bodice with very fine pleating. *Snowshill Collection*

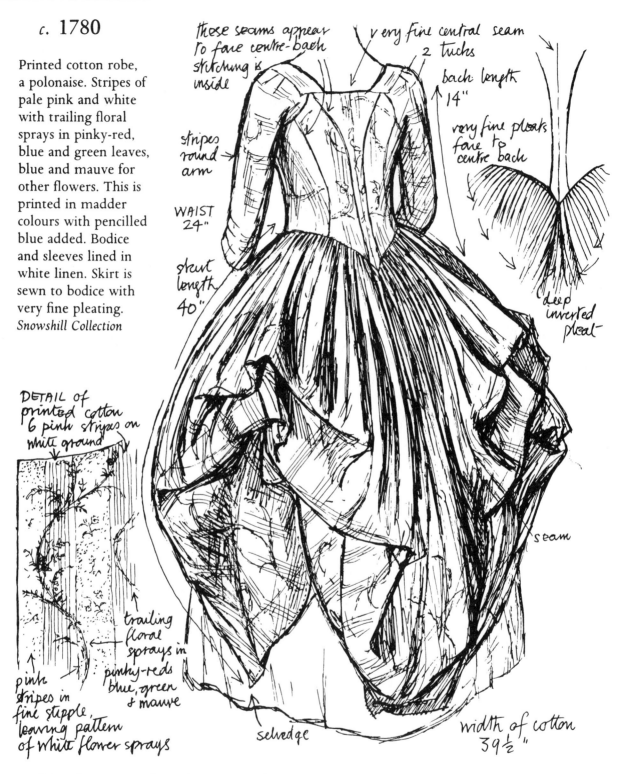

these seams appear to face centre-back stitching is inside

very fine central seam
2 tucks
back length 14"

very fine pleats face to centre back

stripes round arm

WAIST 24"

skirt length 40"

deep inverted pleat

DETAIL of printed cotton 6 pink stripes on white ground

trailing floral sprays in pinky-reds blue, green & mauve

pink stripes in fine stipple, leaving pattern of white flower sprays

selvedge

seam

width of cotton 39½"

Printed cottons such as this were used a great deal for informal dress by the 1780's, when elaborate 'pin-grounds' and finely outlined patterns were obtained in these printed cottons, by the use of metal strip and pins inserted into the wood-blocks. This attractive example,

65

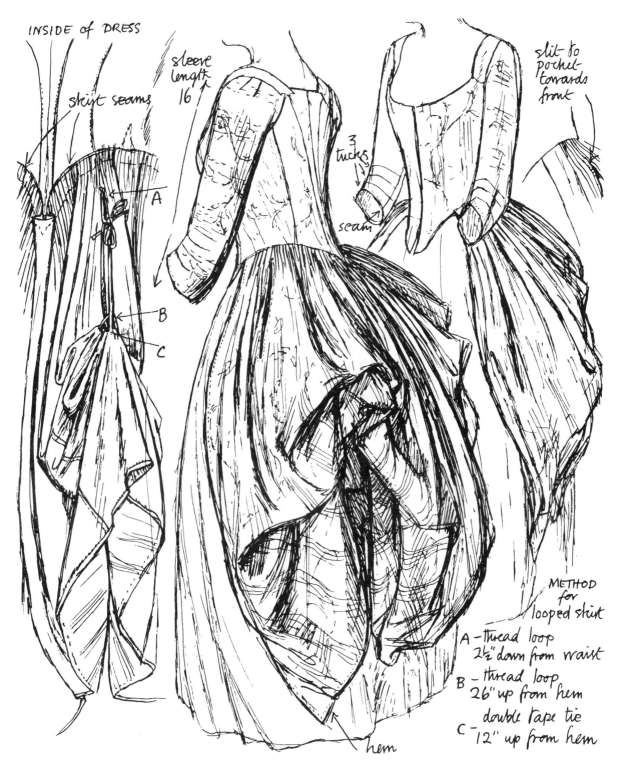

INSIDE of DRESS

skirt seams

sleeve length 16

3 tucks

seam

slit to pocket towards front

A

B

C

METHOD for looped skirt

A – thread loop 2½" down from waist

B – thread loop 26" up from hem

double tape tie

C – 12" up from hem

hem

with its prettily draped skirt, still with its original tape-ties and loops, would probably have been worn over a muslin petticoat. The front of the bodice, by its signs of wear, was pinned together; the back seams face in, to the centre.

18th century

Silver lace robings
c. 1750, with matching
stomacher and cuffs.
1700–50 stomacher,
ivory silk, embroidery
in deep red, brown,
pale yellow, light and
dark green silks, and
silver thread, closely
boned and lined.
A rare pair of French
garters, of late 18th c.
Stockings, fine cream
silk, delicate open-
work at ankle.
Snowshill Collection

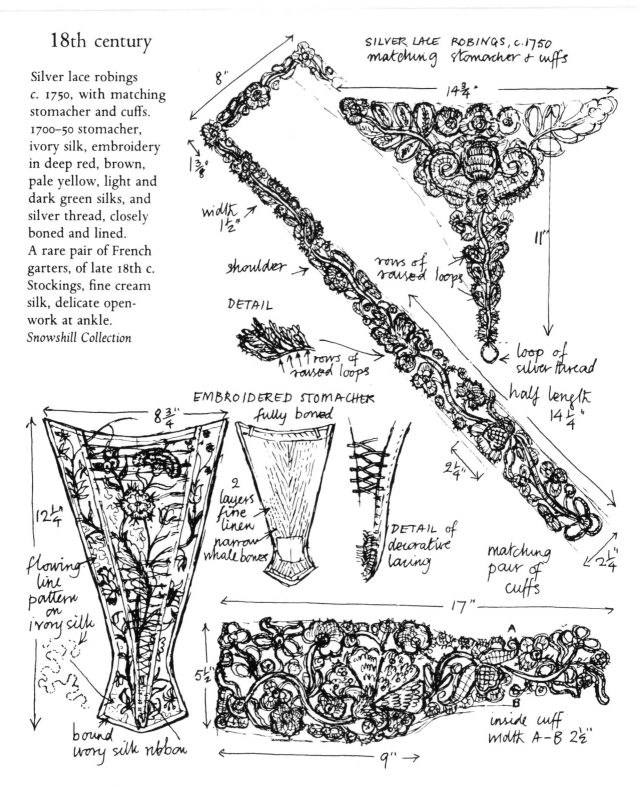

SILVER LACE ROBINGS, C.1750
matching stomacher & cuffs

8"

14¾"

1⅜"

width 1½"

shoulder

rows of raised loops

DETAIL

rows of raised loops

11"

loop of silver thread

half length 14¼"

2¼"

EMBROIDERED STOMACHER
fully boned

8¾"

12¼"

flowing line pattern on ivory silk

bound ivory silk ribbon

2 layers fine linen

narrow whale bones

DETAIL of decorative lacing

matching pair of cuffs

2¼"

17"

5½"

A

B

inside cuff width A-B 2½"

9"

Such silver lace robings are rare; these were made for a dress with winged cuffs of *c.* 1740–50.
The embroidered stomacher also is a fine example of 18th c. needlework. The French garters,
with their tiny brass wire springs, are perfect, and, like the fine cream silk stockings, could

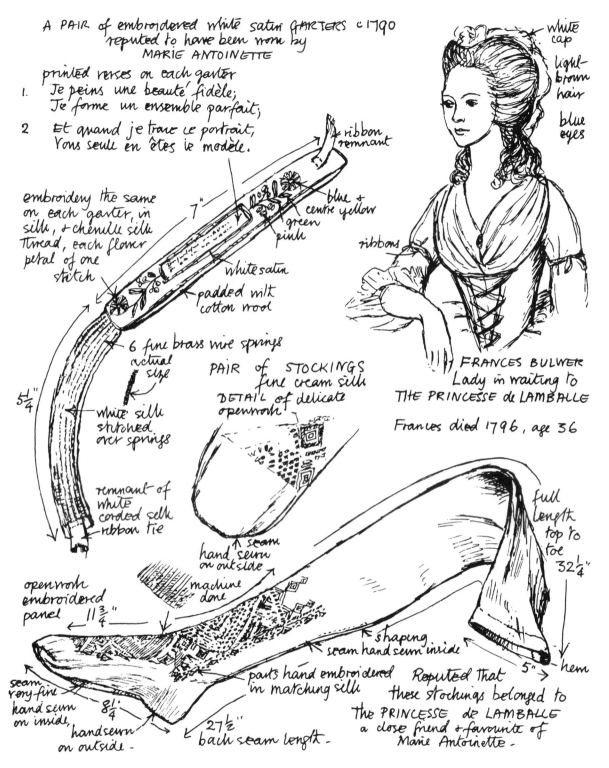

A PAIR of embroidered white satin GARTERS c 1790
reputed to have been worn by
MARIE ANTOINETTE

printed verses on each garter

1. Je peins une beauté fidèle;
   Je forme un ensemble parfait;

2. Et quand je trace ce portrait,
   Vous seule en êtes le modèle.

ribbon remnant

embroidery the same on each garter, in silk, + chenille silk thread, each flower petal of one stitch

7"

blue + centre yellow
green
pink

white satin

padded with cotton wool

6 fine brass wire springs actual size

5¼"

white silk stitched over springs

remnant of white corded silk ribbon tie

PAIR of STOCKINGS
fine cream silk
DETAIL of delicate openwork

seam hand sewn on outside

machine done

white cap
light brown hair
blue eyes

ribbons

FRANCES BULWER
Lady in waiting to
THE PRINCESSE de LAMBALLE

Frances died 1796, age 36

full length top to toe 32¼"

openwork embroidered panel 11¾"

seam very fine hand sewn on inside, 8¼" handsewn on outside

27½" back seam length

parts hand embroidered in matching silk

shaping seam hand sewn inside

5" hem

Reputed that these stockings belonged to THE PRINCESSE de LAMBALLE a close friend + favourite of Marie Antoinette.

perhaps have been brought back to England by Frances Bulwer, after the unfortunate Princess was murdered in 1792; and then remained in the Bulwer family, until they were inherited by Charles Wade of Snowshill in the 20th c.

1780's

White printed cotton, informal dress, woven check pattern. Printed trailing flower sprays on yellow branching or 'twig' background, in natural colours, of mainly red flowers, some blue and white. Green stalks obtained by pencil blue over the yellow. Bodice boned back and front, with front lacing. Bodice and sleeves linen-lined. *Snowshill Collection*

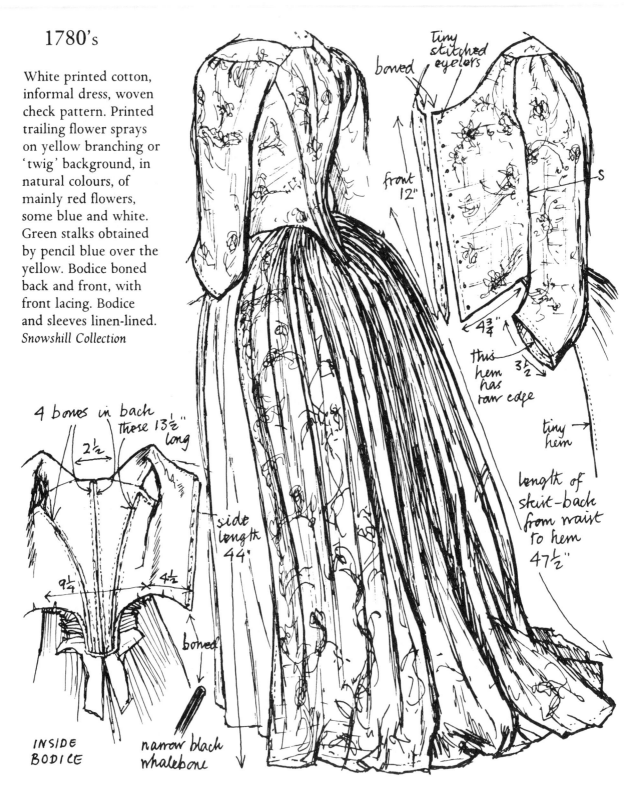

boned

tiny stitched eyelets

front 12"

S

4¾"

this hem has raw edge

3½

tiny hem

length of skirt-back from waist to hem 47½"

4 bones in back these 13½" long

2½

side length 44"

9¼   4½

boned

INSIDE BODICE

narrow black whalebone

Made for a tall, slender woman, this dress hangs in rich yet delicate folds, with the bodice tapering well down at centre back, which is boned for its full length. Bodice front and side-back are cut in one piece. It would have been worn over a muslin robe or petticoat, and a

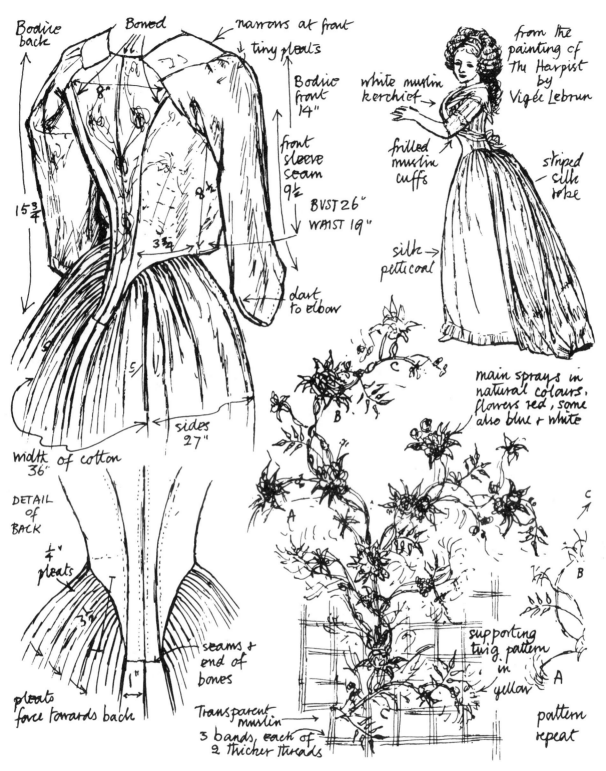

Bodice back

Boned

narrows at front

tiny pleats

8"

8"

Bodice front 14"

front sleeve seam 9½

BUST 26"
WAIST 19"

15¾

3½

dart to elbow

from the painting of The Harpist by Vigée Lebrun

white muslin kerchief

frilled muslin cuffs

striped silk robe

silk petticoat

sides 27"

width of cotton 36"

DETAIL of BACK

¼" pleats

3½

seams & end of bones

1"

pleats force towards back

Transparent muslin 3 bands, each of 2 thicker threads

main sprays in natural colours, flowers red, some also blue + white

supporting twig pattern in yellow

pattern repeat

A   B   C

false rump would have given the necessary fullness at the back. A muslin neckerchief covering the bosom was usual, most likely tied at the back as in the small figure study, with the hair dressed wider and looser than in the 1770's.

2nd half 18th c.

White printed cotton, small child's dress, open in front, hook-and-eye fastening on bodice. Block-printed floral pattern, pinks, mauves, and pencilled blue. Linen lining to bodice and sleeves. Skirt pleated at back. Tiny doll on stick, wax head and arms. Silk dress pasted on paper, braid edging of silk and silver wire. *Snowshill Collection*

from the painting at Windsor of Queen Charlotte & her family

by Zoffany 1775-80

black lace or gauze

ribbons from child

DETAIL showing child with DOLL

this doll has legs & feet with shoes on

width all round hem 81

CHILD'S DRESS BACK VIEW

FRONT

7¼
5½
10¼
7¼

seam

lining to here

front repaired both sides

Joins

wide gusset & joins

wide gusset & joins

21¼

seam

joins seam

Bodice & sleeves lined coarse white linen neatly sewn

3¼
6½

WAIST 22¾

gusset each side

join

round brass wire hooks & eyes

seams

2 small gussets + seam

join & gusset

2 gussets + seam

BACK DETAIL

1"
3¼"

loops white cotton

double inverted pleats

from The Fruit Barrow by H. Walton 1779

child's open robe

A 1"

B

pinks

C

blue leaves & stalks

seams

A charming little child's dress, probably made from remnants, it shows signs of considerable wear; one wonders what story lies behind its preservation. The pattern varies a great deal in the printing. Large flowers are pink, mauve, or blue, but with the smaller flowers, such as

71

pearl pin

HEIGHT of DOLL

8"

← white wig, cotton-wool - 3 rows of curls

pleated white ribbon

lace

wax

green silk bow

pearl pin

wax head & shoulders

linen

pin set in silver sequin in centre of rosettes

stick

pages of old book printed in Latin

fine silver wire trimming on stomacher

finest thin open gauze veil, like a cobweb.

1¼"

2¾"

lace

white satin

fan shaped falling cuff

wax

4"

6½

braid of silk strands white pink & green

scalloped edge to cuff

needlepoint lace ruffles of linen thread, quite strong.

wax arms & hands

white silk with pink stripes

pink silk tacked to paper

braid of silver-gilt.

'A,' no repeats appear the same, being pink or blue or a mixture of both. The hand-painted blue stalks and leaves are carelessly done. On the other hand, the tiny 'doll' is modelled and dressed with delightful taste and finish.

1780-94

Pink printed cotton round gown. Pattern, trailing flower sprays in dark red, blue, and green. Background mainly pink with red pin dot, and yellow small diamond and leaf pattern. Fastening front bodice with an apron-front skirt. Deep wide neckline, bodice and sleeves lined white cotton. Black leather shoes. *Snowshill Collection*

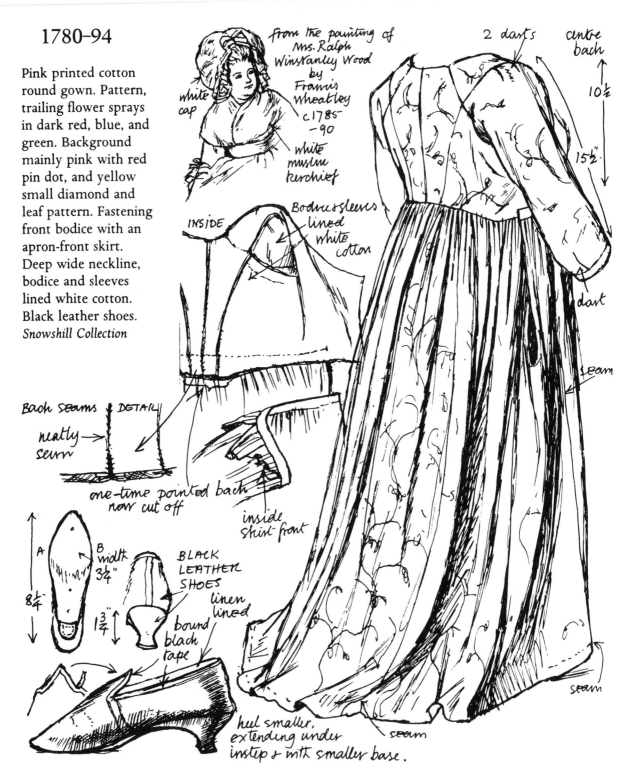

from the painting of Mrs. Ralph Winstanley Wood by Francis Wheatley c 1785-90

white cap

white muslin kerchief

2 darts   centre back

10½

15½"

Bodice & sleeves lined white cotton

INSIDE

dart

seam

Back Seams   DETAIL
neatly → sewn

one-time pointed back now cut off

inside skirt-front

A

B width 3¼"

8¼

1¾"

BLACK LEATHER SHOES
linen lined
bound black tape

heel smaller, extending under instep & with smaller base.

seam

seam

This cotton, with but two blue warp threads in the selvedge, dates about 1780–90. It was made for a short, stout woman, but about 1794 she must have altered the dress to give it a higher, more fashionable waistline. Skirts are no longer open in front; this is a closed robe.

73

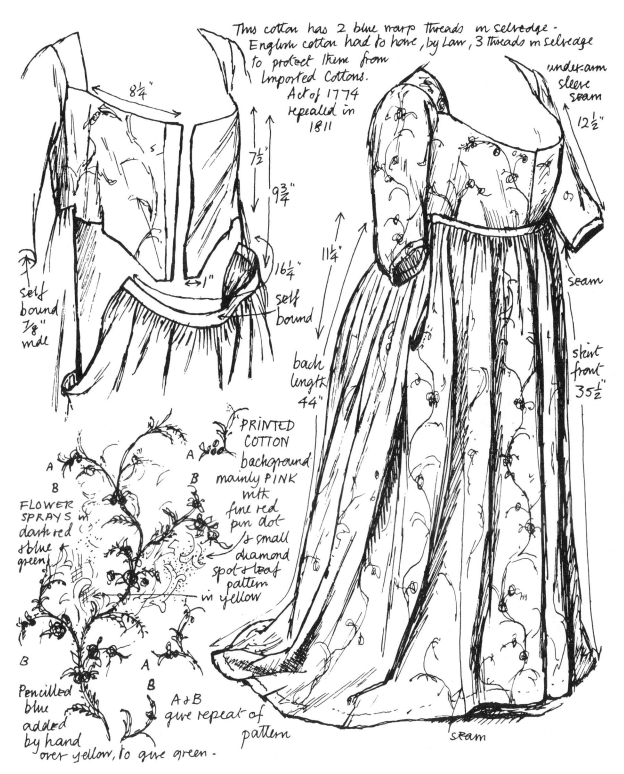

This cotton has 2 blue warp threads in selvedge.
English cotton had to have, by Law, 3 threads in selvedge
to protect them from
Imported Cottons.
Act of 1774
repealed in
1811

8¼"

under-arm
sleeve
seam

12½"

7½"

9¾"

11¼"

16¼"

1"

self
bound
⅞" wde

self
bound

seam

back
length
44"

skirt
front
35½"

seam

FLOWER
SPRAYS in
dark red
& blue
green

A

B

A

B

PRINTED
COTTON
background
mainly PINK
with
fine red
pin dot
& small
diamond
spot & leaf
pattern
in yellow

B

A

B

Pencilled
blue
added
by hand
over yellow, to give green.

A & B
give repeat of
pattern

A bustle pad would still be worn, though smaller, and the bosom covered with a kerchief, and the hair with a mob-cap. Shoes undergo a marked change, the heels becoming smaller and lower, until they eventually disappear.

1790-1800

Earlier printed cotton altered to later style, with high waistline. Delicate interlacing floral pattern with fine black-line stems; flowers pink and pale mauve, leaves and flowers pale blue and yellow. Open robe, low wide neckline. Printed cotton caraco or jacket, intricate formal floral pattern dark red, blue, black.
Snowshill Collection

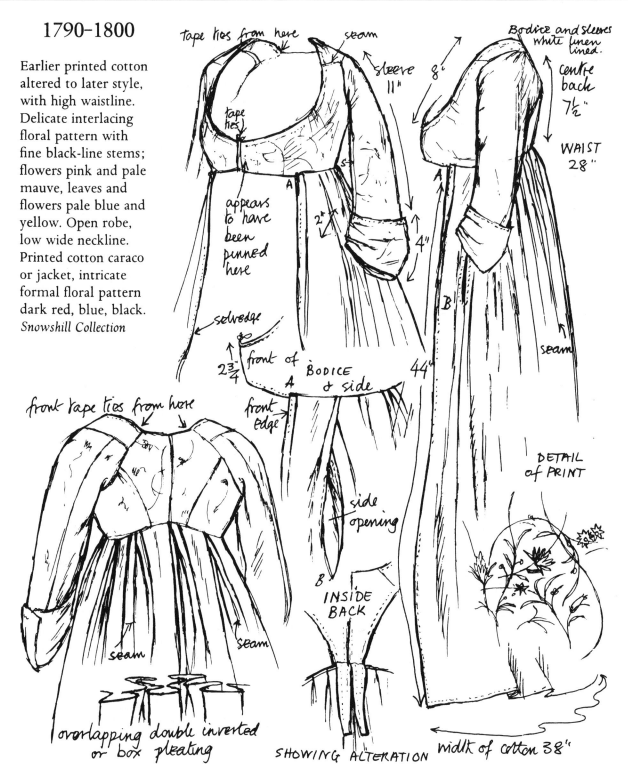

tape ties from here

seam

sleeve 11"

Bodice and sleeves white linen lined.

8"

centre back 7½"

WAIST 28"

tape ties

appears to have been pinned here

5"

2"

4"

A

B

selvedge

2¾"

front of BODICE & side

A

44"

seam

front edge

side opening

B INSIDE BACK

DETAIL of PRINT

front tape ties from here

seam

seam

overlapping double inverted or box pleating

SHOWING ALTERATION

width of cotton 38"

Printed cottons and plain muslins replace silk for all informal wear. Lavish dress seen prior to the French Revolution is gone. Simple styles have a very high waistline, which remains for another 20 years. The caraco, a waisted, thigh-length jacket, was worn as the bodice of a

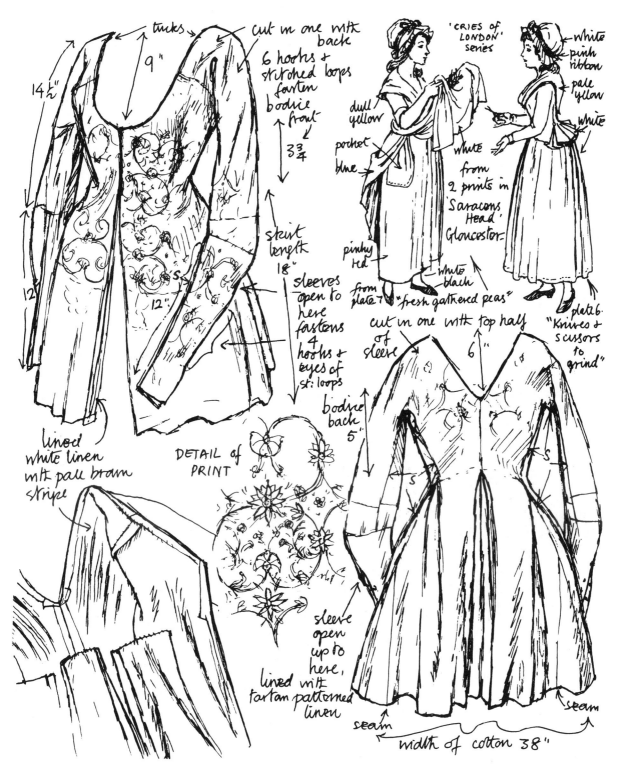

tucks

cut in one with back

6 hooks & stitched loops fasten bodice front

9"

14½"

12

12"

skirt length 18"

sleeves open to here fastens 4 hooks & eyes of st: loops

lined white linen with pale brown stripe

DETAIL of PRINT

sleeve open up to here, lined with tartan patterned linen

'CRIES of LONDON' series

dull yellow

pocket

blue

pinky red

from plate 7

white black

"fresh gathered peas"

white

from 2 prints in 'Saracens Head' Gloucester

white

pink ribbon

pale yellow

white

plate 6.

"Knives & scissors to grind"

cut in one with top half of sleeve

6"

bodice back 5"

S

S

width of cotton 38"

seam

seam

gown, being called a 'caraco dress' when complete with a skirt. It was a popular and useful garment for 'working' women. This example may have belonged to a foreign worker, the cut of the sleeve in with bodice is unusual.

Late 18th c.

Fan, painted skin leaf, ivory sticks and guards, all richly decorated. Fan printed 1789, on white paper. Wooden guards and sticks, country dance tunes.
Richard Radway

Three pairs shoes, very pointed toes, tiny heels. Maker's name on green leather pair. Smaller heels on black cloth shoes and on yellow and pink pair.
Snowshill Collection

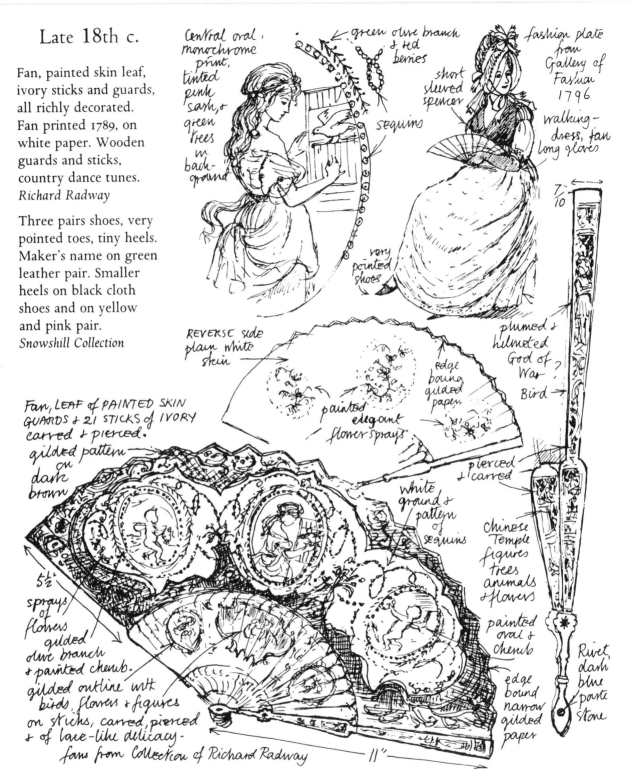

Central oval, monochrome print, tinted pink sash, & green trees in background

green olive branch & red berries

sequins

very pointed shoes

short sleeved spencer

fashion plate from Gallery of Fashion 1796

walking-dress, fan & long gloves

7/10

REVERSE side plain white skin

painted elegant flower sprays

edge bound gilded paper

plumed & helmeted God of War?

Bird →

Fan, LEAF of PAINTED SKIN GUARDS & 21 STICKS of IVORY carved & pierced.

gilded pattern on dark brown

pierced & carved

white ground & pattern of sequins

Chinese Temple figures trees animals & flowers

5½

sprays of flowers gilded olive branch & painted cherub.

gilded outline with birds, flowers & figures on sticks, carved, pierced & of lace-like delicacy.

painted oval & cherub

edge bound narrow gilded paper

Rivet dark blue paste stone

fans from Collection of Richard Radway

— 11" —

The ivory guards and sticks of the beautifully painted skin fan are very richly carved and pierced, the lower decorated part of the sticks being particularly fine. They make a striking contrast to the simple yet charmingly shaped sticks on the 'Country Dance' fan of 1789.

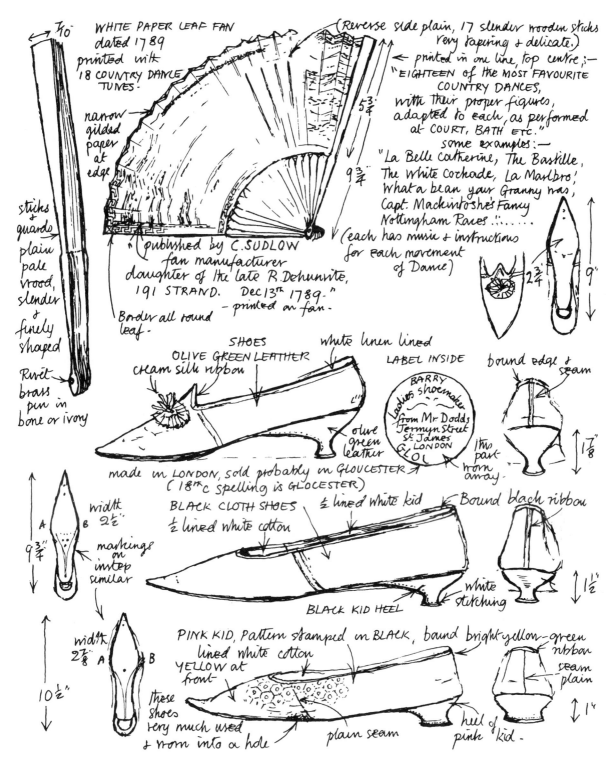

↑ 1/10"

WHITE PAPER LEAF FAN
dated 1789
printed with
18 COUNTRY DANCE
TUNES.

narrow → gilded
paper
at
edge

sticks
+ guards
plain
pale
wood,
slender
+ finely
shaped

Rivet →
brass
pin in
bone or ivory

(Reverse side plain, 17 slender wooden sticks
very tapering + delicate.)

← printed in one line, top centre ;—
"EIGHTEEN of the MOST FAVOURITE
COUNTRY DANCES,
with their proper figures,
adapted to each, as performed
at COURT, BATH etc."
some examples :—
"La Belle Catherine, The Bastille,
The White Cockade, La Marlbro',
What a beau your Granny was,
Capt. Mackintoshe's Fancy
Nottingham Races .:......

(each has music & instructions
for each movement
of Dance)

5 3/4

9 3/4

2 3/4
2 1/4

9"

published by C. SUDLOW
fan manufacturer
daughter of the late R. Dehunvite,
191 STRAND. Dec 13th 1789."
- printed on fan.

Border all round
leaf.

SHOES
OLIVE GREEN LEATHER
cream silk ribbon

white linen lined

LABEL INSIDE

Ladies' shoemaker
BARRY
from Mr Dodds
Jermyn Street
St James
LONDON
GLO[L]

bound edge &
seam

olive
green
leather

this
part
worn
away.

1 7/8"

made in LONDON, sold probably in GLOUCESTER
(18th C spelling is GLOCESTER)

9 3/4"
A   B
width
2 1/2"

markings
on
instep
similar

BLACK CLOTH SHOES
1/2 lined white kid
1/2 lined white cotton

Bound black ribbon

white
stitching

BLACK KID HEEL

1 1/2"

10 1/2"

width
2 7/8" A   B

these
shoes
very much used
+ worn into a hole

PINK KID, pattern stamped in BLACK, bound bright yellow-green
lined white cotton
YELLOW at
front

plain seam

ribbon
seam
plain

heel of
pink kid.

1"

The maker's name printed on the leaf, besides all the dance tunes, makes this fan extremely
fascinating. So too are these pointed shoes; each pair shows the fast decreasing size of the heels
during the '80's and '90's. Heelless ones appear by 1800.

c. 1798–1800

Dark brown printed linen 'two-piece,' of tiny leaf pattern in red, white, and greeny-brown. High-waisted jacket edged with matching frill, also waist-tie. Matching front on inner bodice of linen; hook-and-eye fastening; coarse linen top to separate matching petticoat. Deep, wide neckline. All front fastenings. *Snowshill Collection*

PRINTED LINEN, DARK BROWN GROUND

soft red

white

greeny brown

SKIRT LINED MAUVE LINEN, fine printed pattern

red white purple line

3 frills 1"

12"

waist-band seam only here behind self button

seam

matching 3/4" frill is double

self-faced to waist

27" visible skirt length

1 3/4

10 1/2"

1 1/2"

11"

1"

seam

seam

placing of 1" neck frills self linen right side

Fully lined sleeves white linen

11"

3 1/4"

2 1/2"

seams

close stroked gathers.

seam

seam

seam

Dark-ground printed patterns were fashionable for dress and furnishings from 1790 to 1800. This outfit was made for a short, stout woman. The printed pattern is small and the colouring subdued. A kerchief would have been worn at the neck. Only a small bustle would have

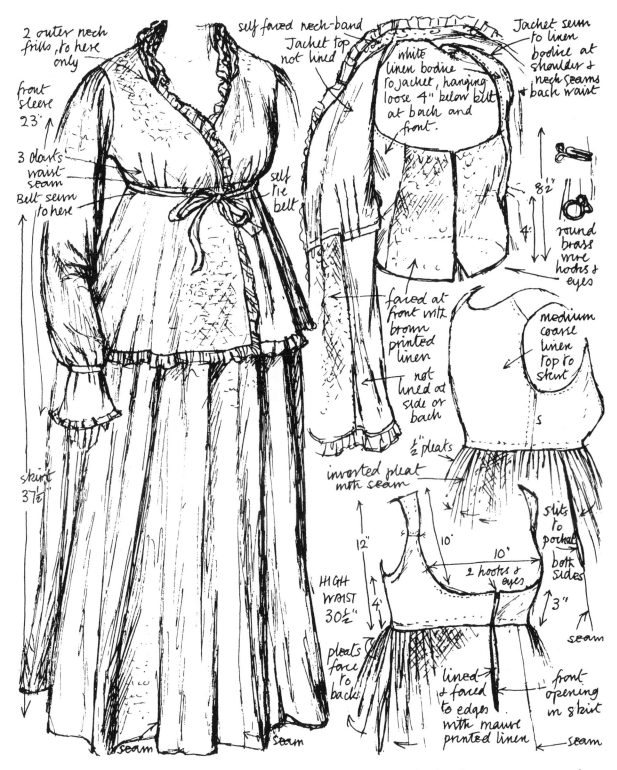

2 outer neck frills, to here only

front sleeve 23"

3 darts waist seam

Belt seam to here

skirt 37½"

self faced neck-band

Jacket top not lined

self tie belt

white linen bodice to jacket, hanging loose 4" below belt at back and front.

Jacket seam to linen bodice at shoulder & neck seams & back waist

8½"

4"

round brass wire hooks & eyes

faced at front with brown printed linen

not lined at side or back

medium coarse linen top to skirt

½" pleats

inverted pleat with seam

slits to pockets both sides

12"

10"

10"

2 hooks & eyes

3"

HIGH WAIST 30½"

4"

seam

pleats face to back

lined & faced to edges with mauve printed linen

front opening in skirt

seam

seam

seam

seam

supported the gathers at the back, as the skirt is even all round. The sleeves are surprisingly long, and are held in at the wrist by the fitting band. The waist is very high, and the stiffly corseted bodice is now no more.

1795-1800

White striped cotton dress, with falling front from waist. Printed in tiny flowing floral pattern in red and blue, with black line, blue and yellow for green. Neckline is high with narrow frill round throat. Bodice front opening, with separate linen under-pieces, joined to back lining. Long, closely fitting sleeves to wrist.
Snowshill Collection

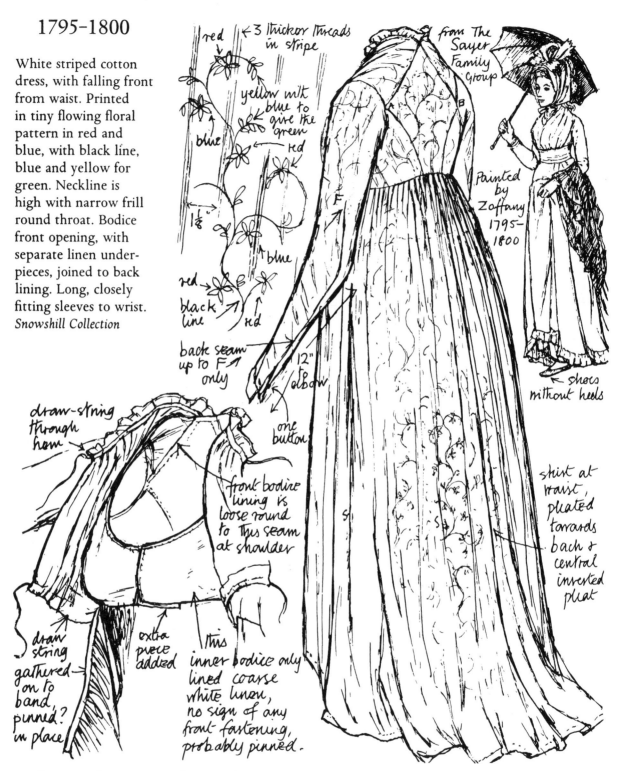

red

← 3 thicker threads in stripe

yellow with blue to give the green

blue

red

1⅛"

blue

red

black line

red

from The Sayer Family Group

B

Painted by Zoffany 1795-1800

← shoes without heels

F

back seam up to F only

12" elbow

one button

skirt at waist, pleated towards back & central inverted pleat

draw-string through hem

front bodice lining is loose round to this seam at shoulder

draw string gathered on to band, pinned? in place

extra piece added

this inner bodice only lined coarse white linen, no sign of any front fastening, probably pinned.

S

S

Dresses take on a new form, high-waisted, long, and slender; full petticoats and stiff stays are done away with. White is the dominating 'colour,' either as plain lawn or muslin, or as background to delicate prints. Until *c.* 1820 colour is usually only in silks. Long sleeves,

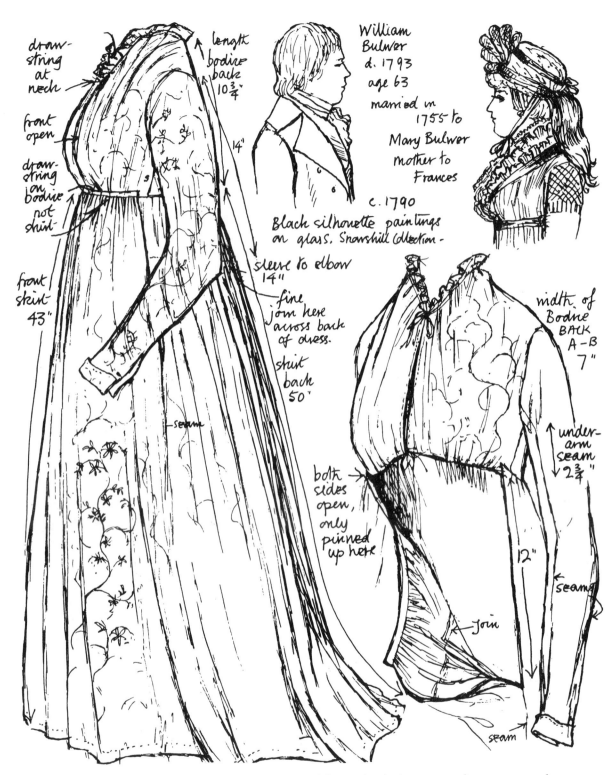

draw-
string
at
neck

front
open

draw-
string
on
bodice
not
skirt

front
skirt
43"

length
bodice
back
10¾"

14"

seam

sleeve to elbow
14"

fine
join here
across back
of dress.

skirt
back
50"

William
Bulwer
d. 1793
age 63
married in
1755 to
Mary Bulwer
mother to
Frances

c. 1790
Black silhouette paintings
on glass. Snowshill Collection.

width of
Bodice
BACK
A – B
7"

under-
arm
seam
2¾"

both
sides
open,
only
pinned
up here

12"

Join

seams

seam

introduced in the '80's, become very fashionable in the '90's; so too, by 1800, are the new heelless shoes. A tiny bustle pad would be tied or pinned to the bodice under the skirt gathers. The front bodice would be pinned.

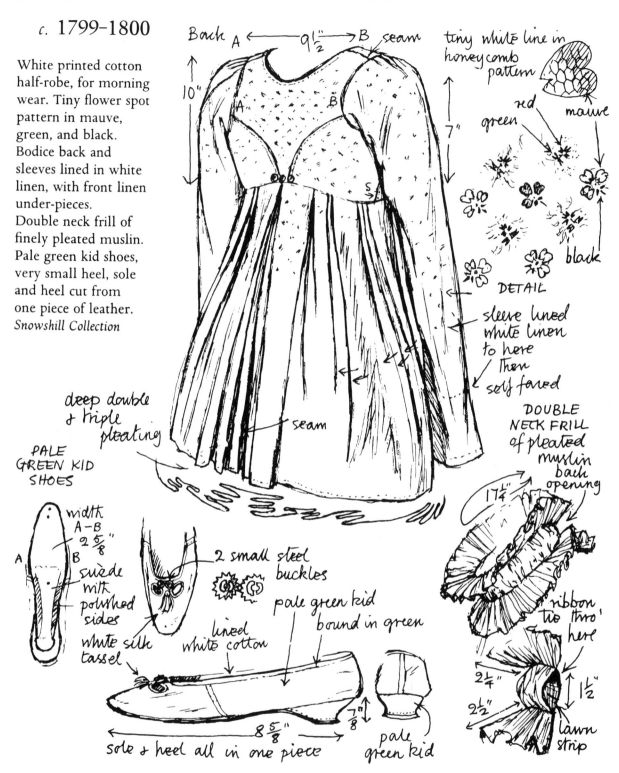

c. 1799–1800

White printed cotton half-robe, for morning wear. Tiny flower spot pattern in mauve, green, and black. Bodice back and sleeves lined in white linen, with front linen under-pieces. Double neck frill of finely pleated muslin. Pale green kid shoes, very small heel, sole and heel cut from one piece of leather. *Snowshill Collection*

Back A ← 9½" → B seam

tiny white line in honeycomb pattern

10"

A   B

7"

red
green   mauve

black

DETAIL

S

sleeve lined white linen to here then self faced

DOUBLE NECK FRILL of pleated muslin back opening

deep double & triple pleating

seam

17¼"

ribbon tie thro' here

PALE GREEN KID SHOES

width A–B 2⅝"

A   B

suede with polished sides

white silk tassel

2 small steel buckles

pale green kid

bound in green

lined white cotton

2¼"

2½"

1½"

lawn strip

8⅝"

⅞"

sole & heel all in one piece

pale green kid

A good example of 'undress' or morning wear. This 'jacket' could have been worn over a white muslin round gown, or have had a separate skirt hooked to it, although these flat brass eyes may be a later addition, as they did not come into use until *c.* 1815. The

83

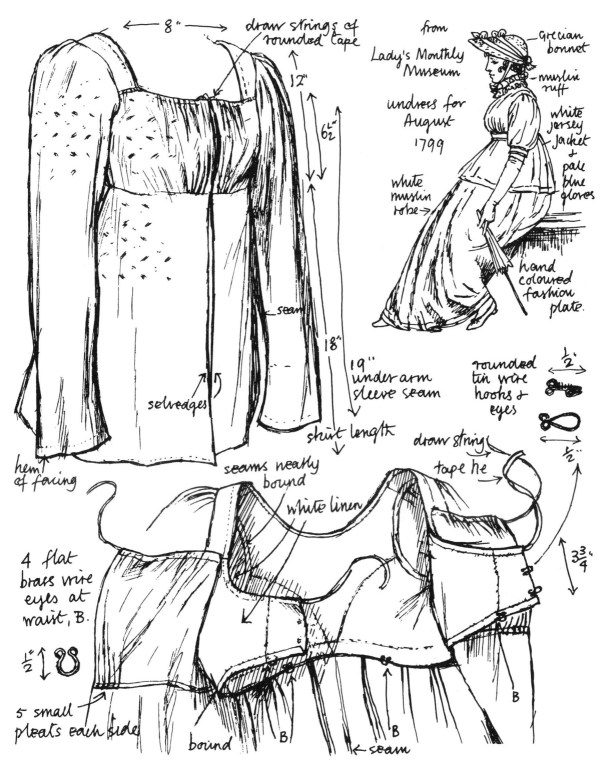

8"

draw strings of rounded tape

12"

6½"

18"

19"
under arm
sleeve seam

seam

selvedges

hem of facing

skirt length

seams neatly bound

white linen

draw strings
tape he

rounded tin wire hooks & eyes

½"

½"

3¾"

4 flat brass wire eyes at waist, B.

½"

5 small pleats each side

bound

B

B

B

seam

from
Lady's Monthly Museum

undress for August 1799

Grecian bonnet

muslin ruff

white jersey jacket + pale blue gloves

white muslin robe →

hand coloured fashion plate.

dainty shoes still have a very tiny heel, but it is soon to disappear for nearly 50 years. The manner of soling these shoes does almost foretell the completely flat, heelless shoe, so soon to be so popular.

1806 From a drawing by Ingres of a family group. Both the women in plain high-waisted dresses, the girl wearing elbow-length mittens. The man is in a double-breasted tail-coat, cut away at the front.

1820 From a hand-coloured print of a 'Group of Parisian Dancers,' for *La Belle Assemblée*, published June 1st. The young woman is in white gauze decorated with blue ribbon, over a white satin slip. The man, all in grey, wears a white shirt and stock.

1824 July fashion-plate in *The Ladies' Pocket Magazine*, shows a dress with lower waist and flounced hem. The study by Dighton *c.* 1830 of James Corry, of No. 2 Montpellier Spa Buildings, in Cheltenham, shows the high velvet collar to his coat and the pantaloon trousers.

2

1800–1835

Gaily coloured woollens, rustling silks, and elaborate embroideries had been worn by English women for centuries, the greater their wealth, the richer and more elaborate their dress. Now, within a few years of some of the most extravagant dresses ever created, the titled woman and the servant dress alike.

Although the tragedy to the Royal House and noble families of France in the late 18th c. had considerable repercussions, changes in the fashionable world had already begun in England. Interest was centred on classical revival, and greater simplicity in dress was already emerging.

From 1800 white muslin gowns grace the feminine form for nearly twenty years; with appropriate hair styles, they are romantic and 'Grecian' in appearance. Stays and petticoats are discarded, and underwear is reduced to the minimum.

The Lady's Monthly Museum, June 1802, gives a contemporary opinion of the 'female demi-nudity . . . the close, all white, shroud looking, ghostly chemise undress of the ladies, who seem to glide like spectres, with their shrouds wrapt tight about their forms, . . . do justify the poet's expression on the following line, "Now sheer *undressing* is the general rage."' Or again, in March 1803, 'a party of high-bred young ladies, who were dressed or rather undressed in all the nakedness of the mode; and could either their limbs or their tongues have been kept quiet, and had they been placed on pedestals or niched in recesses, they might have passed for so many statues very lightly shaded with drapery; . . . it really was as much of hazard of health, as it was trespass against modesty, to come into public *en chemise*, as if they were just out of their beds.' And later, in June of that year, 'a dress may now be made so exceedingly fine and thin, that it may be carried in a pocket-book or conveyed by the two-penny post to any part of the town.'

This brings up the much discussed question of whether or not women damped their dresses. A letter from a very old lady in Devonshire, Miss Ursula Radford, may throw some light on the subject. She writes: 'An old friend of ours, Miss Beatrix Cresswell, whose parents were married in 1845, told this to me . . . her father's mother lived in Northumberland as a child, and a family of cousins from London came to live near them. The London girls wore a "sprinkled chemise" under their frocks, but the grandmother's papa, insisted upon a flannel petticoat for his daughter.'

With the Indian muslins come the Kashmir shawls, large, light, and warm, their richly woven borders a perfect background for the plain high-waisted dresses. But by 1820 elaboration on the bodice, increasing fullness of the sleeve, and decorated hemline bring a return to coloured silks and patterns, tight lacing and embroidered petticoats.

1803-05

White spotted muslin trained dress, with bodice front and skirt in one. The lining of bodice and short little under-sleeves is of white linen. The long muslin sleeves have been cut off at the elbow. Under-pieces of bodice front fasten with draw-string at neck, probably pinned at 'waist.' Tape tie on inside at back.
Snowshill Collection

back width
B ← 6½" → C
gathers
2¾
lace insertion very fine & neat
muslin sleeve full linen lining short & fitting to here
seams
3½"
B
C
A
F
fine gathers
selvedges each side of slit in seam
pleat
seams
full length skirt back 72"
seam
hem
side open.
deep pleat A to
seam
width of muslin 52"
trails on ground 33"

8"
under arm seam
1¾"
A   F
fold →
deep pleat
bodice & skirt front flaps down from here

This graceful trained dress is a good example of the style and construction found 1800–10, and it could have been used for day or evening wear until *c.* 1806, when day dresses with trains are no longer fashionable, although the skirt is often slightly longer at the back than

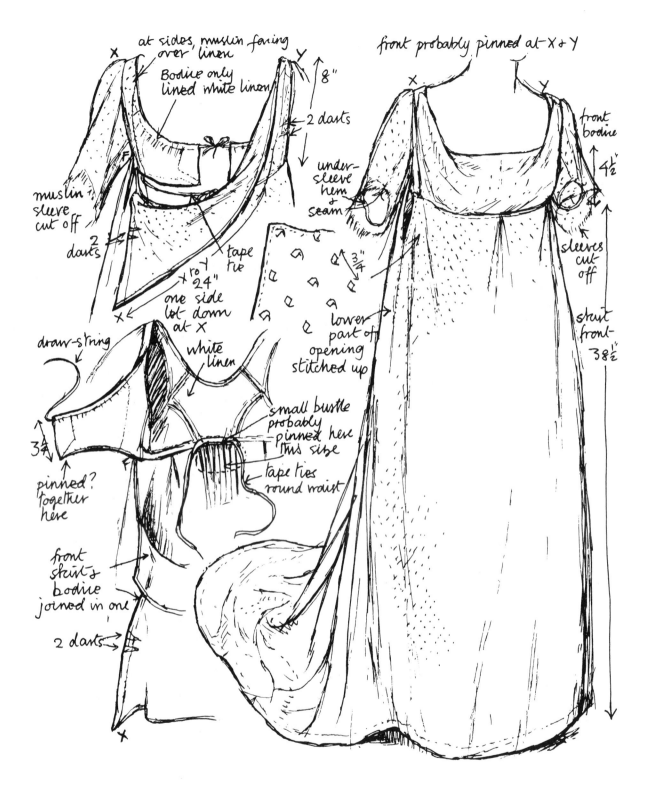

at sides, muslin facing over linen

Bodice only lined white linen

8"

2 darts

X

Y

front probably pinned at X & Y

X

Y

front bodice

4½"

under-sleeve hem & seam

muslin sleeve cut off

2 darts

tape tie

X to Y 24"

one side let down at X

X

white linen

3"

¾

lower part of opening stitched up

sleeves cut off

skirt front 38½"

draw-string

small bustle probably pinned here this size

3¼"

pinned? together here

tape ties round waist

front skirt & bodice joined in one

2 darts

X

at the front. A small bustle pad would still have been needed under this dress to hold out the back gathers. A chemise and waist-petticoat would probably have been the only underwear, with stockings gartered at the knee.

1800-10

White spotted muslin dress, with bodice front joined to apron-front of skirt. Original pins still in position. Bodice lining and half-sleeves of white linen, with front bodice under-pieces pinned together. Bodice back width very narrow, with wide box pleats at skirt back. Bodice side-back cut in one piece with side-front. Sleeves long. *Snowshill Collection*

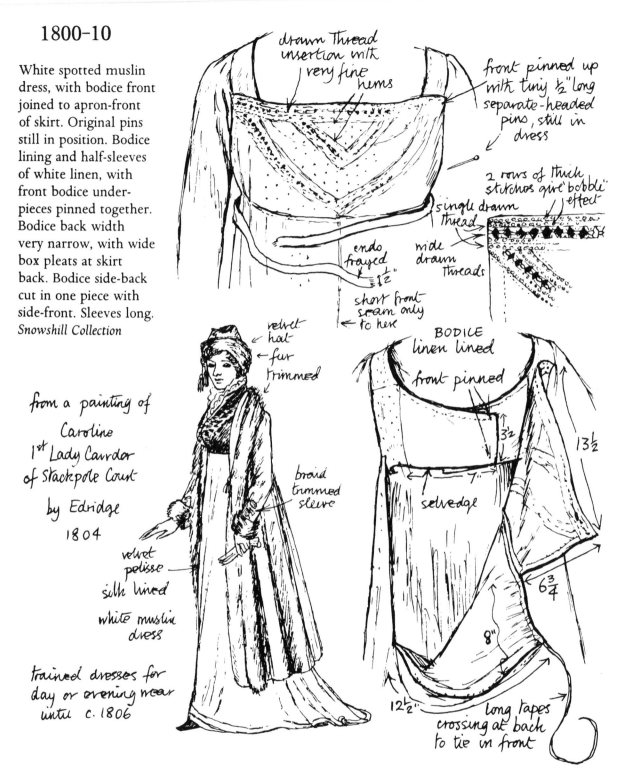

drawn thread insertion with very fine hems

front pinned up with tiny ½" long separate-headed pins, still in dress

2 rows of thick stitches give "bobble" effect

single drawn thread

wide drawn threads

ends frayed 5½"

short front seam only to here

velvet hat
fur trimmed

from a painting of Caroline 1st Lady Cawdor of Stackpole Court by Edridge 1804

braid trimmed sleeve

velvet pelisse
silk lined
white muslin dress

trained dresses for day or evening wear until c.1806

BODICE
linen lined

front pinned

3½

13½

selvedge

7

6¾

8"

12½"

long tapes crossing at back to tie in front

Many varieties of spotted muslins were made. This very simple dress is enriched by the drawn thread-work insertion on bodice and sleeve. The waistline is very high, and again a bustle pad would have supported the box pleats of the skirt at A–B. Plain muslin dresses,

89

DETAIL of spotted muslin at D, on sleeve.

D

$\frac{3}{4}$"

3¼"

centre back 5½"

short linen undersleeve

deep box pleats

long tape ends, to tie in front

side seam under deep pleat

Back width 7½"

D

seam

sleeve 25"

2½"

Belt only stitched at A + B

43"

40" skirt front

from front

side opening under here

seam

muslin 50" wide

seam

seam

seam

side seam

fastening at the back, had been worn by small girls since *c.* 1780, with a wide sash round the waist, and hem at ground-level. They would thus, during the first forty years of their life, **experience** very little change in fashion!

90

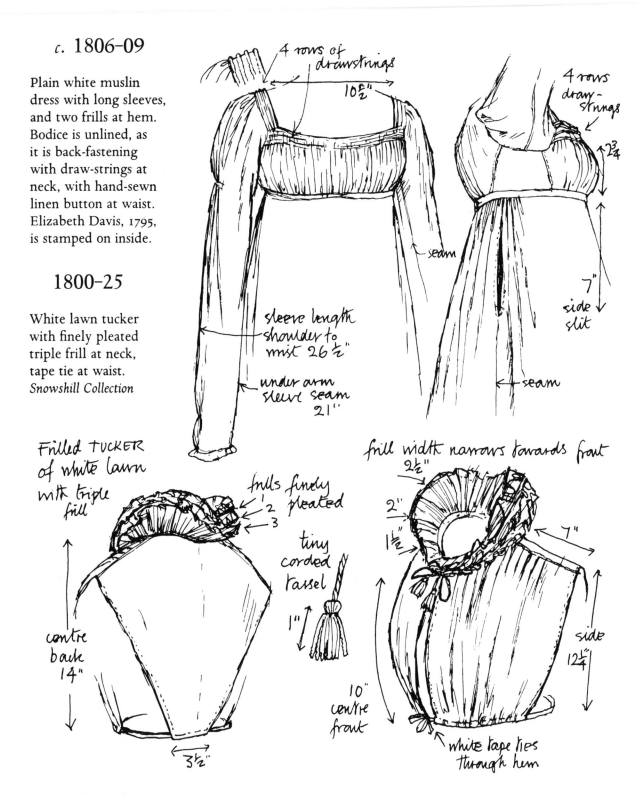

c. 1806–09

Plain white muslin dress with long sleeves, and two frills at hem. Bodice is unlined, as it is back-fastening with draw-strings at neck, with hand-sewn linen button at waist. Elizabeth Davis, 1795, is stamped on inside.

1800–25

White lawn tucker with finely pleated triple frill at neck, tape tie at waist.
Snowshill Collection

4 rows of drawstrings

10½"

4 rows draw-strings

2¾

seam

7"
side slit

sleeve length shoulder to wrist 26½"

under arm sleeve seam 21"

seam

Frilled TUCKER of white lawn with triple frill

frills finely pleated
'1
'2
3

tiny corded tassel

1"

centre back 14"

3½"

frill width narrows towards front
2½"

2"

1½

7"

side 12¼"

10" centre front

white tape ties through hem

This beautifully made dress, with the finest of stitching and gathering, is more of the style *c.* 1806–09 than of the earlier date stamped inside. Another interesting point is that it retains the side-slit, presumably for access to the pocket, although it is usual with these transparent

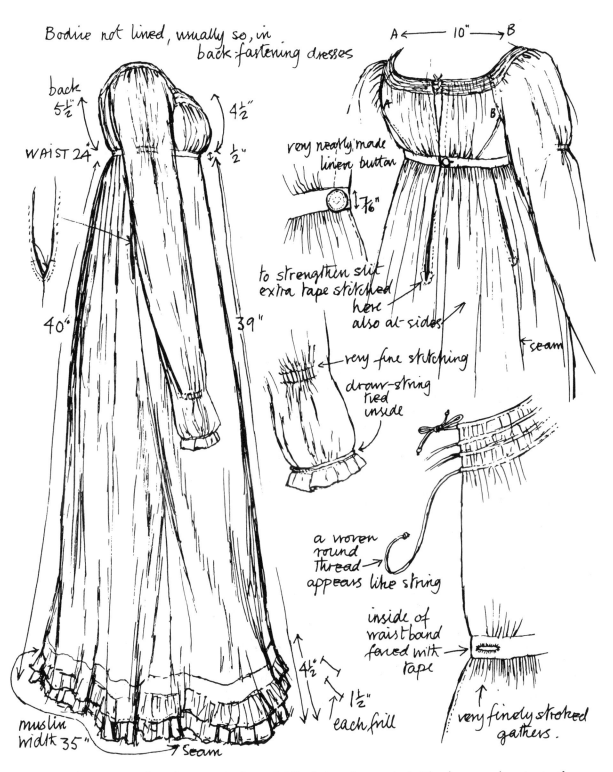

Bodice not lined, usually so, in
back-fastening dresses

back 5½"

4½"

½"

WAIST 24"

40"

39"

A ← 10" → B

A   B

very neatly made
linen button

7/16"

to strengthen slit
extra tape stitched
here
also at sides

seam

very fine stitching

draw-string
tied
inside

a woven
round
thread
appears like string

inside of
waistband
faced with
tape

4½"

1½"
each frill

very finely stroked
gathers.

muslin
width 35"

Seam

figure-clinging muslins for a reticule or 'ridicule' to be carried. The lawn tucker is similar to one that would have been worn with this dress, but this particular example has the waistline at a rather lower level.

c. 1806–09

Full evening dress in plain white muslin, richly embroidered at neck, sleeves, and hem, with heavy gold fringe at hem. High-waisted and back fastening with hooks and eyes of flattened silver wire and draw-string. Tape tie inside. Only sleeves are lined with stiffer coarser muslin. *from Lullingstone Castle in Kent; now at Snowshill Collection*

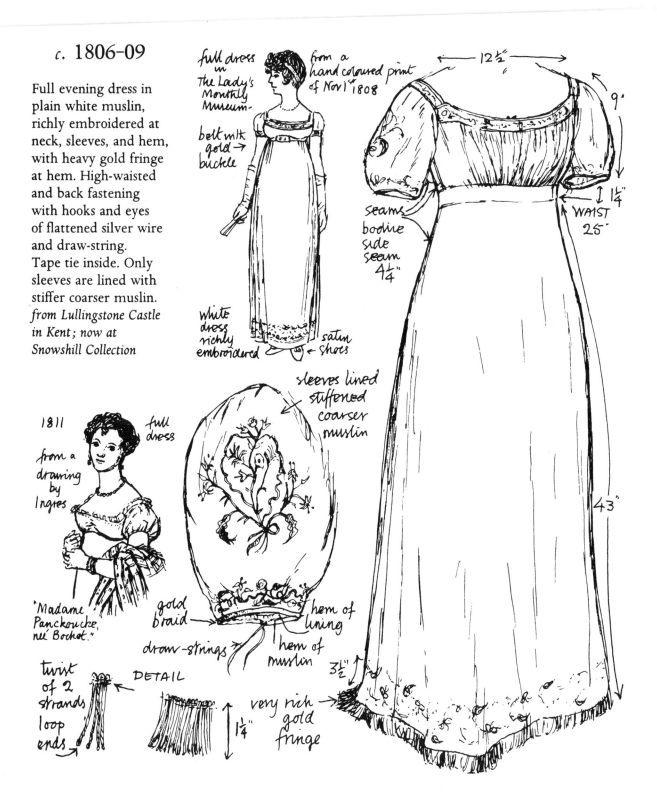

full dress in The Lady's Monthly Museum. from a hand coloured print of Nov 1st 1808

belt with gold buckle

white dress richly embroidered

satin shoes

seams bodice side seam 4¼"

12½"

9"

1¼" WAIST 25"

sleeves lined stiffened coarser muslin

1811 full dress from a drawing by Ingres

"Madame Panckoucke, née Bochet."

gold braid

draw-strings

hem of lining

hem of muslin

43"

3½"

very rich gold fringe

twist of 2 strands loop ends

DETAIL

1¼"

A very simple dress made of the plainest possible muslin, but heavy with the weight of the gold fringe at the hem. The embroidery is exquisite, being sewn with single very fine strands of coloured silks in pink, blue, yellow, green, and grey, for the flowers, buds, and fern, with

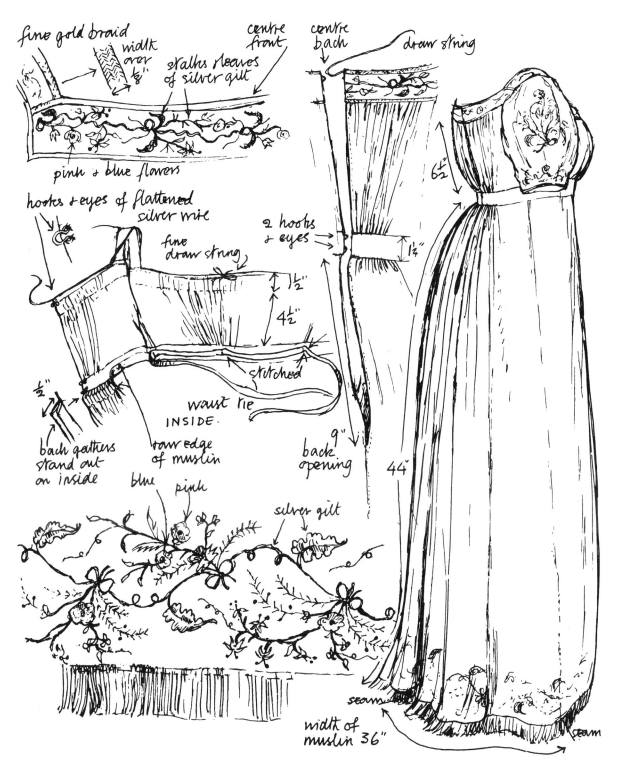

fine gold braid

width over ⅛"

stalks, leaves of silver gilt

centre front

centre back

draw string

pink & blue flowers

hooks & eyes of flattened silver wire

fine draw string

2 hooks & eyes

6½"

1½"

1½"

4½"

stitched

waist tie

INSIDE.

back gathers stand out on inside

raw edge of muslin

½"

back opening

9"

44"

blue

pink

silver gilt

seam

width of muslin 36"

seam

the leaves and stalk in silver-gilt thread. *The Lady's Monthly Museum* 1808 fashion-plate shows a very simple fashionable dress, of 'fine leno over white satin,' belted, and with long buff gloves and a tiny fan.

c. 1810

White muslin dress embroidered in tiny flower motif of brown and blue-grey. The sleeves are very long. Apron-front bodice and skirt, pinned at shoulder. White linen lining to bodice back, with tiny sleeves and narrow under-pieces at front. Frilled hem. Pink satin shoes, no heels, no shaping for left or right feet.
Snowshill Collection

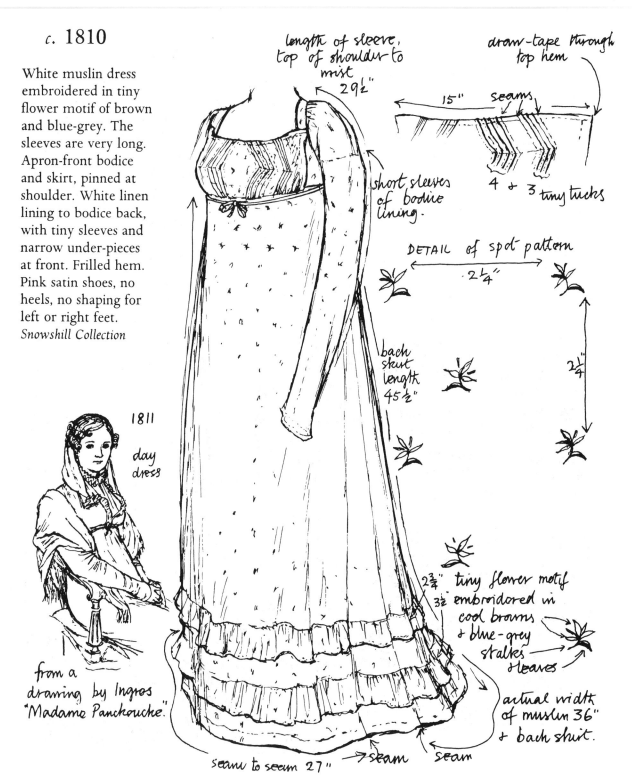

length of sleeve, top of shoulder to wrist 29½"

draw-tape through top hem

15" seams

4 & 3 tiny tucks

short sleeves of bodice lining.

DETAIL of spot pattern
2¼"

2¼"

back skirt length 45½"

1811 day dress

2¾" tiny flower motif
3½ embroidered in cool browns & blue-grey stalks & leaves

from a drawing by Ingres "Madame Panckouche".

actual width of muslin 36" & back skirt.

seam to seam 27" seam seam

White muslin dresses with dainty spot, sprig, or check patterns continue to be in fashion until the '20's. During the years of war with France there is little change, but after 1815 there are hints of new styles to come. There is an increased use of frills at the hemline, and more

95

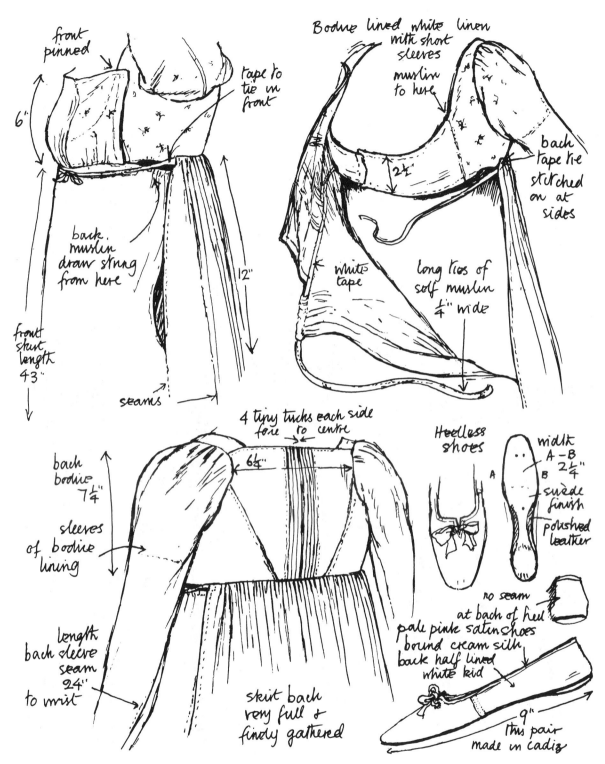

front pinned

6"

tape to tie in front

Bodice lined white linen with short sleeves

muslin to here

back. muslin draw string from here

back tape tie stitched on at sides

2½"

12"

front skirt length 43"

seams

white tape

long ties of self muslin ¼" wide

4 tiny tucks each side fore to centre

6¼"

back bodice 7¼"

sleeves of bodice lining

Heelless shoes

width A – B 2¼"

A

B

suède finish

polished leather

no seam at back of heel

pale pink satin shoes bound cream silk back half lined white kid

length back sleeve seam 24" to wrist

skirt back very full & finely gathered

9" this pair made in cadiz

decoration on the bodice. The waistline reaches its highest level c. 1815–20, then gradually lowers as the hemline increases in width. These heelless shoes, called 'straights,' remain with little change for 50 years. See also Regency dresses pp. 372–374.

1816

Heavy cream cloth caped coat or pelisse. Thick close wool, of felt-like texture, all very finely sewn and finished. Partially lined in black silk. Overlapping front, buttoning neck to hem. High-waisted belt. Slit opening at side with flap. Made to fit a tall woman. *exhibited at Victoria and Albert Museum; lent from Snowshill Collection*

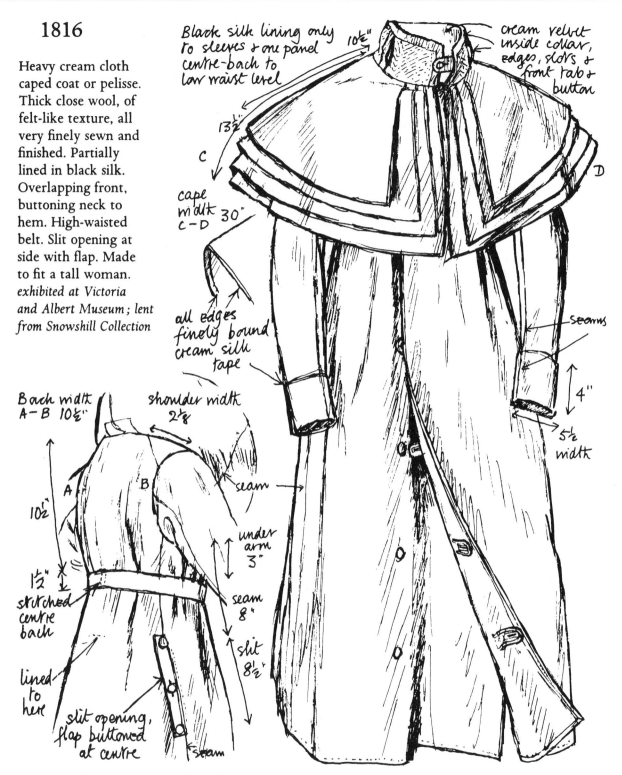

Black silk lining only to sleeves & one panel centre-back to low waist level

10½"

cream velvet inside collar, edges, slots & front tab & button

13½"

C

cape width C-D 30"

D

all edges finely bound cream silk tape

seams

4"

5½ width

Back width A-B 10½"

shoulder width 2⅛

A

B

10½"

seam

under arm 3"

1½"

stitched centre back

lined to hem

seam 8"

slit 8½

slit opening, flap buttoned at centre

seam

Men's box coats are seldom finished so beautifully as this fine and rather rare example of a woman's coat. The edges are left unbound, and, owing to the thickness of the cloth, they do not fray. The tab and slots on the collar are interesting, and none are shown in the fashion

underside of capes

9½"

fashion DETAIL hat & pelisse 1816

velvet slots, back & sides - for scarf ?

3½"

BUST 36"

capes
1
2
3
4

front length 51"

WAIST BELT 30"

Back full length 54"

22½"

27½"

seam

binding
& fine stitching
velvet

Front view showing join of 4th cape to 3rd

4th cape only up to here, stitched to 3rd so finely, can hardly be seen

seam

cream silk binding.

seam

detail of an almost identical pelisse of 1816, which does have the tabs for the concealed front fastening, but they are on the opposite side from this coat. Flat round or bag-shaped reticules were carried.

c. 1815

Day dress, fine white cotton, small woven check pattern in lilac. Double neck frill and very long sleeves, also with double frill at wrist. Apron-front to skirt; bodice fastens in front with cotton under-pieces. Back lined white cotton, also short inner sleeves. Bustle pad sewn in. Two tucks at hem. Dorset button on cuff.
Snowshill Collection

from a print 'The Lake's Nest'

July 29" 1818

printed by William Darton. Jun. London

back width C–D 10"

8¾"

short, fitting inner sleeve of white cotton

C   D

A   B   5"

pleats finely stroked gathers A–B 6"

neck band 15¼"

6"

white cotton

dart

BUSTLE PAD ¾" wide

gathered 12¼ back

23" width of slightly gathered front

seam

back & front each 31" width seam to seam

seam

Many of these simple dresses are beautifully sewn; the stroked gathers, tiny hems on the frills, and the Dorset button on the wrist-band show this to perfection. These fine thread buttons are found on underwear from *c.* 1700, and they remained in use up to *c.* 1830. Sleeves

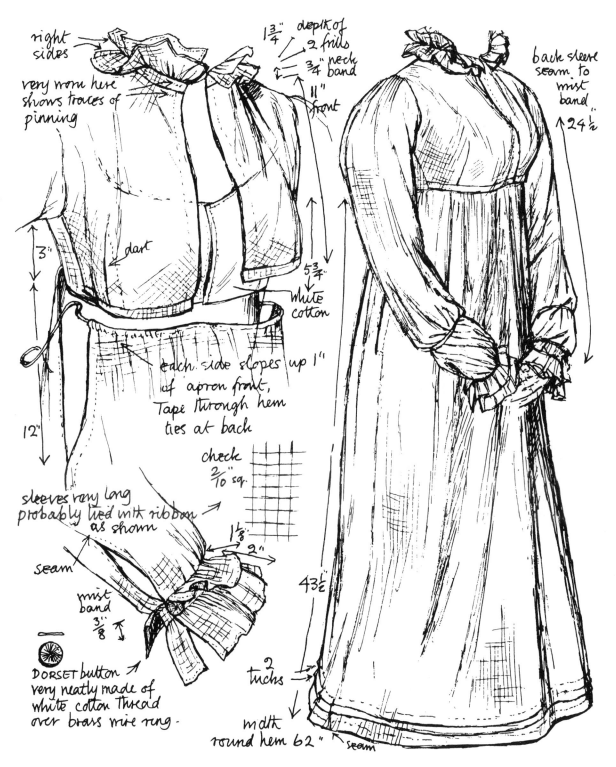

right sides

very worn here shows traces of pinning

$1\frac{3}{4}$" depth of 2 frills

$\frac{3}{4}$" neck band

11" front

dart

3"

12"

each side slopes up 1" of apron front, Tape through hem ties at back

back sleeve seam to wrist band
$24\frac{1}{2}$"

$5\frac{3}{4}$"

White cotton

check $\frac{2}{10}$" sq.

sleeves very long probably tied with ribbon as shown

seam

wrist band

$1\frac{1}{8}$"   9"

$\frac{3}{8}$"

DORSET button very neatly made of white cotton thread over brass wire ring.

$43\frac{1}{2}$

2 tucks

width round hem 62"   seam

are long, almost covering the hand; sometimes ribbons are tied round the arm, giving a pouched appearance. Note here the growing fullness at the top of the sleeve. Many types of shawls or mantles are used, with hat or bonnet.

1815-22

White spotted muslin dress, very high waist, very low neckline. Dress open all down back, button fastening only on bodice, which is unlined. Tucks at hem and on sleeve.

White striped muslin, printed spot flower pattern in lilac with border at hem. Neck frills, piped seams on back, fastening with tape ties at back.

Snowshill Collection

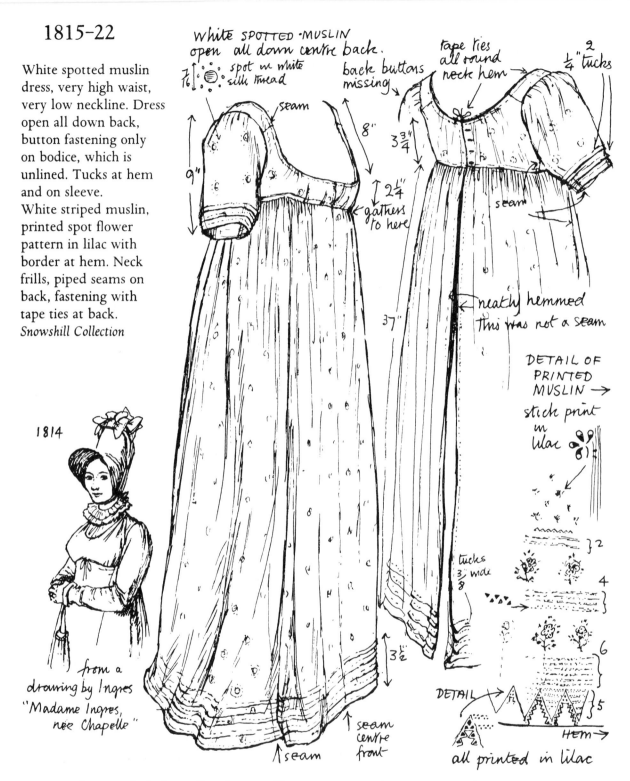

WHITE SPOTTED·MUSLIN
open all down centre back.

$\frac{7}{16}$ spot in white silk thread

back buttons missing

seam

9"

8"

2$\frac{1}{4}$" gathers to here

tape ties all round neck hem

2 $\frac{1}{4}$" tucks

3$\frac{3}{4}$"

seam

neatly hemmed this was not a seam

37"

DETAIL OF PRINTED MUSLIN →

stick print in lilac

tucks 3$\frac{3}{8}$ wide

} 2

} 4

} 6

DETAIL →

} 5

HEM →

all printed in lilac

1814

from a drawing by Ingres
"Madame Ingres, née Chapelle"

3$\frac{1}{2}$"

seam

seam centre front

Two dresses which fit a tall girl or small young woman, but it is unusual to find a woman's dress open down the back, neck to hem. The other printed dress is of a muslin of *c.* 1815; flowing formal designs usually replacing spot prints *c.* 1820. It was probably a front-fastening

PRINTED STRIPED MUSLIN
sleeves & bodice lined white cotton

neck frill DETAIL

seams on back bodice are piped

high WAIST 22"

21"

18"

3"

tape tie

5¾

3½

deep pleat

faced to edge

8¾

one slit

7"

4¾

self button

stitched pleat

length 40"

seam

false hem

width striped muslin 37"

fold

stripes of 6 threads

1"

thin muslin

seam

seam

seam

seam

back 42"

tuck

tuck

dress, altered to the more fashionable back-fastening style of the 1820's, but it is interesting in that it has piped seams; these are rarely found on muslins before 1822. Bodice and sleeves are lined.

102

1817-19

Blue silk and wool dress, made from a shawl, richly woven border in floral cone Kashmir pattern in dull reds, deep golden yellows, light and dark greens. Border motif used on bodice and decorative sleeves, cord and buttons as trimming. Cross-over bodice back and front. Tape ties at back opening.
Snowshill Collection

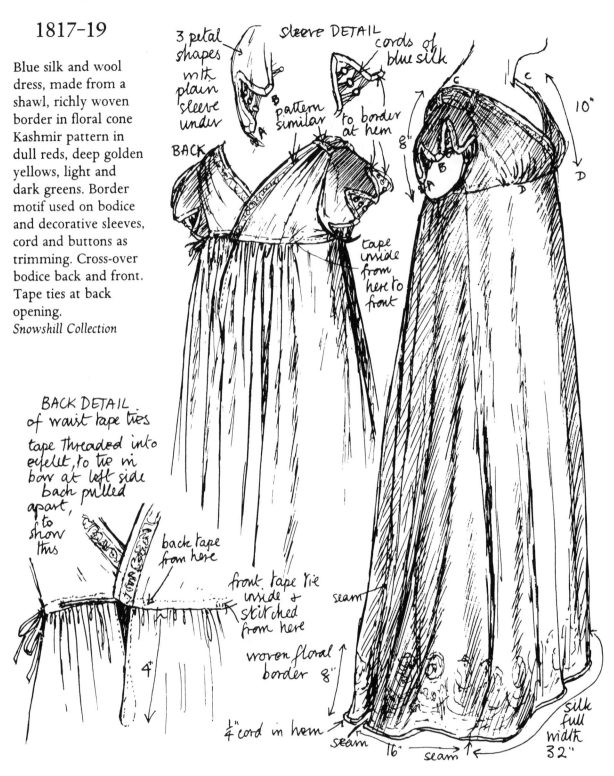

3 petal shapes with plain sleeve under

sleeve DETAIL

cords of blue silk

BACK

B

A

pattern similar

to border at hem

tape inside from here to front

c

c

10"

8"

B

D

D

BACK DETAIL. of waist tape ties

tape threaded into eyelet, to tie in bow at left side back pulled apart, to show this

back tape from here

front tape tie inside + stitched from here

woven floral border 8"

¼" cord in hem

seam

seam

16"

seam

seam

silk full width 32"

4"

The waist reaches its highest level by 1820, and the puffed, petal-shaped sleeves are often found in 1818–20. Colours return, mainly at first in silks; both sleeve and hemline now show increased decoration, and this hem is quite thickly corded. The miniatures of about this date

pattern similar to border at hem

shoulder width

FRONT

2½"

4"

under arm seam 1½"

back skirt 42"

seam

corded hem ¼"

front 40"

from T. Stanley Brown family miniatures Gentleman in white stock & waistcoat, dark grey coat & 'M' cut collar.

DETAIL

gold ear rings & brooch

corded silk ties

Wife in grey dress, white cap of fine spotted muslin or net white collar & tucker, edged with white embroidery. A PAIR of oval miniatures back to back in red leather oval case.

woven floral pattern

this on blue ground

this part on yellow ground

as border on bodice

blue

8"

selvedge

are very detailed, showing the wife wearing a similar bodice with corded silk ties fastening her dress. The husband has the very fashionable 'M' cut collar, first appearing c. 1800 and used on day coats until 1850.

Early 19th c.

Black silk taffeta bonnet, lined in pink silk over wire frame. Black silk soft hood, lined quilted blue silk, button-fastened.
Snowshill Collection

Black silk calash, magenta silk lined over three hoops, with corded piping at back, magenta silk ribbon ties.
Mrs M. Macbeth

Studies of accessories and underwear.

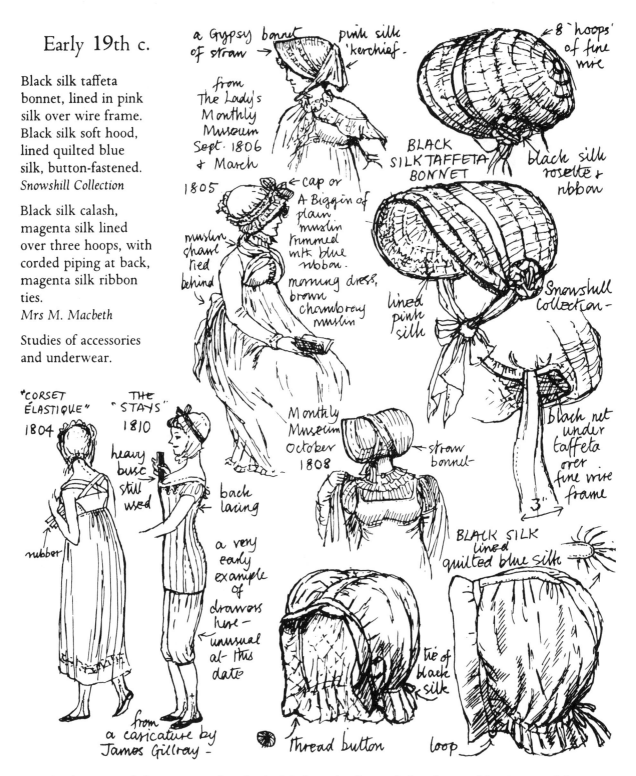

a Gypsy bonnet of straw →

pink silk 'kerchief.

from The Lady's Monthly Museum Sept. 1806 + March

1805

← cap or A Biggin of plain muslin trimmed with blue ribbon.

morning dress, brown chambrey muslin

muslin shawl tied behind →

8 'hoops' of fine wire

BLACK SILK TAFFETA BONNET

black silk rosette + ribbon

lined pink silk

Snowshill Collection —

black net under taffeta over fine wire frame

3"

Monthly Museum October 1808

← straw bonnet

CORSET ÉLASTIQUE 1804 →

THE "STAYS" 1810

heavy busc still used

back lacing

a very early example of drawers here — unusual at this date

rubber

from a caricature by James Gillray —

thread button

loop

BLACK SILK lined quilted blue silk

tie of black silk

At the turn of the century the classical hair style dictated the shape of bonnets and hats, giving at first a horizontal line; later, with the hair dressed on top of the head, high-crowned hats, caps, and bonnets appeared, as the 1805–13 studies show. Prints too give details of

from 'Poetical Sketches of
Scarborough
'The Library' 1813

calash
black
silk
cloak,
edged
lace

reticule

from prints of old CHELTENHAM
Mrs Hannah
Forty
1744-
1816

white

grey
white

Mrs
Rous

brown

for 50 years
pumper
at the old well.

early 19ᵗʰ c
pumper at the old well

edge of black
silk.

BLACK SILK CALASH
lined with magenta silk

all one piece
of silk

3½"

6¾"

3
hoops
centre
one
now
missing

1819

corded
piping

2¼"

2½"

4"

4"

12"

"artificial"
hump
a pad worn even by poor
contemporary illustration—women

magenta
silk ribbons
1⅜"

⅝"

width
11"

from
Mrs. M. Macbeth

height
front
hoop

9½"

foundations and underwear. The busc, used in the 16th c. to keep the front of the stays straight, was still in use in the 19th c., made of wood, bone, whalebone, and steel, or of silver if worn in tropical climates.

1810-20

White spotted muslin spencer, puffed and petal-shaped sleeves over long sleeves, very high-waisted.
Mrs Mary Martin

Cream holland spencer, plain long sleeves, high neck with collar, unlined. Belted, with fringed tassels at back, tape ties in seam, and tapes inside at centre back.
Snowshill Collection

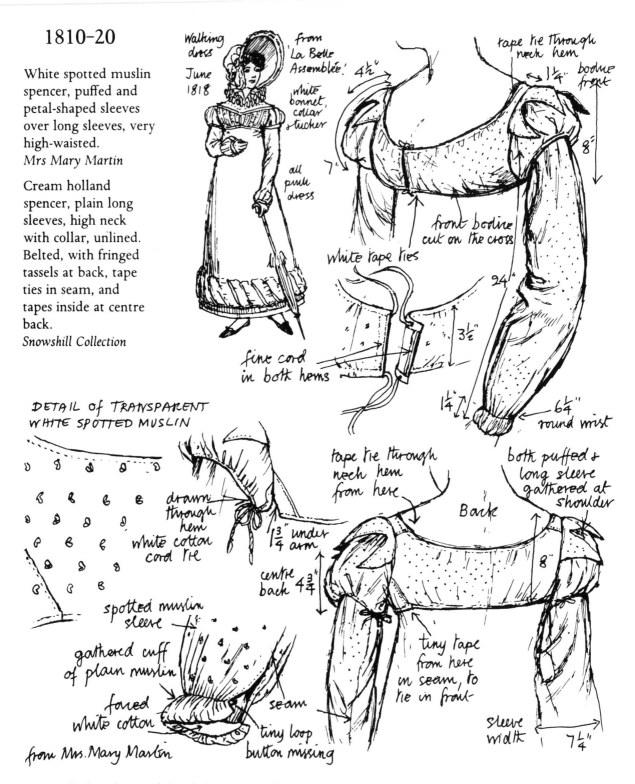

Walking dress June 1818

from 'La Belle Assemblée'

white bonnet, collar, tucker

all pink dress

tape tie through neck hem

1¼" bodice front

4½"

7"

8"

front bodice cut on the cross

white tape ties

24"

fine cord in both hems

3½"

1¼"

6¼" round wrist

DETAIL of TRANSPARENT WHITE SPOTTED MUSLIN

drawn through hem

white cotton cord tie

spotted muslin sleeve

gathered cuff of plain muslin

faced white cotton

from Mrs. Mary Martin

seam

tiny loop button missing

tape tie through neck hem from here

1¾" under arm

centre back 4¾"

Back

both puffed & long sleeve gathered at shoulder

8"

tiny tape from here in seam, to tie in front

sleeve width 7¼"

With the advent of thin light muslins during the 1790's, a short form of jacket to waist-level, called a spencer, was worn, both outdoors, indoors, and for evening wear. They stayed in fashion for about 20 years, while the waist remained high, but went out of use as the waistline

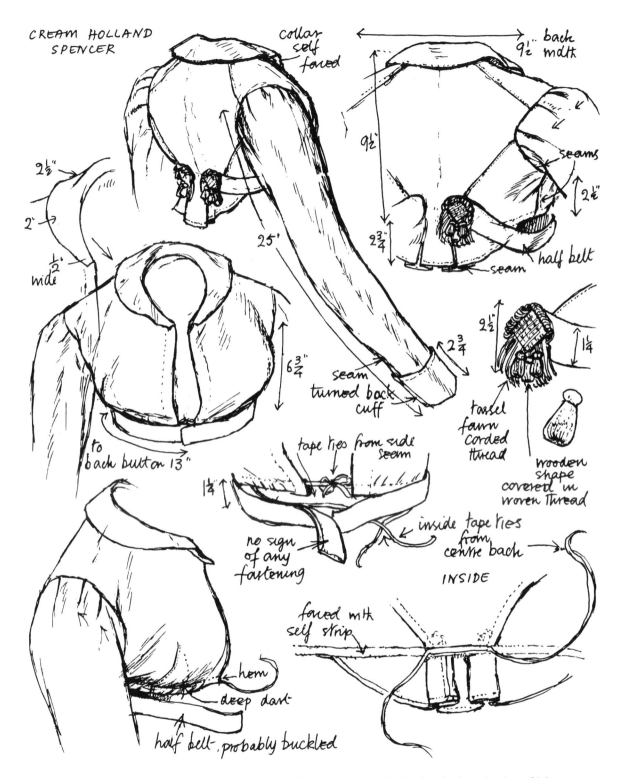

CREAM HOLLAND SPENCER

collar self faced

back mdth

9½"

9½"

seams

2¼"

2½"

2'

½' wide

25'

6¾"

2¾"

seam turned back cuff

to back button 13"

9½"

1¼

tassel faun corded thread

wooden shape covered in woven thread

1¼

tape ties from side seam

no sign of any fastening

inside tape ties from centre back

INSIDE

faced mth self strip

hem

deep dart

half belt, probably buckled

half belt

seam

2¾"

fell. Coloured spencers are usual with white dresses, particularly the darker shades of blue or black. Both these examples are light in colour; another dainty one is shown in the study from Ingres on p. 110.

c. 1818–22

Pale blue silk child's spencer, lined cream silk. Puffed sleeves over long sleeves, edges piped. Ribbon tie at collar, button on belt. Woman's black silk spencer, bodice lined black silk, but sleeves lined in white cotton. Puffed sleeves over long sleeves, piping in satin. Belted. Fine straw bonnet with high crown.
Snowshill Collection

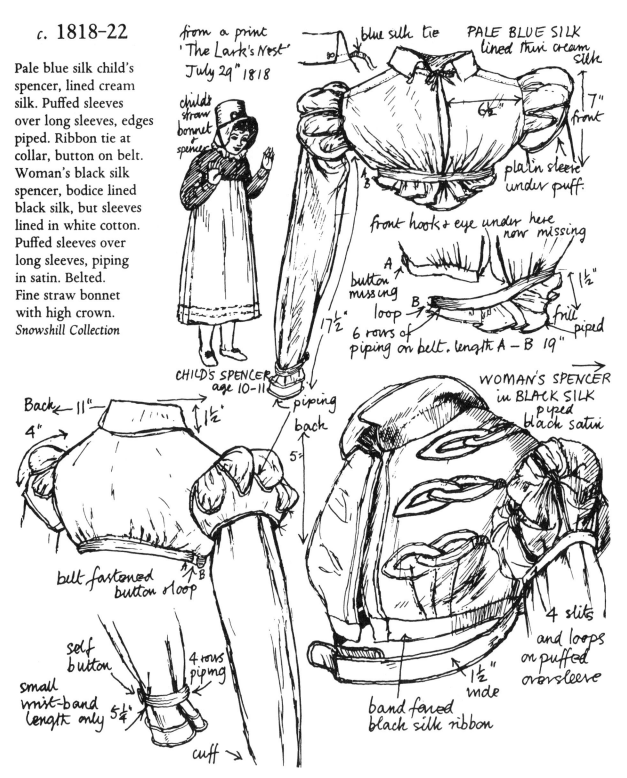

from a print 'The Lark's Nest' July 29" 1818

child's straw bonnet & spencer

blue silk tie

PALE BLUE SILK lined thin cream silk

6½"

7" front

plain sleeve under puff

front hook & eye under here now missing

A

button missing

loop

B

6 rows of piping on belt. length A – B 19"

1½" frill piped

CHILD'S SPENCER age 10–11

17½"

piping back

WOMAN'S SPENCER in BLACK SILK piped black satin

Back — 11"

4"

1½'

5"

belt fastened button & loop

self button

4 rows piping

small wrist-band length only 5¼"

cuff

4 slits and loops on puffed oversleeve

1½" wide

band faced black silk ribbon

Piping was used on dress seams from the early 1820's, and the decoration on the woman's black silk spencer has certainly been enriched by its use. The spencer is here in its final phase before the waistline gradually descends and these very attractive little jackets disappear.

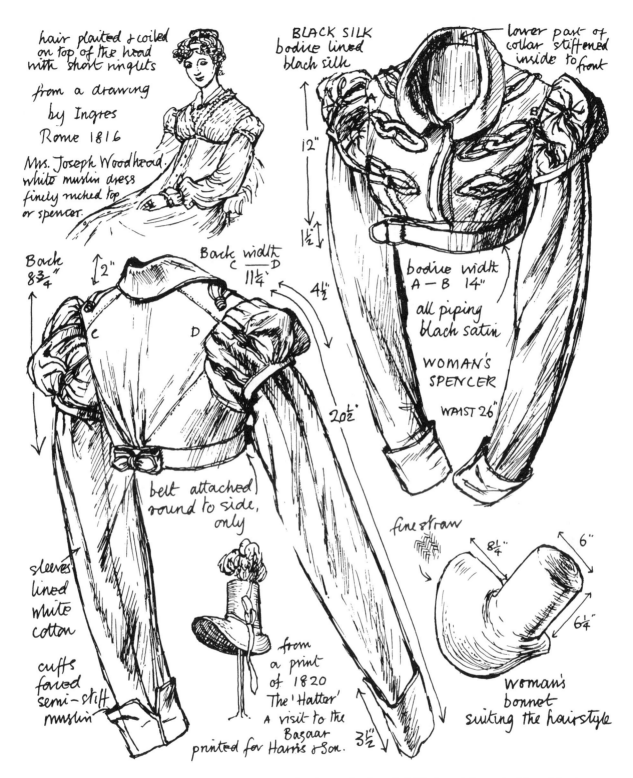

hair plaited & coiled on top of the head with short ringlets

from a drawing by Ingres Rome 1816

Mrs. Joseph Woodhead. white muslin dress finely ruched top or spencer.

BLACK SILK bodice lined black silk

lower part of collar stiffened inside to front

12"

1½"

bodice width A — B 14"

all piping black satin

WOMAN'S SPENCER

WAIST 26"

Back 8¾"

2"

Back width C — D 11¼"

c

D

4½"

20½"

belt attached round to side, only

sleeves lined white cotton

cuffs faced semi-stiff muslin

from a print of 1820 The 'Hatter' A visit to the Bazaar printed for Harris & Son.

3½"

fine straw

8¼"

6"

6¼"

woman's bonnet suiting the hairstyle

The one shown in the 1816 study is very finely ruched and frilled and is probably white to match the dress. The drawing also shows the hair coiled on top of the head, thus setting the angle for the bonnet.

Early 19th c.

Hinged green silk parasol with folding wooden handle and whalebone frame. Golden fawn silk tiny pagoda-shaped parasol, long cane handle, whalebone frame, cord loop. Large black silk pagoda-shaped umbrella, bone ring holder, whalebone frame, with wooden handle, tip broken. *Snowshill Collection*

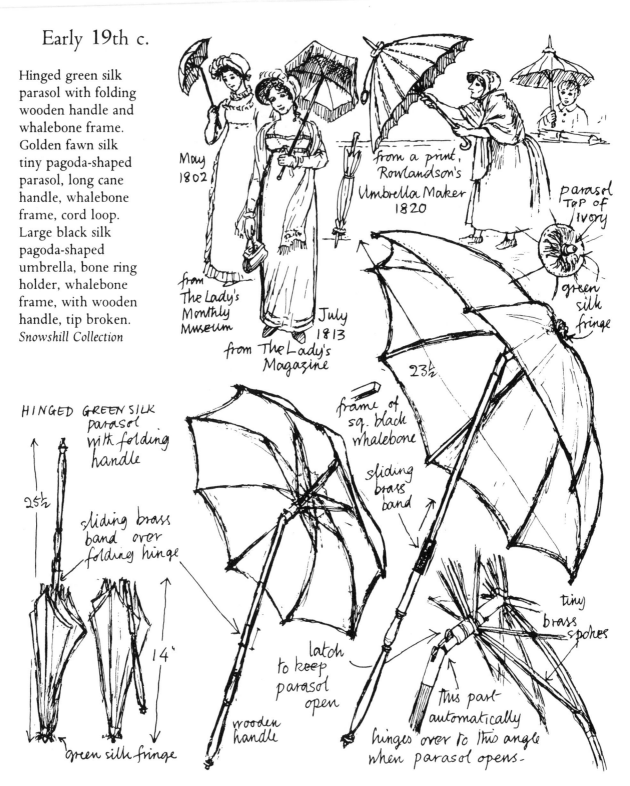

May 1802

from The Lady's Monthly Museum

July 1813

from The Lady's Magazine

from a print, Rowlandson's Umbrella Maker 1820

parasol top of ivory

green silk fringe

frame of sq. black whalebone

sliding brass band

23½

HINGED GREEN SILK parasol with folding handle

25½

sliding brass band over folding hinge

14'

green silk fringe

latch to keep parasol open

wooden handle

tiny brass spokes

this part automatically hinges over to this angle when parasol opens.

The large, heavy umbrellas of the late 18th c. are shown in Rowlandson's study of the *Umbrella Maker* 1820; the black silk medium-sized umbrella shown here has the same ring holder, although this silk tie is sewn to a rib. Pagoda shapes were c. 1800–40, when tiny hinged parasols

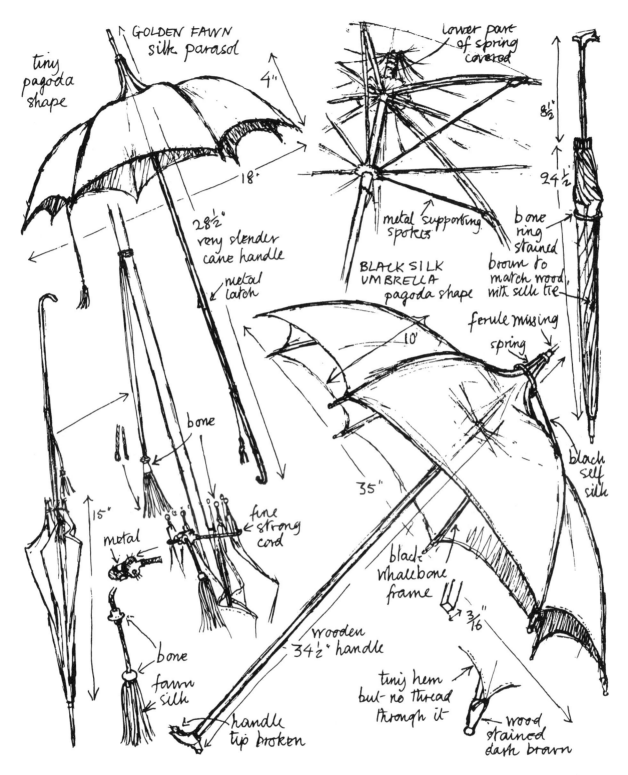

GOLDEN FAWN
silk parasol

tiny
pagoda
shape

4"

lower part
of spring
covered

metal supporting
spokes

18"

28½"
very slender
cane handle

metal
latch

bone

fine
strong
cord

metal

bone

fawn
silk

15"

handle
tip broken

8½"

24½"

bone
ring
stained
brown to
match wood
with silk tie

ferule missing

spring

BLACK SILK
UMBRELLA
pagoda shape

10'

35"

black
self
silk

black
whalebone
frame

³⁄₁₆"

wooden
34½" handle

tiny hem
but no thread
through it

wood
stained
dark brown

also appeared, shown in the 1802 study. This green silk parasol also has a folding handle;
usually this is found from *c.* 1838, although the fringed parasol in the 1813 print appears to
have a similar stick.

1820–30

Ribbed white cotton cap with muslin frills, finely gathered crown, all beautifully sewn. Second cap, all of net, embroidered net frill, and fully gathered crown pulled up by draw-strings in seam.

1800–25

Two white lawn tuckers, double pleated frills, cord ties with tassels. Shoulder frills on one tucker.
Snowshill Collection

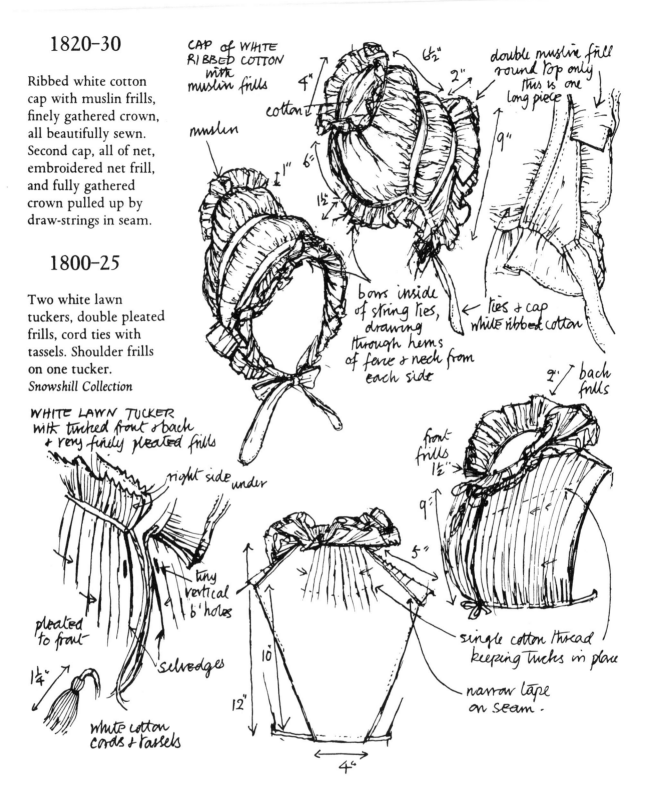

CAP of WHITE RIBBED COTTON with muslin frills

cotton

muslin

1"

6½

1½

4"

6½"

2"

double muslin frill round top only this is one long piece

9"

A

bows inside of string ties, drawing through hems of face & neck from each side

ties & cap white ribbed cotton

WHITE LAWN TUCKER with tucked front & back & very finely pleated frills

right side under

tiny vertical b'holes

selvedges

pleated to front

1¼"

white cotton cords & tassels

10"

12"

4"

front frills 1½"

2" back frills

9"

5"

single cotton thread keeping tucks in place

narrow tape on seam.

The remarkably fine sewing, pleating, and gathering on these accessories have to be seen to be believed. Both caps have the frill round the face and neck in one long piece, overlapping over the forehead, so that it need have no join. The 1822 study shows both cap and tuckers.

white pleated and frilled cap and tucker.

each frill very finely sewn + gathered, + stitched on separately

4½"

2" wide 1" at front

12"

FRILLED LAWN TUCKER very fine pleating

1"

fine cord ties & tassels very tiny 6 holes each side

4½"

9"

tape ties

from an engraving for "Original Poetry for Young Minds." by Miss Horwood LONDON 1822

CAP LAID FLAT

4½"

1¾" 2½"

2"

fine drawstring under frill at A which pulls thro' hem from D

gathers very close at front & side

4½

seams

B

C

D

fine draw strings in hems at B + C. C string pulls from D.

CAP of fine white NET, embroidered net frill in one long piece being double at top only

frill ends here, having no join.

seam

begins here

The cap is very similar to these shown here, but slightly different with inside gathering on the upper part of the crown. The tucker with the shoulder frills was probably worn outside the dress.

1st half 19th c.

Cream silk shawl, woven borders, small-cone design.
Brilliant red woollen shawl, woven border, large floral cones.
Dull crimson silk shawl, floral spot pattern and borders.

1815–20

Dress of white cotton finely woven green floral spot pattern, borders woven in rich red and green.
Snowshill Collection

1805 from painting of Mme Rivière by Ingres

1828 ribbon from painting of Sir George Sitwell & his Family by Partridge

shawl with large motif

yellow blue WOVEN SHAWL DETAIL

green's blue + white

cream silk ground & fringe woven pattern in dull yellow with blue green & crimson

small cone

8½"

border sewn on

shawl width 20" length 102"

narrow edging in Red

yellow   dark green

width 30" Length 115" dull crimson silk, ground & fringe

border sewn on

RED SHAWL Length 72" & width 42"

red wool fringe.

Brilliant red wool, woven border in reds, dark blue yellow & orange.

Large cone 13" long

white background with dot pattern

Kashmir shawls became fashionable in England *c.* 1777, some designs at first being copied in turn by Edinburgh, Norwich, and finally by Paisley weavers. As a wrap, rectangular or square, the shawl remained in favour some 90 years. The Kashmir-designed shawl with plain

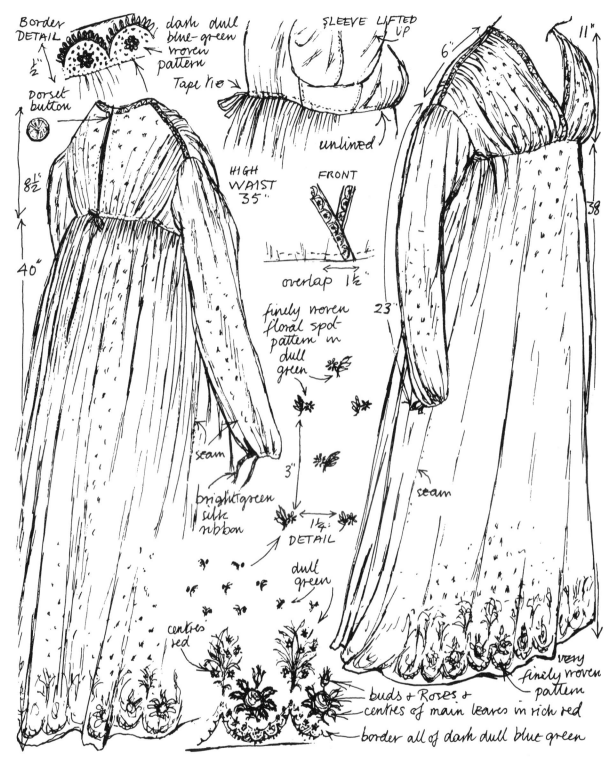

Border
DETAIL

dark dull
blue-green
woven
pattern

SLEEVE LIFTED
UP

11"

1"½

Tape Tie

6"

Dorset
button

unlined

38

8½"

HIGH
WAIST
35"

FRONT

40"

overlap 1½"

finely woven
floral spot
pattern in
dull
green

23

3"

seam

seam

bright green
silk ribbon

1¼"
DETAIL

dull
green

centres
red

buds & Roses &
centres of main leaves in rich red

very
finely woven
pattern

border all of dark dull blue green

field and borders of large floral cones was most popular in the first 20 years of the 19th c.
It can be dated by size and treatment of the cone shape used, besides the quality of the
material, silk or wool.

1822-30

White muslin, woven checkered pattern with spot-printed flower in dull purple. Bodice lined white cotton, short inner white cotton sleeves. Long sleeves with frilled cuff, button fastened. Bodice front-opening apron-front skirt, full gathers at back. Blue netted silk purse, gilt slides and beads, blue silk tassels.
Snowshill Collection

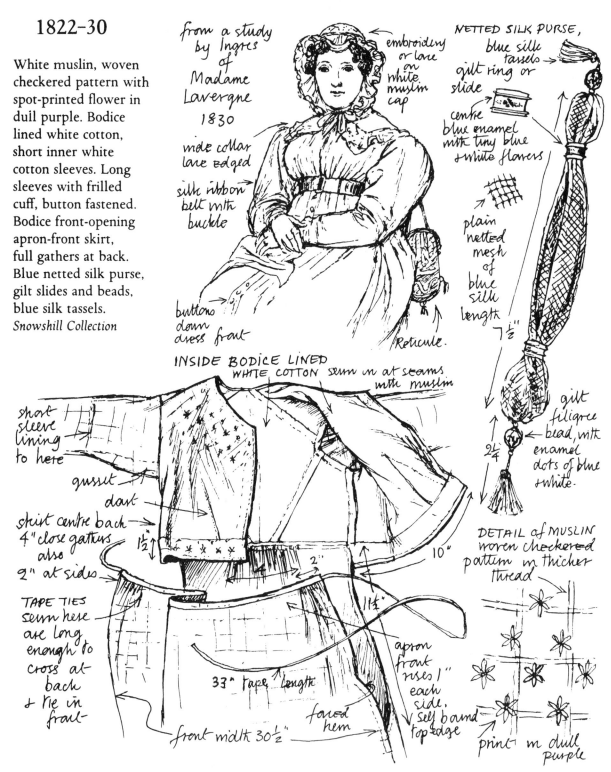

from a study by Ingres of Madame Lavergne 1830

wide collar lace edged

silk ribbon belt with buckle

embroidery or lace on white muslin cap

buttons down dress front

Reticule.

NETTED SILK PURSE, blue silk tassels

gilt ring or slide

centre blue enamel with tiny blue & white flowers

plain netted mesh of blue silk length 7½"

2¼"

gilt filigree bead, with enamel dots of blue & white.

INSIDE BODICE LINED WHITE COTTON seam in at seams with muslin

short sleeve lining to here

gusset

dart

skirt centre back 4" close gathers also 2" at sides

1½"

2"

10"

11½"

apron front rises 1" each side. self bound top edge

TAPE TIES sewn here are long enough to cross at back & tie in front

33" tape length

front width 30½"

faced hem

DETAIL of MUSLIN woven checkered pattern in thicker thread

print in dull purple

Though very plain, this is quite an interesting dress, linking an almost out-of-date printed muslin, with its old fashioned front fastening, to the new piped seams, lowered waistline, and increasing fullness and gathers at the top of the sleeve. The study from Ingres also shows

117

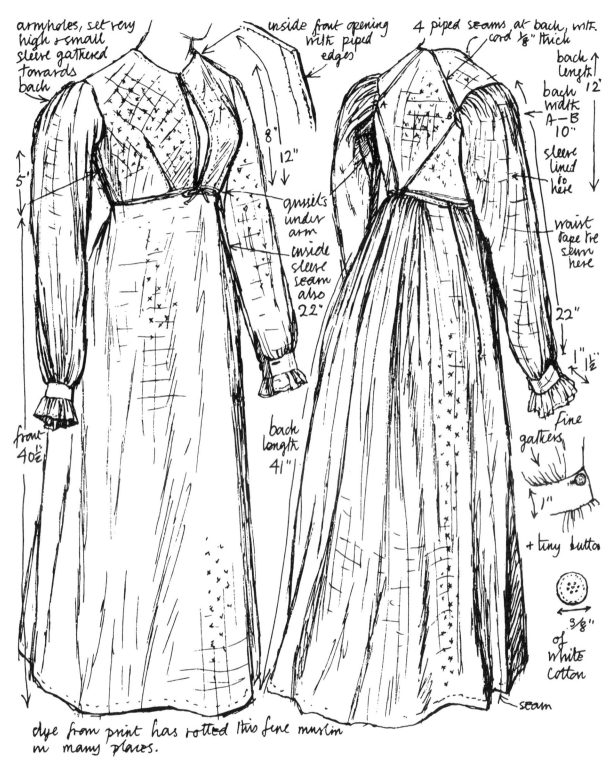

armholes, set very high & small
sleeve gathered towards back

inside front opening with piped edges

4 piped seams at back, with cord 1/8" thick

back length 12"

back width A—B 10"

sleeve lined to here

waist tape tie sewn here

8"

12"

5'

gussets under arm

inside sleeve seam also 22"

22"

1" 1½"

fine gathers

1"

+ tiny button

3/8"

of white cotton

seam

front 40½"

back length 41"

dye from print has rotted this fine muslin in many places.

a mixture of changing styles, for the waistline, by 1826–27, has generally lowered to near normal level. Reticules of various shapes are still carried, but the early 19th-c. netted purse is small, increasing in length later.

c. 1823

Fine cream silk gauze, machine-embroidered pink silk floral pattern, under-dress of white satin padded at hem. High waistline, sash probably of pink satin now missing. Puffs of gauze on satin sleeve. Gauze dress sewn to satin at neck, arm and waist seams. Back-fastening ties, full gathers at back, inner ribbon waist tie. *Snowshill Collection*

net gathered on to silk tape under seams

satin piping

net

6'

pink satin

4 pleats

& satin bound

net facing

net & satin sewn together at waist

fitting undersleeve of satin

3"

BUST 36"

HIGH WAIST 33"

DETAIL of pink silk leaf pattern on gauze

6"

DETAIL of pink silk machined embroidery on gauze

1½

very fine pink silk weft threads, with slightly raised stamped pattern

1½"

net seam

4"

satin seam

4"

4"

4"

satin width 35"

net (or gauze) width 36"

Embroidered net or gauze over white or coloured satin was increasingly used for ball dresses 1816–30. Padded hems are found on silk dresses c.1823–28, and piped seams from 1822. The waistline is high and the skirt plain in front, but gathered

"The Cooke family" 1822

From the painting by Parry

dark gauze over satin

net only is gathered, satin underdress is fitting.

5" net puffs

seams

shirt front 45"

skirt back 47"

neck edging 5 pleats of pink satin

FRONT & gathered net

BACK

7"

silk tape seam inside net, round front waist, draws thro' hem at sides, to tie at back inside.

BACK FASTENING

5½"

INSIDE SATIN SKIRT

seam

net & satin sewn together, here net seam

satin seam

net seam

silk ribbon tie thro' neck hem

inner ribbon waist tie

outer ribbon waist tie

gauze gathered very full at back satin only medium gathered

satin undershirt hem padded with cotton wool

satin seam

↕ 1½

at the back, particularly the gauze. The puff sleeves show increasing elaboration, which balances the extra decoration at the hem. This lovely dress, like many others of net or gauze, is very frail indeed.

c. 1823

Mustard-yellow silk dress, with plain silk bodice and petal-shaped sleeve, with skirt and puff sleeve of matching striped silk. Padded hem of plain silk. Bodice part lined white linen. Ribbon ties at back. Long cream feather ankle-length tippet, large matching muff, lined crimson silk. Feathers black-tipped.
Snowshill Collection

feather tippet & muff
9"

sleeve 'petals' & Bodice of plain satin
2¼"
7"

groups of longer feathers tipped with black hair-like ends

fitting sleeve with gathered puffs, and bound edge, of striped satin, as skirt.

10½"

width 6"

54"

Bodice front lined, loose lining at back
9½"

4¼"

seam dart

Tippet-back
12"

width 10"

feathers stitched in rows, very finely done.

feather length about 2"

satin width 19"

hem padded

Exquisitely light and fine, this feather muff and tippet are probably of marabou, the long creamy feathers being tipped with black. They are a fine example of those fashionable *c.* 1820–30, although large feather and fur muffs are seen in prints and paintings early in the

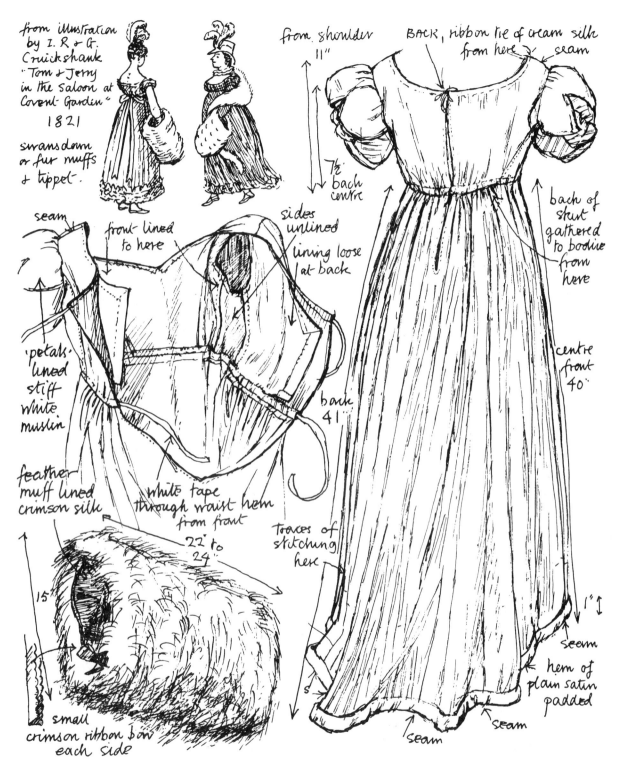

from illustration by I. R & G. Cruickshank "Tom & Jerry in the Saloon at Covent Garden" 1821 swansdown or fur muffs & tippet.

from shoulder 11"

BACK, ribbon tie of cream silk from here

seam

7½ back centre

seam

front lined to here

sides unlined

lining loose at back

back of skirt gathered to bodice from here

'petals' lined stiff white muslin

feather muff lined crimson silk

back 41

centre front 40"

white tape through waist hem from front

22" to 24"

15"

small crimson ribbon bow each side

traces of stitching here

1" ↕

seam

hem of plain satin padded

seam

seam

century, and during the 1780's, with large fur muffs a century earlier in 1630–40. The yellow silk dress shows the lower waistline, fuller sleeves, and increasing width at the hem, particularly at the back.

1822-27

Creamy white dress, of silk and wool, a firm, springy texture. Folds of fine silk net trimming neckline, edges satin-bound, satin bands on skirt. Sleeves piped in satin, skirt frills self-piped and corded. Bodice and sleeves lined in white cotton, shaped petal sleeves lined in stiffened muslin. Sash missing.
Snowshill Collection

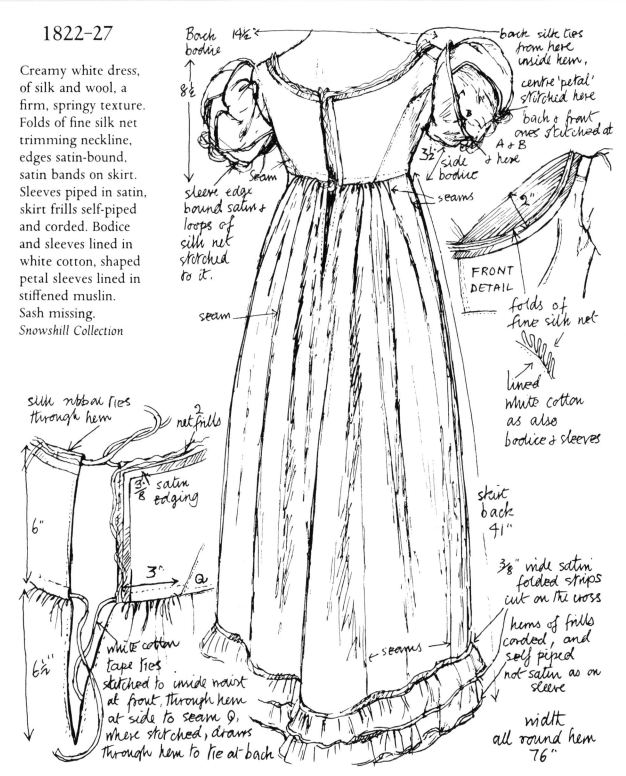

Back bodice 14½

8½

Seam

sleeve edge bound satin & loops of silk net stitched to it.

seam

back silk ties from here inside hem,

centre 'petal' stitched here

back & front ones stitched at A & B & here

A & B

3½ side bodice

seams

FRONT DETAIL

2"

folds of fine silk net

lined white cotton as also bodice & sleeves

skirt back 41"

³⁄₈" wide satin folded strips cut on the cross

hems of frills corded, and self piped not satin as on sleeve

width all round hem 76"

silk ribbon ties through hem

net frills

³⁄₈ satin edging

6"

3"

a

6½"

white cotton tape ties stitched to inside waist at front, through hem at side to seam a, where stitched, draws through hem to tie at back

seams

The material of this dress is worth a second look; for the first time for many years another fabric, other than cotton or silk, is used on a fashionable dress; now wool begins its return to favour, and many fine and delicate examples appear by the 1860's. The miniatures on this

corded edge of sleeve piped in satin

folds of fine silk net

lined stiffened muslin

satin

bodice front 3¼"

stitched here + at A + B

puff sleeves lined white cotton

skirt front 40"

frills 2½"

2½"

seam

width of material 24"

satin bands

seam

hem 1¼"

seam

light brown hair

black velvet ribbon

white dress

Mary Bulwer age 18 Great-grandmother of Charles Wade who made the Collection at Snowshill Manor

blue sash

Miniatures of brother + sister 1827

Edward Bulwer age 21

shirt white

black stock

white

red waist-coat

black waist-coat

M cut collar of blue-grey coat, found on day coats until 1850 + on many evening coats until 1870.

brass buttons

page are very interesting, not only because they show women's hair style and fashionable neck trimming, but because of the family connection with Charles Wade, who had many items from the Bulwer family in his collection.

c. 1826–28

Medium grey-brown silk taffeta cloak, with collar and two capes. Cloak and both capes lined duck-egg blue silk, interlined with fawn cotton and a layer of cotton-wool. Edges of cloak, collar capes and flap to arm-slit, all stitched and piped. Ribbon ties fastening at front, and on inside, with two at centre back. *Snowshill Collection*

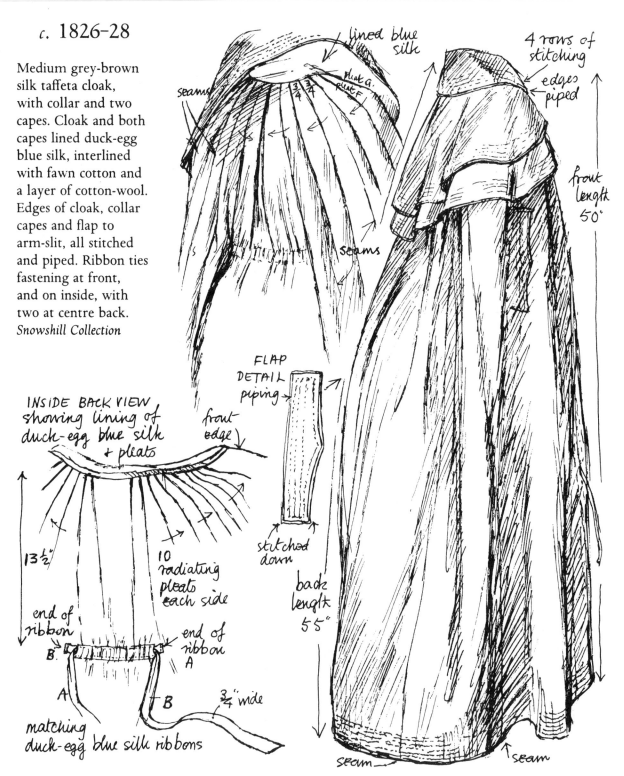

lined blue silk

seams

pleat G.
pleat F
3/4 3/4

seams

4 rows of stitching

edges piped

front length 50"

FLAP DETAIL piping

stitched down

back length 55"

INSIDE BACK VIEW showing lining of duck-egg blue silk + pleats

front edge

13½"

10 radiating pleats each side

end of ribbon

B.

A

end of ribbon A

B

¾" wide

matching duck-egg blue silk ribbons

seam

seam

An attractive caped cloak, which is both light and warm. Under the brown silk is a layer of cotton-wool lightly quilted to a fawn cotton interlining, and sewn to the brown silk with rows of stitching round the edges, the pale blue silk lining being sewn in afterwards. Neither

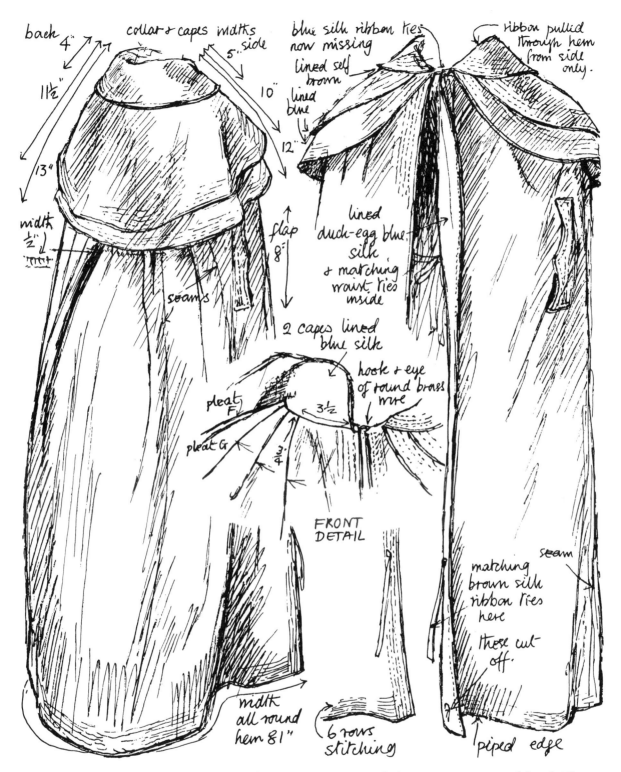

back 4"

collar & capes widths

5" side

blue silk ribbon ties now missing

ribbon pulled through hem from side only.

11½"

lined self brown

10"

lined blue

13"

12"

flap 8"

width ½"

seams

lined duck-egg blue silk & matching waist ties inside

2 capes lined blue silk

hook & eye of round brass wire

pleat F

pleat G

3½

4in.

FRONT DETAIL

matching brown silk ribbon ties here

these cut off.

seam

width all round hem 81"

6 rows stitching

piped edge

the width of the capes nor the hemline is very great, and the waist is at normal level. The method of pulling in the gathers at the back waist, with crossed ties, is found on other capes and wraps of about this date.

c. 1825–35

White printed cotton 'robe-de-chambre,' printed in trailing floral pattern, folded ribbon design in red, blue-green, and mauve. Flowers and black line of fine stems, angular but delicate; pin-dot pattern. Waist tape tie inside crossing at back. Open half-way down front. Robe half-lined. Two-flounce white cotton bustle.
Snowshill Collection

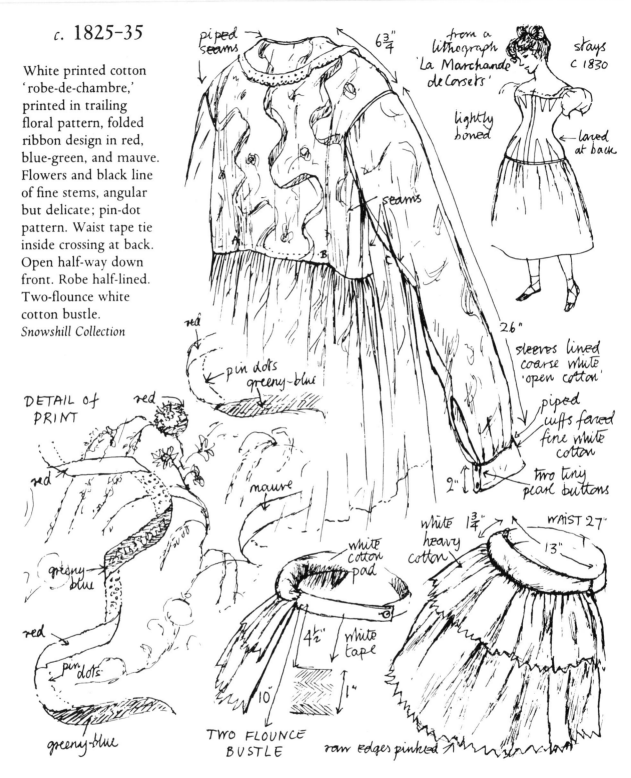

piped seams

6¾"

from a lithograph 'La Marchande de Corsets'

stays c 1830

lightly boned

laced at back

seams

26"

sleeves lined coarse white 'open cotton'

piped cuffs faced fine white cotton

2"

two tiny pearl buttons

red

pin dots greeny-blue

DETAIL OF PRINT

red

red

mauve

greeny-blue

red

pin dots

greeny-blue

white cotton pad

white 1¾"

heavy cotton

WAIST 27"

13"

4½"

white tape

10"

1"

TWO FLOUNCE BUSTLE

raw edges pinked

It is unusual for such a simple robe as this to be preserved, but, compared with the tight-waisted dresses of mid-19th c., this would be most comfortable for maternity wear. The very tiny pearl buttons, appearing here for the first time, are similar to those found on the cuffs

white openwork embroidery

2 flat brass wire hooks & eyes

front opening

button-hole stitched

$3\frac{3}{4}$"

2"

$14\frac{1}{2}$

$2\frac{1}{4}$"

$24\frac{1}{2}$"

seams piped & all round arm hole

white cotton lined yoke & faced edges

A

B

back & sides to C lined white cotton

INSIDE

B

A

C

A

B

C

23"

2 ties crossing on hem at back

Underwear 1825-35

white cotton cap

down filled cotton sleeve-puffs

chemise with short sleeves

3 flounce bustle

white lawn petticoat

$39\frac{1}{2}$"

seam

seam

white cotton pocket

skirt

half-lined thin white cotton

piped hem

embroidered

deep false hem of thicker cotton

seam

from Gallery of English Costume Platt Hall, Manchester

of the printed muslin day dress, with the imbecile sleeves, p. 155, and to the one on the reticule, p. 153. The crossing tape ties inside are the same as those found on the cloaks of this decade. The small studies show the underwear in use during the early '30's.

1825-28

White striped muslin, floral printed pattern trailing design in deep pinky reds and pale blue-grey. Waist lower with wide shoulder-line, fully gathered sleeves and skirt, with frilled and ruched decoration at hem. Bodice and sleeves lined white cotton. Tape tie inside. Fastens hook and eye at back bodice and on wrist. Slit to pocket.
Snowshill Collection

full shoulder width

sleeve length
shoulder to wrist 29"

bodice
centre back 9½

24"
neck self bound on cross seam
10"

armhole set high
2" & small

WAIST 21"

1⅛"

flattened brass wire
large at waist
3 smaller hooks
on bodice with
stitched bars

seams

slit opening to pocket

seams

skirt back 39"

5"
side seam

white cotton lining to sleeves & cuffs bodice & waistband

white tape ties

width all round hem 80"

width of muslin 33"

There is an elegance about this day dress, not only in the cut and fine sewing of the tiny gathers, but also in the printed muslin. This fern-like design is one of the characteristics of the delicate patterns of 1825-30, with nicely restrained colouring. The study from the miniature

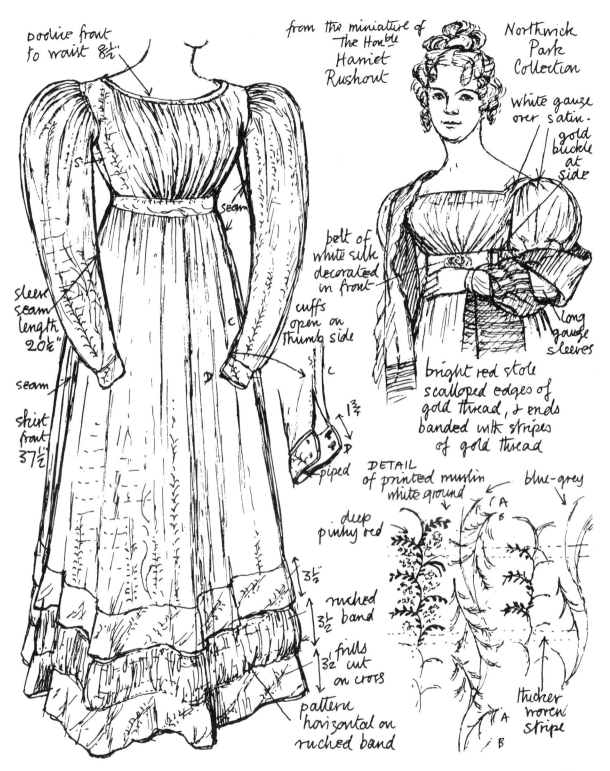

bodice front to waist 8½"

from the miniature of The Honble Harriet Rushout

Northwick Park Collection

white gauze over satin.

gold buckle at side

sleeve seam length 20½"

seam

skirt front 37½"

belt of white silk decorated in front

cuffs open on thumb side

3¾

piped

long gauze sleeves

bright red stole scalloped edges of gold thread, & ends banded with stripes of gold thread

DETAIL of printed muslin white ground

blue-grey

deep pinky red

A
B

3½"

ruched band 3½"

frills 3½" cut on cross

pattern horizontal on ruched band

thicker woven stripe

A
B

in the late Capt. Spencer Churchill's Collection shows the fashionable hair style with 'Apollo knots' and ringlets, 1824–33. White continues popular for evening wear, also gauze over satin, with striped printed muslins for day.

1825-30

Dull red woollen cloth cloak, with cape and matching sleeves. Front only is lined in matching silk, also shoulder yoke. Sleeves are lined in bright crimson silk. Neck and waist ties inside of matching ribbon. All edges bound and piped in matching silk. Hook-and-eye fastening on front of cape part only. *Snowshill Collection*

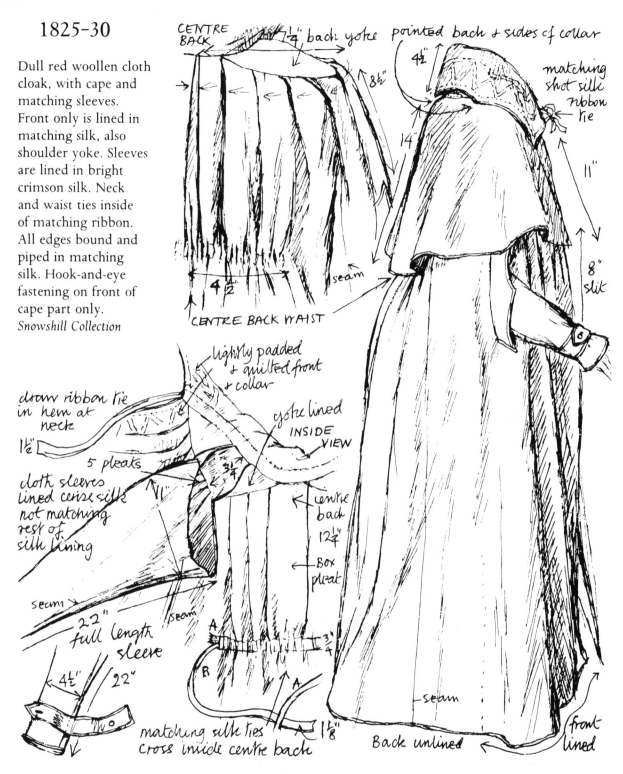

CENTRE BACK

1¼" back yoke

pointed back & sides of collar

4½"

matching shot silk ribbon tie

8½"

14"

11"

8" slit

seam

4½"

CENTRE BACK WAIST

lightly padded & quilted front & collar

draw ribbon tie in hem at neck

1½"

5 pleats

cloth sleeves lined cerise silk not matching rest of silk lining

yoke lined

INSIDE VIEW

3¾"

1"

centre back

12¼"

Box pleat

seam

22" full length sleeve

seam

A

3¾"

4½"

22"

B

A

matching silk ties cross inside centre back

1⅛"

Back unlined

seam

front lined

The sewn-in matching sleeves are indeed a useful addition to a caped cloak; these are long, covering the hand to the knuckles even when the wrist-band is fastened; the pleats at the shoulder show the growing fullness of all sleeves at this period. The inner waist-tie has the

131

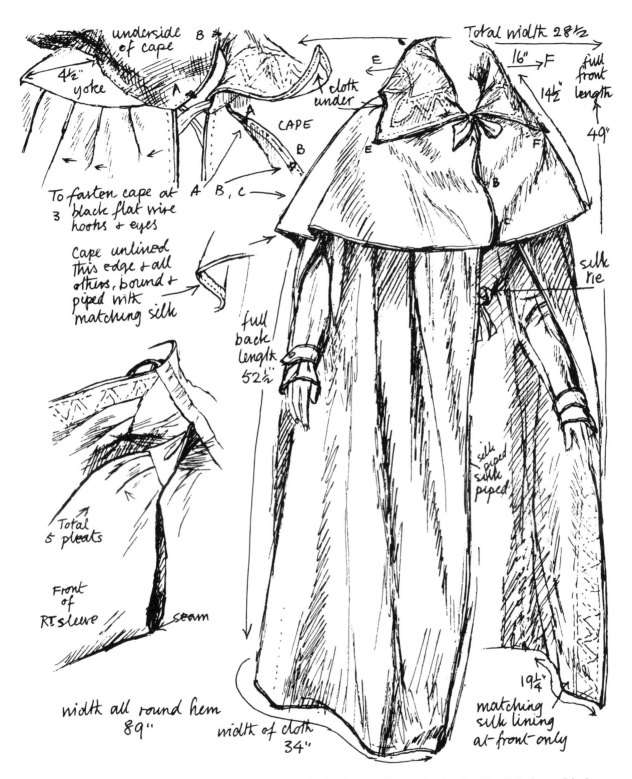

underside of cape B

4½ yoke

A

cloth under

CAPE B

E E

Total width 28½

16" F

14½"

full front length 49"

B

silk tie

To fasten cape at 3 black flat wire hooks & eyes

A B, C

Cape unlined this edge & all others, bound & piped with matching silk

full back length 52½"

silk piped silk piped

Total 5 pleats

Front of RT sleeve

seam

19¼"

matching silk lining at front only

width all round hem 89"

width of cloth 34"

familiar cross-over method; when tied, the cloak fits snugly to the back. The lightly padded and quilted collar and inside front lining have the fashionable vandyked pattern found on many dresses of 1826–27.

1826–28

Blue woollen cloth coat or pelisse, for tall, thin girl. Front opens half-way down skirt, hook and bar under buttons. Bodice and sleeves lined in grey cotton, skirt lined thin white silk, all sewn in with cloth at seams. Collar lined brown silk. Buttons and piping of light navy-blue silk. Girl's straw bonnet trimmed blue ribbon.
Snowshill Collection

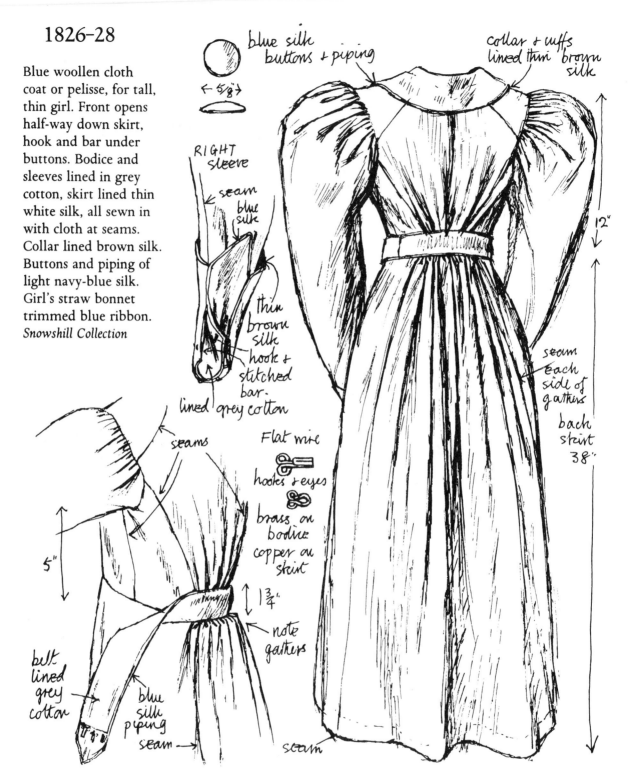

blue silk buttons & piping

collar & cuffs lined thin brown silk

← 5/8 →

RIGHT SLEEVE

seam

blue silk

thin brown silk

hook & stitched bar.

lined grey cotton

12"

seam each side of gathers

back skirt 38"

seams

Flat wire

hooks & eyes

brass on bodice copper on skirt

5"

1¾"

note gathers

belt lined grey cotton

blue silk piping

seam →

seam

Although the belt measures 22″, the inside waist is much smaller, owing to the thick pad of gathers turned inwards from the top of the skirt, giving almost the effect of a bustle. The sleeves are very long, being half the total length of the pelisse, and the cuffs are extremely

133

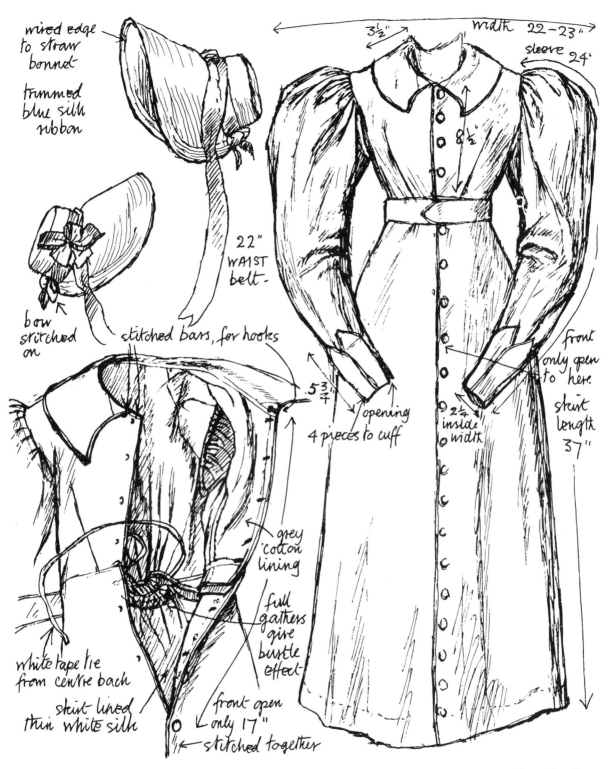

wired edge to straw bonnet

trimmed blue silk ribbon

bow stitched on

22" WAIST belt -

stitched bars, for hooks

width 22-23"

3½"

sleeve 24"

8½"

5¾"

opening

4 pieces to cuff

front only open to here

skirt length 37"

2¼" inside width

grey cotton lining

full gathers give bustle effect

white tape tie from centre back

skirt lined thin white silk

front open only 17"

stitched together

fitting and narrow; the original wearer must have been a very thin girl. This simple style of straw bonnet, with a now much smaller crown, is perfect in shape, although it belonged to a doll of about this same date (see child, p. 138).

1825-30

Red printed cotton day dress, pattern in white with touches of blue, in delicate floral trailing design with Chinese pagoda motifs. Full sleeves, bodice very richly ruched and piped, both being lined in white cotton. Skirt closely gathered at back. Hem frilled to knee-level, edges all piped. Inner waist-ties.
Snowshill Collection

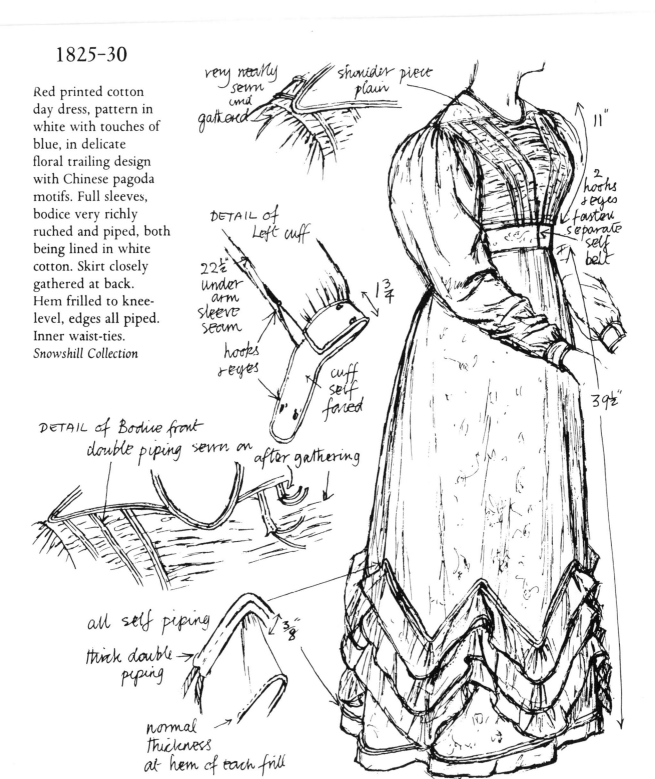

very neatly sewn and gathered

shoulder piece plain

11"

2 hooks & eyes fasten separate self belt

DETAIL of Left cuff

22½" under arm sleeve seam

hooks & eyes

cuff self faced

1¾"

39½"

DETAIL of Bodice front
double piping sewn on after gathering

all self piping
thick double piping

³⁄₈"

normal thickness at hem of each frill

A very good example of a day dress showing the increased decoration of the bodice and hemline, with typical ruching and thick piping, also the V shape to the trimming on the bodice. The 'gigot' sleeves are set into small high armholes, and are very fully gathered

135

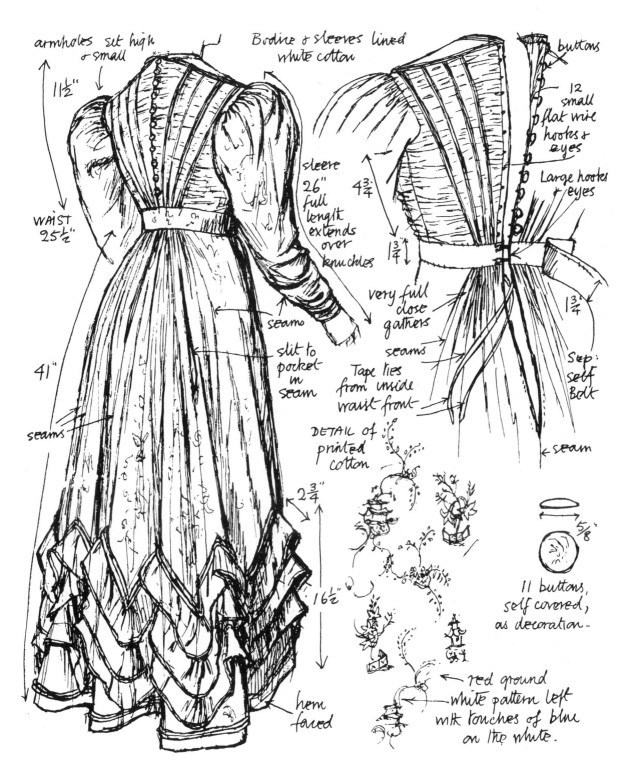

armholes set high & small

11½"

Bodine & sleeves lined white cotton

buttons

12 small flat wire hooks & eyes

Large hooks & eyes

WAIST 25½"

sleeve 26" full length extends over knuckles

4¾"

1¾"

very full close gathers

seams

Tape ties from inside waist front

1¾"

Sep: self Belt

41"

seams

slit to pocket in seam

seam

DETAIL of printed cotton

2¾"

16½"

5/8

11 buttons, self covered, as decoration—

hem faced

← red ground white pattern left with touches of blue on the white.

on the shoulder, although they are not at the maximum width. The rather harsh colouring of this dress is balanced by the fineness of the sewing. It was found, with others, locked away in a chest of drawers, unopened for years.

1827-28

Black ground, printed cotton day dress, with wild flower sprays in yellows, pinks, green, and some blue, very delicate in design. Bodice back and front with V-shaped bands and gathers. Normal waistline. Bodice and sleeves lined in brown cotton. Deep flounce at hem with thick piping. Gigot sleeves, very long.
Snowshill Collection

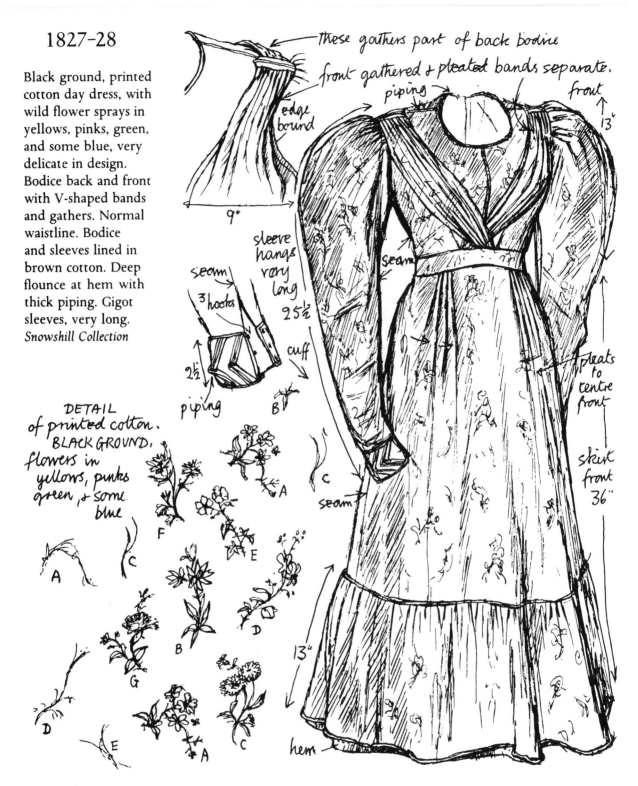

these gathers part of back bodice

front gathered + pleated bands separate.

piping

front

13"

edge bound

9"

sleeve hangs very long 25½

seam

3 hooks

2½

piping

cuff

B

C

seam

DETAIL of printed cotton. BLACK GROUND. flowers in yellows, pinks green, + some blue

A

C

F

E

D

B

G

D

E

A

C

seam

pleats to centre front

skirt front 36"

13"

hem

At first glance this day dress appears very sombre, but the charming flower sprays bear closer inspection and take away some of the heaviness of the dress. The sleeves are extremely long and show traces of having been tied or gathered, as in the study. The skirt has a new

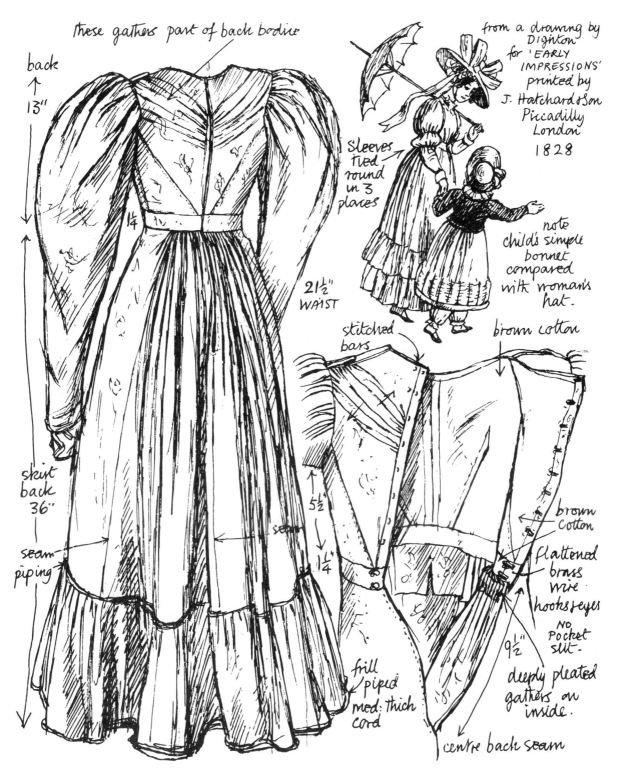

these gathers part of back bodice

back

13"

1¼

1¼

21½" WAIST

skirt back 36"

seam piping

seam

from a drawing by Dighton for 'EARLY IMPRESSIONS' printed by J. Hatchard & Son Piccadilly London 1828

Sleeves tied round in 3 places

note child's simple bonnet compared with woman's hat.

stitched bars

brown cotton

5½

1¼

9½"

frill piped med: thick cord

brown cotton

flattened brass wire hooks & eyes

NO pocket slit.

deeply pleated gathers on inside.

centre back seam

note as well as the bodice, having now some pleated fullness at front waist, here giving a 'follow through' movement to the bodice gathers. This dress, like the red cotton, had been shut away, perhaps thought too ugly to hang with the others.

1825-35

Fine white pelerine of embroidered muslin.
Mrs M. S. Mallam

White watered-silk reticule, embroidered in silks, pink, green, copper, and yellow. Large white silk bonnet, trimmed in white satin and pale blue ribbons.

c. 1830-35

Green silk parasol, pagoda shape, metal stick, ivory handle.
Snowshill Collection

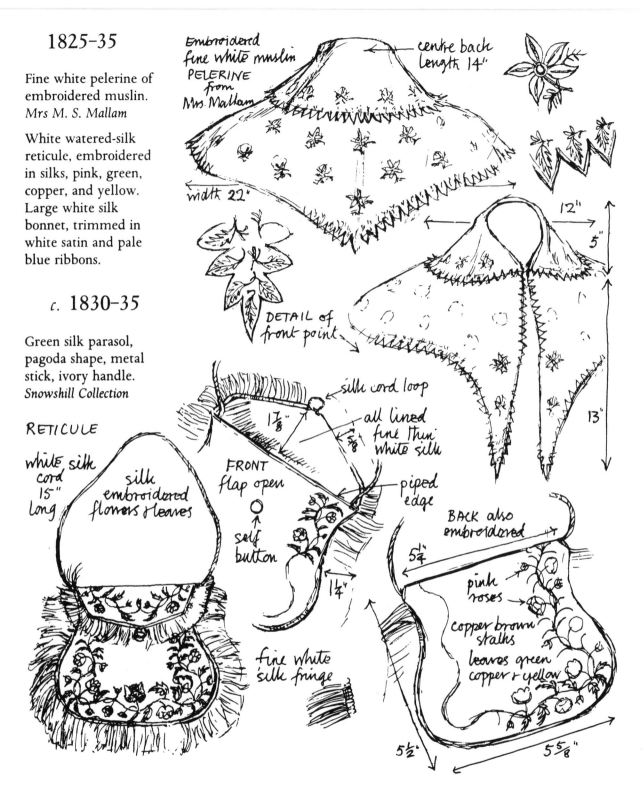

Embroidered fine white muslin PELERINE from Mrs. Mallam

centre back length 14"

width 22"

DETAIL of front point

12"   5"

13"

all lined fine thin white silk

silk cord loop

$1\frac{7}{8}$" $\frac{5}{8}$"

piped edge

RETICULE

white silk cord 15" long

silk embroidered flowers & leaves

FRONT flap open

self button

$1\frac{1}{4}$"

fine white silk fringe

BACK also embroidered

$5\frac{1}{4}$"

pink roses

copper brown stalks

leaves green copper & yellow

$5\frac{1}{2}$" $5\frac{5}{8}$"

Fine white embroidered collars or pelerines spread over the increasingly wide shoulders; this dainty example is not of maximum width. Reticules, usually embroidered and often fringed, were carried until increasingly full skirts made it possible for pockets to be worn again.

139

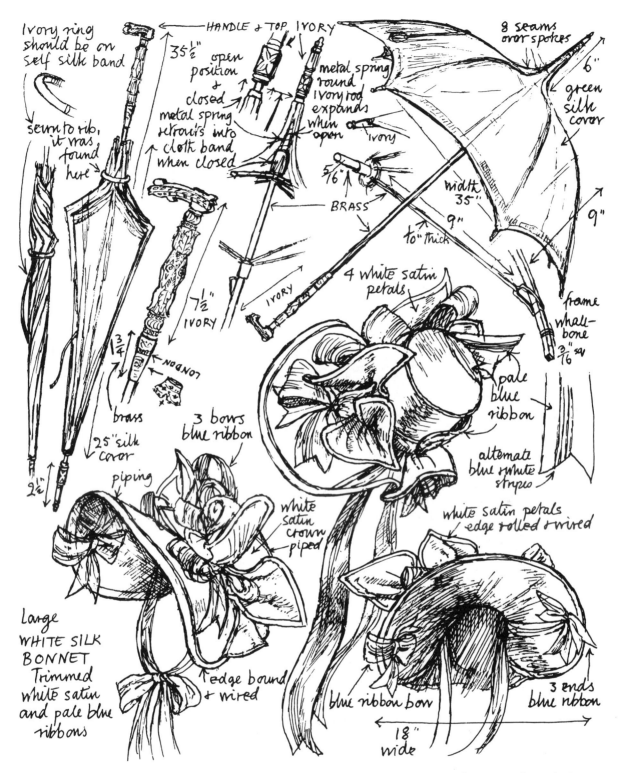

Ivory ring should be on self silk band

sewn to rib, it was found here

HANDLE & TOP IVORY

35½" open position & closed

metal spring retracts into cloth band when closed

metal spring round ivory rod expands when open

IVORY

BRASS

8 seams over spokes

6" green silk cover

width 35"

 to" thick

9"

9"

frame whalebone 3/16" sq.

7½" IVORY

3/4

LONDON

brass

IVORY

⅜"

4 white satin petals

pale blue ribbon

alternate blue white stripes

white satin petals edge rolled & wired

25" silk cover

2½"

3 bows blue ribbon

piping

white satin crown piped

edge bound & wired

Large WHITE SILK BONNET Trimmed white satin and pale blue ribbons

blue ribbon bow

18" wide

3 ends blue ribbon

Pagoda-shaped parasols, fashionable from *c.* 1800, remained in use until *c.* 1840; the tubular metal stick with ivory handle is found *c.* 1835. Large silk bonnets, perhaps because they are so large, and therefore difficult to store, are more rarely preserved.

1827-28

Lilac silk taffeta dress with tartan stripes in cream and green, with some pink. Bodice and sleeves, waistband and cuffs, lined white cotton. Edges and seams are piped; the deep hem is padded. Large gigot sleeves. Slit to pocket in skirt. Waist tape tie.
Snowshill Collection

Black satin shoes, square toe, satin baby ribbon ties.
Mrs M. Macbeth

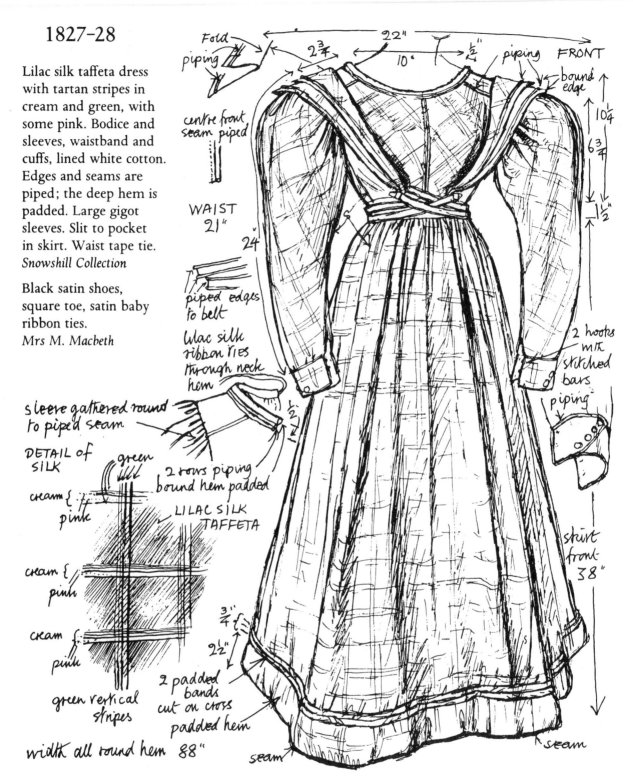

Fold piping

centre front seam piped

WAIST 21"

24"

piped edges to belt

Lilac silk ribbon ties through neck hem

sleeve gathered round to piped seam

DETAIL of SILK

cream {
pink

cream {
pink

cream {
pink

green vertical stripes

2 rows piping
bound hem padded

LILAC SILK TAFFETA

green

2 padded bands cut on cross padded hem

width all round hem 88"

22" 10" ½" piping FRONT

bound edge

10¼"

6¾"

1½"

2¾"

2 hooks with stitched bars

piping

skirt front 38"

¾"

22½"

seam

seam

The smallness of the waist is emphasized by the bodice decoration, huge sleeves, and increasingly wide skirts, now gathered all round at the waist. Padded hems are rarely seen after 1828, and the gigot-type sleeve, which appeared *c.* 1824, lasted to about 1836, with a

BACK

$10\frac{1}{4}$"

8"

Lilac silk ribbon tie

fine black satin ribbon ties 18" long

BLACK SATIN SHOES

tiny tape ties

piped seams

$1\frac{7}{2}$

$2\frac{1}{2}$

$3\frac{3}{4}$

seams

worn by Lady Hetta Forbes c. 1830

"Droit"

$1\frac{3}{4}$

10"

$2\frac{3}{8}$

skirt back $39\frac{1}{2}$

bound slit to separate pocket

stitched eyelets

hook

lined

dart

$1\frac{1}{2}$

2"

8"

hooks + eyes

9"

narrow white tape drawstrings round waist

seam

seam

seam

similar type again appearing in the 1890's. Shoes continue to be heelless, but the toes became square by the '30's, and at this time are still not made for left or right feet, but a tiny label in French often indicates which is which.

1825-29

Lilac silk taffeta dress for evening wear. Long lilac gauze sleeves, over taffeta puff sleeve. Bodice trimmed with lilac satin and frill of lace at neckline. Hem trimmed with padded satin bands, with folds of ribbon and gauze. Puffed sleeves and bodice back lined in white linen. V-shaped bodice decoration. Ties at neck and waist. *Snowshill Collection*

A

taffeta puff sleeve

gauze

Back silk ties from B

A

satin

lace gathered ½" in from edge

B

2"

fine white silk net embroidered in white silk

taffeta

FRONT DETAIL

pale lilac silk taffeta

⅝

1⅝

5 panels tapered lilac satin ribbon

2 pleats

double piped in taffeta

7¾"

9¾"

seam

⅜

seam

seam

very long gauze sleeves 31"

seam

s

seam

silk width 19"

Long transparent gauze sleeves are one of the most fashionable features of evening dress at this period; they had first appeared some ten years earlier than this, but were then not so full at the shoulder. These are made very long, hanging in graceful folds round the forearm.

143

1 3/4"
4 hooks of flattened black wire
sleeves & bodice back lined fine white linen
front unlined
white silk ribbon tie in front hem
8 1/2"
1 1/2"
gauze seam stitched to puff sleeve length lilac gauze
31"
4 1/2"
taffeta pleat + fold of gauze
satin buttons
pale lilac silk ribbon inside ties
8"
lilac gauze sleeves
lilac silk ribbon
edge pinhed
bound narrow satin
eyelet
1/2"
satin
taffeta double piping
hook
lilac gauze sleeves
double gauze
fold of taffeta
width all round hem 90"
padded satin ribbon
2 3/4"
seam
seam
s.

The wide decorated hemline balances the width of the shoulders, the pleating and padding helping the skirt to swing outwards. Several petticoats are worn under these more full-skirted dresses; stays pinch in the waist.

1825–29

Lilac silk taffeta evening dress with long gauze sleeves. Black kid heelless shoes, trimmed with blue ribbon, square toe.

1829–30

Fine cream silk dress of stockinette, for a young girl. Delicate trailing floral print on fine rectangular woven ground. Green satin trimming on bodice and skirt. *Snowshill Collection*

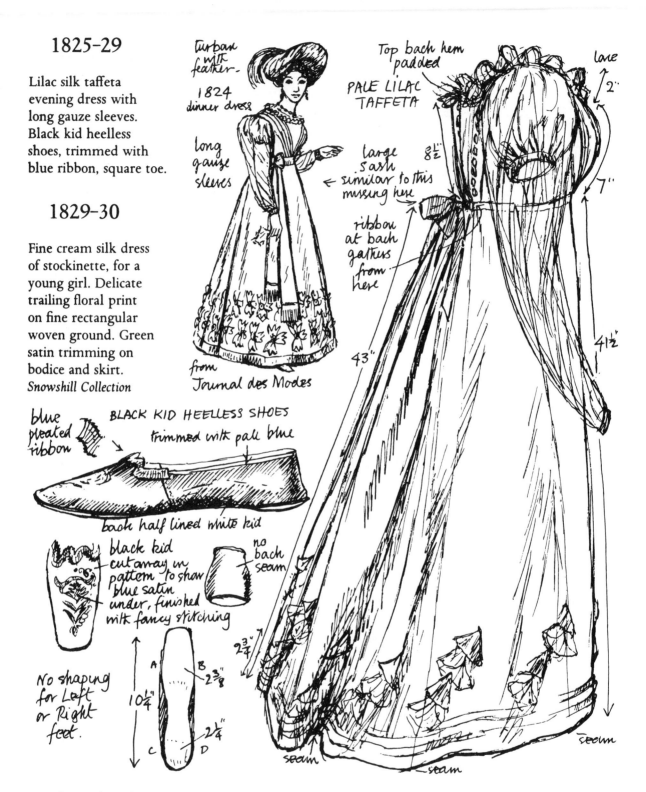

turban with feather.

1824 dinner dress

long gauze sleeves

from *Journal des Modes*

Top back hem padded

PALE LILAC TAFFETA

large sash similar to this missing here

ribbon at back gathers from here

lace

2"

8½"

7"

4½"

43"

2¾"

seam

seam

seam

blue pleated ribbon

BLACK KID HEELLESS SHOES trimmed with pale blue

back half lined white kid

black kid cut away in pattern to show blue satin under, finished with fancy stitching

no back seam

No shaping for Left or Right feet.

10¼"   A   B   2⅜"

2¼"

C   D

The V-shaped pleating and decoration on the bodice, seen also in the 1824 fashion-plate, remains in use in various forms for over another 20 years. It indicates the downward trend which appears in the pointed waistline on dresses in the mid '30's. The young girl's dress

epaulette edge bound green silk braid

neck and skirt trimmed with green satin folded & cut on the cross

from the painting of the children of John Walter Esq at Bear Wood

armhole neatly hemmed

lined white cotton

front tape ties

5½"

9½"

BACK white tape ties

1¾"

WAIST 20½"

8

1¾"

33"

c 1826-29

front pleats of SKIRT

front neck tape-tie

9½"

green satin

CENTRE FRONT

BACK fastening.

glazed cotton

flat brass wire hooks

9½"

Bodice & skirt lined white cotton

hem of stockinette

cotton lining

6¼"

WOVEN PATTERN DETAIL

back opening in seam

very fine cream silk STOCKINETTE 33" wide

1½"

1¾"

FRONT SKIRT pleated back skirt very closely gathered

shows a change from waist gathers to pleating; also it has the higher level of skirt decoration. This dress, fortunately fully lined, may have been a form of 'pinafore' dress, a sleeved habit shirt being worn underneath.

1828-30

Primrose-yellow gauze over-dress, trimmed with golden-yellow satin cut on the cross, and fine blonde lace. An evening gown with very full puffed sleeves, edged with the lace. Wide satin sash with bow and long hanging loop. Decorated from hem to knee-level with panels edged in satin. The under-dress is missing. *Snowshill Collection*

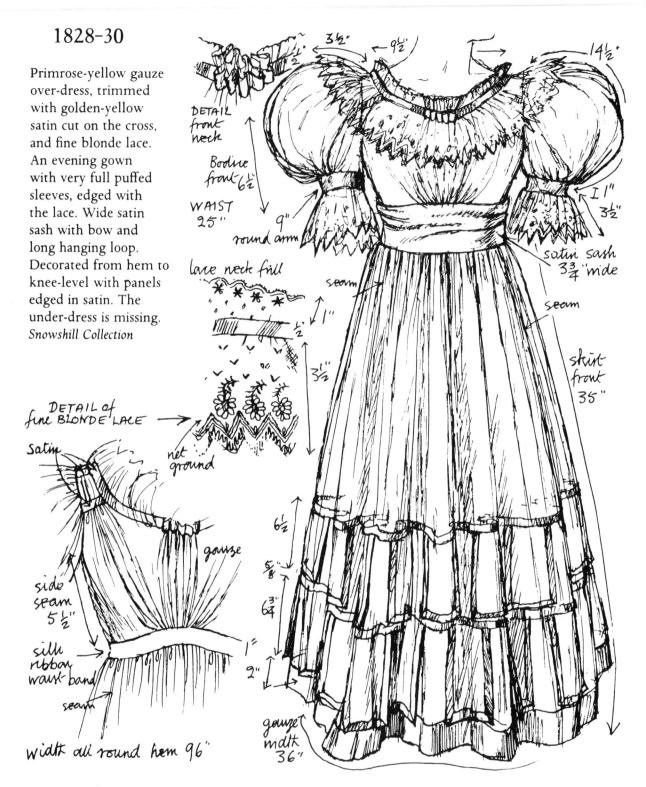

DETAIL front neck

Bodice front 6½"

WAIST 25"

round arm 9"

3½"   9½"   14½"

I 1"   3½"

satin sash 3¾" wide

seam

seam

skirt front 35"

lace neck frill

net ground

3½"   ½   1"

DETAIL of fine BLONDE LACE

satin

gauze

side seam 5½"

silk ribbon waist band

seam

6½

⅝"

6¾"

1"   9"

gauze width 36"

width all round hem 96"

A matching satin under-dress with short puffed sleeves would have completed this lovely gauze evening dress. The gathering of the bodice and skirt on to the ribbon waistband is full and close, and the dress hangs wide at the hem, measuring all round 96". With these

147

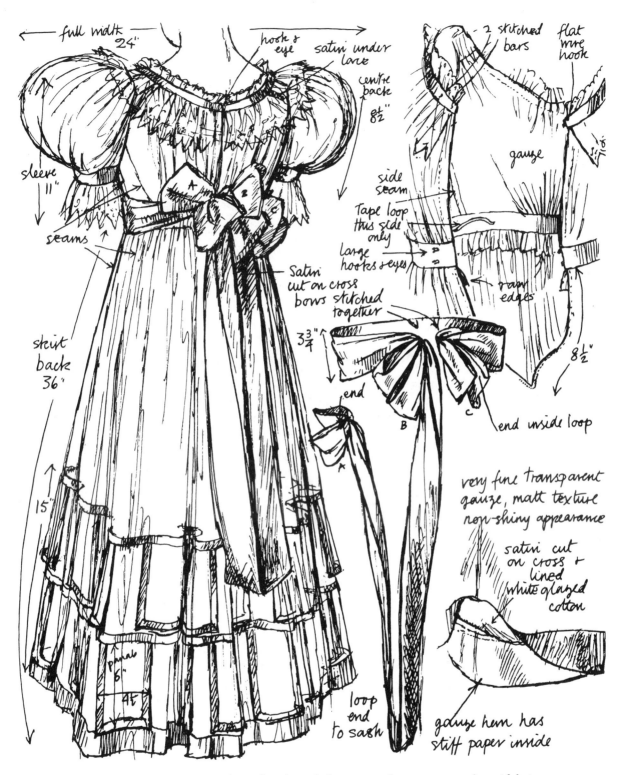

full width 24"

hook & eye

satin under lace

centre back 8½"

sleeve 11"

seams

skirt back 36"

15"

panels 6"

4½

2 stitched bars

flat wire hook

gauze

side seam

Tape loop this side only

large hooks & eyes

raw edges

8½"

Satin cut on cross bows stitched together

3¾"

end

end

end inside loop

B

C

very fine transparent gauze, matt texture non-shiny appearance

satin cut on cross + lined white glazed cotton

loop end to sash

gauze hem has stiff paper inside

wider skirts, decoration reaches knee-level, and then is used no more as the width increases; this is particularly so on day dresses. Extra waist-petticoats are worn, often with rows of thick piping above the flounced hem.

1829-31

Lilac and white striped evening dress, with dainty floral print on white stripe. Very full puffed sleeves of white satin, under very fine gathered silk net edged with embroidered net. Tiny white satin apron trimmed with lilac. Narrow padded rolls at hem. Fastening of hook & eye at back. White satin collar, lined stiffened cotton. *Snowshill Collection*

1831 fashion plate

lace

gauze

from "Le Follet Courrier des Salons"

join in white satin sleeve

5¼"

BACK VIEW WITH COLLAR & with COLLAR REMOVED

white satin

lilac ribbon

↕ 1⅛"

seams

seam

lilac stripes only, show on full gathers at back

DETAIL of flower print in lilac, tan, gold & green on white stripe

lilac satin stripe

1"

2½

stitched bars for 4 hooks

BACK FASTENING

10½"

4 tiny hooks

inner tape ties

transparent white stripe with weft thread thicker.

padded rolls at hem white & lilac satin

1¾"

width round hem 110"

Only a small, slender woman could have worn this very dainty dress, which now is unfortunately in a very frail condition, particularly the cobweb fine lace. When first seen, this dress was without the collar. But as I was sorting through a box containing ribbons and scarves

149

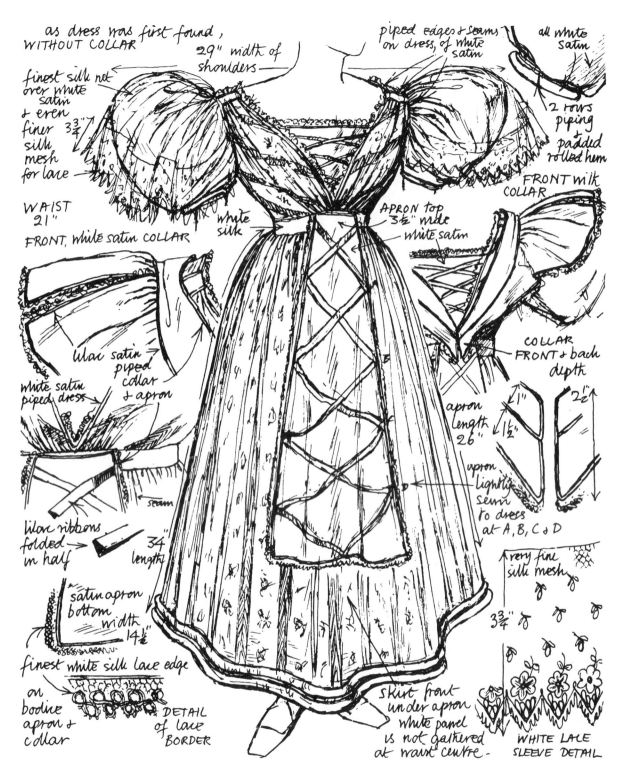

as dress was first found, WITHOUT COLLAR

29" width of shoulders

piped edges & seams on dress, of white satin

all white satin

finest silk net over white satin & even finer 3¾" silk mesh for lace

2 rows piping & padded rolled hem

FRONT with COLLAR

WAIST 21"

FRONT, white satin COLLAR

white silk

APRON top 3½" wide white satin

lilac satin piped collar & apron

white satin piped dress

seam

COLLAR FRONT & back depth

1"   2½"

1½"

apron length 26"

apron lightly sewn to dress at A, B, C & D

lilac ribbons folded in half

34" length

satin apron bottom width 14½"

very fine silk mesh

3¾"

finest white silk lace edge

on bodice apron & collar

DETAIL of lace BORDER

skirt front under apron white panel is not gathered at waist centre.

WHITE LACE SLEEVE DETAIL

some months later, the white satin collar was found, and matched by the narrow lilac piping, very fine lace edging, and quality of satin. The sleeves, here at their maximum width, are lined with stiffened cotton.

150

1830–33

Purple-black gauze dress, striped, machine-woven leaf pattern, narrow piping and binding of purple-black satin speckled with pale fawn. Bodice draped at front in to matching corded silk waistband. Sleeve and skirt sewn in flat pleats, wide on skirt with gathers at back. Wide gigot sleeve.
Chastleton House; lent to Snowshill Collection

narrow band of purple satin

pleated gauze / all seams piped in matching purple satin

9½"

max: width round sleeve 31"

matching waistband of corded silk ribbon, also speckled as satin

1½"

back open to here in seam

2 small flat black wire hooks

piped

piping

fine gathers

flat pleats

2 very large hooks & eyes of flattened black wire

width all round hem 96"

seam

seam

DETAIL of GAUZE

finest silk gauze stamped texture on woven pattern

The huge sleeves and distinctive satin used on this dress made it possible for it to be recognized and reunited with the satin under-dress in the Snowshill Collection. When found in the drawer at Chastleton House with various examples of lace it was folded away surprisingly

narrow band matching
purple satin
edges piped

pleated
gauze

pleated
gauze

double
piping

sleeve
pleats
face to
back

WAIST 27½"

matching
satin
underdress

& puffed
sleeves

width 27-28"

double piping
in purple satin
all round
armhole

shirt
front
41"

skirt
pleats
face
to front

skirt
back
43½"

gathers
from
here

seam
piped
in
satin

stitched
together

small
hook &
eye

edge bound
in matching
purple satin

seam

seam

small hem

Waist belt or sash is missing, probably of the matching satin

small, so fine is the silken gauze. The wide type of pleating on the skirts of both gauze and satin is the same, and the flat pleating on the sleeves is a little unusual. This wide, graceful skirt is free of all form of trimming.

1830–33

Purple-black satin under-dress, matching gauze overdress from Chastleton House. Very full puff sleeves, pleated to dress, stiff brown net lining. Glazed cotton lining to skirt, this pleated and gathered at waist. Matching reticule, embroidered in silks, chenille, ribbon-work, and fish scales, lined in pink silk.
Snowshill Collection

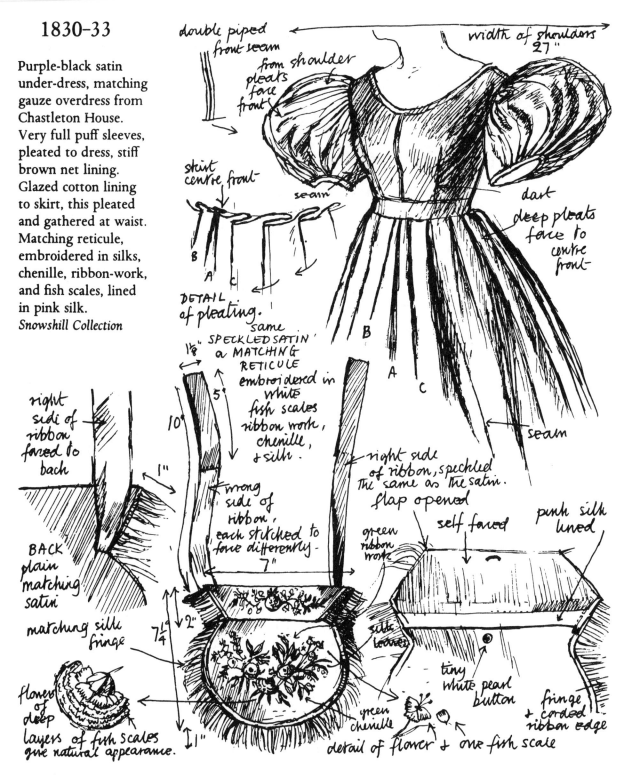

double piped front seam

from shoulder pleats face front

width of shoulders 27"

skirt centre front

seam

dart

deep pleats face to centre front

B
A C

DETAIL of pleating.

same 'SPECKLED SATIN' a MATCHING RETICULE embroidered in white fish scales ribbon work, chenille, + silk.

1⅛"

5"

10"

B
A C

seam

right side of ribbon faced to back

1"

wrong side of ribbon, each stitched to face differently.
7"

right side of ribbon, speckled the same as the satin. flap opened

green ribbon work

self faced

pink silk lined

BACK plain matching satin

matching silk fringe

7¼" 2"

silk leaves

tiny white pearl button

fringe + corded ribbon edge

flowers of deep layers of fish scales give natural appearance.

1"

green chenille

detail of flower + one fish scale

The satin skirt is pleated a little more richly than the gauze, giving the skirt slightly greater width at the hem. The missing sash may have been similar to the one in the fashion-plate of 1831 (p. 149). The embroidered reticule or handkerchief sachet is made from the identical

153

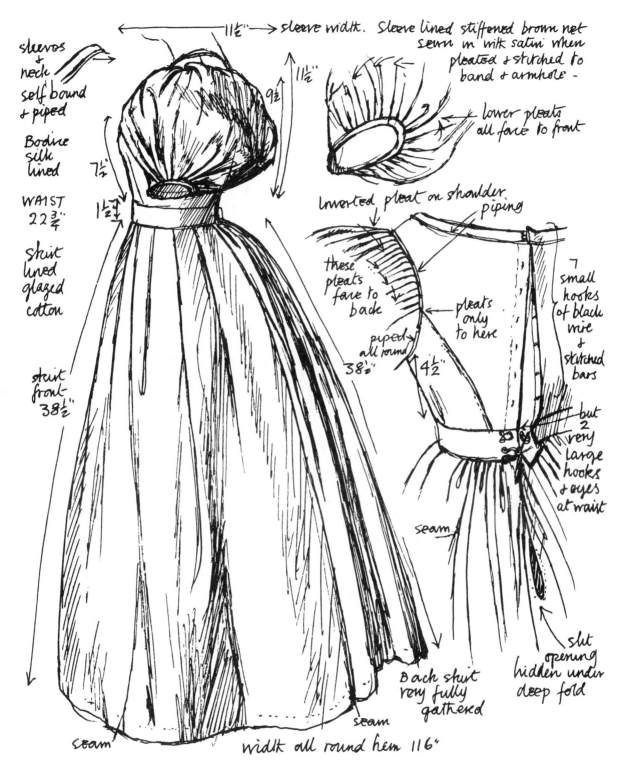

sleeves + neck self bound + piped

Bodice silk lined

WAIST 22¾"

skirt lined glazed cotton

skirt front 38½"

7½"

1½"

11½" → sleeve width. Sleeve lined stiffened brown net sewn in with satin when pleated + stitched to band + armhole –

11½"

9½

lower pleats all face to front

Inverted pleat on shoulder. piping

these pleats face to back

pleats only to here

piped all round 38½"

4½"

7 small hooks of black wire + stitched bars

but 2 very large hooks + eyes at waist

seam

slit opening hidden under deep fold

Back skirt very fully gathered

seam

seam

seam

width all round hem 116"

satin, speckled in exactly the same way; probably this is by accident rather than design, as the gauze too has this irregular blotched effect. The embroidery, with the use of ribbon, chenille, and silk and tiny white fish scales, is rare and very attractive.

1829-33

White checkered muslin day dress, printed in flowing floral pattern, in pinks, blue, green, and mauve. Bodice, lined white cotton, has gathered band from shoulder to waist. Large cape collar, lined plain muslin. Sleeves very full, shoulder to wrist, cuff with tiny pearl buttons. Seams and edges piped. Skirt with pocket slits.
Snowshill Collection

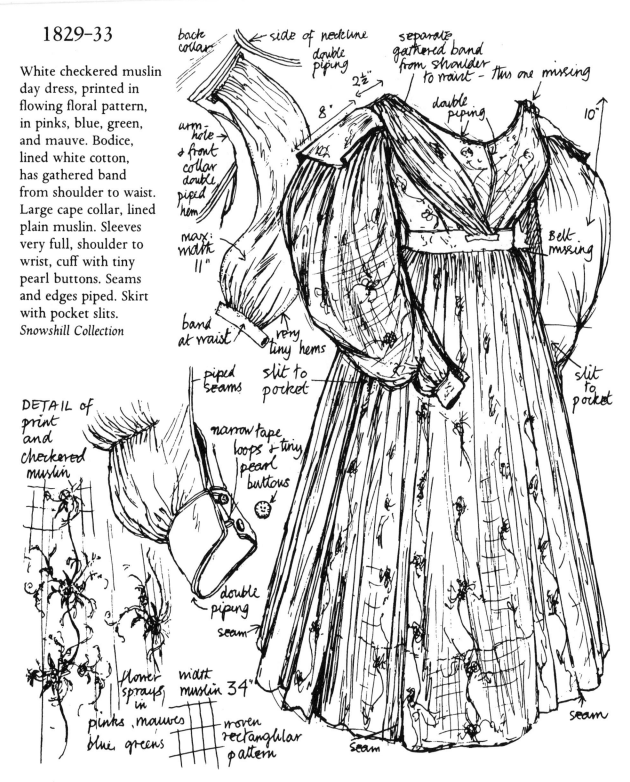

back collar
side of neckline
double piping
separate gathered band from shoulder to waist – this one missing
double piping
10"
2½"
8"
arm-hole
front collar double piped hem
max: width 11"
Belt missing
band at waist
very tiny hems
slit to pocket
slit to pocket
piped seams
slit to pocket
DETAIL of print and checkered muslin
narrow tape loops & tiny pearl buttons
double piping seam
flower sprays in pinks, mauves blue, greens
matt muslin 34"
woven rectangular pattern
seam
seam
seam

This rather charming floral pattern makes this muslin an attractive material and helps the vast 'imbecile' sleeves (found 1829-35) to hang in graceful folds. Both sleeves and skirt are very finely and closely gathered, and the skirt, like the sleeves, is of some considerable width!

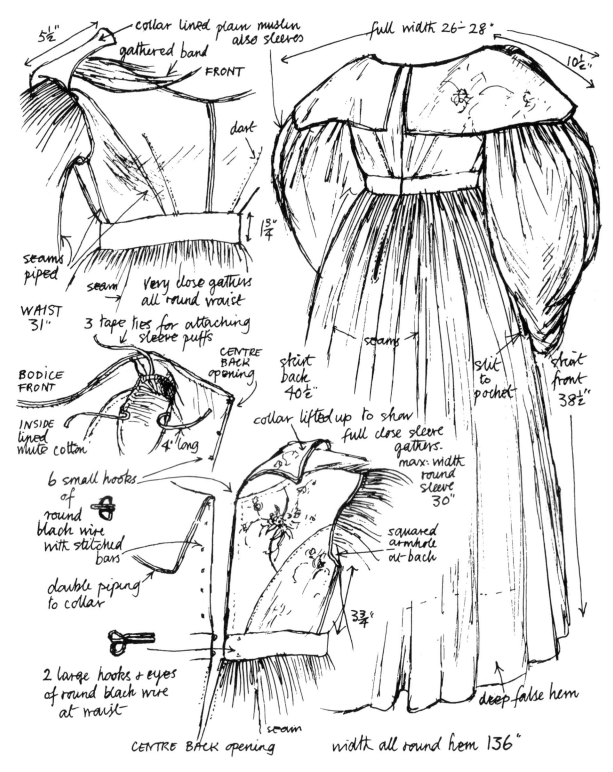

5½"

collar lined plain muslin also sleeves

gathered band

FRONT

dart

full width 26-28"

10½"

1¾"

seams piped

seam

Very close gathers all round waist

WAIST 31"

3 tape ties for attaching sleeve puffs

CENTRE BACK opening

skirt back 40½"

slit to pocket

skirt front 38½"

BODICE FRONT

INSIDE lined white cotton

4" long

collar lifted up to show full close sleeve gathers.

max: width round sleeve 30"

6 small hooks of round black wire with stitched bars

double piping to collar

squared armhole at back

3¾"

seams

2 large hooks & eyes of round black wire at waist

deep false hem

CENTRE BACK opening

seam

width all round hem 136"

It is still supported on a number of petticoats. The tape ties inside the armhole are for securing the huge sleeve puffs, used 1825–35 (p. 128). The double piping on the bodice and cuffs is very finely done.

1833–35

White embroidered
muslin pelerine, with
floral spot pattern on
top collar and round
border of under-collar.
Mrs M. S. Mallam

1835–39

Plain navy-blue silk
taffeta mantle, with
wide collar, fastening
only with waist ribbon
tie. Wool interlining,
navy-blue silk lined,
edges bound in navy-
blue velvet.
Snowshill Collection

DETAIL of embroidery

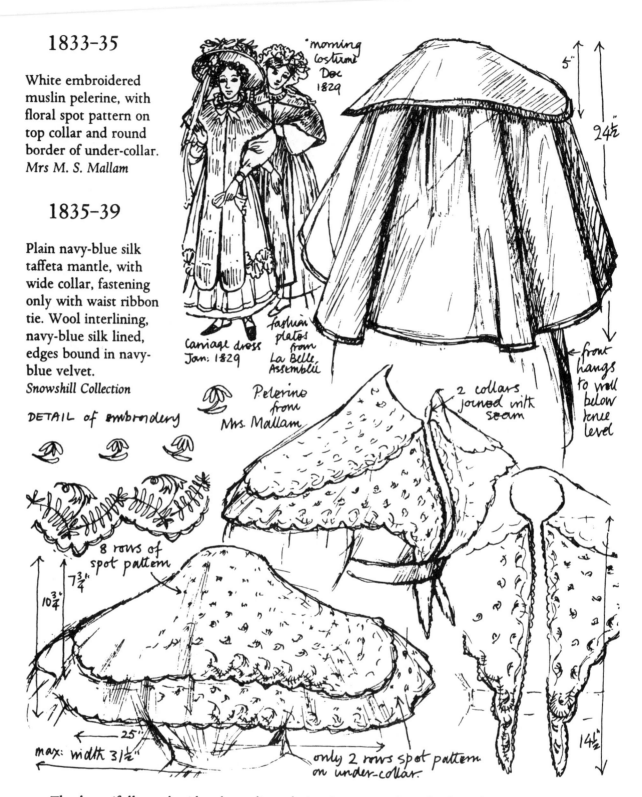

'morning costume Dec 1829

Carriage dress Jan: 1829

fashion plates from La Belle Assemblée

Pelerine from Mrs Mallam

2 collars joined with seam

front hangs to well below knee level

8 rows of spot pattern

7¾"

10¾"

max: width 31½"

25"

only 2 rows spot pattern on under-collar.

5"

24½

14½

The beautifully embroidered muslin pelerine is very wide indeed, and it accentuates the full width of the shoulder-line of the early '30's. Buckled belts were fashionable, and held the long ends of the pelerine in place. The taffeta mantle has the wide collar and full cape

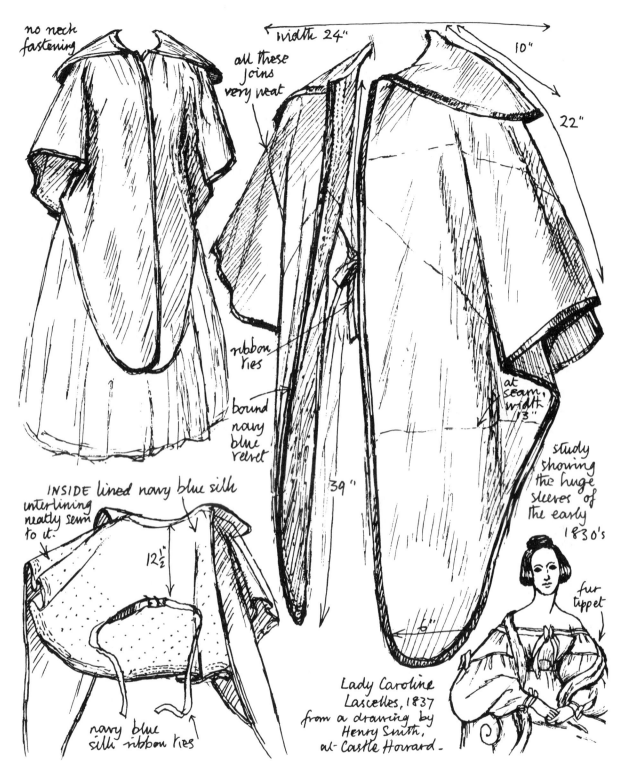

no neck fastening

all these joins very neat

width 24"

10"

22"

ribbon ties

bound navy blue velvet

at seam, width 13"

study showing the huge sleeves of the early 1830's

39"

6"

INSIDE lined navy blue silk

interlining neatly sewn to it.

12½"

navy blue silk ribbon ties

fur tippet

Lady Caroline Lascelles, 1837 from a drawing by Henry Smith, at Castle Howard.

necessary for covering the very wide sleeves. Mantles with long hanging ends, similar to this, remained in fashion for many years; the borders were often frilled or fringed during the '40's and '50's. This example is both warm and light.

1830-35

Dark grey-brown, or 'Spanish brown,' silk taffeta mantle, with wide collar edged with black velvet pile on brown ground. Waist drawn in at back with tape tie inside. Front ties of silk, neck to hem; lined matching brown glazed cotton and interlined with coarse woollen cloth of open texture.
Snowshill Collection

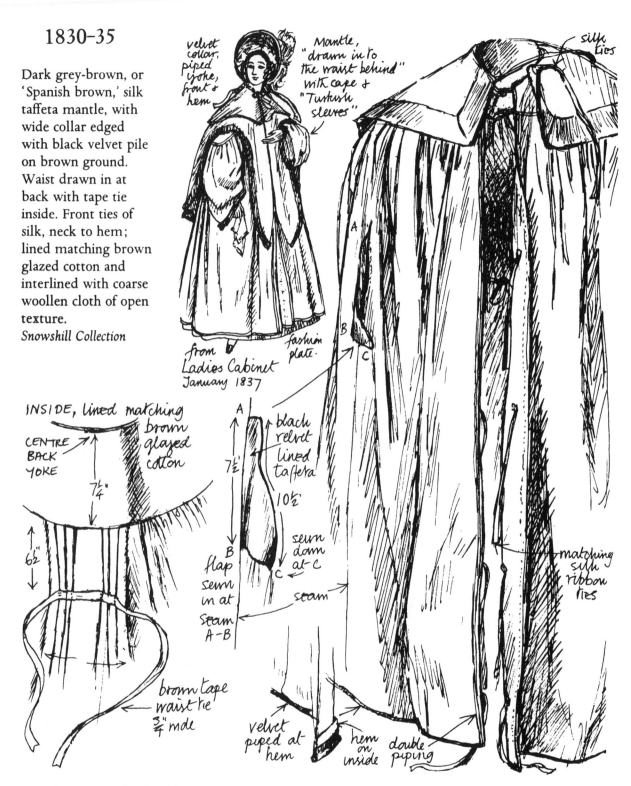

velvet collar, piped yoke, front & hem

Mantle, "drawn into the waist behind" with cape & "Turkish sleeves"

silk ties

from Ladies Cabinet January 1837

fashion plate.

INSIDE, lined matching brown glazed cotton

CENTRE BACK YOKE

7¼"

6½"

brown tape waist tie ¾" wide

A

7½"

B

flap sewn in at Seam A-B

black velvet lined taffeta

10½"

sewn down at C

C

seam

velvet piped at hem

hem on inside

double piping

matching silk ribbon ties

The very wide shoulder-line reached its maximum width *c.* 1833, but silk mantles such as this were still in use in 1837, when we can read in *The Ladies' Cabinet* that they 'have lost nothing of their vogue,' and 'rich satin with applications in velvet of a darker shade' and

159

back collar 26½"

depth front yoke + front length 50"

1¾ depth

back length 55"

collar depth centre back

11"

2½"

10"

velvet

width all round hem 119"

seam

seam

seam

lined matching glazed cotton + interlined

collar front

6"

7"

7½"

62"

CENTRE BACK OUTSIDE

piped

yoke width 20"

7"

6"

¾

gathers on shoulder, pleats at back

5" length, velvet waist-band sewn on back with tape inside

another of cashmere, as shown in the drawing here, were the height of fashion. Mantles really were voluminous; there is another like this one at Snowshill, lined in pale blue silk, with a deep cape to hip-level.

1834–35 'November Modes,' a fashion-plate in *The Beau Monde*, showing the huge sleeves and the widening skirts of the '30's. *The Country Gentleman*, a lithograph by Dighton, is of Mr L. C. Fulwer Craven of Brockhampton Park, near Cheltenham.

1863 Mr Street and Grace, from T. Stanley Brown's family album. Her wide-sleeved, velvet-trimmed dark silk dress would have been worn over a full cage crinoline. He wears frock coat, waistcoat, and trousers, a male fashion that changes little in Victoria's reign.

1870's from 2 illustrations in *Our Fathers*; the young lady at a game of croquet, in a looped-up dress over a bustle. The couple are at an 'Exhibition of perishable wicker coffins.' He wears a top-hat and morning coat, and trousers with a narrow stripe at the side.

3

1835–1870

The wheel of fashion now turns full circle; after nearly eighty years dresses with tiny waists have their billowing skirts once more distended over a hooped foundation. During the '30's the bustle supporting the back gathers increases in size, and by 1840 a stiff horsehair skirt is often worn below the growing number of petticoats; this is replaced in 1856 by an under-skirt held out on whalebone hoops, a little tricky to manage at times, but it reduces the need for extra petticoats. The steel hoops and finer watch-spring steels which soon follow are light and flexible, more easily managed, and rather delightful to wear. Victorian women, neatly stepping in their dainty boots or shoes, hidden under wide spreading skirts, appear to float along rather than to walk.

At first these crinolines are domed, widening at the hem towards the '60's, although they tend to become smaller around 1862. By '67, just before their decline, they swell out at back and sides, but remain flat in front. Finally, skirt fullness is concentrated at the back, and the bustle returns yet again.

One of the most notable happenings that occur during this period is the invention of the sewing-machine. Nowadays it is rather taken for granted, but for countless years, far back in time, every stitch, in every garment made, every sheet, quilt, or curtain, was sewn by hand. It is not until the mid-19th c. that machines for sewing are invented, and the history of the development of this useful mechanism is fascinating.

Machine-sewn dresses appear in England from 1860, and some early advertisements are worth recording. A very appealing one in *The Lady's Own Paper* 1868 is obviously directed at the conscience of the Victorian male. It praises the qualities of the 'Florence Sewing Machine.' 'The man who sports a costly watch, or expensive jewelry, when his wife, with weary fingers and heavy heart, is wearing away her life at midnight, stitching for the children while they sleep, for want of a Sewing Machine, is shamefully thoughtless, or worse—heartless. . . . Buy a "Florence" for your friend, your sister, or wife, it will shorten her toil and lengthen her life.'

Some materials or garments have interesting connections, being kept perhaps for years before being used or handed down to a favourite niece or daughter. These days fashion changes too rapidly, but a century and more ago such things as shawls or muslins remain 'wearable' for many years. Mrs Warren Hastings, who died aged 90, left her possessions and property to the Imhoff family, her daughter-in-law Lady Imhoff, and some items to her niece Marion Winter. The shawl and muslin dress (pp. 177 & 195) were given by Lady Imhoff herself to Mrs Whitmore Jones of Chastleton House, whose daughter, Mrs J. D. Harris, wrote down these details. What we do not know is who it was who had this muslin made up into such a charming dress.

1836-37

Crisp deep cream silk evening dress, sleeves short with pleated puffs, low neckline, draped pleated front. Bodice laced at back, with bones front, back, and sides. Bodice and sleeves lined glazed cotton, skirt pleated and gathered to wide waistband, is lined with stiffened muslin. Wide belt or sash is missing.
Snowshill Collection

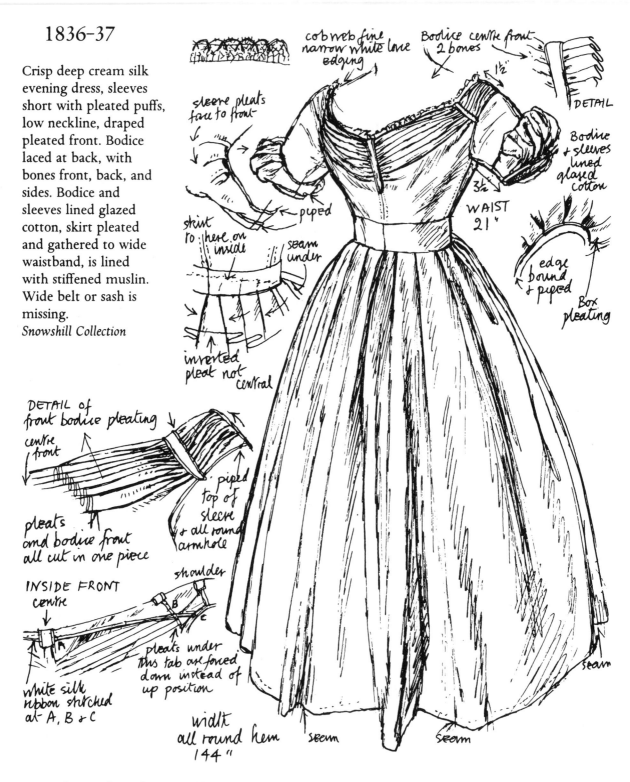

cob web fine narrow white lace edging

Bodice centre front 2 bones

DETAIL

sleeve pleats face to front

piped

Bodice + sleeves lined glazed cotton

1½

3½

WAIST 21"

edge bound + piped

Box pleating

skirt to there on inside

seam under

inverted pleat not central

DETAIL of front bodice pleating

centre front

pleats and bodice front all cut in one piece

piped top of sleeve + all round armhole

INSIDE FRONT centre

shoulder

pleats under this tab are forced down instead of up position

white silk ribbon stitched at A, B & C

width all round hem 144"

seam

seam

seam

A dainty dress for a small, slender woman, it has the new, fitting sleeve, the puff at the elbow being the only trace of the full sleeve of the earlier '30's. The bodice has the fashionable pleated front, seen also on the 1837 fashion-plate, p. 170. The wide, flat pleating of this skirt,

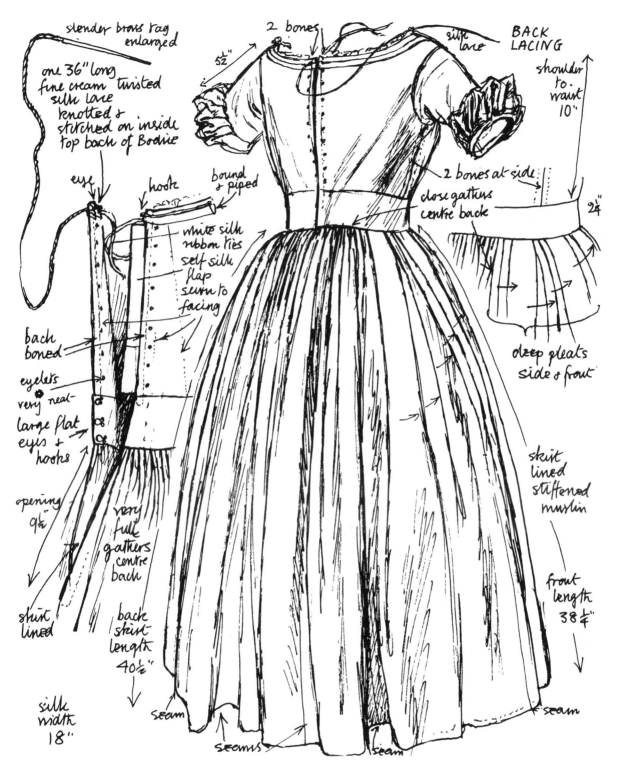

slender brass rag enlarged

one 36" long fine cream twisted silk lace knotted & stitched on inside top back of Bodice

2 bones

silk lace

BACK LACING

5½"

shoulder to waist 10"

eye

hook

bound & piped

2 bones at side

close gathers centre back

2¼"

white silk ribbon ties self silk flap sewn to facing

deep pleats side & front

back boned

eyelets very neat

large flat eyes & hooks

opening 9½"

very full gathers centre back

back skirt length 40½"

skirt lined

skirt lined stiffened muslin

front length 38¼"

silk width 18"

seam

seams

seam

seam

seam

with its close, full gathers at the back, has the front inverted pleat set off-centre, indicating that at some time the dress was let down by inserting this rather wide waistband. The rest of the sewing is fine and neat.

1837-39

Printed cotton, black
ground, trailing floral
print in lilac, harsh
green, tan, orange,
and dull yellow.
Morning dress with a
ruched and piped
decorated bodice, with
sleeves richly gathered
above the elbow, bodice
lined glazed linen,
skirt half-lined.
Back fastening, hook
and stitched bar, slit
to pocket in skirt.
Personal Collection

corded piping

folded edge only but has effect of double piping

fine white embroidered muslin tucker

piped seams

5 rows of ruching

piped hems

¼" binding

bodice centre front 7½

9"

BUST 39"
WAIST 34"

seam

14½"

2¼

skirt length back & front 41½"

DETAIL of printed cotton
BLACK ground

tan & orange

green spray

dull yellow & medley of other colours

lilac

tan & orange

lilac
green & tan
lilac
green & tan
lilac

lilac
seam

width all round hem 140"

seam

It is fortunate that such a simple morning dress as this should be preserved, as it does perhaps
reflect the fashion of the day more accurately than a wedding-gown. The printing of this
floral pattern is fairly typical of the mid '30's, not only in the use of its rather harsh colouring

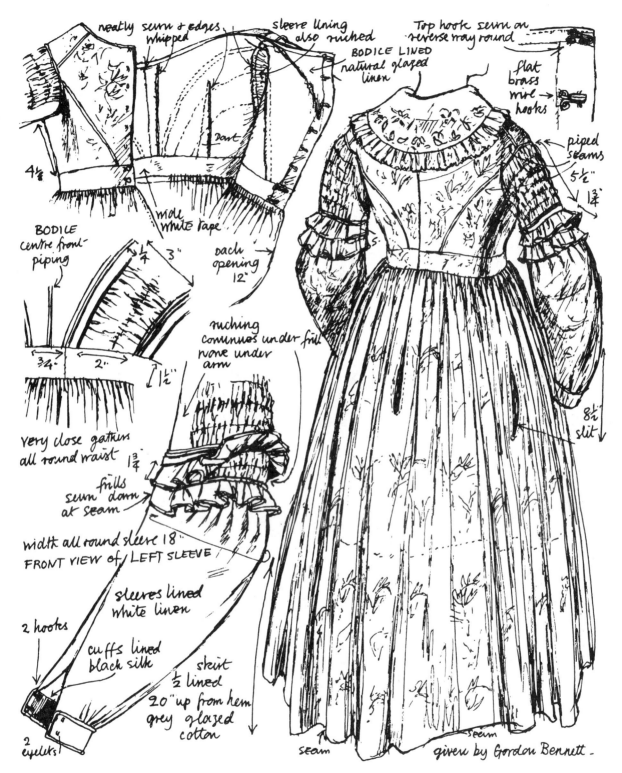

neatly sewn + edges whipped

sleeve lining also ruched

Top hook sewn on reverse way round

BODICE LINED natural glazed linen

flat brass wire hooks

piped seams

5½" 1¾

4⅝

part

BODICE centre front piping

mid white tape

back opening 12"

1¼ 3"

¾ 2"

1½"

ruching continues under frill none under arm

very close gathers all round waist

1¾

frills sewn down at seam

width all round sleeve 18"
FRONT VIEW of LEFT SLEEVE

sleeves lined white linen

cuffs lined black silk

skirt ½ lined 20" up from hem grey glazed cotton

2 hooks

2 eyelets

8½ slit

seam

seam

given by Gordon Bennett.

and solid green, but in the slight inaccuracy of the actual printing. The sleeves are well worth noting, as they clearly show the collapse of the earlier sleeve; the cut is identical, but the rows of gathering alter the shape entirely.

1837-39

White embroidered muslin tucker, single collar, edge frilled. Pair of pockets, white linen, on waist-tape.
Personal Collection from Gordon Bennett

White satin heelless shoes, very slight shaping of soles. Brown satin parasol, black woven pattern.
Snowshill Collection

Green silk parasol, also ivory-tipped.
Mrs M. Macbeth

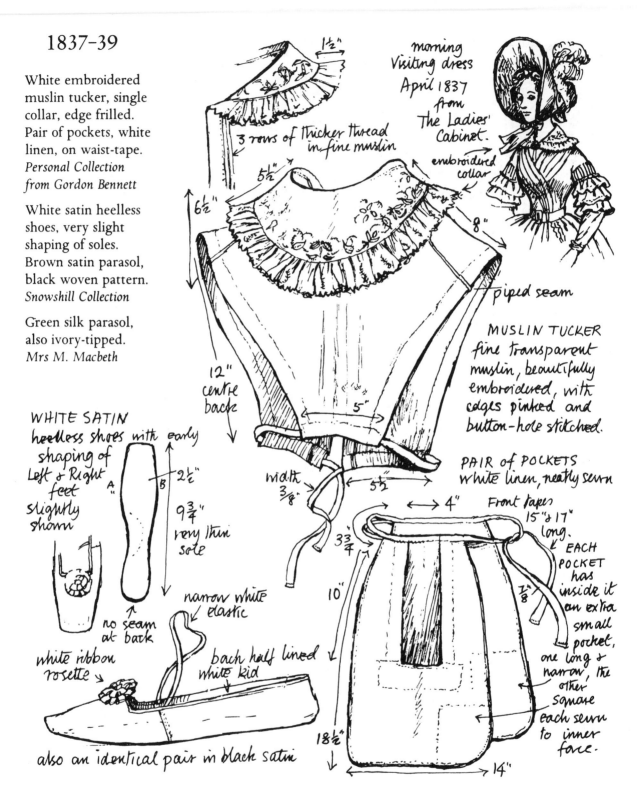

1½"

3 rows of thicker thread in fine muslin

morning Visiting dress April 1837 from The Ladies' Cabinet.

embroidered collar

5½"

6½"

8"

12" centre back

5"

piped seam

MUSLIN TUCKER
fine transparent muslin, beautifully embroidered, with edges pinked and button-hole stitched.

WHITE SATIN heelless shoes with early shaping of Left & Right feet slightly shown

2½"

9¾" very thin sole

A B

no seam at back

narrow white elastic

white ribbon rosette

back half lined white kid

width 3/8"

PAIR of POCKETS
white linen, neatly sewn

4"

Front tapes 15" & 17" long.

EACH POCKET has inside it an extra small pocket, one long & narrow, the other square each sewn to inner face.

7/8"

3¾"

10"

18½"

14"

also an identical pair in black satin

Both the dainty embroidered muslin collar and the pair of pockets were kept with the black printed cotton day dress; the tucker must have been a favourite one, as it has been much worn and very finely darned. The pockets are still very much the same shape as those of the

167

Frame – black whalebone 8 supporting metal spokes

3½

Bonnet with large tilted up brim + long handled parasol

morning dress June 1837

from a fashion plate in The Ladies' Cabinet

Ribbon bow, as here or brooch, would fasten the tucker in front.

ivory

1½"

fits one finger

21"

full length 32" wooden handle

2" ivory

1"

½"

BROWN SATIN pattern woven in black

brown silk tassel

cord was sewn here

GREEN SILK cover

21"

ivory

wooden handle

full length 29"

metal ring

tiny green silk tassel

black whalebone square

ivory tip

ivory handle

13½

1" silk fringe of brown + black

18th c., but this pair has a tiny extra pocket inside each of them. The small parasols are typical of this decade, the long, slender handle tipped with ivory being replaced in the '40's by the smaller elaborate carriage parasol, with folding stick.

168

1837-40

Printed white muslin with woven stripe in cream silk, flower sprays in deep rose pink and yellow, with green leaves and spot pattern in green. Bodice and sleeves, closely pleated panels with puffs at elbow. Bodice lined in white cotton, upper sleeve lined coarse muslin. Finely piped seams. Boned bodice.
Snowshill Collection

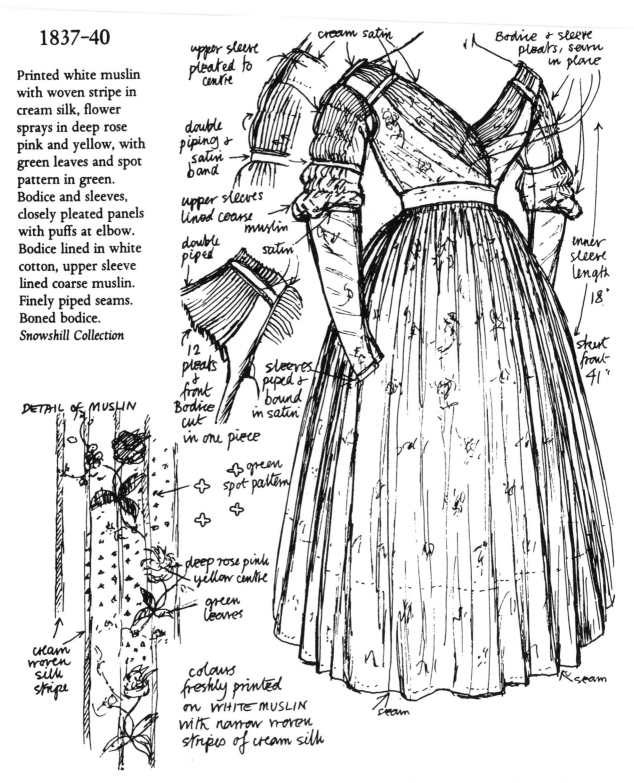

cream satin

upper sleeve pleated to centre

Bodice & sleeve pleats, sewn in place

double piping & satin band

upper sleeves lined coarse muslin

double piped

satin

inner sleeve length 18"

skirt front 41"

12 pleats & front Bodice cut in one piece

sleeves piped & bound in satin

DETAIL of MUSLIN

green spot pattern

deep rose pink yellow centre

green leaves

cream woven silk stripe

colours freshly printed on WHITE MUSLIN with narrow woven stripes of cream silk

seam

seam

The bodice, now boned at back and sides, with tiny waist and ever tightening sleeves, shows a return to restriction in dress, with low-set armholes and boned corsets. Back fastening continues on dresses until the end of the '40's; piped seams are popular. Different materials

169

hairstyle March 1837

from The Ladies' Cabinet

flowers entwined round hair

for dinner dress

satin piped seams

2 narrow bones at each side of centre back

7 small hooks & eyes of flat brass wire

$1\frac{3}{4}$"

$5\frac{1}{2}$"

3"

satin band

WAIST 21"

at waist 2 large flat brass wire hooks & eyes

skirt back $41\frac{1}{2}$

BODICE lined white cotton

small armhole

seam   dart

Boned

12

$10\frac{1}{2}$"

$4\frac{1}{2}$

boned $1\frac{1}{2}$"

tape

Tie stitching to keep gathers close

seam

seam

seam

seam

seam

seam

seam

skirt has no pocket slit

deep false hem of white muslin

width all round hem 125"

width of muslin 25"

lend themselves to various methods of pleating and gathering; in this muslin they are set very fine and close indeed. Silks are sewn in flat, wider pleats during the '30's, but by the '40's narrower pleating is more usual.

1837-38

Creamy white silk afternoon dress. Floral printed pattern with trailing black-line stems, deep crimson flowers, with green leaves. Tiny pointed waistline to bodice, which is boned at back. Very low-set sleeve, puffed at elbow with frill. Dress fully lined in white cotton. Day boots of cotton. Black satin dress shoes. *Snowshill Collection*

BODICE
centre front
tiny pointed waist
front point not stitched to pleats
pleats stitched to linen tape and lining
skirt front pleats ½" to ¾" wide, face to centre
fitting sleeve cotton lined
finely sewn bars
A
self silk
B
white tape

very narrow piping in white silk
neck edging & all seams piped
closer pleats
skirt 38"
A
B

DETAIL
thin creamy white silk printed in deep crimson & green, with flowing, delicate black line stems
leaves green
flower petals & dots deep crimson

alternate sprays upside down every alternate row.

seam
seam
width all round hem 128"

This is a good example of the type of dainty floral pattern fashionable for a few years, but even more important is the new line shown in this dress; it has a tiny pointed front to the bodice. Fashion-plates in *La Belle Assemblée* foretold this as early as 1828. The sleeves are set

171

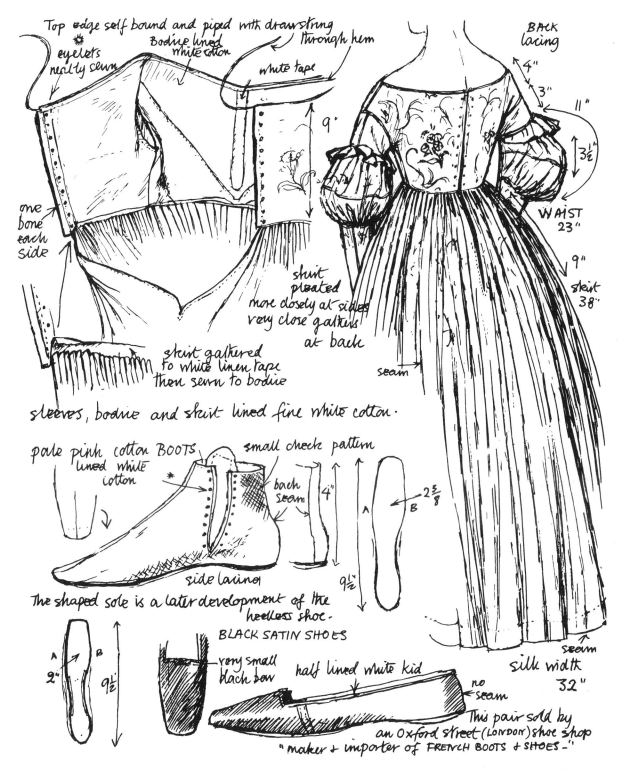

Top edge self bound and piped with drawstring through hem

eyelets neatly sewn

Bodice lined white cotton

white tape

9"

one bone each side

skirt pleated more closely at sides very close gathers at back

skirt gathered to white linen tape then sewn to bodice

sleeves, bodice and skirt lined fine white cotton.

BACK lacing

4"

3"

11"

3½"

WAIST 23"

9"

skirt 38"

seam

pale pink cotton BOOTS lined white cotton

small check pattern

back seam

4"

B 2⅝

side lacing

9½"

The shaped sole is a later development of the heelless shoe.

BLACK SATIN SHOES

A B
2" 9½"

very small black bow

half lined white kid

no seam

seam

silk width 32"

This pair sold by an Oxford Street (London) shoe shop "maker & importer of FRENCH BOOTS & SHOES.-"

very much lower, making any arm movement difficult; they are more fitting, the earlier fullness reduced to puff and frill. Black or white satin shoes or boots were for formal wear until the '60's, cloth or leather for day.

1840's–'50's

Two white cotton caps, one edged with closely gathered muslin frills, the other with lace. Also a linen chemise with flap front, round-shaped neck at back.
Snowshill Collection

One net cap, white embroidered, lace edging, and long lace lappets.
Mrs M. Macbeth

Chemisette of white embroidered cambric.
Mrs M. S. Mallam

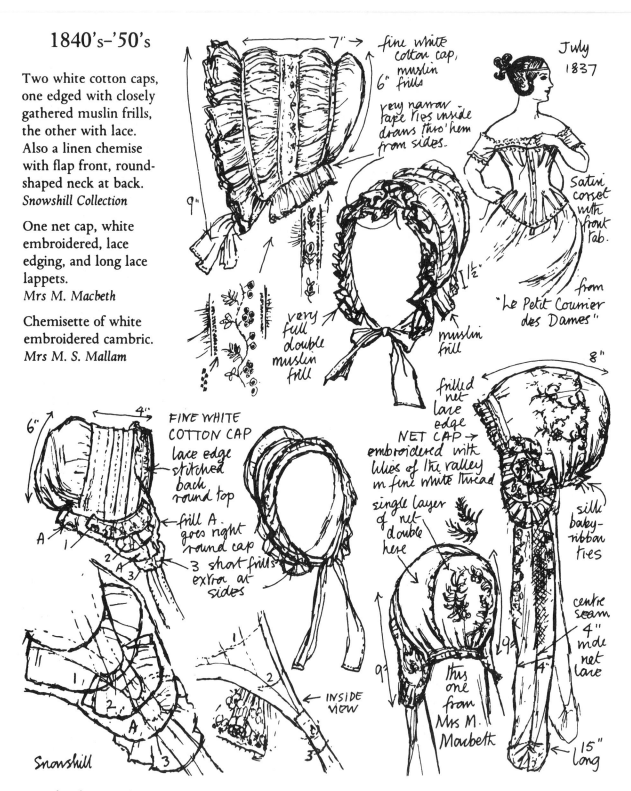

fine white cotton cap, muslin frills

6" frills

7"

very narrow tape ties inside drawn thro' hem from sides.

9"

very full double muslin frill

muslin frill

1½"

July 1837

Satin corset with front tab.

from "Le Petit Courrier des Dames"

6" 4"

FINE WHITE COTTON CAP
lace edge stitched back round top

frill A goes right round cap

3 short frills extra at sides

A 1
2 A
3

A

1
2
A
3

1
2

INSIDE VIEW

3

Snowshill

frilled net lace edge

NET CAP →
embroidered with lilies of the valley in fine white thread

single layer of net double here

8"

silk baby-ribbon ties

centre seam 4" wide net lace

4"

9"
9"

this one from Mrs M. Macbeth

15" long

The changing hair style again shows its effect on the shape of bonnet and cap; these examples of the cotton and the net caps are exquisitely finely sewn and gathered, and are fashionable at this time, but younger women no longer favour them in the '60's. Long, wide linen chemises,

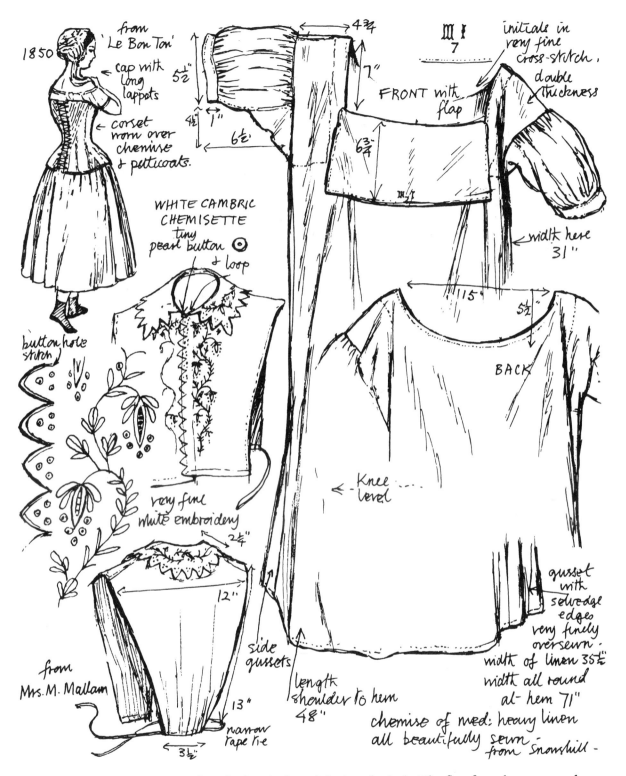

1850

from 'Le Bon Ton'

cap with long lappets

corset worn over chemise & petticoats.

WHITE CAMBRIC CHEMISETTE
tiny pearl button ⊙
& loop

button hole stitch

very fine white embroidery

from Mrs. M. Mallam

5½"

4½" 1"

6½"

4¾"

7"

FRONT with flap

6¾"

Ⅲ Ⅰ 7

initials in very fine cross-stitch. double thickness

width here 31"

115"

5½"

BACK

Knee level

gusset with selvedge edges very finely oversewn. width of linen 35½" width all round at hem 71"

chemise of med: heavy linen all beautifully sewn. from Snowshill -

2¼"

12"

side gussets

length shoulder to hem 48"

13"

narrow tape tie

3½"

such as this, are quite usual in the late '40's and during the '50's. The flap front hangs over the front of the corset, protecting the dress. The chemisette would be worn over this, under the dresses of the 1850's.

c. 1841–43

Fine cream wool with silk stripe, printed floral pattern in red and green. Fringe of green silk, rosettes and bands of green satin. Boned bodice lined white cotton, sleeves lined glazed cotton, separate half-sleeves. Back fastening. Pelerine, green silk fringe, cord and tassels, lined in glazed cotton.
Snowshill Collection

pelerine lined glazed cotton tab loop centre back for waist tie

green silk cord length 16"

piped seam

green cord

piped

pelerine front 10" and back 16"

WAIST 25"

5½"

silk

pleats, self & green satin sewn to bodice

self piped

1"

green piped

green cord decor: hidden darts

green satin rosettes

1¾" on sleeve

1" on bodice front

bound edges

¾"

green silk fringe

extra dark

green cord

width all round hem 124"

seam

The lower and more pointed waistline, emphasized with lines of pleated bands, the bodice, boned at front and sides, and the use of striped material, all make this a typical day dress of the early '40's. Another feature is the detachable lower sleeve, with the upper sleeve

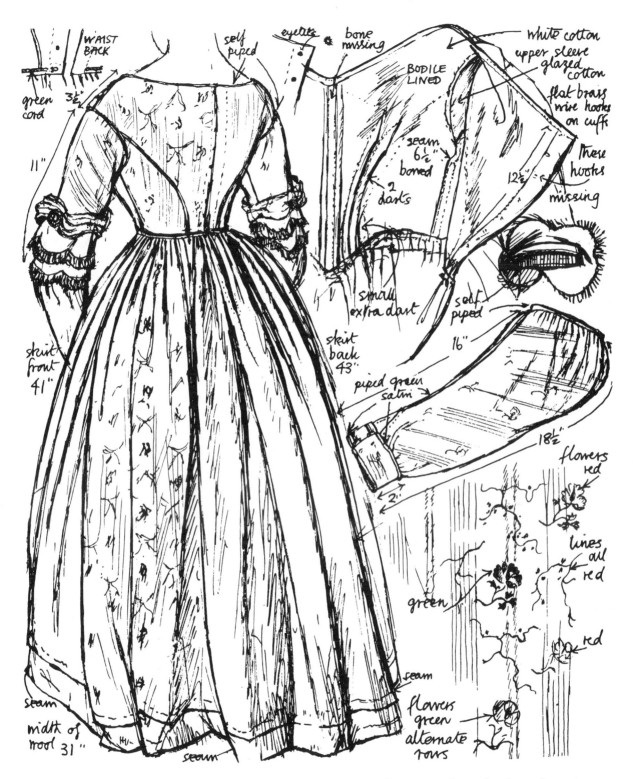

decorated with bands, tucks, and fringes. The separate pelerine matching the dress, fastening with cord and rich tassels, adds to the effect of the fashionable sloping shoulder-line. The sewing here is not as fine as is usually found.

c. 1846

Drawn white silk bonnet, cream woollen shawl, woven pattern. *Snowshill Collection*

Earlier cream silk shawl, printed floral pattern, orange, green, red, mauve, and black, lined pattern in blue. Cream silk fringe. *Once owned by Mrs Warren Hastings; given by her daughter-in-law, Lady Imhoff, to Mrs Whitmore Jones, of Chastleton House*

Cashmere shawl 1843

silk evening shawl richly printed pattern

wreath-like band of green leaves & tiny red flowers

background lace-like honeycomb pattern of blue line.

cream silk fringe

large ornate sprays of orange leaves red flowers & purple tulips with black line, and green leaves

from a fashion plate of "a Public Promenade Dress" in The Ladies' Cabinet

at Chastleton House.

The lovely silk shawl at Chastleton House is kept with a muslin evening dress which is linked with Mrs Warren Hastings, and this shawl is reputed to have belonged to her. This is quite possible, as shawls were worn in the late 18th c., as well as in the 19th, over the wide-spreading

cream
woollen
day
shawl
63½"
square
with
woven
pattern

Drawn white silk bonnet
with cane hoops.
- INSIDE round face
cream net-frill & loops of
cream gauze ribbon

curtain of matching
cream silk,
edged with pillow lace.

stiff
cream
silk
ribbons

wired
edge
to fine cream
pillow lace

all lines &
edges
angular

This woven
pattern reversed
each alternate
row

3¼"

10"

woven
pattern
in bright red
& blue, with
a little green

Snowshill Collection

4¾"
cream silk
knotted fringe

skirts. The woven woollen shawl was worn by Mary Julia Sellick at the wedding of her sister
Anna to Capt. John Ross Ward, *c.* 1846. The white silk bonnet could well have been worn
also at a wedding of about this date.

1840–50

Shot-silk taffeta mantle, in fawn-grey with self-frilled edges gathered over piping cord. Front with tapering ruched band narrow at waist, with hook-and-eye fastening.
Fancy straw bonnet trimmed red velvet and red and pink velvet leaf shapes; red velvet curtain, red silk ribbons.
Snowshill Collection

Self trimming ruched
2½"
edges pinked & scalloped

2½"
unlined
22"
piped seam
A
B
C
G
H

gathered over thin cord
3"
edges pinked & scalloped
3"
3"
bound hem up to C

H
G
top of bound hem of front at C

fastening at waist front 2 round wire hooks & eyes
hook
hook
A
B

This mantle has a neatly devised form of sleeve, with the frilled and scallop-shaped edging and cape-like back, giving a rich effect to an otherwise plain and simple garment. During this decade shot silk was very popular. The 1841 figure shows a similar form of mantle,

from
1841
fashion
plate

The Ladies'
Mirror

front
length
42"

back
length
35"

Fancy
straw
bonnet
with
dark
red velvet
& pink & red
velvet
leaf shapes

8"

edge
wired

pink
silk
ruched
over
wire

Red silk ribbon
ties

deep red
velvet

dark
red
silk
ribbons

DETAIL
of
STRAW

OUTSIDE

orange
thread

self bound
edge

19"

2½"

22½"

H
G

with frilled edges, but nearer in shape to the earlier shawl or wrap with long scarf-ends—
in fact, not very different from the 18th c. 'cloak.' The bonnet shape is typical of the '40's,
rounded, framing the face.

1840-45

Fine cream wool dress, woven pink silk stripe printed floral pattern in plain soft colours, yellow, red, green, and mauve. Delicate black-line dot pattern. Bodice boned at sides, waist pointed in front. Bodice and sleeves lined white cotton. Epaulette, with sleeve closely ruched under it at top. Skirt lined white muslin.
Snowshill Collection

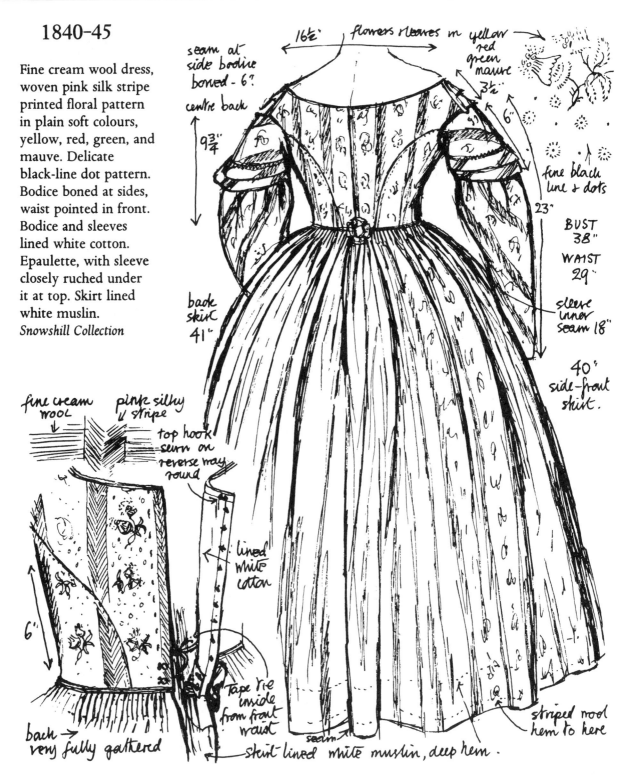

seam at side bodice boned - 6"

centre back

9¾"

16½"

flowers & sleeves in yellow red green mauve

3½"

6"

fine black line & dots

23"

BUST 38"

WAIST 29"

sleeve inner seam 18"

40" side-front skirt.

back skirt 41"

fine cream wool

pink silky stripe

top hook sewn on reverse way round

lined white cotton

6"

tape tie inside from front waist

back → very fully gathered

seam

striped wool hem to here

skirt lined white muslin, deep hem.

There is an identically patterned material in this collection, made into a dress of 1829–31, on p. 149. The colours are the same except for a mauve stripe in place of the pink, as here; the wearer then had only a 21″ waist! The sleeves on this day dress are still very full at the

181

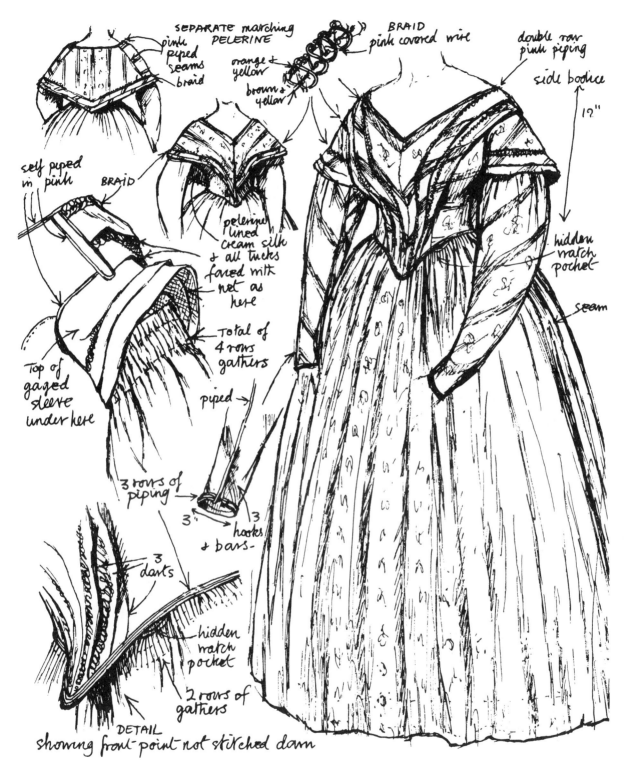

SEPARATE matching PELERINE

pink piped seams braid

BRAID pink covered wire

double row pink piping

side bodice

orange & yellow

brown & yellow

12"

self piped in pink

BRAID

pelerine lined cream silk & all tucks faced with net as here

hidden watch pocket

seam

Total of 4 rows gathers

Top of gaged sleeve under here

piped →

3 rows of piping →

3"   3

hooks & bars.

3 darts

hidden watch pocket

2 rows of gathers

DETAIL
showing front point not stitched down

top, closely ruched and hidden under the tiny over-sleeve. The separate pointed front to this bodice conceals the very tiny watch pocket, found now in many dresses of the '50's and '60's, and on into the early '80's.

1840-45

Fully dressed doll, real hair with head and shoulders of wax. Bonnet, with flounced dress and petticoats, long cotton drawers. Black velvet bag, steel beaded with tiny fringe; also a black satin bag with steel and jet beads.
Mr F. Norris; lent to Personal Collection

Black velvet bag with tiny gilt beads.
Miss A. Anderson

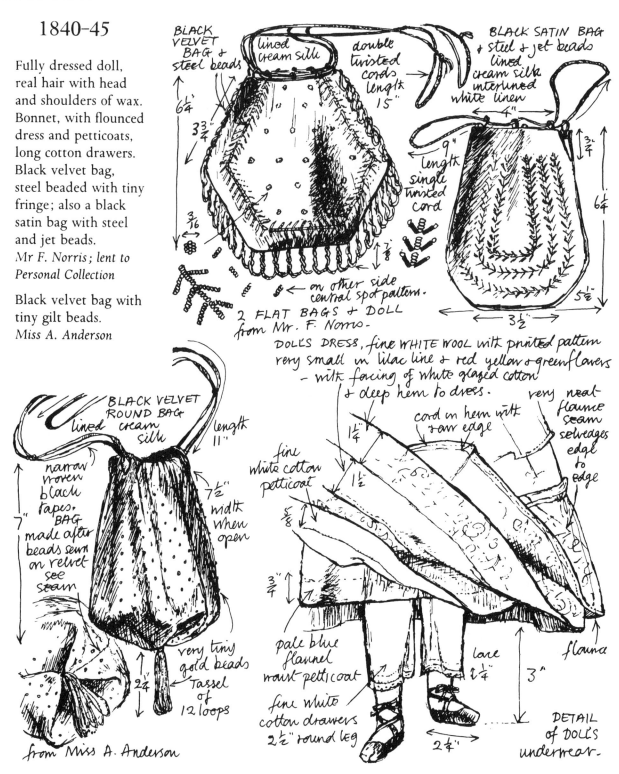

BLACK VELVET BAG & steel beads · lined cream silk · double twisted cords length 15"

6¼' 3¾' 3/16

BLACK SATIN BAG & steel & jet beads lined cream silk interlined white linen 4" 3¾' 6¼' 5½' 3½'

9" length single twisted cord

on other side central spot pattern.
2 FLAT BAGS & DOLL from Mr. F. Norris.

DOLL'S DRESS, fine WHITE WOOL with printed pattern very small in lilac line & red yellow & green flowers – with facing of white glazed cotton & deep hem to dress.

BLACK VELVET ROUND BAG lined cream silk · length 11"
narrow woven black tapes. BAG made after beads sewn on velvet see seam
7" 7½' width when open 2¼'
very tiny gold beads Tassel of 12 loops

from Miss A. Anderson

cord in hem with raw edge
1½ 1½ 5/8
very neat flounce seam selvedges edge to edge
fine white cotton petticoat
¾
pale blue flannel waist petticoat
fine white cotton drawers 2½" round leg
lace 1¼
2¼'
flounce
3"
DETAIL of DOLL'S underwear.

No child could resist loving sweet 'Charlotte Norris,' who is dressed exactly as a little girl of this date would be, complete with long cotton drawers. During the '40's these drawers became shorter and more frilled. In the early '40's small rounded or flat bags became

183

pink braid as on dress,
pink silk lined,
PALE PINK BONNET
of muslin with
tiny woven stripe
of 3 threads.
these used for ruching

$2\frac{3}{8}$

$3\frac{1}{2}$

lace

$1\frac{1}{8}$

3"

piped seams

5"

4"

silk BRAID pink & shaded green
GLOVES

$1\frac{3}{4}$

$1\frac{3}{16}$

both flounces cut on cross, seams with pattern matching -

$4\frac{1}{2}$

$4\frac{1}{2}$

narrow cord in hem

flounce seam

"CHARLOTTE" NORRIS from Mr. F. Norris

full height 23"

black baby ribbon

red leather up to elbow.

front skirt length 11"

dark brown real hair curled

WAX HEAD & SHOULDERS

3"

$5\frac{3}{4}$

$3\frac{1}{2}$

gathering & ruching

narrow & ½" wide pink satin ribbons

shoulder width 5"

$2\frac{1}{2}$

black velvet ribbon for shoes

6 tiny pins as back fastenings

fashionable, of dark blue or black velvet, embroidered with tiny gilt or steel beads; but, with pockets in the fuller-skirted dresses, they became less necessary, returning with the use of muslins in the '50's and smoothly gored skirts of the '60's.

Mid 19th c.

Short black silk mittens, long white silk mittens.
Mrs M. Macbeth

Short black net mittens. Fine green kid gloves; wrist-length, one button.
from Gordon Bennet to Personal Collection

Two purses of coloured beads on net. Round 'shaggy bead' purse, tiny sovereign purse, both with steel beads. Two long purses with steel beads & tassels.
Snowshill Collection

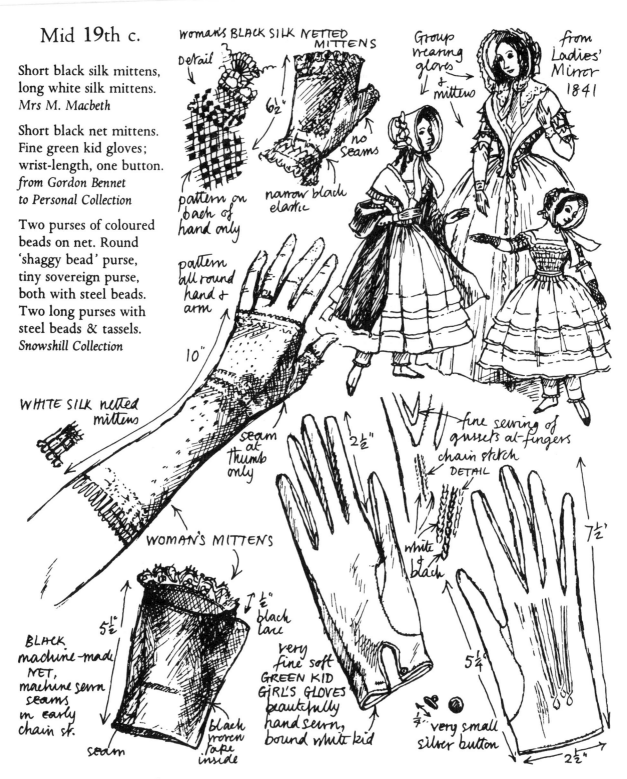

WOMAN'S BLACK SILK NETTED MITTENS

Detail

6½"

no seams

Group wearing gloves & mittens

from Ladies' Mirror 1841

pattern on back of hand only

narrow black elastic

pattern all round hand & arm

10"

WHITE SILK netted mittens

seam at thumb only

WOMAN'S MITTENS

2½"

fine sewing of gussets at fingers

chain stitch DETAIL

white & black

7½"

BLACK machine-made NET, machine sewn seams in early chain st.

seam

5½"

½" black lace

black woven tape inside

very fine soft GREEN KID GIRL'S GLOVES beautifully hand sewn, bound white kid

5¼"

¼" very small silver button

2½"

Mittens are worn during the 1830's and '40's for both day and evening, but they go out of fashion in the '50's and '60's. Gloves are also worn throughout the day, even for dancing and dining, although green ones such as these would be for day wear until the mid '60's,

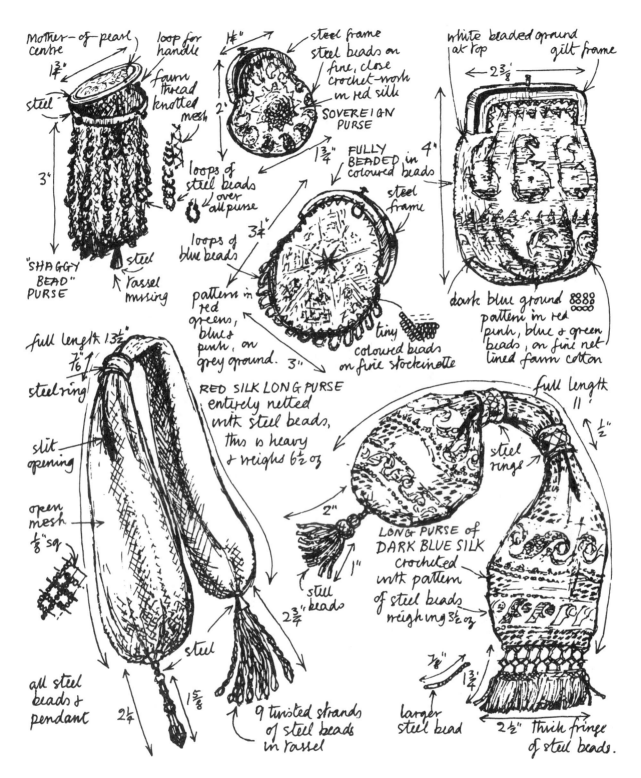

mother-of-pearl centre

loop for handle

1¾"

faun thread knotted mesh

steel

3"

"SHAGGY BEAD" PURSE

steel

tassel missing

1½"

steel frame

steel beads on fine, close crochet-work in red silk

2"

SOVEREIGN PURSE

1¾"

loops of steel beads over all purse

loops of blue beads

3¼"

pattern in red greens, blues pink, on grey ground.

3"

tiny coloured beads on fine stockinette

FULLY BEADED in coloured beads

steel frame

4"

white beaded ground at top

gilt frame

2⅜"

dark blue ground pattern in red pink, blue & green beads, on fine net lined faun cotton

full length 13½"

⅞6"

steel ring

slit opening

open mesh ⅛" sq

all steel beads & pendant

2¼"

1⅝"

steel

9 twisted strands of steel beads in tassel

RED SILK LONG PURSE entirely netted with steel beads, this is heavy & weighs 6½ oz

2"

1"

steel beads

2¾"

LONG PURSE of DARK BLUE SILK crocheted with pattern of steel beads weighing 3½ oz

full length 11"

steel rings

1½"

⅞"

larger steel bead

1¾"

2½" thick fringe of steel beads.

when longer ones are favoured. Purses completely sewn over with tiny coloured beads date *c.* 1835–50, the small sovereign and 'shaggy bead' purses with steel beads *c.* 1835–70. Steel beads are extensively used during the '50's & '60's.

1849–50

Deep violet printed, fine wool, a barège; woven tartan pattern, with pink rosebud spot pattern and deep patterned flounces. Silk fringe of violet, brown, and grey on bodice and sleeves; back fastening with short neck opening in front. Fully lined and boned bodice, muslin under-skirt sewn in at waist.
Snowshill Collection

self piping

stitched to dress on piped seam

short neck opening

top hook faced upwards

15 hooks + eyelets

seam

BACK

large hooks & eye

tiny watch pocket set in seam of dress

muslin under-skirt, sewn in at waist

larger pocket set in seam of dress

← A
piped
B

full skirt length 40"

deep violet ground with printed pink rosebuds.

tartan pattern of closely woven stripes, on open, almost transparent wool, fine as muslin, called "barège". width all round hem 132"

A

B

10" flounces
10"

Although this day dress has the back fastening found in the '40's, it has many features found in the 1850's: the widening sleeves under which muslin half-sleeves would be worn and the deeply flounced skirt with richly patterned borders, which were specially printed or woven

187

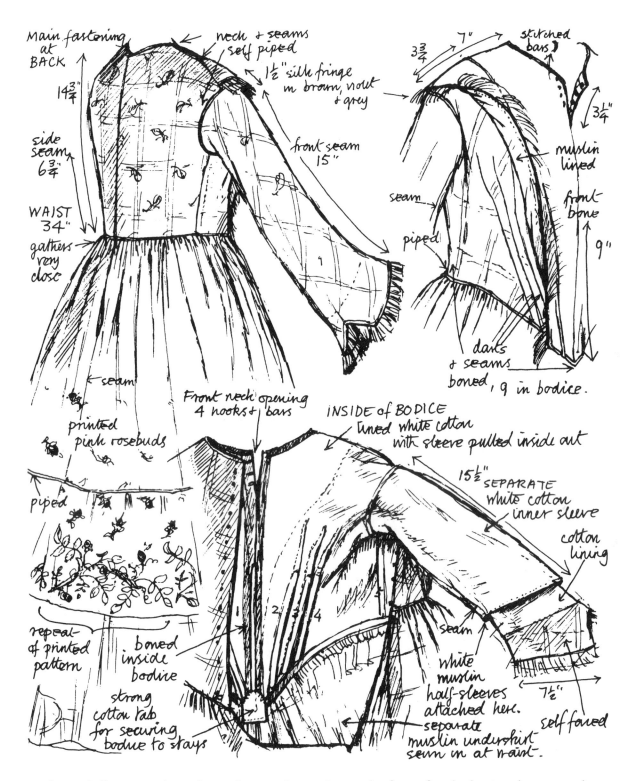

Main fastening at BACK

neck + seams self piped

1½" silk fringe in brown, violet + grey

14¾"

side seam 6¾"

front seam 15"

WAIST 34"

gathers very close

seam

printed pink rosebuds

piped

repeat of printed pattern

strong cotton tab for securing bodice to stays

Front neck opening 4 hooks + bars

boned inside bodice

3¾   7"   stitched bars

3¼"

muslin lined

seam

piped

front bone

9"

darts + seams boned, 9 in bodice.

INSIDE of BODICE lined white cotton with sleeve pulled inside out

15½" SEPARATE white cotton inner sleeve

cotton lining

seam

white muslin half-sleeves attached here.

separate muslin undershirt sewn in at waist.

7½"

self faced

for such flounces. Also it has a short neck opening at the front, foreshadowing the new style front fastening of the '50's. Flounces on already very full skirts increase their width, and pockets are easily hidden in their folds.

1851-54

Fine cream wool day dress, printed spot pattern in brown and pink, trimmed with golden brown silk fringe. Fastening at back. Bodice, skirt, and upper sleeves lined white cotton. Wide draped front, bell-shaped sleeves. Very full skirt, three flounces. Hem bound woollen braid. White kid elastic-sided boots.
Snowshill Collection

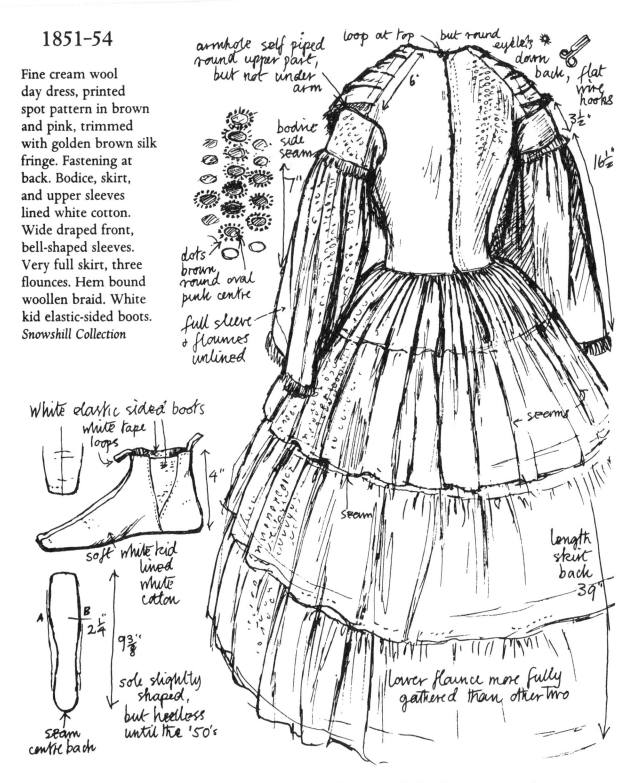

armhole self piped round upper part, but not under arm

loop at top

but round eyelets down back, flat wire hooks

6"

3½"

16½"

bodice side seam

7"

dots brown round oval pink centre

full sleeve & flounces unlined

seams

seam

seam

length skirt back 39"

lower flounce more fully gathered than other two

White elastic sided boots

white tape loops

4"

soft white kid lined white cotton

A   B
2¼"

9⅜"

sole slightly shaped, but heelless until the '50's

seam centre back

With the exception of the back fastening, this dress has all the characteristics of the '50's, high neckline as well as the flounced skirt and much wider type of sleeve. Under-sleeves of white muslin, probably embroidered, were always worn with such sleeves as this. A

front bodice
from shoulder

17"

centre bodice
back
16"

7"

self piped

underside of
front folds

white
cotton
&
extra
piece

sleeve
front
seam

10"

16½

golden brown
silk fringe

1"

skirt
front
37"

lining

hem edged with
woven wool
binding.

width all round hem
125"

piped

WAIST
27"

top flounce
at side
8½

10½"

12½"

seams

seam

seams

width of wool
25"

horsehair petticoat would help to support the several petticoats worn under these dresses until 1856, when the crinoline frame replaced it. Elastic-sided boots appeared after 1837, and heels reappeared in the 1850's.

1848-64
Dark green silk ugly.

c. 1838-65
Dark brown silk carriage parasol, with fringe of black silk.
Personal Collection.
Ugly from Gordon Bennett

1840-50
Deep rich red satin and cloth bonnet with feather trimming.

1860-64
Straw spoon bonnet.

1865-67
Tiny yellow bonnet.
Snowshill Collection

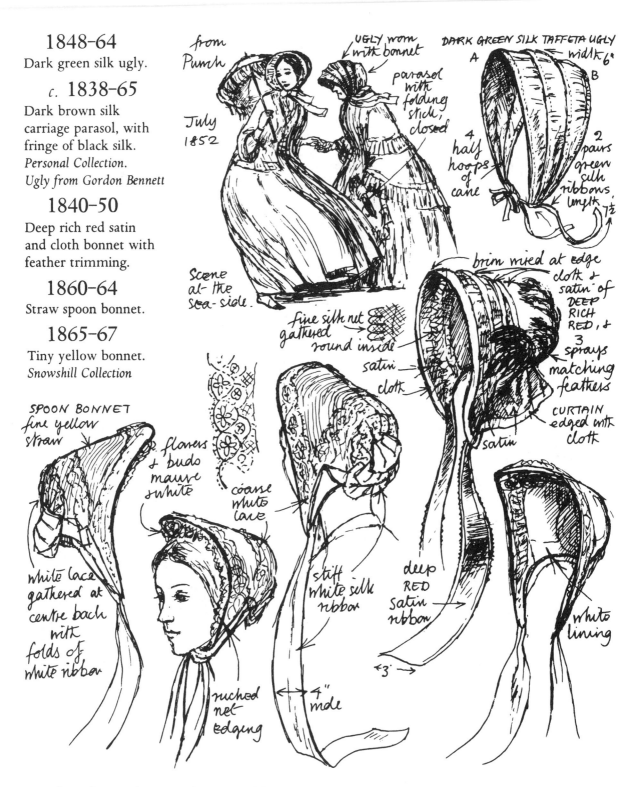

from Punch

July 1852

UGLY worn with bonnet

parasol with folding stick, closed

DARK GREEN SILK TAFFETA UGLY
A
width 6"
B
4 half hoops of cane
2 pairs green silk ribbons
length 7½"

Scene at the sea-side.

fine silk net gathered round inside

brim wired at edge
cloth & satin of DEEP RICH RED, & 3 sprays matching feathers
satin
cloth
CURTAIN edged with cloth
satin

SPOON BONNET
fine yellow straw
flowers + buds mauve white
coarse white lace
white lace gathered at centre back with folds of white ribbon
ruched net edging
stiff white silk ribbon
4" wide
deep RED satin ribbon
←3→
white lining

The ugly and the parasol were used for the same purpose, to protect the fair owner from the sun. The ugly, worn round the front of the bonnet, gave added protection, particularly when small-brimmed or spoon bonnets became fashionable. But the ugly died out as bonnets

191

DARK BROWN SILK
BLACK SILK FRINGE
metal spokes

22"

white lace & mauve poppy, Belgian straw bonnet

from The Englishwoman's Domestic Magazine June 1861

green

glass dew drops

21" wide

full length 28"

wooden stick

2" metal slide

green silk ribbons

3 white daisies, petals of feathers

whalebone ribs 11½"

black silk bone

1"

to fit one finger

white undersleeves

satin ends of decorative "bow"

dress grey & white shot silk

FOLDING PARASOL

folded georgette on satin loop

yellow satin & wool

white lace

blue flowers & poppies & daisies

green ferns

2 layers white lace

2 long ends cross under fancy "bow" they do not tie

all yellow, long ends of fine wool "georgette" also the pleated frill

flowers on separate band.

narrow ties of white silk fringed ribbon

decreased in size and hats gained in popularity. During the '50's younger women at the seaside or in the garden (p. 200) preferred the wide-brimmed round straw hat. Some tiny parasols were often very elaborate.

1852-68

Fine white cashmere hooded cloak, lined pink silk, quilted to interlining. Trimmed fringed corded pink and white silk ribbon and pink and white silk tassels. Fastening hook and eye. Small inner pocket one side. Bonnet, fine white plaited horsehair, white silk ribbon, blue flowers, and fine black lace.
Snowshill Collection

WHITE CASHMERE & PINK SILK

front & side length 27½"

from 'Punch' Spring 1852

13"

straight of cloth

"...showing how the pretty hoods, now worn by Ladies, might be made useful, as well as ornamental."

BACK LENGTH 30"

WHITE BONNET, with blue flowers, white ribbon & black lace

frilled black lace

ribbons missing

wider black lace & rosette at back

fine, narrow black lace edging & frill.

straw with glass beads & droplets →

centre of black lace rosette.

Blue flowers & leaves with white lace

white ribbon this side

very fine white net lace frilled at top

white silk ribbon

curtain white silk, edged narrow black lace. lined white silk

Punch made various amusing comments on this apparently popular garment when it first appeared in 1852. Several examples, similar to this but with a single tassel, are at Snowshill, some all in white, one of black silk. As seen in the fashion-plate of 1868, this type of cloak

193

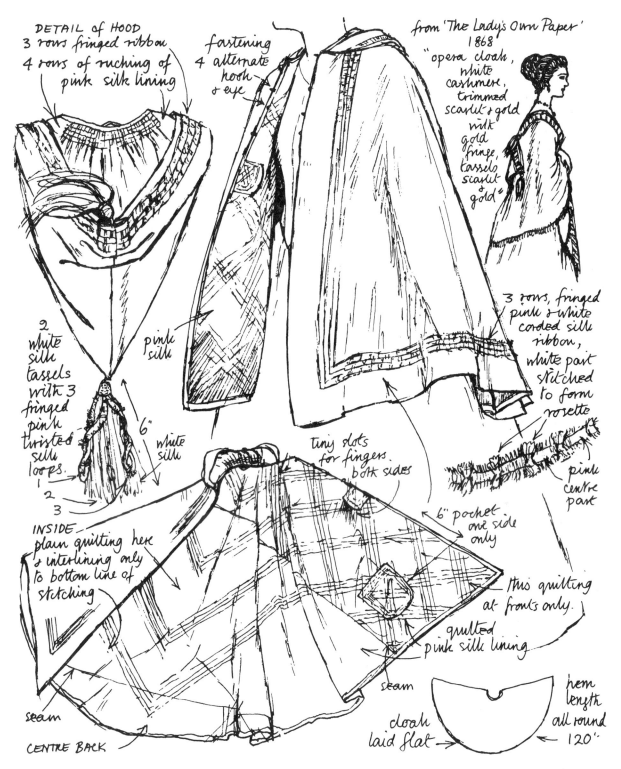

DETAIL of HOOD
3 rows fringed ribbon
4 rows of ruching of
pink silk lining

fastening
4 alternate hook
& eye

from 'The Lady's Own Paper'
1868
"opera cloak,
white
cashmere,
trimmed
scarlet & gold
silk
gold
fringe,
tassels
scarlet
&
gold"

2
white
silk
tassels
with 3
fringed
pink
twisted
silk
loops.
1
2
3

pink
silk

6"

white
silk

3 rows, fringed
pink & white
corded silk
ribbon,
white part
stitched
to form
rosette

pink
centre
part

Tiny slots
for fingers.
both sides

6" pocket
one side
only

this quilting
at fronts only.

quilted
pink silk lining

INSIDE
plain quilting here
& interlining only
to bottom line of
stitching

seam

CENTRE BACK

seam

cloak
laid flat

hem
length
all round
120"

remained a warm and useful covering for many years. During the '50's bonnets changed in shape, revealing more of the face, with a smaller crown and curving-away brim; these were worn well back on the head (shown on p. 197).

194

1856–57

White embroidered muslin evening dress, fully boned and lined bodice, lacing at the back, short puff sleeves. Low pointed waistline back and front. Skirt unlined, very finely embroidered, in white outline stitch with some openwork, tiny flower all-over spot pattern. Tape tie inside front. Lace bertha missing.
Chastleton House

lace bertha was probably here, as traces of stitches remain.
piped seams

full length bodice 16½"

unlined skirt, gathered on tape band then sewn to bodice

Top of sleeve only slightly gathered

Bodice boned front, back & sides

full gathers here

9½"

4¾"

double piping

boned front with tape ties inside to secure dress front to corsets

seam

fashion plate from *Petit Courrier des Dames* 1850

full evening dress and a Theatre dress from "*Le Follet*" 1857

back fastenings on evening dress, also some waists pointed back and front, from '56.

skirt side-back 43"

seam

The lovely muslin from which this dress is made once belonged to Mrs Warren Hastings; how it came to Chastleton House is told at the beginning of this chapter. Many materials would appear old-fashioned after some years, but although white muslin had dominated

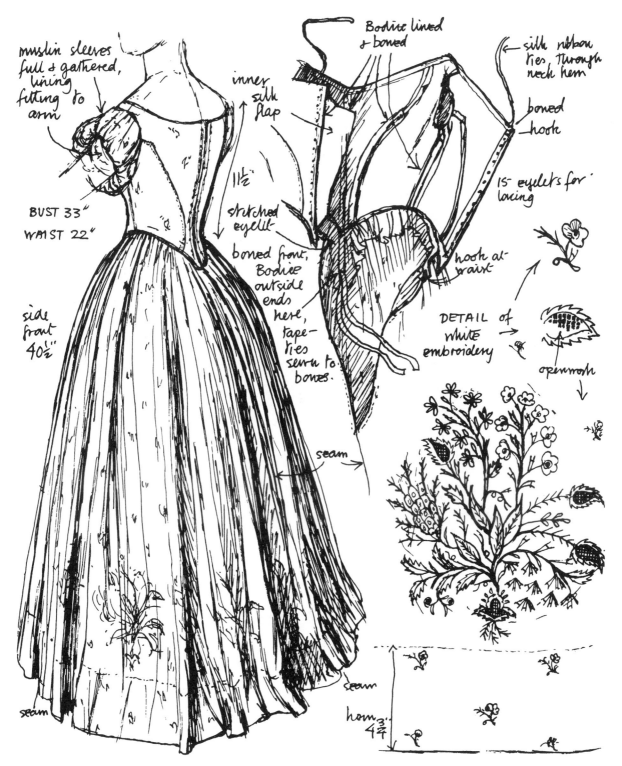

muslin sleeves full & gathered, lining fitting to arm

inner silk flap

Bodice lined & boned

silk ribbon ties through neck hem

boned hook

15 eyelets for lacing

BUST 33"
WAIST 22"

11½

stitched eyelet

boned front, Bodice outside ends here, tape ties sewn to bones.

side front 40½"

hook at waist

DETAIL of white embroidery

openwork

seam

seam

seam

hem 3¾

women's dress for so long, and was no longer worn during the day, for evening wear it was fashionable still. This is a Society woman's dress; the small studies show the hair style, bertha, and pointed bodice of the 1850's.

1857-60

Large crinoline frame of Welsh cloth, with 5 very fine flexible ½" steel hoops set low at hem; back fastening. *Chastleton House*

Fawn crinoline of open netted thread, with 4 narrow ⅜" steels, set low at hem, fastening at back. Fawn cloth small crinoline, with 4 steels, ½" wide, front fastening. *from Mr F. Norris to Personal Collection*

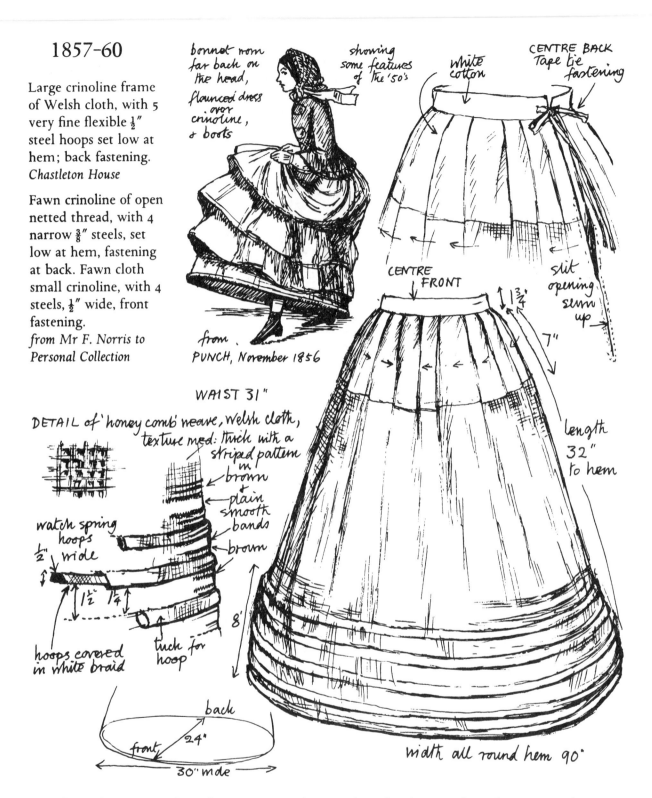

bonnet worn far back on the head, flounced dress over crinoline, & boots

showing some features of the '50s

from PUNCH, November 1856

white cotton

CENTRE BACK Tape tie fastening

slit opening sewn up

CENTRE FRONT

1¾

7"

length 32" to hem

WAIST 31"

DETAIL of 'honey comb' weave, Welsh cloth, texture med: thick with a striped pattern in brown + plain smooth bands brown

watch spring hoops ½" wide

1½   ¼

hoops covered in white braid

tuck for hoop

8'

width all round hem 90°

back

front   24°

30" wide

The early cage crinoline of 1856, improved a year later by the use of watch-spring steels, is commented on in *The Englishwoman's Domestic Magazine*, 1861: 'crinolines are more necessary than ever, the best ones are made of very narrow steels,' and 'those skirts of wider steel run

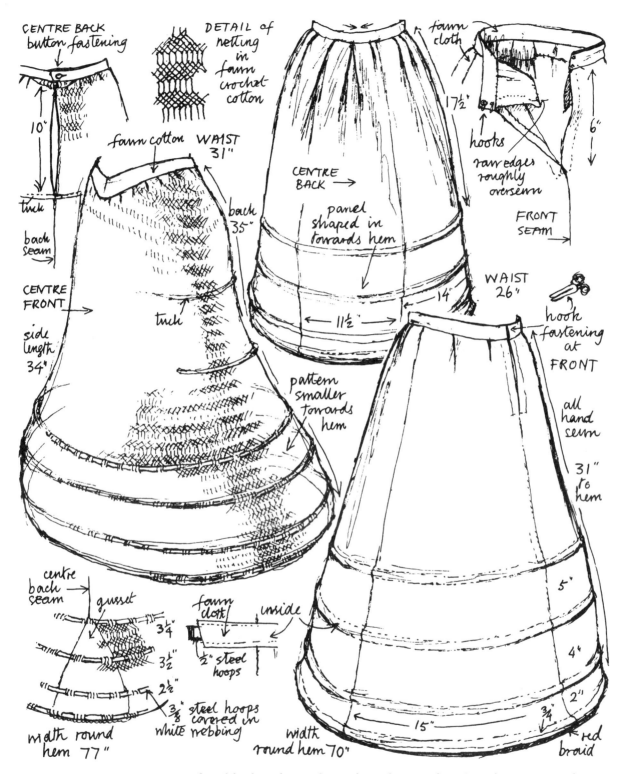

CENTRE BACK
button fastening

10"

tuck

back
seam

DETAIL of
netting
in
faun
crochet
cotton

faun cotton   WAIST
31"

back
35"

CENTRE
FRONT

side
length
34"

tuck

pattern
smaller
towards
hem

CENTRE
BACK

panel
shaped in
towards hem

14"

11½"

faun
cloth

17½"

hooks

raw edges
roughly
oversewn

FRONT
SEAM

6"

WAIST
26"

hook
fastening
at
FRONT

all
hand
sewn

31"
to
hem

centre
back
seam

gusset

3¾"

3½"

2½"

⅜" steel hoops
covered in
white webbing

width round
hem 77"

faun
cloth

inside

½" steel
hoops

width
round hem 70"

5"

4"

2"

¾"

red
braid

15"

in open net, are very comfortable, but do not keep their shape so long.' And, to wear under unlined silk or muslin dress, 'a moderate size steel petticoat and of course a plain one over it, ... with one or more flounces at the hem.'

c. 1857-65

Crinoline, watch-spring hoops, white webbing, red band at hem, also white silk stockings, Dr's spectacles in case.
Mrs M. Macbeth

Folding spectacles in green shagreen case.
T. Stanley Brown

Linen chemise.
the Late Mrs V. Hands

Down-quilted skirt.
Mrs M. J. King

Down-quilted skirt, and blue cloth boots.
Snowshill Collection

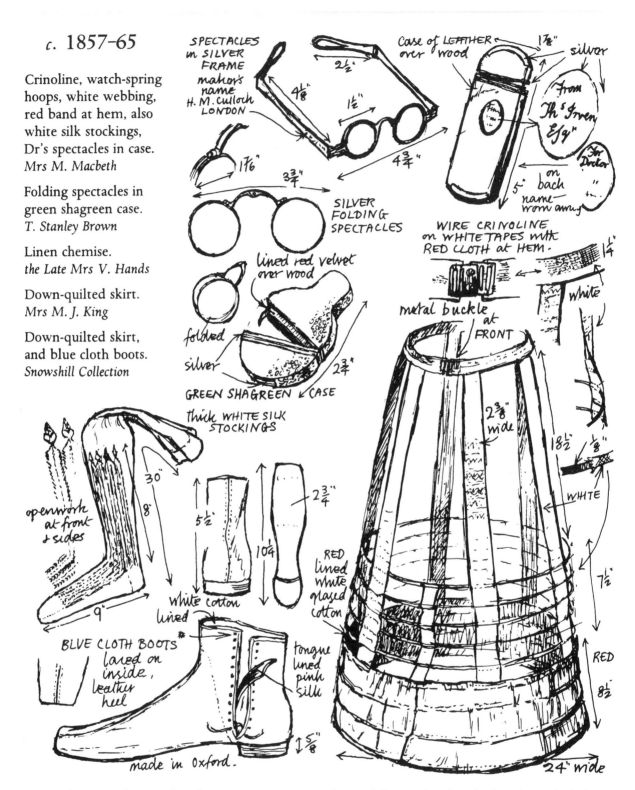

SPECTACLES in SILVER FRAME maker's name H. M. Culloch LONDON

Case of LEATHER over wood

1⅞" silver

From Th.ˢ Orven Esq"

for Doctor "

on back name worn away

5"

2½"

4⅛"

1½"

4¾"

1⅞"

3¾"

SILVER FOLDING SPECTACLES

lined red velvet over wood

folded

silver

2¾"

GREEN SHAGREEN CASE

WIRE CRINOLINE on WHITE TAPES with RED CLOTH at HEM.

1¼"

white

metal buckle at FRONT

2⅜" wide

18½"

⅛"

WHITE

7½"

RED

8½"

thick WHITE SILK STOCKINGS

30"

8"

openwork at front & sides

9"

5½"

10¼"

2¾"

White cotton lined

RED lined white glazed cotton

BLUE CLOTH BOOTS laced on inside, leather heel

tongue lined pink silk

made in Oxford.

⅝"

24" wide

Both pairs of spectacles, dates uncertain, are so beautifully made, they had to be included; shagreen was used in the 18th c. for similar cases, such as for manicure sets. White openwork stockings of silk or cotton were usual, and boots were worn with the crinoline, which was

199

self faced

14"

LINEN CHEMISE

4¾"

4"

from PUNCH
June 1857

skirt looped up
inside with cords
showing
coloured
petticoat

machine
sewn

8½"

6"

machine sewn

length
38"
to hem

quilted onto
red cotton
inside
Double tape ties
right round in
waist hem

30½" wide
main
seams
hand sewn

FRONT, with
tape tie through hem
printed cotton -
machine
sewn

knee
level

red
ground,
with
green,
blue &
brown

FRONT

7½"

2
gussets
finely
sewn
in.

BACK

yellow
blue & black
on
RED GROUND.

35⅝"
wide

BACK
length
33"
& front
30"

RED BRAID

FRONT
length
33"
back
35"

3"

seam

BOOTH & FOX'S DOWN SKIRT, size 36"
Trade mark & Exhibition awards
LONDON 1862 . DUBLIN 1865.

piped
edge
80" round -
all machine sewn

Width
round hem 80"

sometimes red, to catch the eye! Both the down-quilted cotton petticoats or skirts are machine-sewn, and would be wonderfully warm for winter wear. The linen chemise, with tucks and embroidery, is of a shorter length 1860–70.

1864-67

Brilliant red flannel
crinoline with 4 steel
hoops; hem bound in
black braid, trimmed
black velvet ribbon,
front fastening.
*from Mr F. Norris to
Personal Collection*

Large cage crinoline,
26 watch-spring steels
width $\frac{1}{10}$", red webbing
and binding, laced
at front. Very light and
flexible, maker's name
on waistband.
Snowshill Collection

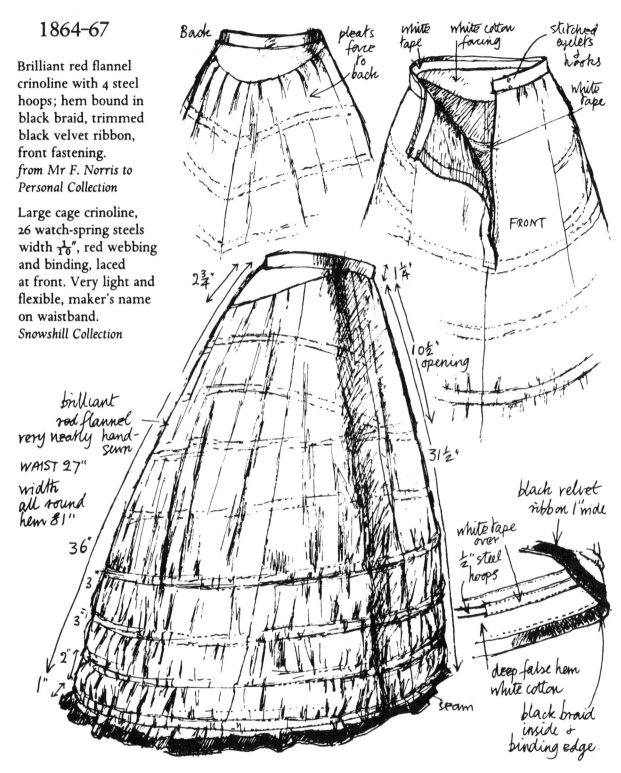

Back
pleats
force
to
back

white
tape   white cotton
facing   stitched
eyelets
hooks
white
tape

FRONT

$2\frac{3}{4}$" $1\frac{1}{4}$"

$10\frac{1}{2}$"
opening

$31\frac{1}{2}$"

brilliant
red flannel
very neatly hand-
sewn

WAIST 27"

width
all round
hem 81"

36"

3

3

2"

1"

white tape
over
$\frac{1}{2}$" steel
hoops

black velvet
ribbon 1" wide

deep false hem
white cotton

black braid
inside &
binding edge.

seam

Red petticoats were quite a feature of the '60's, before the decline of the crinoline in the winter
'67–'68. But even as late as April 1868 Thomson's were advertising in *The Lady's Own Paper*,
'No more crinoline accidents,' offering 'A new Safety crinoline, which no written or pictorial

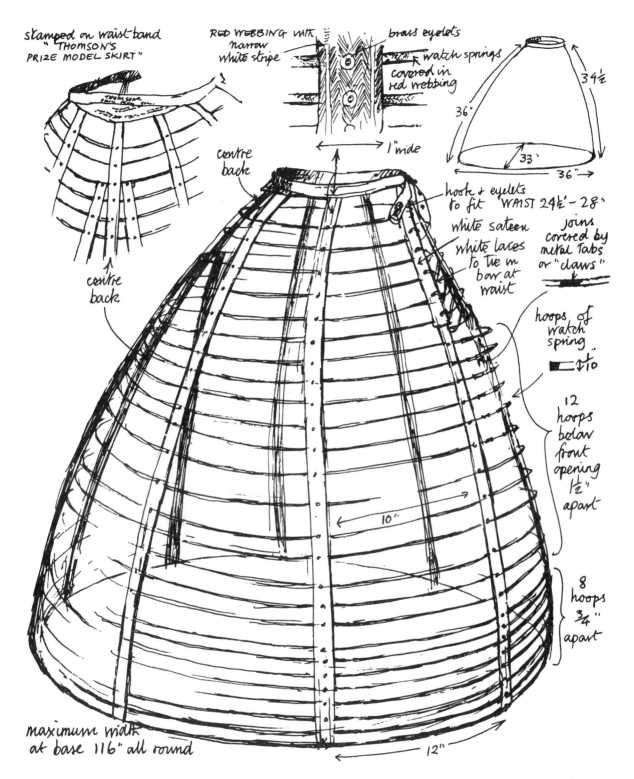

stamped on waist-band
"THOMSON'S
PRIZE MODEL SKIRT"

RED WEBBING with narrow
white stripe

brass eyelets

watch springs
covered in
red webbing

1" wide

34½

36"

33"

36"

centre
back

centre
back

hooks & eyelets
to fit WAIST 24½" – 28"

white sateen

white laces
to tie in
bow at
waist

joins
covered by
metal tabs
or "claws"

hoops of
watch
spring
·10

12
hoops
below
front
opening
1½"
apart

8
hoops
¾"
apart

10"

maximum width
at base 116" all round

12"

description can possibly convey—complete freedom of motion—No possibility of the feet becoming entangled—made in two shapes.' But, in spite of this, the famous Thomson's crinolines went out of fashion, being replaced in the '70's by the bustle.

202

1855–65

Under-sleeves of white cambric, with guipure work, fastened at wrist with tiny pearl button.
Miss J. Procter

Reticule embroidered in woolwork and beads, another in silk cross-stitch with beads and sequins.
Four tiny hats, ribbons, feathers, veil, and flowers for trimming. Blue and white feather fan, with painted wooden handle.
Snowshill Collection

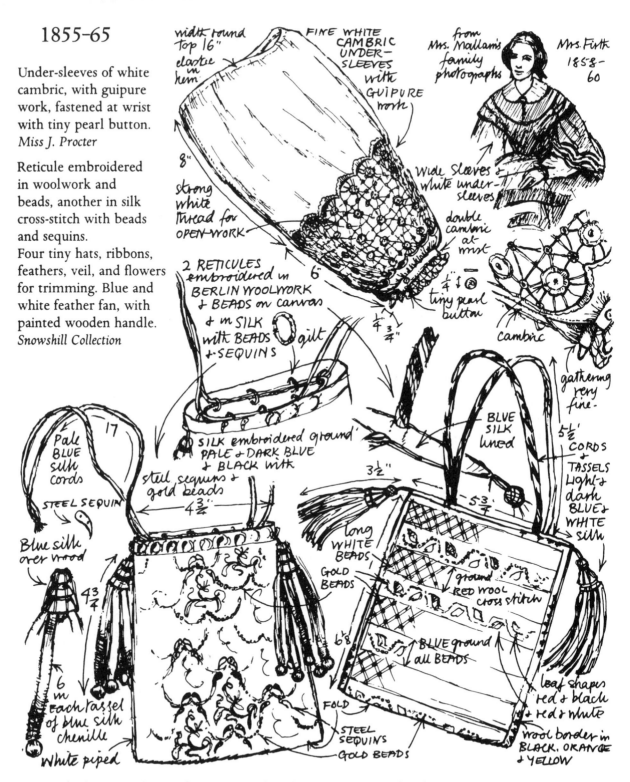

width round Top 16"
elastic in hem

FINE WHITE CAMBRIC UNDER-SLEEVES with GUIPURE work

from Mrs. Mallam's family photographs

Mrs. Firth 1858-60

8"

strong white Thread for OPEN-WORK

Wide Sleeves & white under-sleeves

double cambric at wrist

6"

1/4" 3/4"

tiny pearl button

2 RETICULES embroidered in BERLIN WOOLWORK & BEADS on canvas & in SILK with BEADS & SEQUINS

gilt

cambric

gathering very fine.

5 1/2' CORDS & TASSELS Light & dark BLUE & WHITE silk

BLUE SILK lined

Pale BLUE silk cords

17

STEEL SEQUIN

Blue silk over wood

SILK embroidered ground PALE & DARK BLUE & BLACK with steel sequins & gold beads 4 3/4"

3 1/2"

5 3/4"

4 3/4

long WHITE BEADS
GOLD BEADS

ground RED WOOL cross stitch

6 in each tassel of blue silk chenille

White piped

FOLD

6 8

BLUE ground all BEADS

STEEL SEQUINS GOLD BEADS

leaf shapes red & black + red & white

wool border in BLACK, ORANGE & YELLOW

With the open sleeve of the '50's and early '60's, white under-sleeves are a very important accessory, plain or embroidered, open like the sleeve itself, or closed at the wrist as here; very many fine examples have survived. Very tiny pearl buttons are still used. Embroidered

fashion plate August 1861

from "The Englishwoman's Domestic Magazine"

white under-sleeves

white STRAW HAT, black velvet bow & black & white feathers. HAIR in chignon.

PALE BLUE CLOTH over STRAW & RED ostrich feather

thin black elastic

BLACK spotted VEIL same on both hats

"cloak" of light alpaca trimmed with green.

AT BACK, BLACK VEIL lightly sewn to long blue silk ribbon

YELLOW STRAW HAT

BLUE ostrich feather & blue velvet

BLUE VELVET & blue silk lined

BLUE corded silk ribbons

white ostrich feather

fine black elastic

folded black satin ribbon on black spotted veil.

3 EARS OF CORN, & WHITE feather tipped with black, 3 RED POPPIES, 1 BLUE cornflower

ALL DOVE GREY SILK RED frill under brim

FEATHER FAN BLUE TIPPED, with WHITE in centre. a screen type fan.

15" max. width

BLACK painted wooden handle.

8¼"

similar fan in painting by James Collinson 1857 "The Empty Purse".

2 lengths narrow black elastic with jet button

BACK

lilac ribbon under veil. Bow of lilac & yellow ribbon HAT PAINTED PINK over yellow straw.

bags return to favour with the use of thinner materials, and later, when more smoothly fitting skirts are worn in the '60's. From c. 1857 younger women fancy the more fashionable hat, though bonnets are still considered correct for formal occasions.

c. 1851–55

Wool tartan jacket or bodice with basque. Skirt missing. Colours rich greens, purple, red, black, white, and blue. Trimmed dark green velvet ribbon, green silk fringe. Fastening hook and bar. Lined.

c. 1856–57

Lilac silk bodice, lined and boned, wide sleeve silk fringe trimming. Skirt missing.
from Mr F. Norris to Personal Collection

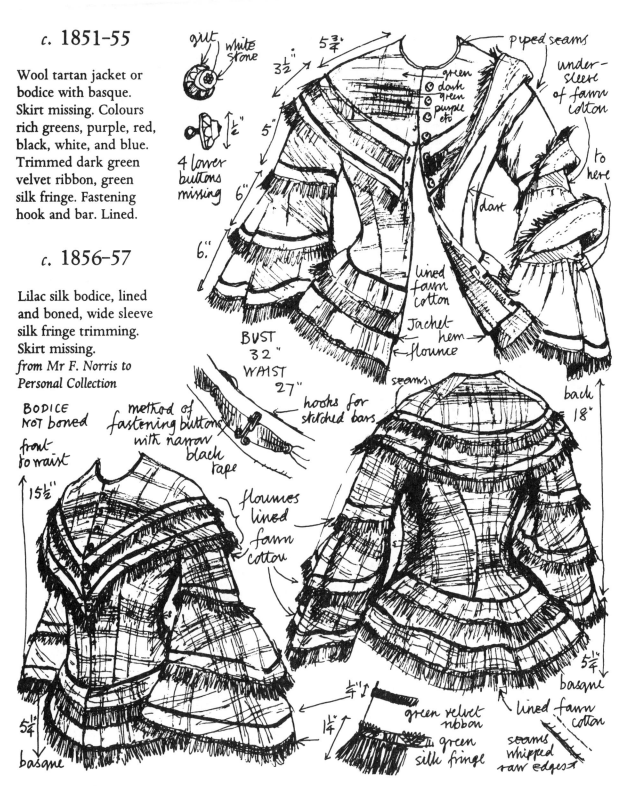

During the '50's dresses are made with separate bodice and skirt; unfortunately both these richly coloured tops have the skirts missing. They are beautifully sewn, with little sign of wear. The tartan one is not boned.

205

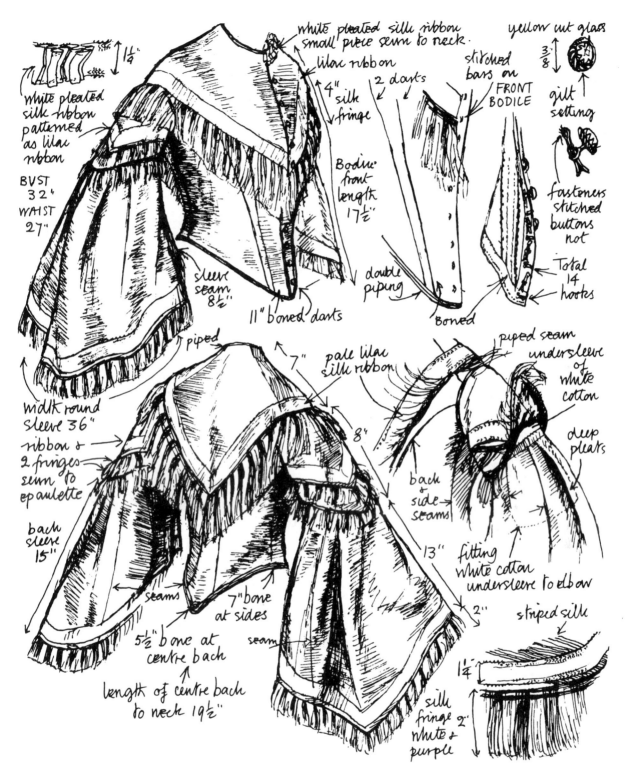

white pleated silk ribbon
small piece sewn to neck.

white pleated silk ribbon patterned as lilac ribbon

1¼"

lilac ribbon

4" silk fringe

2 darts

stitched bars on FRONT BODICE

yellow cut glass

3/8

gilt setting

fasteners stitched buttons not

Total 14 hooks

BUST 32"
WAIST 27"

Bodice front length 17½"

sleeve seam 8½"

11" boned darts

double piping

Boned

piped

piped seam

undersleeve of white cotton

7"

pale lilac silk ribbon

8"

deep pleats

mid'k round sleeve 36"

ribbon & 2 fringes sewn to epaulette

back & side seams

back sleeve 15"

13"

fitting white cotton undersleeve to elbow

2"

striped silk

seams

7" bone at sides

5½" bone at centre back

seam

1¼

silk fringe 2" white & purple

length of centre back to neck 19½"

The lilac bodice is boned and has the wide type of sleeve found in the '50's, also the deeply pointed waist, back and front, which is found on evening dresses of this date. The buttons on both bodices are decorative and removable. Skirts would be back-fastened.

1855–57

White watered silk, rich stiff quality. A wedding-dress with separate jacket and skirt. Bodice boned front and sides; wide sleeves and basque. Trimming of pleated white satin ribbon, deep silk fringe, with double net frills on sleeve. Back fastening to skirt, box pleating at waist into band, gathers at back.
Chastleton House

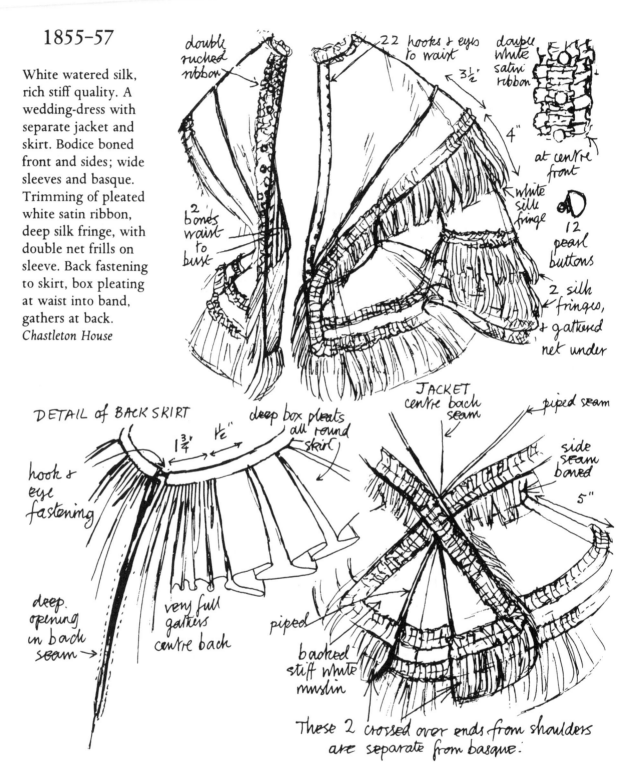

double ruched ribbon

22 hooks & eyes to waist

double white satin ribbon

3½"

4"

at centre front

white silk fringe

12 pearl buttons

2 silk fringes, + gathered net under

2 bones waist to bust

DETAIL of BACK SKIRT

hook & eye fastening

1¾" ½"

deep box pleats all round skirt

deep opening in back seam →

very full gathers centre back

JACKET centre back seam

piped seam

side seam boned

5"

piped

backed stiff white muslin

These 2 crossed over ends from shoulders are separate from basque.

This dress shows the type of back-fastening skirt worn with the jacket-bodices of the '50's, which are always front fastening. Deeply fringed V-shaped trimmings are very fashionable. The large decorative pearl buttons hide the hook-and-eye fastening. Pearl buttons were

207

from an ambrotype 1853-60

Donald Hall's family photographs

day dress with wide sleeves & white undersleeves

seam piped

white satin ribbon edges pinked.

fine silk net frill

backed stiff white muslin

white satin ribbon

14"

14"

5"

47" skirt side length + 49" centre back length

seam

seam

seam

seam

pocket in skirt

SLEEVE DETAIL
4 overlapping net frills

2 silk fringes

skirt front length 40"

side seam with pocket at top hidden under fringe.

manufactured *c.* 1855; previous to this only very small ones are found on cuff or reticule. Fine net or muslin under-sleeves would have been worn. The bride's veil would have hung down her back; it was not worn over the face until the '60's.

1858–60

Black silk taffeta dress, sleeves and flounces edged in black velvet. Front-fastening dress, pocket under flounce and tiny watch pocket. Epaulettes over sleeves, these seamed front and back, full but tapering to wrist. Bodice front cut in one piece, boned, lined in brown cotton. Skirt is lined stiffened coarse brown muslin.
Snowshill Collection

all bodice front cut in one piece lined brown cotton

front fastening 16 hooks & eyelets skirt opening side-front

watch pocket

front neck

2½"

15½"

all round sleeve

10"

waist piped

seams

3½"

F

A

B

pocket under top flounce

edges

bound black velvet

A

B

June 1860

mauve silk fanchon on straw bonnet

white tulle cap

rows of draw pleats

flat silk puffs

from "The Englishwoman's Domestic Magazine –" Mauve silk dress, trimmed darker mauve.

hem bound black velvet with braid at edge.

A crisp, rustling dress, made for a tall, slender woman. Epaulettes from *c.* 1858 accentuate a drooping shoulder-line and the flounces emphasize the horizontal lines of the skirt. An interesting detail is not only the tiny watch pocket set in the waistline seam, but the larger

FRONT
bar eyelets
front boned
fold
pleats
length of back
17"
4"
S
side & front boned
hook & eye
watch pocket

neck edge piped also sleeve. seam
under epaulette
sleeve pleated
WAIST 24"
seam
all 3 flounces 13" at front & sides 13½" at back
seam
width all round hem 132"
seam
seam

May 1860
Girl age 8-9 yrs
bertha crosses in front & sash ties in front

from "The Englishwomans Domestic Magazine" pink & white striped dress, trimmed rose coloured silk Drawers with muslin embroidery

pocket in the front hidden under the first flounce. Towards the end of the '60's, when smoothly fitting skirts are worn, these pockets cannot be concealed and reticules return. Sleeves, with two seams, are narrower.

210

c. 1859

Fine soft figured silk day dress, of medium cool brown. Bodice has pleated front bands; the waistline is higher and straight. Skirt sewn to bodice in close fine gathers, side-front fastening with pocket in skirt. Bodice front fastening. Dress fully lined white linen. Closed, but full sleeves with only one seam, lined brown linen.
Mrs M. Macbeth

5½"

14"

9"

piped seam

40½"

41"

detail from "The Duet" by Frank Stone. showing hairstyle & collar & brooches worn on this type of dress

15"

3⅜"

gathered more fully at back

BODICE DETAIL
each fold of pleat sewn to fine brown stiff muslin

pleats sewn up to here & WAIST to here

hook with stitched bar

centre back seam

width of silk 20"

seam

seam

seam

A day dress, worn by Mrs Macbeth's great-grandmother, is elegant in its simplicity and well reflects an everyday style of this period. The bodice has the general line of the '50's, also the closed but full bishop sleeve, which came in about 1855 as an alternative to the wide

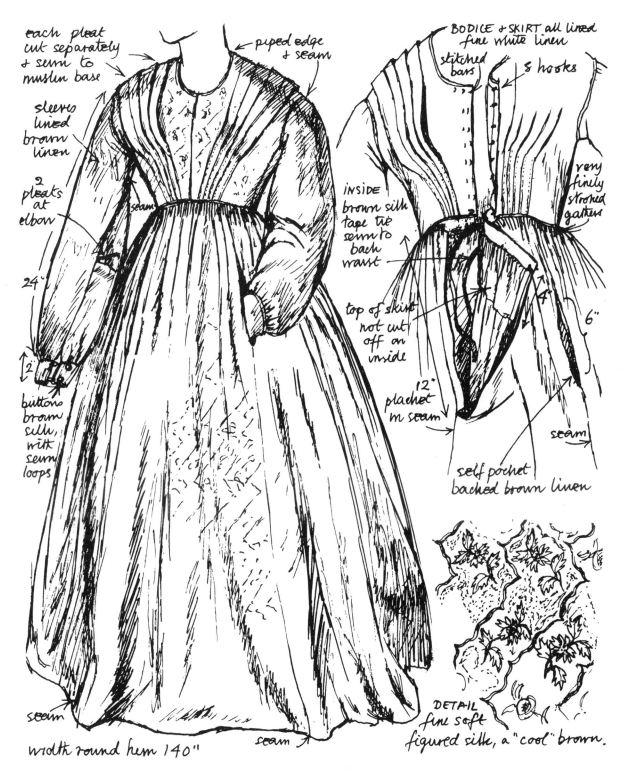

each pleat cut separately + seum to muslin base

piped edge + seam

BODICE + SKIRT all lined fine white linen

stitched bars

8 hooks

sleeves lined brown linen

2 pleats at elbow

seam

INSIDE brown silk tape tie seum to back waist

very finely stroked gathers

24"

2

buttons brown silk, with seum loops

top of skirt not cut off on inside

12" placket in seam

4"

6"

seam

self pocket backed brown linen

seam

DETAIL fine soft figured silk, a "cool" brown.

width round hem 140"

seam

seam

pagoda or bell sleeves; it has one seam. The raised straight waistline is found after 1859, but the skirt is then set in to a waistband, and not sewn direct to the bodice as here, in such fine close gathers.

1864-65

White transparent wool
as muslin, checkered
in white silk, printed
in soft red-line pattern
with rose sprays in
red, buds and leaves
in orange-red and in
green. Afternoon
crinoline dress, very
full skirt pleated
and gathered. Bodice
trimmed black lace
over green ribbon; the
cotton lining has short
sleeves. Skirt unlined.
Snowshill Collection

armholes very small

7¼"

from "The Englishwoman's Domestic Magazine" March 1861

black lace & red flowers

black lace

Dress in 2 shades of green

seam

seams

seams

DETAIL of transparent fine white wool, as muslin checkered in white silk

roses & lines printed in soft red

buds + leaves in orange + green

weft threads show more than warp

Although this skirt is so full, the whole dress is very light and delicate, matching the pattern
and material. The fashionable use of black lace over the bright green ribbon on the sleeves
is attractive. The skirt and the bodice, as is usual, are both sewn to the waistband, although

213

tiny button covered in green silk thread

top of white cotton bodice lining to here

16"

WAIST 25"

Bodice front fastening & skirt side-front open to here

length front skirt 41½"

width of material 23½"

seam

ruched panel between lace is extra, giving double muslin here

15½"

13½"

black lace over green silk ribbon

piped seams

narrow white lace neck edging

central panel is loose, with material of dress & lining, sewn together in this seam

side seam boned to here

7"

1"

3"

1"

triple inverted pleat

length centre back skirt 47"

very close gathers

4 pleats

width all round hem 186"

seam

seam

the dressmaking hints in *The Englishwoman's Domestic Magazine*, June 1860, are not **exactly** followed: 'in mounting skirt to body, fulness must be arranged in 5 or 6 pleats on each side of the front, with 3 or 4 large box pleats at back.'

1864-65

White transparent wool as muslin, checkered and with printed rose sprays and narrow stripes. Crinoline dress with pleated and gathered skirt, which is unlined. Bodice lined white cotton. Black satin shoes with small flat heels, soles shaped and thicker.
Snowshill Collection

White cotton stockings with initial and date.
Mrs M. S. Mallam

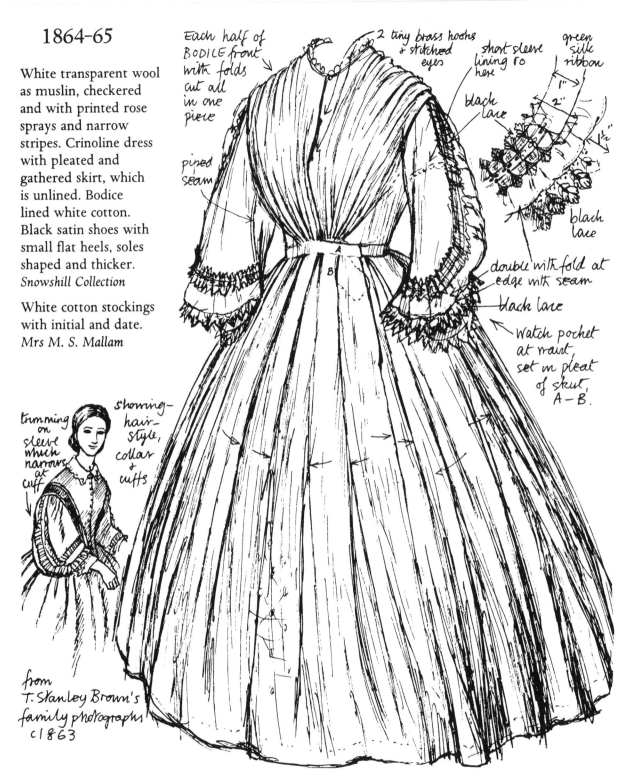

Each half of BODICE front with folds cut all in one piece

piped seam

2 tiny brass hooks & stitched eyes

short sleeve lining to here

green silk ribbon

black lace

1"

2"

1½"

black lace

double with fold at edge with seam

black lace

Watch pocket at waist, set in pleat of skirt, A – B.

A

B

trimming on sleeve which narrows at cuff

showing hair style, collar & cuffs

from T. Stanley Brown's family photographs c1863

Various sleeve fashions appear during the late '50's to early '60's, with the tendency for them to become less wide; the fullness being caught in with either trimming or puffs. The bodice front is cut in one piece of material, the gathers being neatly held in place by almost invisible

215

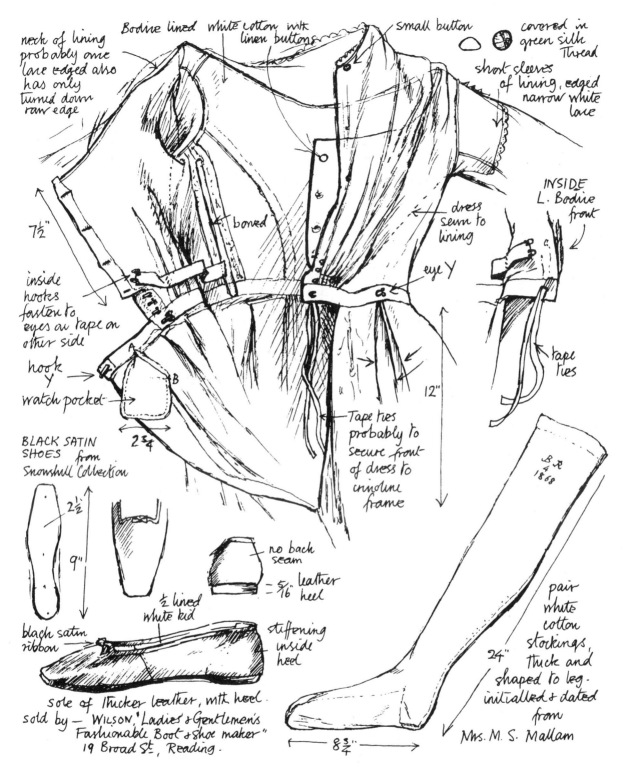

neck of lining probably once lace edged also has only turned down raw edge

Bodice lined white cotton with linen buttons

small button

covered in green silk Thread

short sleeves of lining, edged narrow white lace

7½"

boned

dress sewn to lining

INSIDE L. Bodice front

inside hooks fasten to eyes on tape on other side

eye Y

12"

tape ties

hook Y

watch pocket

B

A

BLACK SATIN SHOES from Snowshill Collection

2¾

Tape ties probably to secure front of dress to crinoline frame

B R 4 1868

2½

9"

no back seam

5/16" leather heel

½ lined white kid

black satin ribbon

stiffening inside heel

pair white cotton stockings, thick and shaped to leg. initialled & dated from Mrs. M. S. Mallam

24"

sole of thicker leather, with heel. sold by — WILSON, "Ladies & Gentlemen's Fashionable Boot & Shoe maker" 19 Broad St, Reading.

8¾"

stitching to the cotton under-bodice, which has short, lace-edged sleeves. Shoes, still with squared toes, have thicker soles and small heels. Thinner-soled shoes are used for dancing. White stockings were used with shoes, coloured ones with boots.

c. 1865–66

Lilac shot-silk taffeta crinoline dress, with black lace trimming on bodice, sleeves, and skirt-back. Fitting sleeves with two seams, tiny puffs at shoulder. Bodice boned front and side, lined white linen, also sleeves. Skirt lined glazed white cotton, fastening side-front, watch pocket and pocket in skirt. Black braid at hem.
Snowshill Collection

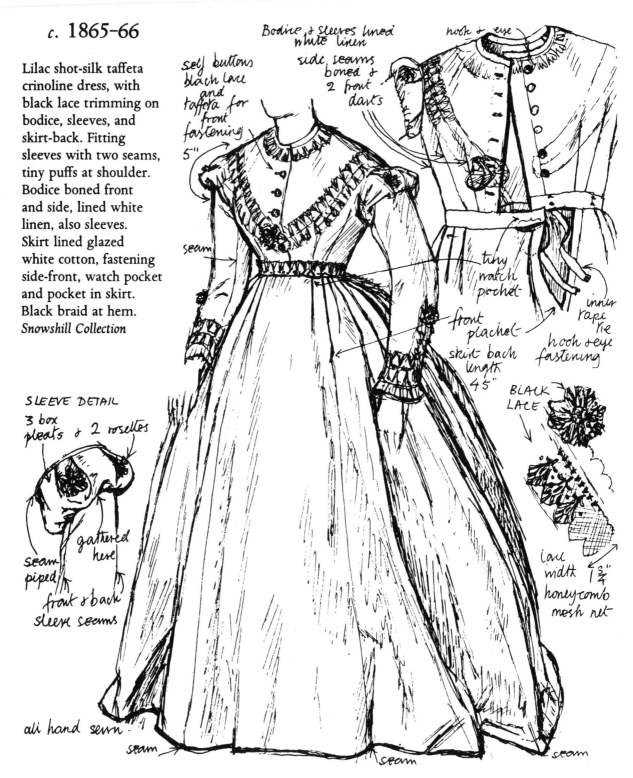

Bodice & sleeves lined white linen

side seams boned & 2 front darts

hook & eye

self buttons black lace and taffeta for front fastening 5"

seam

tiny watch pocket

front placket

skirt back length 45"

inner tape tie hook & eye fastening

BLACK LACE

lace width 1¾" honeycomb mesh net

SLEEVE DETAIL

3 box pleats & 2 rosettes

gathered here

seam piped

front & back sleeve seams

all hand sewn.

seam

seam

seam

This is another of the dresses found locked away in the chest of drawers. It is a lovely example of the '60's, with the skirt emphasis well at the back, and worn over a crinoline. But even as early as 1860, *The Englishwoman's Domestic Magazine* tells us, 'Some ladies are now leaving off

217

½" ⅓
6"
seam
5¾"
boned
pleats
face to
centre-
back
1" wide
close gathers at
back
hook & eye fastening
on separate belt
skirt fully
lined, white
glazed cotton
seam
hem bound narrow
black woollen braid

DOUBLE LACE
frill

from
family photograph
of my
grandmother's
cousin.

1866
silk
taffeta
dress
trimmed
with
black

14"

14½"

probably
white frill
here, as at
wrist

11½"

1½"

WAIST
26½"

lace edge
to white
net frill

pocket
in
seam

39½

seam

seams

the "iron" crinoline,' but Parisian ladies are wearing under their dresses 'muslin petticoats
with small flounces up to the waist, each flounce mounted on a piece of steel.' . . . But, in spite
of that, crinolines were not discarded until '68.

218

1865-67

Delicate pink alpaca evening dress. Large matching bow at back, long sash-ends to near ankle-level. Trimmed narrow white satin vandyked edging, & golden brown fringe. Bodice and sleeves lined white linen, front and sides boned. Front fastening. Pocket in skirt, also tiny watch pocket. This dress is all machine-sewn. *Snowshill Collection*

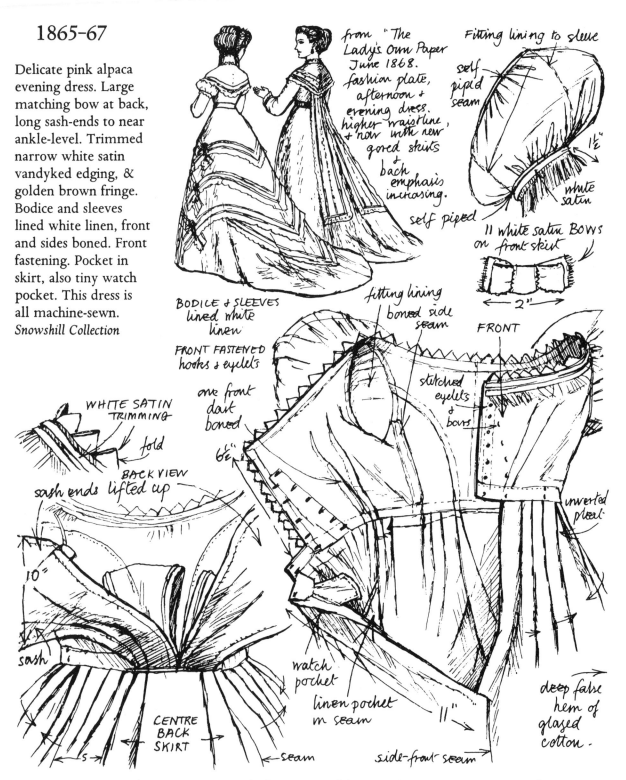

from "The Lady's Own Paper June 1868. fashion plate, afternoon & evening dress. higher waistline, + now with new gored skirts & back emphasis increasing.

self piped

Fitting lining to sleeve

self piped seam

1½"

white satin

11 white satin BOWS on front skirt

2"

BODICE & SLEEVES lined white linen

FRONT FASTENED hooks & eyelets

one front dart boned

6½"

fitting lining boned side seam

FRONT

stitched eyelets & bars

inverted pleat

WHITE SATIN TRIMMING

fold

BACK VIEW

sash ends lifted up

10"

sash

CENTRE BACK SKIRT

5

watch pocket

linen pocket in seam

seam

side-front seam

11"

deep false hem of glazed cotton.

Machine sewing becomes quite usual after 1865, and by 1868 there are many makes of sewing-machine available. The trailing skirt is fashionable, and long sash ends, with the declining crinoline, but gores replace pleats and gathers. We read in *The Lady's Own Paper*, 1868: 'we

all machine
sewn.
ALPACA, pink warp
& white weft.
28" wide.

golden-
brown
silk
fringe

WAIST
22"

2 hooks
& eyes

↑ front
skirt
38"

watch
pocket

placket
to
here

11 →
BOWS

white satin
trimming

6½' 11"

SASH
matches
dress

golden-brown silk fringe →

2
darts

linen
pocket
in
seam

watch pocket
& placket
under
folds

s

centre
back
.53½

seam

seam

HEM
bound black
velvet ribbon

seam

seam

seam

156"
width round
hem

are sorry to chronicle that very gay colours are in vogue for dress in Paris, because we never
think them so elegant . . . as delicate neutral tints.' And they recommend 'light grey alpaca,
mauve satin pipings, vandykes and fringes.'

c. 1868

White muslin dress, spot pattern printed in pale blue-green. Hand-sewn, unlined. Plain fitting sleeves with two seams. Pocket in skirt above knee-level, tiny watch pocket at waist. Six very small pearl buttons fasten bodice front, with skirt placket at left front. Three flounces on skirt, hem bound white woollen braid.
Snowshill Collection

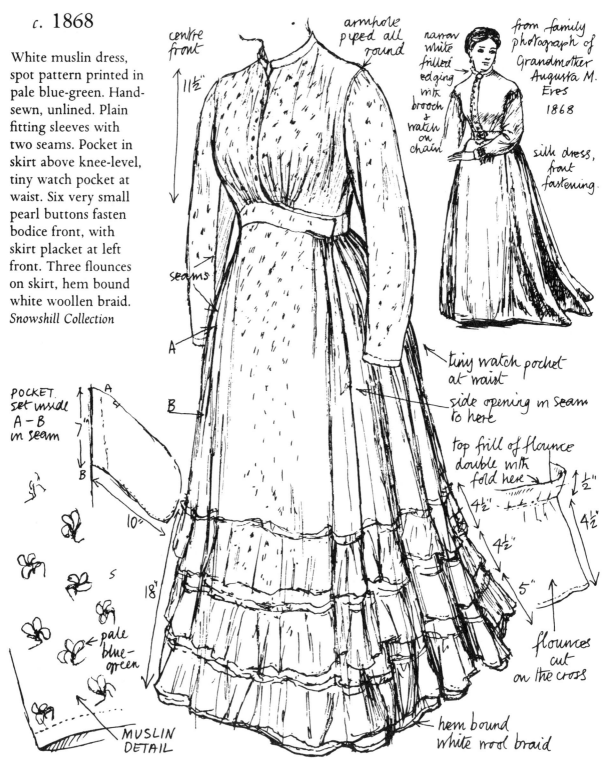

centre front

armhole piped all round

11½"

seams

A

B

POCKET set inside A – B in seam

A

B

10"

18"

pale blue-green

MUSLIN DETAIL

narrow white frilled edging with brooch & watch on chain

from family photograph of Grandmother Augusta M. Eves 1868

silk dress, front fastening.

tiny watch pocket at waist

side opening in seam to here

top frill of flounce double with fold here

½"

4½"

4½"

4½"

5"

flounces cut on the cross

hem bound white wool braid

A simple day dress, not easy to date; perhaps made in the early summer of 1868, soon after the collapse of the crinoline in the winter of '67. Flounces at the bottom of the skirt are becoming fashionable again during 1868, and sleeves are fitting. This dress hardly appears

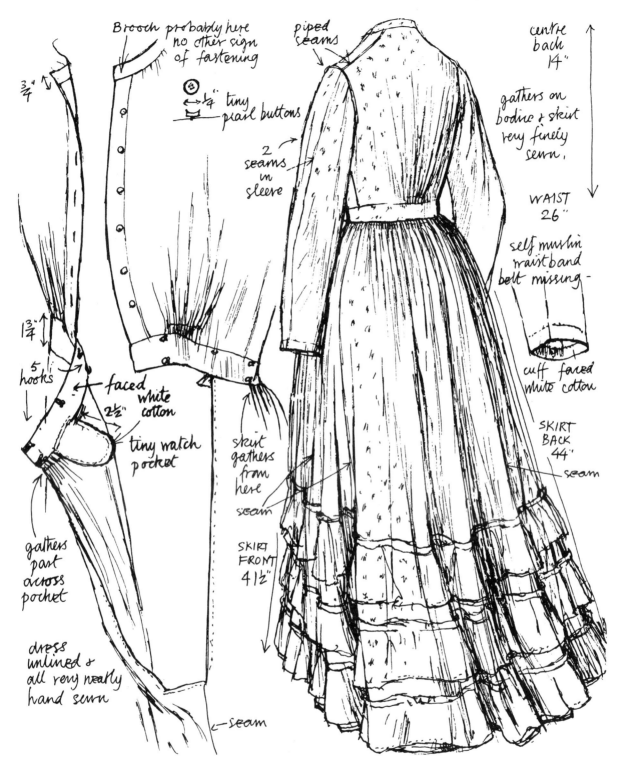

3/4"

Brooch probably here
no other sign
of fastening

⌀ ¼" tiny
pearl buttons

2
seams
in
sleeve

piped
seams

centre
back
14"

gathers on
bodice & skirt
very finely
sewn.

WAIST
26"

self muslin
waistband
belt missing —

cuff faced
white cotton

1 3/4"

5
hooks

faced
white
cotton

2½"

tiny watch
pocket

skirt
gathers
from
here

seam

SKIRT
BACK
44"

seam

gathers
past
across
pocket

SKIRT
FRONT
41½"

dress
unlined &
all very neatly
hand sewn

← seam

to have been worn, which is possible, for during that year over-skirts, extra trimming, and draperies were looped up over the bustle, and women were once more 'caged' and padded, this time at the back. This skirt is not made for a bustle (p. 229).

c. 1870

White silk taffeta, a wedding-dress, front-fastening separate bodice; back-fastened skirt, separate apron front with bow and long sash-ends, back fastening. Apron and skirt lined stiffened muslin. Bodice lined white cotton. Trimmed deep cream silk bows and fringe. Large fine wedding-veil, lace on machine-made net.
Mrs M. J. King

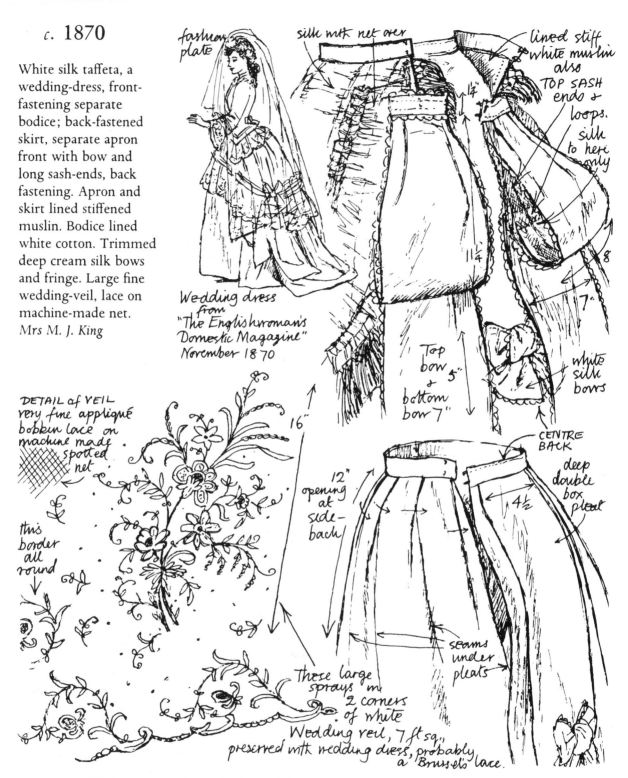

fashion plate

silk with net over

lined stiff white muslin also TOP SASH ends & loops. silk to here only

Wedding dress from "The Englishwoman's Domestic Magazine" November 1870

1¼

11¼

8

7"

Top bow 5" & bottom bow 7"

white silk bows

DETAIL of VEIL very fine appliqué bobbin lace on machine made spotted net

this border all round

16"

12" opening at side-back

CENTRE BACK deep double box pleat

4½

seams under pleats

These large sprays in 2 corners of white Wedding veil, 7 ft sq., preserved with wedding dress, probably a Brussels lace.

A graceful dress in rustling silk, beautifully preserved even with the wedding-veil, orange blossom wreath, and tiny posy-holder. Deep cream trimmings on white might have been used, in the early '70's, when two shades of the same colour are often found on one dress.

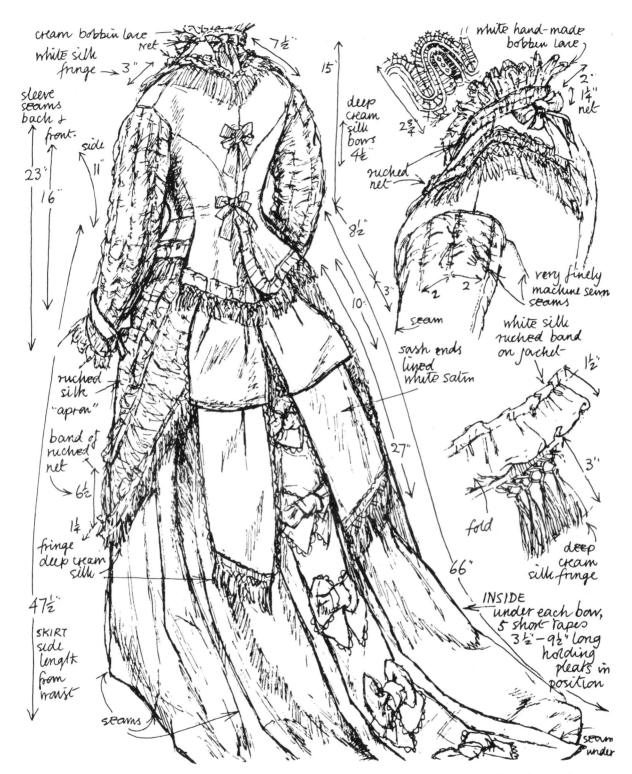

cream bobbin lace
net
white silk fringe → 3"
7½"

sleeve seams back & front.
23"
16"
side 11"

15
deep cream silk bows 4½"
ruched net

white hand-made bobbin lace
2"
1¼" net
2¾"

8½"
3"
10'

seam
2   2
very finely machine sewn seams

white silk ruched band on jacket

1½"
3"
fold
deep cream silk fringe

ruched silk "apron"

band of ruched net
6½"

1¼

fringe deep cream silk

sash ends lined white satin

27"

47½"
SKIRT side length from waist

seams

66"

INSIDE under each bow, 5 short tapes 3½" – 9½" long holding pleats in position

seam under

These fringes and bows may have darkened with age. The back-fastening skirt has a deep double box pleat at back, waist to hem, the pleats held in position inside, by short tapes, sewn across, behind each of the bows.

224

c. 1870

White silk taffeta wedding-dress, three separate parts. Bodice trimmed with silk fringes and ruched white net. Sleeves all of ruched silk, cuffs of plain silk. Bobbin lace at neck and cuff. Apron of ruched silk trimmed with ruched net, fringe and silk bows. White silk bows on pleats of back skirt. White crinolette.
Mrs M. J. King

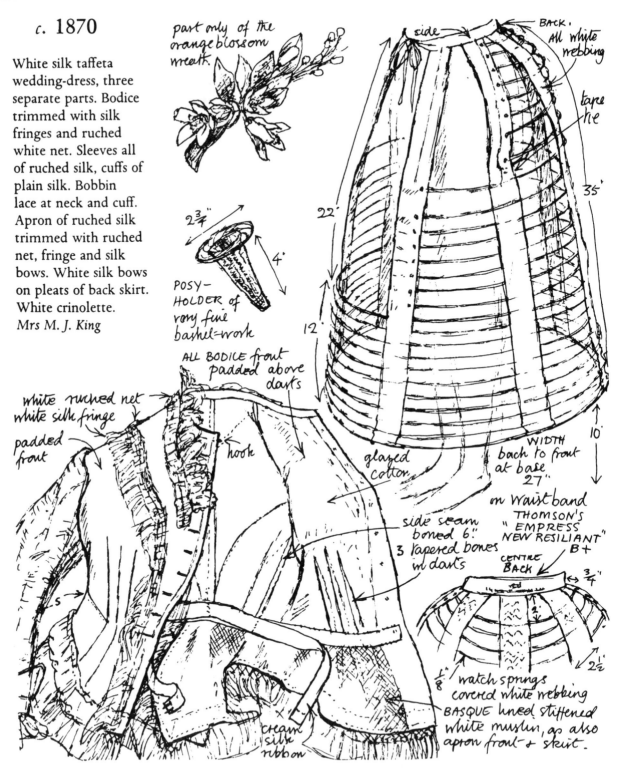

part only of the orange blossom wreath.

POSY-HOLDER of very fine basket-work

2¾"

4'

side

BACK. All white webbing

tape tie

35'

22'

12

ALL BODICE front padded above darts

white ruched net
white silk fringe

padded front

hook

glazed cotton

WIDTH back to front at base 27"

10

on waistband
THOMSON'S "EMPRESS NEW RESILIANT" B+

side seam boned 6"
3 tapered bones in darts

CENTRE BACK

¾"

2½

⅛" watch springs covered white webbing
BASQUE lined stiffened white muslin, as also apron front + skirt.

cream silk ribbon

Fringes and decorative bows are favourite trimmings of the early '70's; so too is ruched net; unfortunately this is so fine that it has not lasted as well as the silk. Inside the Thomson's crinoline frame there is a single tape tie holding the front back. This is really half-way between

225

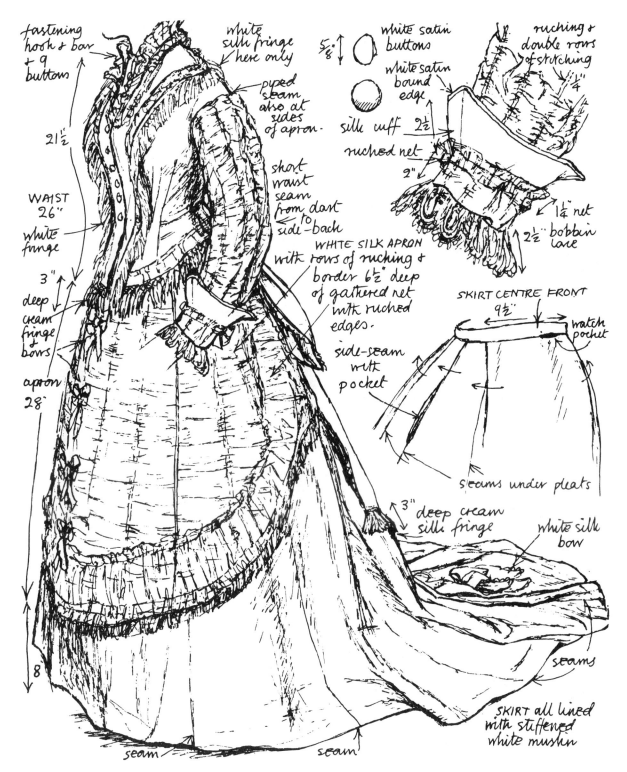

fastening hook & bar + 9 buttons

white silk fringe here only

white satin buttons

$\frac{5}{8}$"

white satin bound edge

ruching & double rows of stitching

$1\frac{1}{4}$"

piped seam also at sides of apron.

silk cuff $2\frac{1}{2}$

ruched net

2"

$1\frac{1}{4}$ net

$2\frac{1}{2}$" bobbin lace

21$\frac{1}{2}$

WAIST 26"

white fringe

short waist seam from dart to side-back

WHITE SILK APRON with rows of ruching & border 6$\frac{1}{2}$" deep of gathered net with ruched edges.

SKIRT CENTRE FRONT 9$\frac{1}{2}$"

watch pocket

3"

deep cream fringe & bows

side-seam with pocket

apron 28"

seams under pleats

3" deep cream silk fringe

white silk bow

8

seam

seam

seams

SKIRT all lined with stiffened white muslin

a crinoline and a bustle frame. The tape ties inside the skirt pleats are an early form of the complicated tape ties which develop later. The bodice and skirt become separate again, a necessity, owing to the heavy pleating of the skirt.

1876 Emily Hall and a relation, from T. Stanley Brown's album. Her dress, bodice and skirt cut in one, with fashionable outside pocket, has lavish pleated and velvet trimming, all made more possible by the increasing use of the sewing-machine since 1860.

1888 July 21st, at 'her Grace's Garden Party,' an illustration from *Punch* of that year. The return of the bustle gives added curves to the female form; this contrasts with the straightness of the masculine frock coat and the narrow creased trousers.

1895–96 Mary Gertrude Street, from T. Stanley Brown's album. Her fur-trimmed, high-necked dress is the very height of fashion. The men, in morning and lounge coats, are fashion-plates from T. H. Holding's book of 1897, *The Direct System of Ladies' Cutting*.

4

1870–1900

The sewing-machine, developed in America from the 1840's, is used there far more extensively than it is in England, where many women still prefer their clothes to be hand-sewn. But by the '70's it has a marked effect on dressmaking in general.

Flounces, frills, pleating, and ruching are used in abundance, and by 1880 *The Ladies' Treasury* insists 'in no case, however, is a dress made of only one material. All dresses without exception are made with two distinct materials.'

Interest is still centred on a woman's waist, and the bodice, by its mere plainness and perfect fit, is accentuated firstly by the vast amount of trimmings and drapery which enfold the figure from the hips downward, and later, 1895–96, by the huge leg-of-mutton sleeves. The ladies' tailor, T. H. Holding, assures us in 1897, 'it is quite clear that comfort is not an essential with women, but the fit is everything. . . . You cannot pay a woman a greater compliment than to make her so tight in the waist that she is miserable.'

But these tightly swathed dresses do bring some improvements, and women's underwear becomes far less bulky; although remaining frilly below the knees for some years yet, it is simplified and figure-fitting; the latter particularly applies to the corsets, which must have been intolerably uncomfortable. The bustle or crinolette of the early '70's disappears 1876–82, but is revived with renewed protuberance from 1882, reaching its maximum size in '85, then dying out by 1889, being latterly called a 'tournure' or 'dress-improver.'

Despite all this impedimenta, women, towards the end of the century, do enjoy a far greater amount of freedom and out-of-door activity than ever before, with bicycling being one of the major diversions during the '90's, even among the upper classes, until it is taken up by all and sundry.

But the popularity of the 'bloomers' of American origin is another matter; T. H. Holding, in his *Direct System of Ladies' Cutting*, is quite informative: 'Bloomers, fortunately or unfortunately, are not popular in England. Many efforts have been made during the past three years, to bring them into use as on the Continent, but English ladies insist on cycling in skirts.' He describes some of them: 'the Touring Skirt is one that does not blow outward, especially if aided by straps at the knee'; while one, as made for the Duchess of Connaught, 'behaves splendidly'; another 'makes a good deal of flapping and windage,' while a fourth 'which is about 4½ yards wide, in the wind, it must be the most awful torture possible, to the wearer— nay, I have seen the skirt "moving" and heard it flapping, while the tendency to lift is something appalling to contemplate.' (See p. 381, Cycling in the 1890's.)

c. 1872–74

White gauze dress, silky texture, trimmed rich grass-green satin with wide sash. Flower spot pattern in purple with yellow and green. Bustle, 3 cane hoops and bustle pad, dress sewn to it. Separate skirt with 'apron front' trimming, and slit to a pocket; fastening at side back. Bodice altered.

from Miss A. Chatwin to Personal Collection

Dress hand sewn

from a catalogue 'Fashion Book' published by Cavendish House, Cheltenham in 1872

satin cloth costume in bronze price 98/-

Bodice altered

15½"

slit opening A to B

length skirt front 38"

skirt opening

BUSTLE with pad + 3 hoops sewn in to dress, with skirt sewn to bustle at E, F & G

1st hoop
2nd hoop
3rd hoop

1½"

5½"

2½"

green ruched ribbon

purple
pale yellow
green centre, leaves & stalks

weft thread thicker

hem

narrow green braid

flowers face alternate way every other row

6½"

length skirt back 44"

1½"
5½"

flounce
hem of dress

centre seam

It is extremely interesting to find a perfect bustle, with small pad as well as cane hoops, sewn into the skirt of a dress. The separate top has been altered, but the skirt is fragile. All the dress is hand-sewn, and the flower-embroidered pattern is nicely done. Flounced dresses,

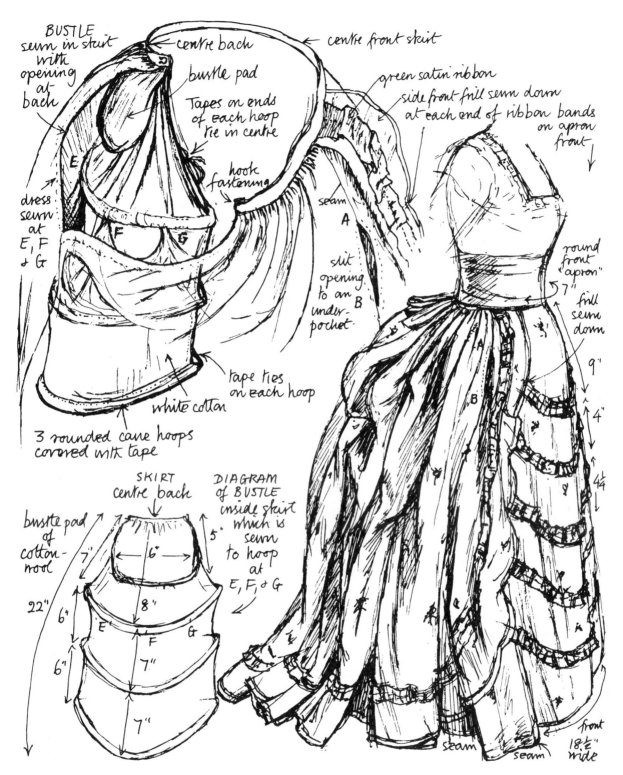

BUSTLE sewn in skirt with opening at back

centre back

centre front skirt

bustle pad

Tapes on ends of each hoop tie in centre

green satin ribbon

side front frill sewn down at each end of ribbon bands on apron front

hook fastening

seam A

slit opening to an under-pocket.

B

round front 'apron'

7"

frill sewn down

9"

4"

44

dress sewn at E, F & G

E

F

G

tape ties on each hoop

white cotton

3 rounded cane hoops covered with tape

SKIRT centre back

DIAGRAM of BUSTLE inside skirt which is sewn to hoop at E, F, & G

bustle pad of cotton-wool

22"

7"

6"

6"

5"

6"

8"

E

F

G

7"

7"

B

seam

seam

front 18½" wide

with either a separate over-skirt or with trimming which gives an 'apron' effect, were very fashionable at this time. With this new line to the dress, hair styles change, and with them the hat or bonnet. Shoes now have heels.

1874-75

Black muslin, white spot pattern, dress of 'half-mourning' worn by Mrs W. Charles Macready. Trimmed black lace, ribbon, black and white silk fringe; worn over a bustle frame. Bodice and sleeves lined in black silk; skirt is unlined. Bodice boned front and sides. Dress all machine-sewn. Underskirt missing.
Snowshill Collection

flounce lined black muslin

SIDE BODICE

black lace & ribbon black & white fringe

seams

side 4½"

13¼"

back waist gathered under bustle flounce

side pleats

pocket in seam has piped edges

WAIST 31½"

double bow of black silk

BLACK SILK BOW edges scalloped & pinked

CENTRE BACK Bow stitched here

Bustle flounce

9½"

12"

seam

seam

centre back seam

flounce cut on cross

William Charles Macready, the actor, born 1793, died in Cheltenham 1873; this dress was probably worn by his widow as 'half-mourning'; the touch of white on black denotes this. Full mourning lasted a year and a day. In 1823 he had married Catherine F. Atkins (d. 1852);

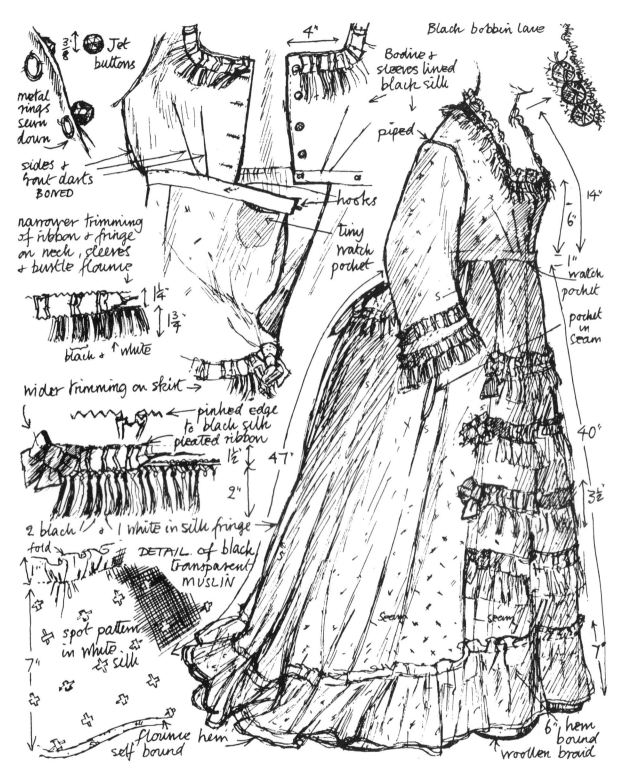

Jet buttons

$\frac{3}{8}$

metal rings sewn down

sides & front darts BONED

narrower trimming of ribbon & fringe on neck, sleeves & bustle flounce

$1\frac{1}{4}$

$1\frac{3}{4}$

black & ↑ white

wider trimming on skirt →

pinked edge to black silk pleated ribbon

$1\frac{1}{2}$

$47''$

$2''$

2 black & 1 white in silk fringe →

fold

DETAIL of black transparent MUSLIN

spot pattern in white silk

$7''$

flounce hem self bound

4''

Black bobbin lace

Bodice & sleeves lined black silk

piped

hooks

tiny watch pocket

$14''$

$6''$

$1''$

watch pocket

pocket in seam

$40''$

$3\frac{1}{2}$

seam

seam

$7''$

6" hem bound woollen braid

in 1860 he married Cecile Spencer (b. 1827, d. 1908). This dress has the fashionable square neckline, flounced skirt, and trimming which simulates an over-skirt or apron, and pockets. Under-sleeves would have been worn.

232

1873–75

Thomson's crinolette, watch-spring hoops, projecting frame at back. Bands of red woollen cloth, deep band at hem. Shoes with small heel, brass-covered, square toe, patterned fabric.
Snowshill Collection

White cotton crinolette for trained dress, half-hoops of steel at back. Laced inside.
Chastleton House: lent to Snowshill Collection

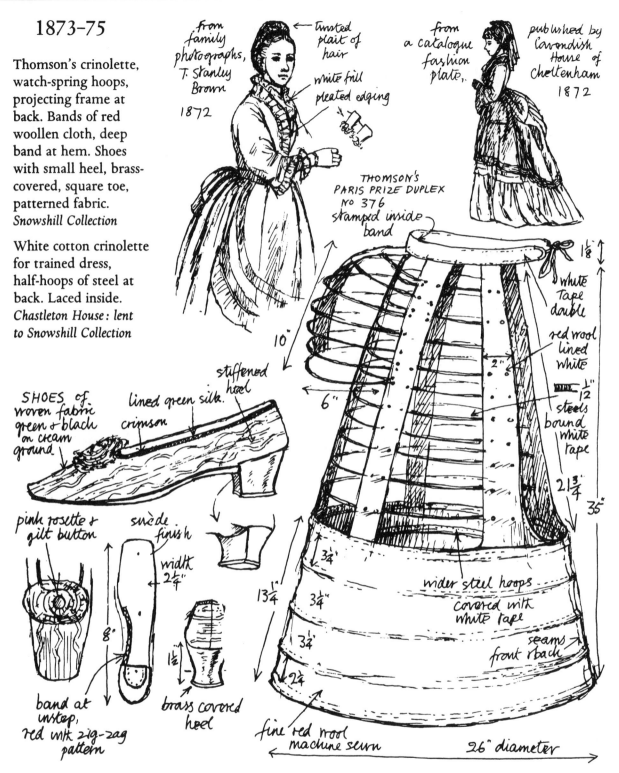

from family photographs, T. Stanley Brown
1872

← twisted plait of hair

white frill pleated edging

from a catalogue fashion plate,

published by Cavendish House of Cheltenham
1872

THOMSON'S PARIS PRIZE DUPLEX No 376 stamped inside band

1⅛

white Tape double

red wool lined white

2"

1/12 steels bound white Tape

21¾

10"

6"

35"

SHOES of woven fabric green & black on cream ground

lined green silk.

crimson

stiffened heel

pink rosette & gilt button

suède finish

width 2¼"

8"

1½

3¼"

3¼"

3¼"

2¼

13¼"

band at instep, red with zig-zag pattern

brass covered heel

fine red wool machine sewn

wider steel hoops covered with white Tape

seams front & back

26" diameter

This type of red crinolette, worn under day dresses of the early '70's, is similar to the crinoline, in that it hangs from the waist, but the white cotton one is laced up inside, so that the over-lapping half-hoops are held firmly out at the back, with the front petticoat part drawn tightly

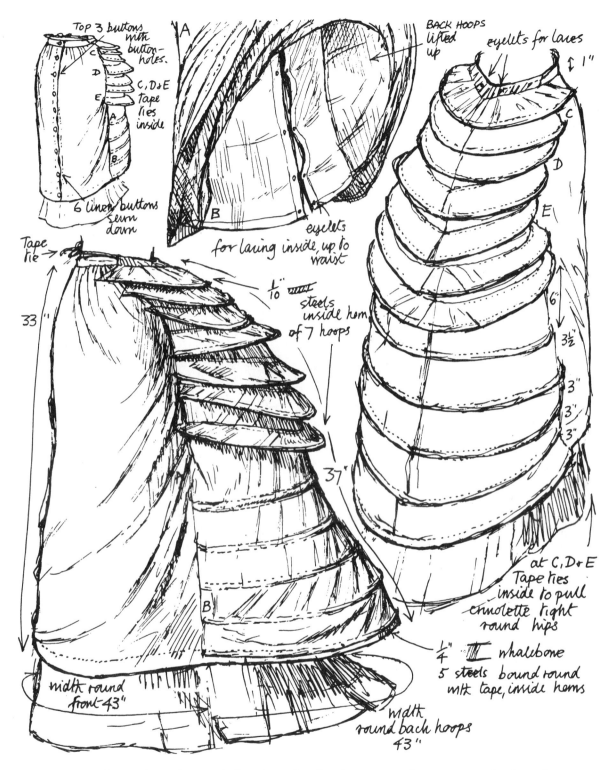

Top 3 buttons with button-holes.

C

D

C, D & E Tape lies inside

E

A

B

6 linen buttons sewn down

A

B

eyelets for lacing inside, up to waist

BACK HOOPS lifted up

eyelets for laces

↕ 1"

C

D

E

6"

3½"

3"

3"

3"

Tape tie →

33"

¼₀" ▨ steels inside hem of 7 hoops

37"

B

width round front 43"

at C, D & E Tape ties inside to pull crinolette tight round hips

¼" Ⅲ whalebone 5 steels bound round with tape, inside hems

width round back hoops 43"

round the figure from hip to below knee-level. The two eyelets at centre back waist are probably for securing it to the corset. Heels on shoes become higher during the 1870's, their first reappearance after some 50 years.

1870–75

Black silk mantle edged in black crape over corded silk with fringes and tassels of black silk with black satin bow. Unlined. Shaped to wear over a bustle; inner tape tie at waist.

1860–70 black satin shoes with heel, black satin bow.
Snowshill Collection

1876 gold and black mourning ring.
T. Stanley Brown

rolled curls.

brooch on black velvet ribbon

locket on chain

from T. Stanley Brown's family photographs 1870

silk braid

also
GOLD RING with black enamel at front with 5 pearls + tiny gold beads

MOURNING RING for a daughter who died in 1876 Alice Bertha Hall

fine plait of her hair

fringe

folded edge

crape

2"

black silk fringe

black crape over corded silk

9"

PATTERN showing INSIDE of MANTLE

darts + seams bound

13"

black tape waist tie

WAIST.

28" front edge

deep pleat + seams

unlined

centre seam

black satin

bow lifted up

tassel

15"

9"

9"

seam

5½

faced stiff black muslin

The mantle of medium-heavy dull-surfaced silk has been very much worn. The crape on the front facings was probably removed because of wear. It is more than likely a widow's mantle, which, when new, had the fashionable fringe, tassel trimmings, and bow over the

235

'for an elderly lady'

from a catalogue published by Cavendish House, Cheltenham 1872

lace edged velvet mantle

satin dress

Mrs Margetson, T. Stanley Brown's family photographs. 1870 epaulettes not worn after this.

cameo locket & earrings

bow at neck missing

3 eyes & hooks

corded silk only crape removed?

front length 28"

crape band sewn on here

3/4"

1 1/4"

length centre back 27"

side length 24"

tassel

2"

black satin bow

tiny black beads

width 2 1/2"

9 1/4"

no seam

1 1/8"

stiffened

lined black cotton + black kid

black satin shoes, heel also

bustle. The mock 'hood' at the back echoes those worn on mantles twenty years earlier. The use of mourning rings is recorded in a will of 1487; they were in use in 16th, 17th, and 18th c., when they were wider than this, and very popular.

1875-76

Candy-stripe silk dress. Princess style, trained robe in plum colour and white. Trimmed plum-coloured satin, frilled edging and lace. Bodice boned & half-lined to hips. All neatly machine-sewn. Satin front pleated and ruched, with panels on skirt. Tape ties inside. *worn by Mrs Milvane's mother; given by her to the Snowshill Collection*

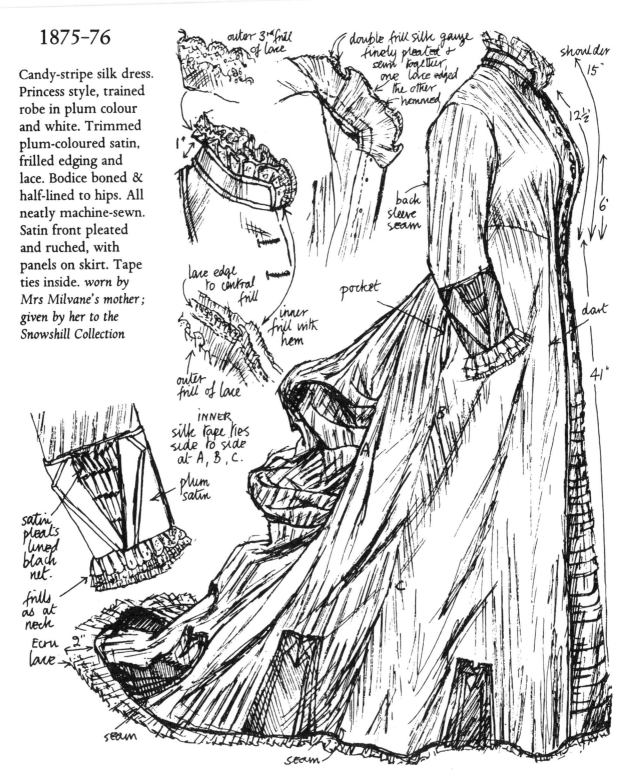

outer 3rd frill of lace

double frill silk gauze finely pleated & sewn together, one lace edged the other hemmed

shoulder 15"

12½"

1"

back sleeve seam

6'

dart

41"

lace edge to central frill

inner frill with hem

pocket

outer frill of lace

INNER silk tape ties side to side at A, B, C.

plum satin

satin pleats lined black net.

frills as at neck

Ecru lace 2"

seam

seam

During 1875-80 sheath-like dresses fit closely to the figure from neck to hip, the bustle slips half-way down the skirt. All fullness is gathered, puffed, swathed, or draped, low down on the dress, held in position by tapes (see early form of this, p. 224). In *The Ladies' Treasury*,

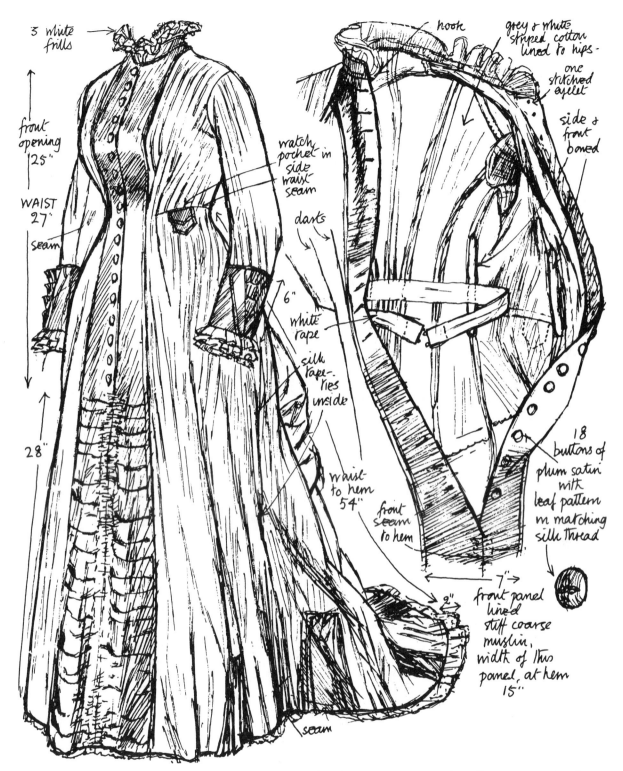

3 white frills

front opening 25"

WAIST 27"

seam

28"

watch pocket in side waist seam

darts

6"

white tape

silk taperies inside

waist to hem 54"

hook

grey & white striped cotton lined to hips

one stitched eyelet

side & front boned

front seam to hem

7"

2"

18 buttons of plum satin with leaf pattern in matching silk thread

front panel lined stiff coarse muslin, width of this panel at hem 15"

seam

1876, we are told: 'our skirts are now so tight that our sitting and walking are seriously inconvenienced . . . the smallest steps in walking are indispensable, and it is impossible to sit any way, but on one side.'

1875-76

Candy-stripe silk dress, back view of tailored sheath-like gown with low-set trained bustle. Detail of inside with vertical & horizontal tape ties, holding dress at centre back. Deep hem of coarse stiff white muslin. Pleated muslin, lace edged round hem. Pocket on inside. Study of the 'tournure,' polite name for bustle in 1876. *Snowshill Collection*

very neat matching joins

dart

double inverted pleat

April 1876 from The Ladies' Treasury

21" centre back

seam

TOURNURE of cambric from The Ladies' Treasury 1876

steel half-hoops

worn under a trained robe

satin panels centre back length

side

9"

front 8"

10"

satin pleated

satin panels lined stiff black muslin

seams

lace on stiffly pleated cream muslin

bound in woollen braid

'Long trains, even for ordinary walking purposes, are universally worn, these must be held up with one hand, or thrown *à l'Amazone* over one arm.' (*The Ladies' Treasury*, 1876.) With the increasing use of the sewing-machine, dresses are adorned with a variety of pleats, fringes,

239

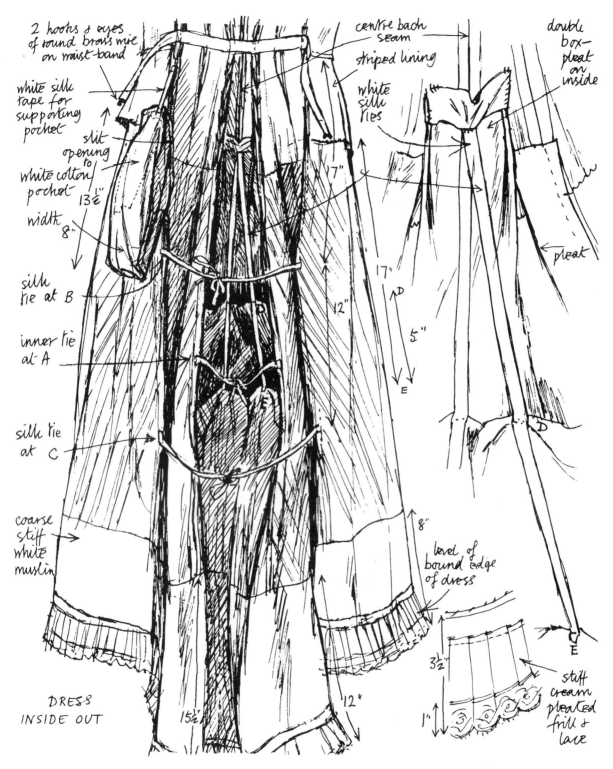

2 hooks & eyes of round brass wire on waist-band

white silk tape for supporting pocket

slit opening to white cotton pocket

13½

width 8"

silk tie at B

inner tie at A

silk tie at C

coarse stiff white muslin

DRESS INSIDE OUT

15½

centre back seam

striped lining

white silk ties

7"

17"

12"

5"

D

E

8"

level of bound edge of dress

12"

double box-pleat on inside

pleat

D

E

3½"

1"

stiff cream pleated frill & lace

and frills. Various materials are used on one dress, of perhaps the same colour or stronger contrast; colours in dresses tend to become brighter. During 1876 it was considered very fashionable to have an elaborate pocket on the outside.

240

1880–82

Printed cotton day dress, white with sprig pattern of red rose buds and fawn (faded green ?). Tunic dress with wide pleated apron front, over separate pleated skirt. Low draped bustle, tape ties inside; all machine-sewn, a Lancashire cotton. *Worn by Mrs Walsh of Lancashire, mother of Mrs Alfred Coley of Birmingham.* Miss Nora Hawker

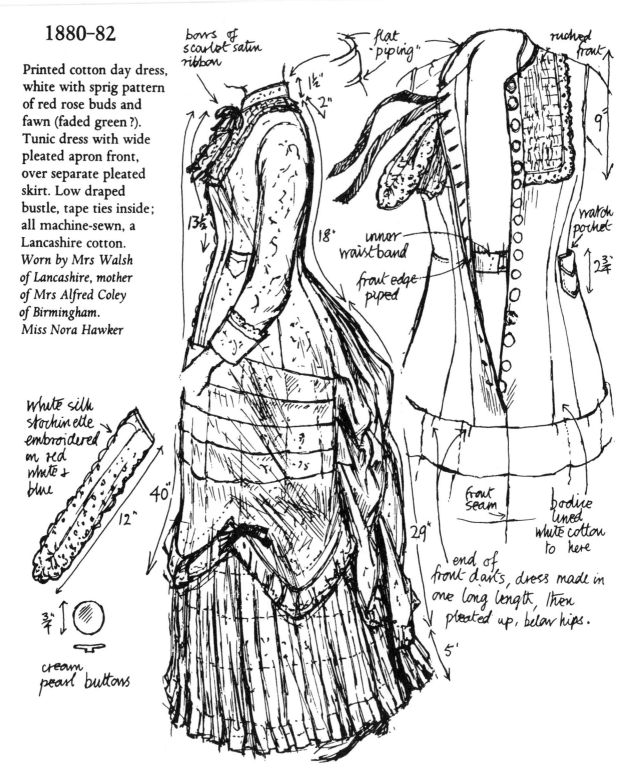

bows of scarlet satin ribbon

flat piping

ruched front

1½"

2"

9"

13½"

18"

inner waistband

front edge piped

watch pocket

2¾"

white silk stockinette embroidered in red white & blue

12"

40"

29"

front seam

bodice lined white cotton to here

end of front darts, dress made in one long length, then pleated up, below hips.

5'

¾"

cream pearl buttons

The square neckline of the '70's is still found on this summer dress of the early '80's. It has the fashionable standing collar, later to become higher and boned, and which is worn until *c.* 1911. The front-fastening tunic dress has the apron front with pleated line at the hip, with

a hint down at the side of the 'pannier' skirt, soon to be revived. The draperies at the back are caught up by tape ties inside. The box-pleated separate skirt is short, without a train, a style which appeared in 1878 for walking dresses.

1880-82

Printed cotton day dress, white sprig pattern. Tunic top, pleated front, small draped bustle, with separate pleated skirt. Satin ribbons of red, frills embroidered in red, white and blue trim the dress. Pocket in skirt at side back. Detail of pleating with inside view of dress, showing sets of tape ties.
Miss Nora Hawker

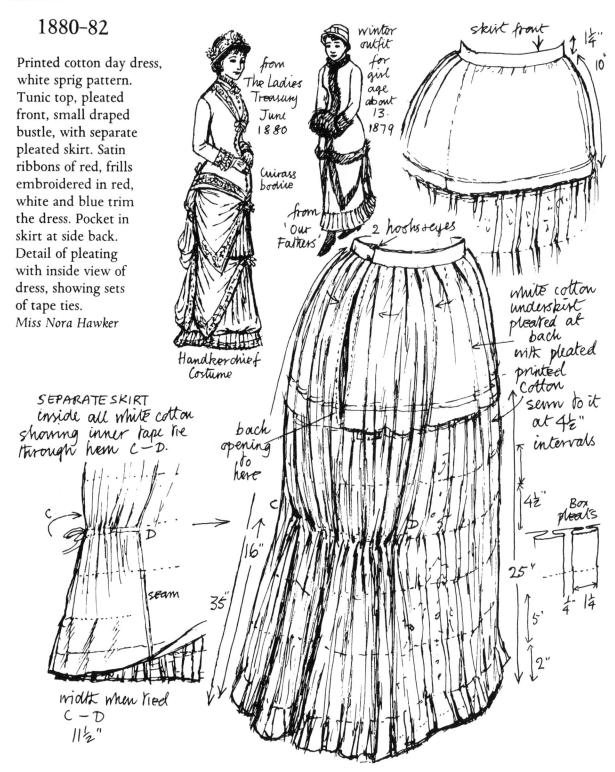

from The Ladies Treasury June 1880

Cuirass bodice

from 'Our Fathers'

Handkerchief Costume

winter outfit for girl age about 13. 1879

skirt front

1¼"

10"

2 hooks & eyes

white cotton underskirt pleated at back with pleated printed cotton sewn to it at 4½" intervals

4½"

25"

5"

2"

Box pleats

¼ 1¼

back opening to here

16"

35"

C

D

SEPARATE SKIRT
inside all white cotton showing inner tape tie through hem C – D.

C

D

seam

width when tied
C – D
11½"

Trained dresses are still worn in 1879 and early '80's for garden parties or evening wear, but by the '80's the trainless dress is usual for ordinary day wear. The pointed line to the draped over-skirt or tunic is very popular, and is called the 'handkerchief costume.' The tape ties

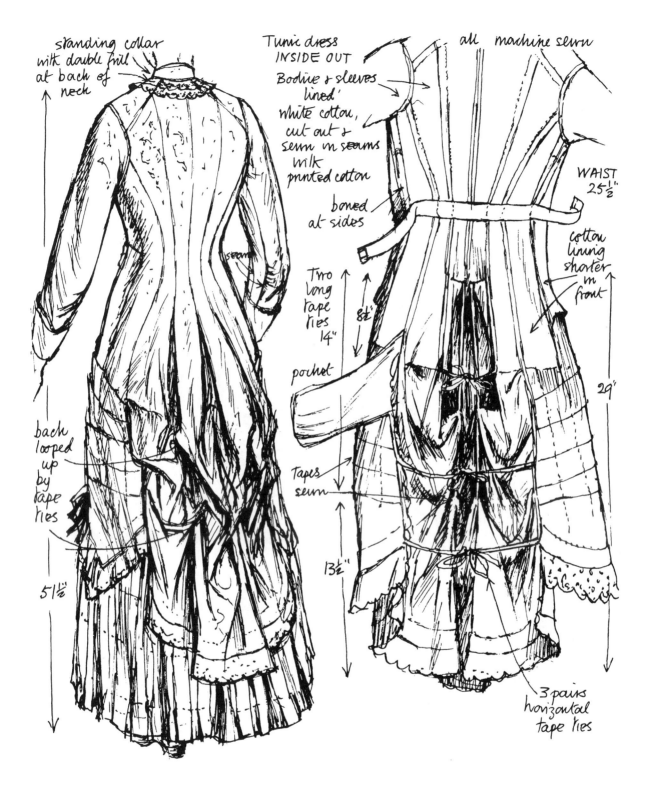

standing collar
with double frill
at back of
neck

Tunic dress
INSIDE OUT
Bodice & sleeves
lined'
white cotton,
cut out &
sewn in seams
with
printed cotton

boned
at sides

all machine sewn

WAIST
25½"

cotton
lining
shorter
in
front

seam

Two
long
tape
ties
14"

8¼"

29"

pocket

back
looped
up
by
tape
ties

Tapes
sewn

51½"

13½"

3 pairs
horizontal
tape ties

inside these dresses appear very involved, but they consist of pairs of tapes drawing the skirt tightly round the knees, with vertical tapes looping up the bustle. By 1883 sleeves on day dresses are shorter above the wrist.

Grey cotton day dress, printed in grey lines giving a watered-silk effect. Cuirasse bodice, skirt draped, ruched, and with pleated frills at hem, bottom frill of bright red cotton. Sheath dress, tie-back skirt draped from hip to mid-calf. Puffed low bustle with inside tape ties. Sleeves with ruched band from wrist to elbow. Back-fastened.
Snowshill Collection

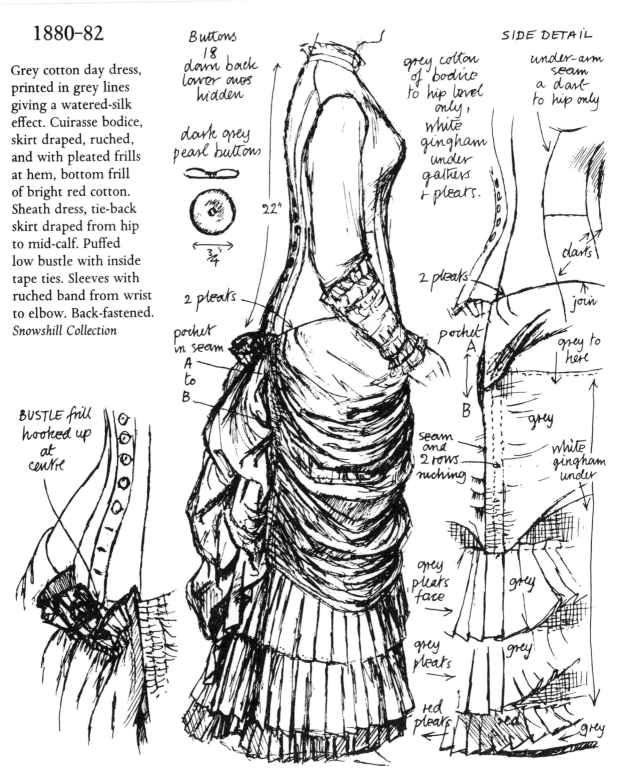

Buttons
18
down back
lower ones
hidden

dark grey
pearl buttons

22"

¾"

2 pleats

pocket
in seam
A
to
B

BUSTLE frill
hooked up
at
centre

grey cotton
of bodice
to hip level
only,
white
gingham
under
gathers
+ pleats.

2 pleats

pocket
A
↓
B

seam
and
2 rows
ruching

grey
pleats
face →

grey
pleats →

red
pleats ←

SIDE DETAIL

under-arm
seam
a dart
to hip only

darts

join

grey to
here

grey

white
gingham
under

grey

grey

red

grey

Yet another of the dresses folded away in the chest of drawers. At first glance it appeared what it is, just another cheap little cotton dress; not until it was put on a 'figure' did it emerge in all its charm of sweeping feminine curves and rich drapery. A fine example of the line of

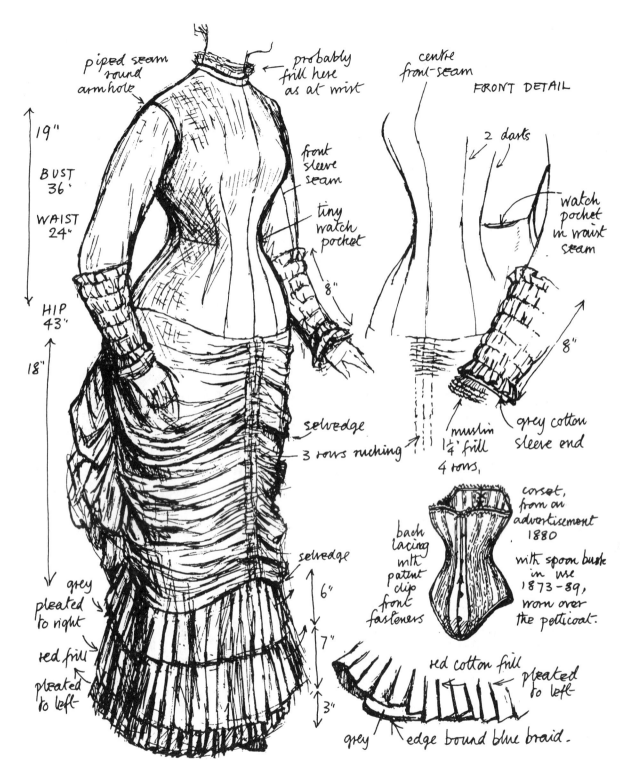

piped seam round armhole

probably frill here as at wrist

centre front-seam

FRONT DETAIL

19"

BUST 36'

WAIST 24"

HIP 43"

18"

front sleeve seam

tiny watch pocket

8"

2 darts

watch pocket in waist seam

8"

selvedge

3 rows ruching

muslin 1¼' frill 4 rows,

grey cotton sleeve end

selvedge

6"

7"

3"

grey pleated to right

red frill

pleated to left

back lacing with patent clip front fasteners

corset, from an advertisement 1880

with spoon busk in use 1873-89, worn over the petticoat.

red cotton frill

pleated to left

grey

edge bound blue braid.

the early '80's. *The Ladies' Treasury*, 1880, comments: 'the amount of work in this dress can hardly be conceived' (fashion-plate, p. 247). The corset advertisement shows how the figure was controlled; stockings were still gartered.

1880-82

Grey cotton day dress with cuirasse bodice, and ruched, draped, and pleated skirt, sewn to white cotton ground with grey and red frills at hem. Back-fastening dress with buttons, neck to hips. Inside view showing tape ties, with pocket set in bustle folds. Child's pink cotton dress, with ruching, frills, and 'bustle.'
Snowshill Collection

from T. Stanley Brown, family photograph of 1880

white frill

brooch

white lace cuff

watch pocket

gold chain

velvet

from The Ladies' Treasury June 1880

Cambric dress

silk frills

silk dress

top neck fastening hook & eye

piped

DETAIL of TAPES under back drapery

tapes sewn to grey cotton

GREY COTTON DRESS

pocket

2 pleats

4 pairs of tape ties

tapes sewn to grey cotton

pocket

INSIDE Tape tie

1st grey pleated frill

white gingham

all dress grey cotton

red frill

These tie-back skirts restrict movement as much as the hobble skirt does in 1910, and the effect is felt on the underwear. Voluminous petticoats and the long, wide chemise could no longer be worn under these fitting dresses; instead a new garment, 'combinations,' emerged,

247

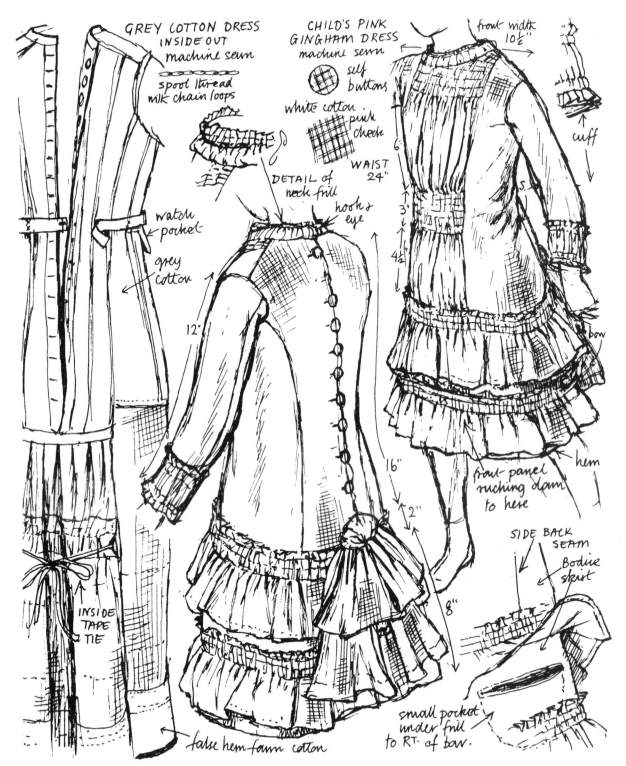

GREY COTTON DRESS
INSIDE OUT
machine sewn

spool thread
milk chain loops

watch
pocket

grey
cotton

12"

INSIDE
TAPE
TIE

false hem fawn cotton

DETAIL of
neck frill

hooks
eye

16"

2"

CHILD'S PINK
GINGHAM DRESS
machine sewn

self
buttons

white cotton
pink
check

WAIST
24"

front width
10½"

cuff

6

3

4½

S

bow

front panel
ruching down
to here

hem

SIDE BACK
SEAM

Bodice
skirt

8"

small pocket
under frill
to RT. of bow.

which combined both chemise and drawers in one. The touch of bright red at the hem of
this dress is a glance backward at the red petticoats glimpsed in the '60's. The child's dress
is included, it is so like the woman's.

1870's–80's

Open-leg drawers, of white cotton, long, below knee; with tucks, frills, and broderie anglaise. Cotton combinations, shaped to figure, legs wide and embroidered. Button fastened inside leg and on shoulder.
from Miss A. Eccles to Personal Collection

1884–88

Dull-red cotton bustle or 'tournure,' or a 'dress-improver.'
Personal Collection

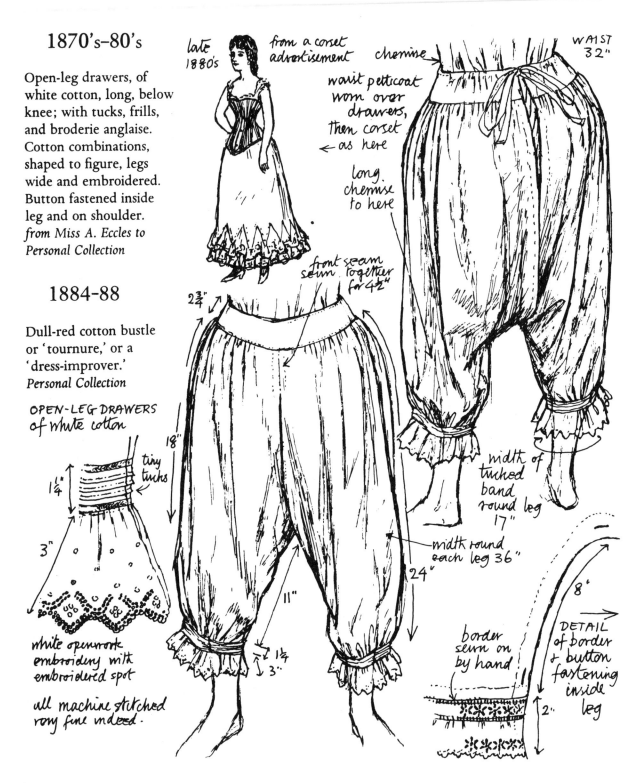

late 1880's

from a corset advertisement

chemise

waist petticoat worn over drawers, then corset ←as here

long chemise to here

WAIST 32"

front seam sewn together for 4½"

2¾"

OPEN-LEG DRAWERS of white cotton

tiny tucks

1¼"

18"

3"

11"

24"

1¼"
3"

width of tucked band round leg 17"

width round each leg 36"

white openwork embroidery with embroidered spot

all machine stitched very fine indeed.

8"

border sewn on by hand

DETAIL of border & button fastening inside leg

2"

Open-leg drawers, worn from quite early in the 19th c., particularly by children, were not generally used until the crinoline of the mid-1850's appeared. Women up till then had mostly found the long chemise and many petticoats quite adequate. Length of leg varied, but such

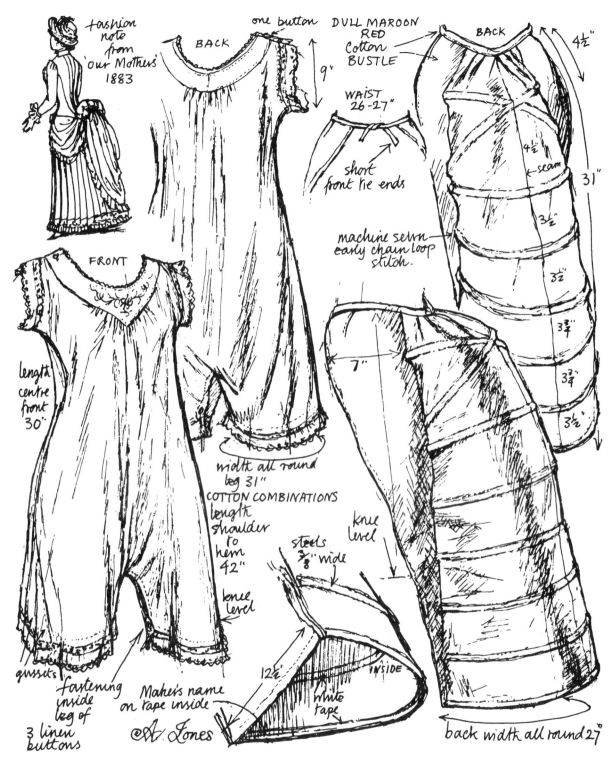

fashion note from 'Our Mothers' 1883

BACK

one button

9"

DULL MAROON RED Cotton BUSTLE

WAIST 26-27"

short front tie ends

machine sewn early chain loop stitch.

BACK

4½"

4½"

← seam

3½"

31"

3½"

3¾"

3¾"

3½"

FRONT

length centre front 30"

width all round leg 31"

COTTON COMBINATIONS
length shoulder to hem 42"

knee level

7"

knee level

steels ⅜" wide

12½"

INSIDE

white tape

gussets

fastening inside leg of 3 linen buttons

Maker's name on tape inside
A. Jones

back width all round 27"

drawers were worn until c. 1900, though side-fastening knickers were also in use in the '70's. Combinations appear c. 1877, and are far less bulky under the fitting dresses. Suspenders were not attached to corsets until c. 1901.

1885-87

Striped cream satin wedding-dress, boned sleeveless bodice, skirt separate with draped over-skirt and gathered back drapery over bustle of steel half-hoops and bustle pad, sewn inside skirt. Embroidered net over-skirt. Plain satin under-skirt covered in net at front, with deep pleated frill at hem. *from Miss A. Chatwin to Personal Collection*

neck and sleeves altered

front lacing

WAIST 24"

boned darts

embroidered net, over under-skirt

back width 9¾"

7½

12"

1½

5"

self piped edges

striped satin

understkirt of net, over plain satin, under embroidered net skirt.

ruched frill, at hem of understkirt

embroidered net gathered at side waist.

c 1883

from family photograph of T. Stanley Brown

lace frills

light floral pattern

piped edges

A

B

C

lace frills

floral pattern

The sheath-like dress of the early '80's gives way to a new form of bustle which projects sharply out at the back *c.* 1883-88, with drapery looped up over the hips, with rich folds at the back of the skirt, held in position with tapes and elastic. High necklines are usual; only

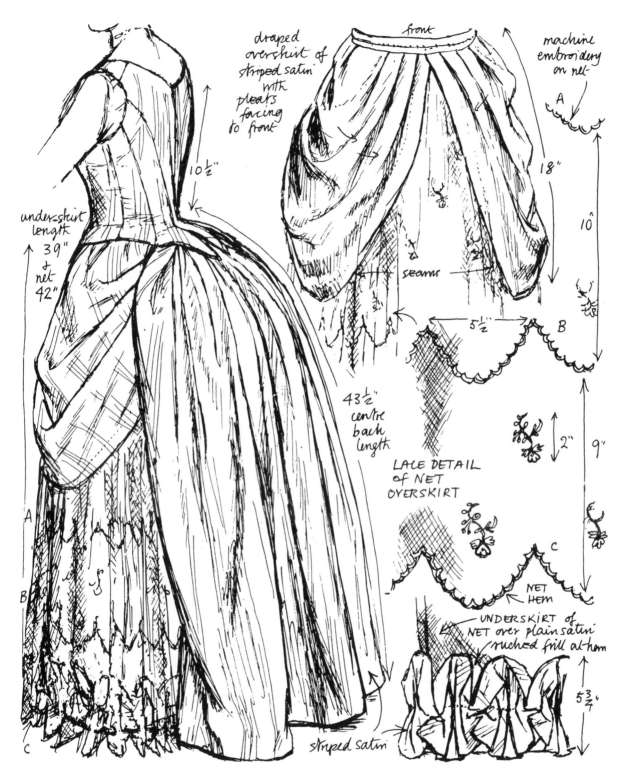

draped overskirt of striped satin with pleats facing to front

front

machine embroidery on net

A

10½"

18"

10°

under-skirt length 39" + net 42"

seams

5½"

B

9"

2"

43½" centre back length

LACE DETAIL of NET OVERSKIRT

A

B

C

NET HEM

C

UNDERSKIRT of NET over plain satin ruched frill at hem

5¾"

striped satin

evening dresses after *c.* 1885 are low-necked, when some dresses are also sleeveless. Three-quarter-length sleeves become fashionable after 1883, when frills on the sleeve, at neck, and on bodice front are popular.

1885–87

Striped cream satin wedding-dress. Detail of front-laced boned bodice, and skirt with draped panniers over hips; full gathering of back skirt over bustle of steel half-hoops and pad of white cotton filled with straw. Inside of skirt showing tape ties on elastic, and pocket at side back. *from Miss A. Chatwin to Personal Collection*

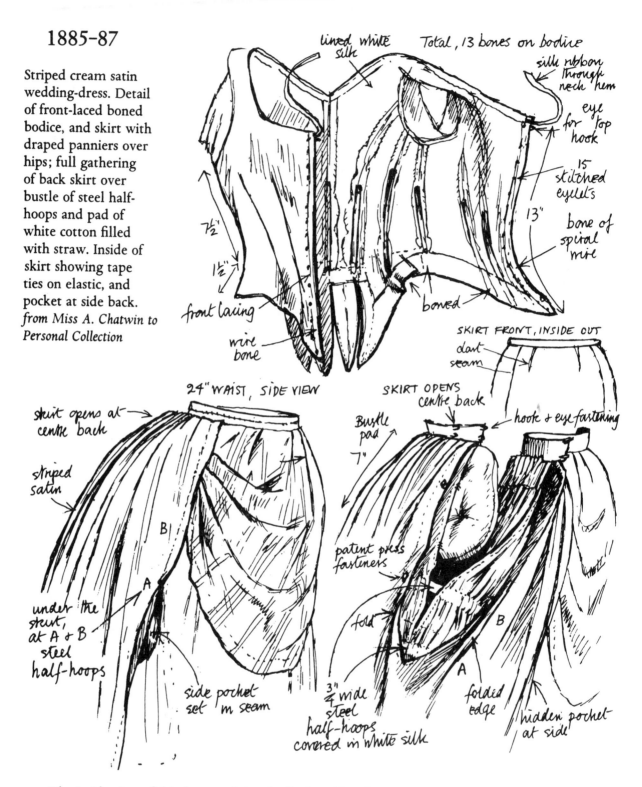

lined white silk

Total, 13 bones on bodice

silk ribbon through neck hem

eye for top hook

15 stitched eyelets

13"

bone of spiral wire

7½"

1½"

front lacing

wire bone

boned

SKIRT FRONT, INSIDE OUT

dart seam

SKIRT OPENS centre back

hook & eye fastening

24" WAIST, SIDE VIEW

skirt opens at centre back

striped satin

B

A

under the skirt, at A & B steel half-hoops

side pocket set in seam

Bustle pad 7"

patent press fasteners

fold

3" wide steel half-hoops covered in white silk

B

A

folded edge

hidden pocket at side

The inside view of this dress explains the 'built-in' bustle construction. Not all dresses had this, but had a separate bustle (p. 250). It is likely that this wedding-dress was used later for evening wear; it is much worn and in a frail condition. On day dresses the standing collar is usual,

253

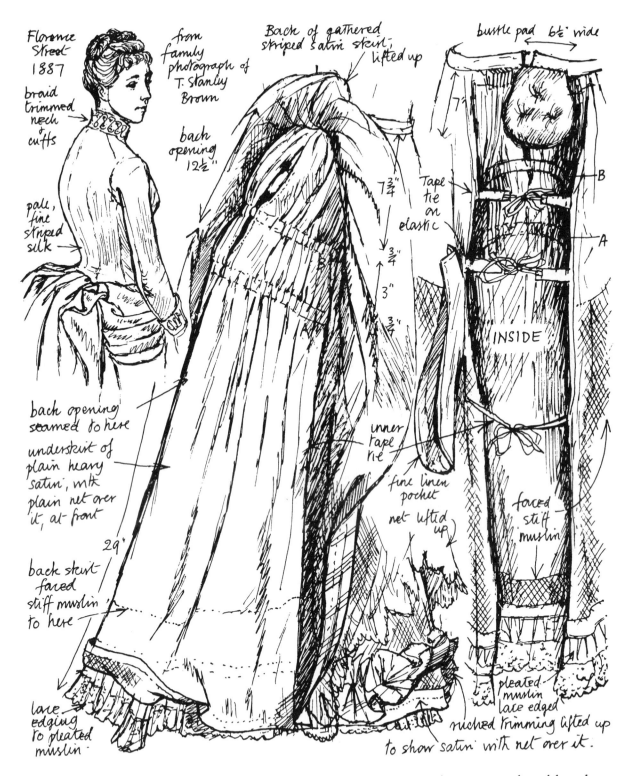

Florence
Street
1887

braid
trimmed
neck
&
cuffs

from
family
photograph of
T. Stanley
Brown

back
opening
12½"

Back of gathered
striped satin skirt,
lifted up

bustle pad 6½" wide

pale,
fine
striped
silk

7"

7¾"

Tape
tie
on
elastic

B

A

¾"

3"

¾"

INSIDE

back opening
seamed to here

underskirt of
plain heavy
satin, with
plain net over
it, at front

inner
tape
tie

fine linen
pocket
net lifted
up)

faced
stiff
muslin

29"

back skirt
faced
stiff muslin
to here

lace
edging
to pleated
muslin.

pleated
muslin
lace edged

ruched trimming lifted up
to show satin with net over it.

and remains in fashion for the next twenty years. Braid trimmings become popular, although at first all the emphasis is on the skirt with its pleats and drapery, for day and evening wear.

254

1889-90

Striped dress of dark blue satin and fawn open-mesh silk net; with dark blue velvet front to bodice and three panels on right side-front of skirt, with double and triple inverted pleats. High-necked bodice, lined and fully boned. Small puffs at top of sleeve, fawn cotton under-skirt sewn in.

from Miss A. Chatwin to Personal Collection

sleeves & bodice lined fawn cotton

altered at neck fastening

centre back seam

18"

16"

WAIST 24"

side-back opening to A, pocket A-B

Total 13 bones

SKIRT INSIDE OUT

BACK

B

F

E

fawn cotton under-skirt

B

dark blue satin & fawn net stripes

double inverted pleat seam in place & triple inverted pleat seam to knee level.

tape

1"   1 1/10"

golden-fawn silk net open texture

centre back 42"

pocket brown cotton alpaca

A

B

3 dark blue velvet panels

Striped dresses continued in fashion throughout the '80's, with the use, as in this dress, of two materials. The sleeves, still worn short above the wrist since 1883, are cut fitting and shaped to the elbow, seen well here. One feature worth noting is the extra puff or fullness

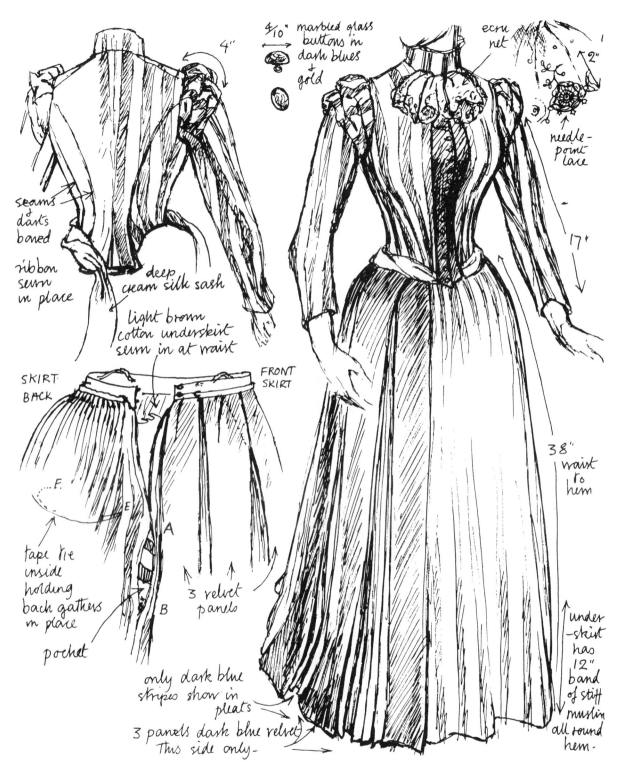

$^{4}/_{10}$" marbled glass buttons in dark blues & gold

ecru net

2"

needle-point lace

17"

seams & darts boned

ribbon sewn in place

deep cream silk sash

light brown cotton underskirt sewn in at waist

SKIRT BACK

FRONT SKIRT

F.

E

A

B

tape tie inside holding back gathers in place

pocket

3 velvet panels

38" waist to hem

under-skirt has 12" band of stiff muslin all round hem.

only dark blue stripes show in pleats

3 panels dark blue velvet this side only-

on the sleeves at the shoulder, indicating where the interest will be centred during the next few years. The skirt, still closely gathered at the back, hangs uncluttered by draperies. A small bustle is probably worn underneath.

256

c. 1890

Pale grey flannel dress, pinky-fawn tartan of thicker flecked thread and thin pink line. Separate bodice and skirt. Sash and bow of golden-fawn corded silk ribbon. Trimming on bodice of golden-fawn braid, edged in bronze gilt beads. *Commander Hart*

Bronze kid shoes with bronze and gilt beads. *from Miss A. Chatwin to Personal Collection*

Back width 9¼
↑ length
15"
S

golden-fawn BRAID edged with bronze gilt beads, braid spirals at wrist

3 dull gilt buttons on cuff

seam

seams

darts

inside pocket, supported by tape from waist

front

↑5" pocket, not set in seam

seam

A
B

SHOES of BRONZE KID. edges cotton bound

2"

8½" cut - bronze

very tiny gilt beads

2⅝

suède finish

A B

width A - B 2⅝"

skirt back 39"

seam

elastic inside from A to B keeping skirt front-right and back gathers in place

A

B

centre back seam

elastic inside on seam

SKIRT LINED golden-fawn cotton, seam in at seams with cloth, similar to bodice.

A winter day dress for a small woman. Very well tailored, with every seam and dart in the bodice boned; fully lined with elastic tie at skirt back, keeping the folds firmly in position. The medium-high neckline, rounded yoke decoration on the bodice, with its flat pleated

dress protectors · tape loops · fawn cotton facing · lined fawn & white cotton · back collar · front collar · 1½" ↕

ruched "puffed" bands between braid · tiny watch pocket in orange silk · 9" · 34½" · 14"

Total 12 bones in bodice

back sleeve seam 22"

WAIST 24½" · fawn cotton · hook for skirt · maker's name in gold (faded)

darts

front sleeve seam 16"

tiny beads of bronze gilt · each side of braid · braid. · Bodice gathered & ruched. · pinky-fawn stripes

line pale pink on grey

sleeve full under arm

SASH & BOW of golden fawn corded silk ribbon, folded round waist

Bodice pleats face to centre → · 17 hooks with 5 metal eyes, & upper ones stitched

skirt front 36"

seam from centre back

and gathered front, are all found on dresses of this time; the sleeves too show signs of increasing fullness on the shoulder. The bronze kid decorated shoes of c. 1890–1900 would be worn with dark brown silk stockings.

April 15th, 1890

Cream silk and net wedding-dress, worn by Miss Hawker's mother. Silk braid trimming, ruched silk gauze & finely pleated frills at hem. Separate skirt and bodice, both parts mounted on white cotton. Bodice is fully boned, fastening at left front. Skirt with taffeta frill at hem, fastens centre back. Delicate net sleeves.
Miss Nora Hawker

Flat silk braid, pattern different back from front

FRONT BODICE DETAIL

7 rows of ruched gauze

14½

gathered gauze over

spotted net

net over silk

dart

frill of gauze

braid on net

skirt side back 43"

silk cord round braid

6 bands of ruched gauze on net.

centre front

NET over SILK, sewn in at seams

also silk & cotton. sewn in together

hem of silk

INSIDE of SILK SKIRT which is mounted on strong fine white cotton sateen facing to Taffeta

Taffeta frill

edge pinked

3 rows ruching

edge scalloped & pinked

frill at hem

plain hem

Trailing skirts return, with increasing emphasis and width at the hemline, though fullness remains at the centre back. A taffeta flounce inside at the hem adds both crispness and a soft rustle to the skirt, which by the late '90's is usually silk-lined. Braid trimmings are used

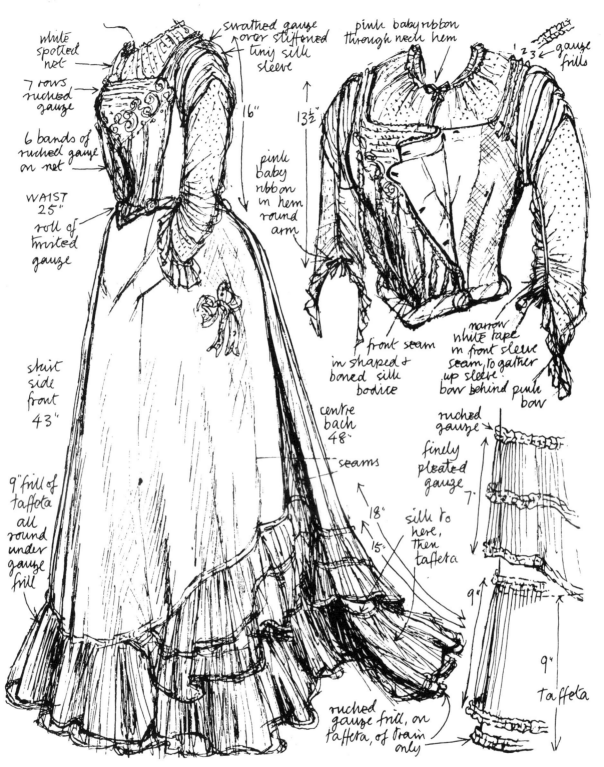

white spotted net

7 rows ruched gauze

6 bands of ruched gauze on net

swathed gauze over stiffened tiny silk sleeve

pink baby ribbon through neck hem

'1 2 3' gauze frills

16"

13½"

WAIST 25"
roll of twisted gauze

pink baby ribbon in hem round arm

skirt side front 43"

9" frill of taffeta all round under gauze frill

centre back 48"

seams

front seam in shaped & boned silk bodice

narrow white tape in front sleeve seam, to gather up sleeve bow behind pink bow

ruched gauze

finely pleated gauze

7.

18"

silk to here, then taffeta

15"

9"

9" taffeta

ruched gauze frill, on taffeta, of train only

on dresses, jackets, skirts, and capes in early '90's. It is interesting that the fashion of fastening bodice in front and skirt at the back is continued in Edwardian dress, even when later it is no longer made in two parts.

1890

Cream silk and net wedding-dress, worn by Miss Hawker's mother. Showing skirt and bodice fastening. White cambric petticoat, also belonging to her, but a little later in date, fastening at side front. Lace frill at hem.
Miss Nora Hawker

1890's silver purse with inside of kid. *from Miss A. Eccles to Personal Collection*

side-front fastening

3 hooks & eyes

WHITE CAMBRIC PETTICOAT

inside tape loop at centre back

WAIST 26½

evening dress

from 'Punch' February 1891

¾"

11½"

seam

length centre back 44½"

15/16"

4¼"

2¼"

3½"

engraved lines

3 5

all inside of fine tan kid

⅛"

SILVER PURSE & chain with finger ring.

White lace frill, machine made on net.

lace frill 4½"

7"

4"

cambric frill

hem

front length 41½"

seam

seam

centre back seam & gussets

The deep back pleat and long, sweeping hemline make the back of the skirt very heavy, and it therefore is hooked to the inner waistband of the bodice. The silk part of the bodice is well tailored and fitted and is fully boned, but the net is left loose and pouched in front;

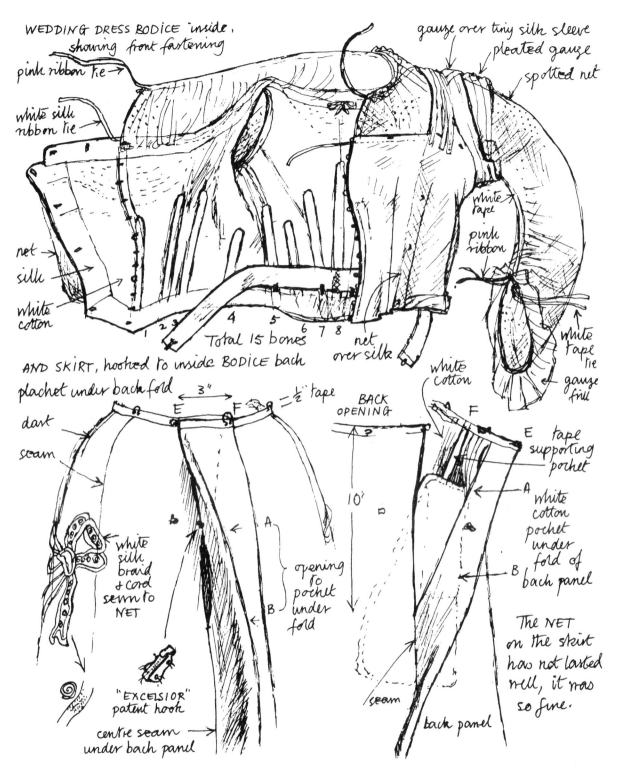

WEDDING DRESS BODICE *inside*, showing front fastening

pink ribbon tie →

white silk ribbon tie

net

silk

white cotton

1 2 3   4   5   6 7 8

Total 15 bones

gauze over tiny silk sleeve

pleated gauze

spotted net

white tape

pink ribbon

net over silk

white tape tie

gauze frill

AND SKIRT, hooked to inside BODICE back placket under back fold

dart

seam

3"

A E F G = 1½" tape

white silk braid + cord sewn to NET

"EXCELSIOR" patent hook

centre seam under back panel

opening to pocket under fold

A
B

BACK OPENING

10'

white cotton

E tape supporting pocket

A white cotton pocket under fold of back panel

B

The NET on the skirt has not lasted well, it was so fine.

seam

back panel

this becomes quite a feature of dresses during the first few years of the 20th century. Various beautiful little guinea purses are made, of metal or mesh; those of the '90's have a finger ring in the handle.

1892-93

Pale yellow-green figured silk evening dress, worn by Miss Francis Louise Walton of Birmingham at age of 17 years. She was later Mrs Arthur McKewan. Bodice is lined and fully boned, back-fastened with trimming of brilliant orange velvet ribbon and cream lace. Separate skirt, lined and back-fastened.
Miss Nora Hawker

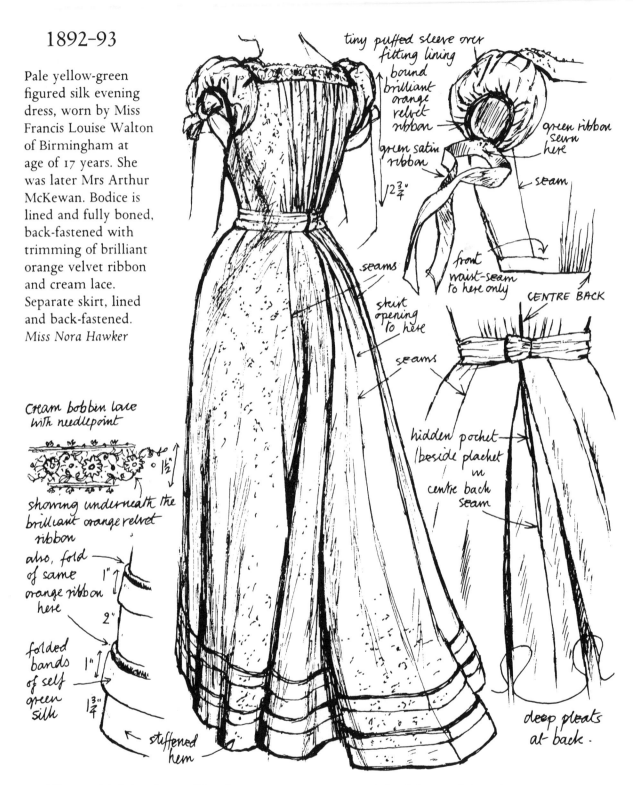

tiny puffed sleeve over fitting lining

bound brilliant orange velvet ribbon

green satin ribbon

green ribbon sewn here

seam

12¾"

front waist-seam to here only

CENTRE BACK

seams

skirt opening to here

seams

hidden pocket beside placket in centre back seam

deep pleats at back.

Cream bobbin lace with needlepoint

1½

showing underneath the brilliant orange velvet ribbon

also, fold of same orange ribbon here

1"

2"

1"

1¾"

folded bands of self green silk

← stiffened hem

The youthful simplicity of this dress is very attractive, and the delicacy of the colour is enhanced by the touch of brilliance in the orange ribbon. Although the bodice appears plain, it is very carefully tailored; each seam and hidden dart is boned. The fact that this dress is so well

263

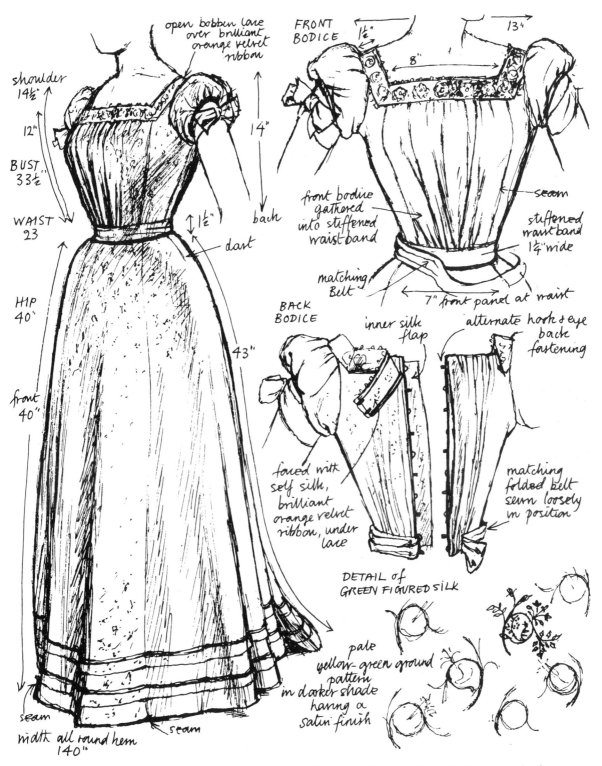

shoulder 14½

12"

BUST 33½

WAIST 23

HIP 40"

front 40"

open bobbin lace over brilliant orange velvet ribbon

14"

back

1½"

dart

seam

seam

width all round hem 140"

43"

FRONT BODICE

1½"

13"

8"

front bodice gathered into stiffened waist-band

seam

stiffened waist-band 1¼" wide

matching Belt

7" front panel at waist

BACK BODICE

inner silk flap

alternate hook & eye back fastening

faced with self silk, brilliant orange velvet ribbon, under lace

matching folded belt sewn loosely in position

DETAIL of GREEN FIGURED SILK

pale yellow-green ground pattern in darker shade having a satin finish

lined has helped to preserve it. The small puff sleeves have a short fitting straight lining. Like many evening dresses, the bodice is back-fastened; day dresses are usually fastened in front.

1892-93

Pale yellow-green figured silk evening dress worn by Miss Francis Louise Walton, showing inside of boned bodice and of lined, gored skirt, with pocket in back seam and frill at hem, of pleated muslin and lace. Separate, bright orange watered-silk petticoat, fastening at side, with ruching and frill at hem.
Miss Nora Hawker

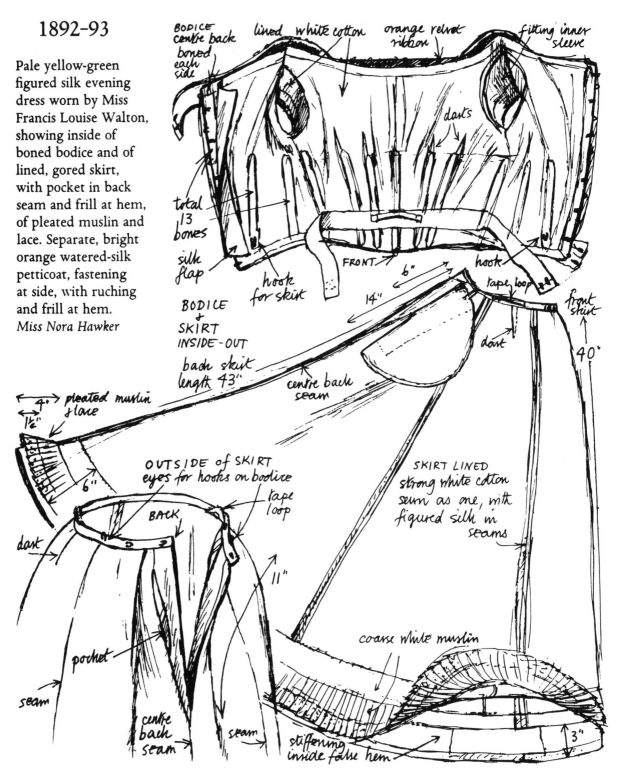

BODICE centre back
boned each side
lined white cotton
orange velvet ribbon
fitting inner sleeve
darts
total 13 bones
silk flap
hook for skirt
FRONT
6"
14"
hook
tape loop
front skirt
40"
BODICE & SKIRT INSIDE-OUT
back skirt length 43"
centre back seam
dart
4" pleated muslin & lace
1½"
6"
OUTSIDE of SKIRT
eyes for hooks on bodice
tape loop
BACK
dart
11"
SKIRT LINED strong white cotton sewn as one, with figured silk in seams
pocket
seam
centre back seam
seam
coarse white muslin
stiffening inside false hem
3"

The square neckline on this evening dress shows the increasing interest in width, some day dresses having a square or round yoked effect, achieved with trimming, not construction (p. 258). The separate orange silk taffeta petticoat, although not worn with this dress, is of

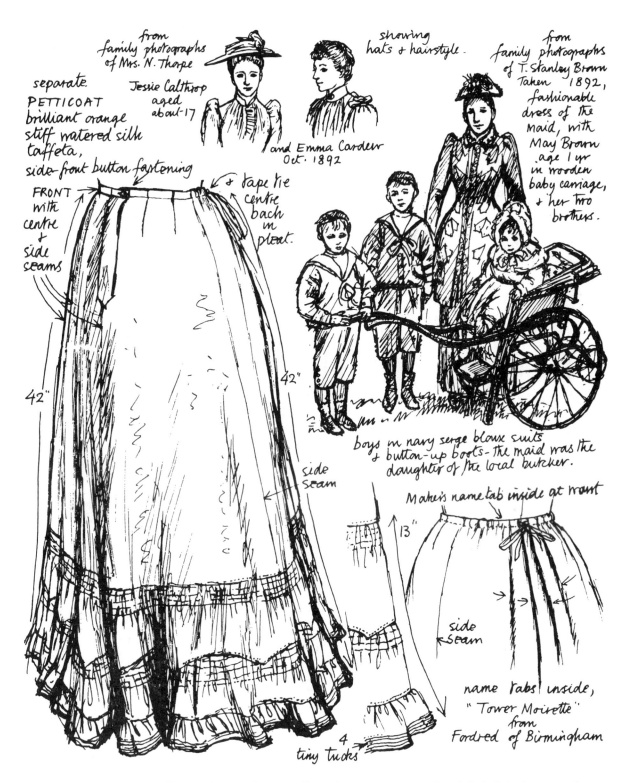

from
family photographs
of Mrs. N. Thorpe

Jessie Calthrop
aged
about 17

showing
hats & hairstyle.

and Emma Carder
Oct. 1892

from
family photographs
of T. Stanley Brown
Taken 1892,
fashionable
dress of the
maid, with
May Brown
age 1 yr
in wooden
baby carriage,
& her two
brothers.

separate.
PETTICOAT
brilliant orange
stiff watered silk
taffeta,
side-front button fastening

FRONT
with
centre
& side
seams

& tape tie
centre
back
in
pleat.

42"

42"

side
Seam

boys in navy serge blouse suits
& button-up boots – the maid was the
daughter of the local butcher.

Maker's name tab inside at waist

13"

side
Seam

4
tiny tucks

name tabs inside,
"Tower Moirette"
from
Fordred of Birmingham

a type that could well have been; this one fits a larger woman. The delightful photographs of 1892 show the fashionable hair style and hat, and the new raised sleeve. The maid can now be almost as well dressed as her mistress.

1892

Cream silk wedding-dress, embroidered in cream beads and tiny pearls. Draped bodice front, large puffed sleeves. Separate long-trained skirt, all fully lined; bodice boned. Matching satin shoes. *worn by Mrs Elizabeth Bruce White on her marriage in Edinburgh to Professor Philip White of Bangor University; given by her daughter-in-law, Mrs Gwen White, to Personal Collection*

BACK centre width 10"

7"

Mrs Bruce White wearing the dress in 1889 before sleeves and the skirt-front were altered. From a family photograph.

19"

2 seam

SLEEVE DETAIL

deep tuck up to here

12" skirt side-back opening + tape tie inside on seam

4" tiny pocket in seam. double inverted pleat

back sleeve seam 14" long

hand-sewn gathers

bound hem to frill

folded edge

1"

5¾"

4¼" hem

seam

frill

side-back seam

hem of underskirt with pleated lace under.

dress hem, under frill

underside of Train

When this dress was worn at the wedding in 1889 the full upper part of the sleeve was caught in and lightly stitched to the lining, as shown in the figure study, but later, when really full sleeves became fashionable, the stitches were unpicked, and the upper part of the sleeves

BODICE
CENTRE
front

17"

BUST
32"

WAIST
24"

43"

top sleeve width
side-front
8"

8"

10"

skirt fastens
under fold
side-
back

hook & eye
fastening

skirt
length
side back,
with train
54"

embroidery
of cream beads
& pearls

fine gathering
on bodice

side
bodice
14"

tuck

sleeve
seam
10"

9
seam

A
B
C

This side
plain

A
B
C

inner
waist-band

2"
3 folds
of chiffon

DETAIL
of embroidery
on cuff
cream
beads

+ pearls

no left or right
foot-shaping

suède
finish

SHOES
of matching satin.

1"
5¾"

seams
pleated lace
under hem of underskirt.

10½"

10"

spread outward in rich folds, completing the outward movement from the seams of the bodice and the sweeping lines of the skirt. The front part of this skirt continues right round under the long folds of the train.

268

1892

Cream silk wedding-dress worn by Mrs E. Bruce White. Matching cream silk patterned jacket, trimmed with swansdown, large silk ribbon bows on shoulders; lined with cream figured cotton. Fitting back, straight front with small sleeve. Inside view of boned bodice, inside of skirt showing under-skirt, train, and trimming. *Personal Collection*

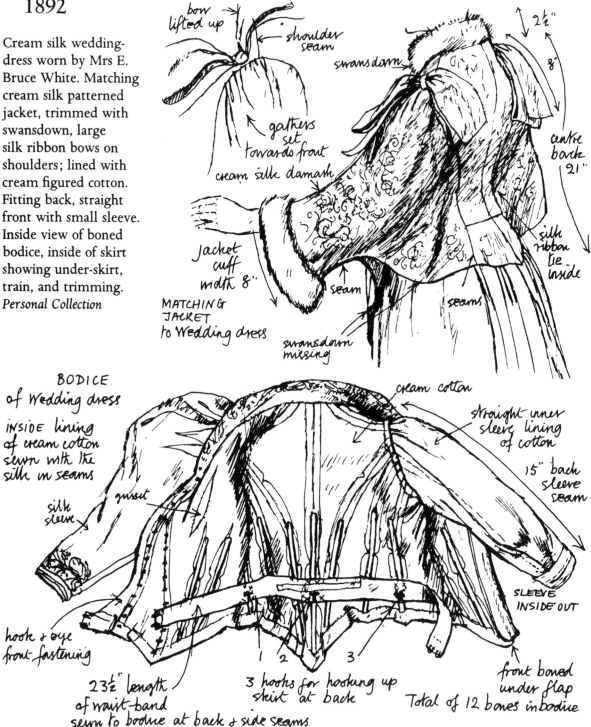

bow lifted up

shoulder seam

2½"

swansdown

8"

centre back 21"

gathers set towards front

cream silk damask

silk ribbon tie inside

Jacket cuff width 8"

seam

seams

MATCHING JACKET to Wedding dress

swansdown missing

BODICE of Wedding dress

INSIDE lining of cream cotton sewn with the silk in seams

cream cotton

straight inner sleeve lining of cotton

15" back sleeve seam

silk sleeve

gusset

hook & eye front fastening

SLEEVE INSIDE OUT

23½" length of waist-band sewn to bodice at back & side seams

3 hooks for hooking up skirt at back

1 2 3

front boned under flap

Total of 12 bones in bodice

The inside view of the skirt shows how the fullness of the train is controlled by the back skirt panel, also fully gathered, but held in place by tape ties and elastic. The upper part of the skirt was also altered; the draped front panel was unpicked and lifted, as shown, so that the

269

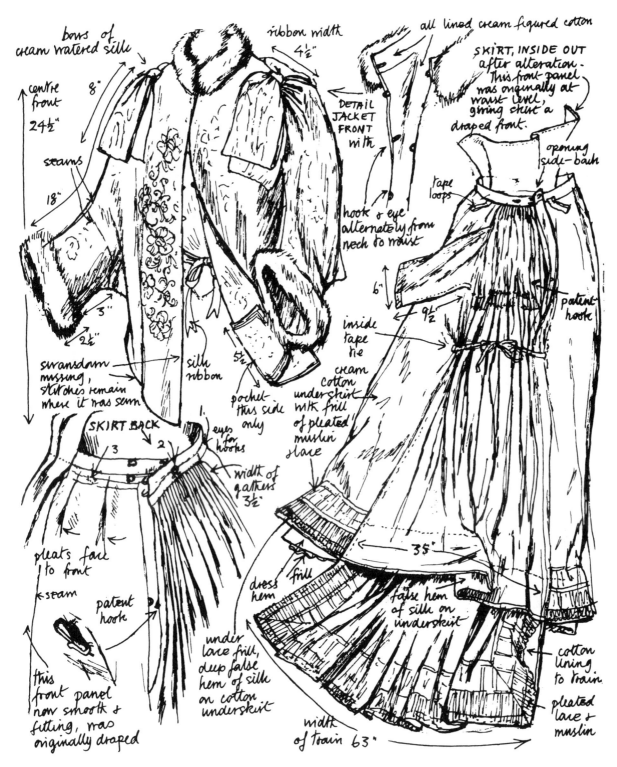

bows of cream watered silk

centre front 24½"

ribbon width 4½"

all lined cream figured cotton

SKIRT, INSIDE OUT after alteration. This front panel was originally at waist level, giving skirt a draped front.

8"

DETAIL JACKET FRONT with

opening side-back

tape loops

seams

18"

hook & eye alternately from neck to waist

6"

9½"

patent hook

3"

2½"

swansdown missing, stitches remain where it was sewn

silk ribbon

5½"

pocket — this side only

inside tape tie

cream cotton underskirt with frill of pleated muslin lace

SKIRT BACK

3   2

1.

eyes for hooks

width of gathers 3½"

35"

pleats face to front

seam

patent hook

dress hem

false hem of silk on underskirt

cotton lining to train

under lace frill, deep false hem of silk on cotton underskirt

pleated lace & muslin

this front panel now smooth & fitting, was originally draped

width of train 63"

skirt set smoothly round from side to side, but this extra piece from the front was never cut off. The skirt is hooked to the bodice waistband. The jacket, once with swansdown right round it, has the very fashionable shoulder-bows.

270

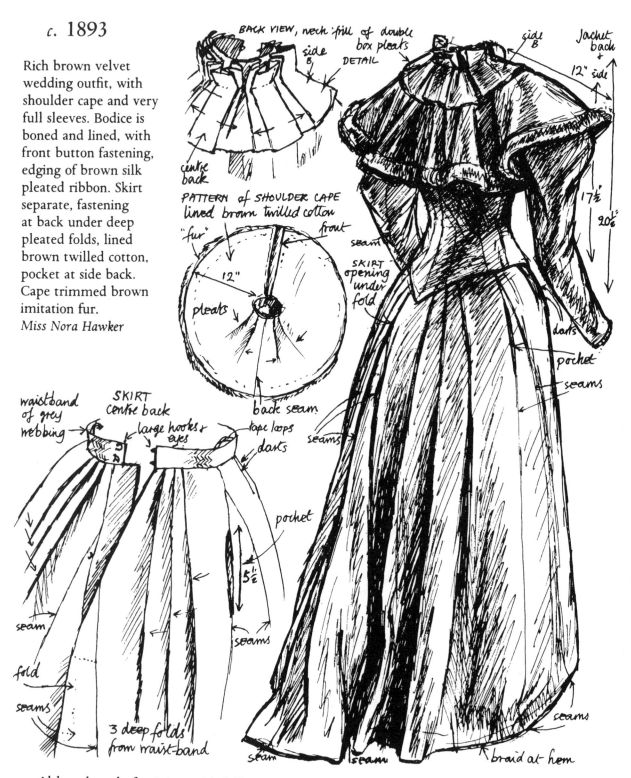

c. 1893

Rich brown velvet
wedding outfit, with
shoulder cape and very
full sleeves. Bodice is
boned and lined, with
front button fastening,
edging of brown silk
pleated ribbon. Skirt
separate, fastening
at back under deep
pleated folds, lined
brown twilled cotton,
pocket at side back.
Cape trimmed brown
imitation fur.
Miss Nora Hawker

BACK VIEW, neck frill of double box pleats DETAIL

side B

side B

centre back

PATTERN of SHOULDER CAPE
lined brown twilled cotton

"fur"

front

12"

pleats

back seam

side B

Jacket back +

12" side

17½

20½

seam

SKIRT opening under fold

darts

pocket

seams

seams

waistband of grey webbing

SKIRT centre back

large hooks & eyes

tape loops

darts

pocket

5½

seams

seam

fold

seams

3 deep folds from waist-band

seam

seam

seams

braid at hem

Although truly feminine, with full curves and tiny waist, this outfit is strictly tailored, with
quite a masculine touch about the closely buttoned front of the bodice, high neckline, and
rather severe collar. The woman's popular tailored coat 'must fit snug everywhere,' to quote

271

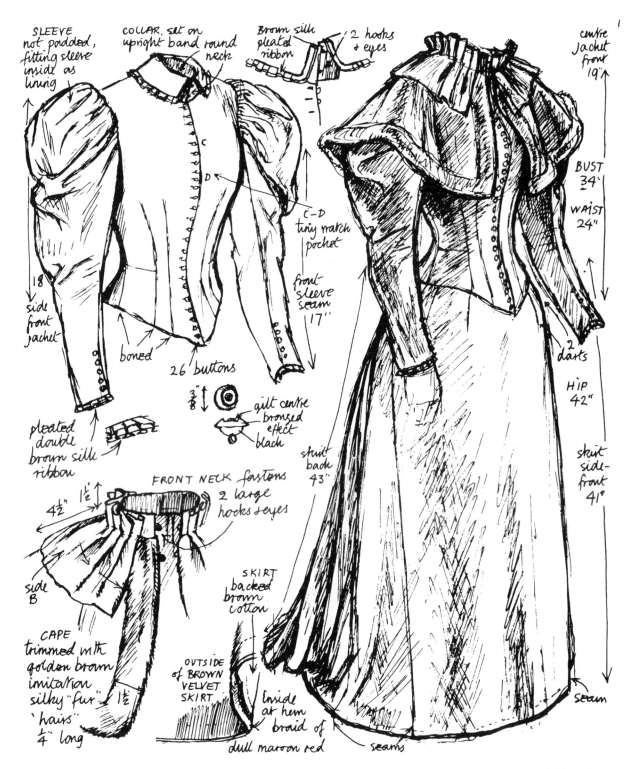

SLEEVE
not padded,
fitting sleeve
inside as
lining

COLLAR, set on
upright band round
neck

Brown silk
pleated ribbon

2 hooks
+ eyes

centre
Jacket
front
19"

c

D

BUST
34"

WAIST
24"

18
side
front
jacket

C-D
tiny watch
pocket

front
sleeve
seam
17"

2
darts

HIP
42"

boned

26 buttons

3"/8

gilt centre
bronzed
effect

black

skirt
back
43"

skirt
side-
front
41"

pleated
double
brown silk
ribbon

FRONT NECK fastens
2 large
hooks + eyes

4½"   1½"

side
B

SKIRT
backed
brown
cotton

skirt
side-
front
41"

CAPE
trimmed with
golden brown
imitation
silky "fur"
'hairs'
¼" long

1½"

OUTSIDE
OF BROWN
VELVET
SKIRT

inside
at hem
braid of
dull maroon red

seams

seam

from T. H. Holding; everywhere, in fact, except for sleeves. These are now very full and influence the shape of coat or cape, the latter being most fashionable, from small ones such as this to those of hip-level.

c. 1893

Rich brown velvet wedding outfit, detail of bodice showing the seams and boning. Petticoat of striped heavy cotton, in navy blue, red, and gold, deep flounce, corded and stiffened, back pleated and fastening with braid tape tie. White cotton drawers. *Miss Nora Hawker*

Fashion notes to show corsets, combinations, hair style, and hat.

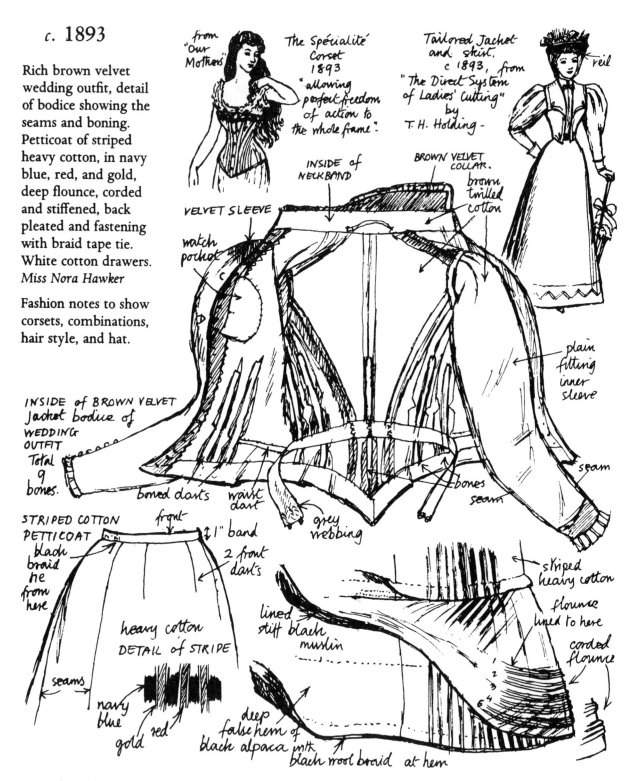

from "Our Mothers"

The Spécialité Corset 1893 "allowing perfect freedom of action to the whole frame".

Tailored Jacket and skirt, c 1893, from "The Direct System of Ladies' Cutting" by T.H. Holding —

veil

BROWN VELVET COLLAR.

INSIDE of NECKBAND

brown twilled cotton

VELVET SLEEVE

watch pocket

INSIDE of BROWN VELVET Jacket bodice of WEDDING OUTFIT Total 9 bones.

plain fitting inner sleeve

seam

boned darts   waist dart

grey webbing

bones seam

STRIPED COTTON PETTICOAT

black braid tie from here

front

1" band

2 front darts

heavy cotton DETAIL of STRIPE

navy blue   gold   red

seams

lined stiff black muslin

deep false hem of black alpaca with black wool braid at hem

striped heavy cotton

flounce lined to here

corded flounce

When looking at women's underwear of the '90's we can understand the difficulties of the lady's tailor if he has to measure her for 'Riding Trousers, Gaiters or Cycling Knickers.' Quoting from T. H. Holding, 'On no account attempt to take [measure] the knee... if a

273

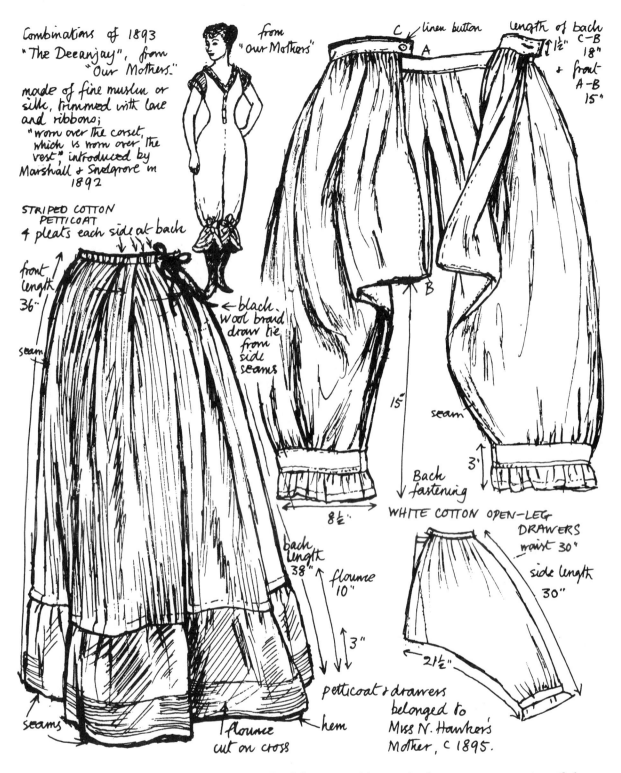

Combinations of 1893 "The Deeanjay", from "Our Mothers."
made of fine muslin or silk, trimmed with lace and ribbons;
"worn over the corset, which is worn over the vest" introduced by Marshall & Snelgrove in 1892

from "Our Mothers"

C — linen button — A

length of back C–B 1½" 18"
+ front A–B 15"

STRIPED COTTON PETTICOAT
4 pleats each side at back

front length 36"

seam

← black wool braid draw tie from side seams

B

15"

Back fastening

seam

3"

8½"

back length 38"

flounce 10"

3"

WHITE COTTON OPEN-LEG DRAWERS
waist 30"
side length 30"

← 2½"

seams

flounce cut on cross

hem

petticoat & drawers belonged to Miss N. Hawker's Mother, c 1895.

lady has a pair of knickerbockers on, the fulness would give the knee too great a size. If she has not knickerbockers on, she may have ordinary open drawers, and to measure her so clad would not be quite decent. . . . In the next place she may, or may not garter above the knee.'

274

c. 1893–95

Fine white cotton wrap or négligée. Full wide sleeves edged with lace, button fastening up to shoulder. Wide collar with lace edging, lace down front to hem. Front fastening large pearl buttons. Fitting inner bodice to waist of white cotton, linen-button fastening. Back of wrap with deeply pleated panel from neck to hem.
Snowshill Collection

front self-faced inside, neck to hem

small linen button hidden

6"

6½"

3"

large pearl buttons top ones missing

small linen button, loop on sleeve

loop

3 deep pleats

sewn to lining

seams

inner BODICE front & back fitting to waist linen buttons

sewn at shoulder seam

inner bodice front sewn to side seams

inner bodice at back fitting to waist

seam

seam

The very wide sleeves of this wrap are rather uncommon; there is a tiny loop on the hem, to fasten the sleeves up, with a very small linen button on the armhole. A feature sometimes seen in the '90's is the deep pleat at the back, sewn in at the neck seam under the collar, so

large pearl
buttons

narrow lace

fitting bodice inside
front & back
to waist.

collar of
single
thickness

1"

7"

3"

sleeves
looped
up

white
lace
on net
ground

back
length
57°

seam

front
length
50½"

Back
hangs loose
from shoulders

seams

that the wrap hangs gracefully from the shoulders to a slight train. The inner bodice or lining
is well tailored, and has a name-tape, 'J. Bird,' in blue machine-stitch sewn inside on the
front hem.

1893-95

Fine soft white silk négligée, trimmed with lace and ribbon. Fully lined fine white cotton. Fitting inner straight sleeve and a short sleeve under full long sleeves with deep lace cuff. Long sash of white satin. Deeply pleated back with silk one length from shoulder to hem.
worn by Mrs Milvane's mother; given by her to Snowshill Collection

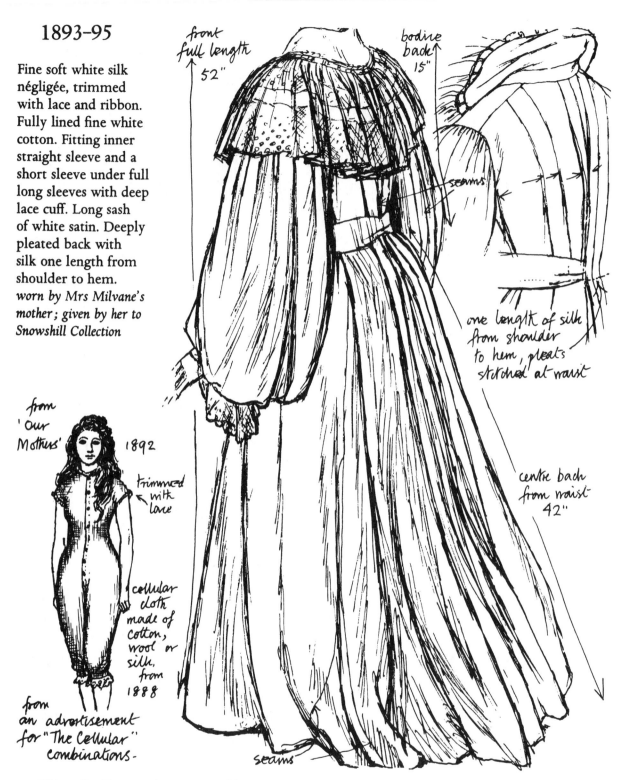

front full length 52"

bodine back 15"

seams

one length of silk from shoulder to hem, pleats stitched at waist

centre back from waist 42"

from 'Our Mothers' 1892

trimmed with lace

cellular cloth made of cotton, wool or silk, from 1888

from an advertisement for "The Cellular" combinations.

seams

This soft silk wrap has an air of languid richness, and although the sleeves are so full, they are graceful and attractive, and have none of the ugliness of some of the huge imbecile sleeves of the 1830's. The deep lace and silk frill of the collar follows the fashion of width across the

277

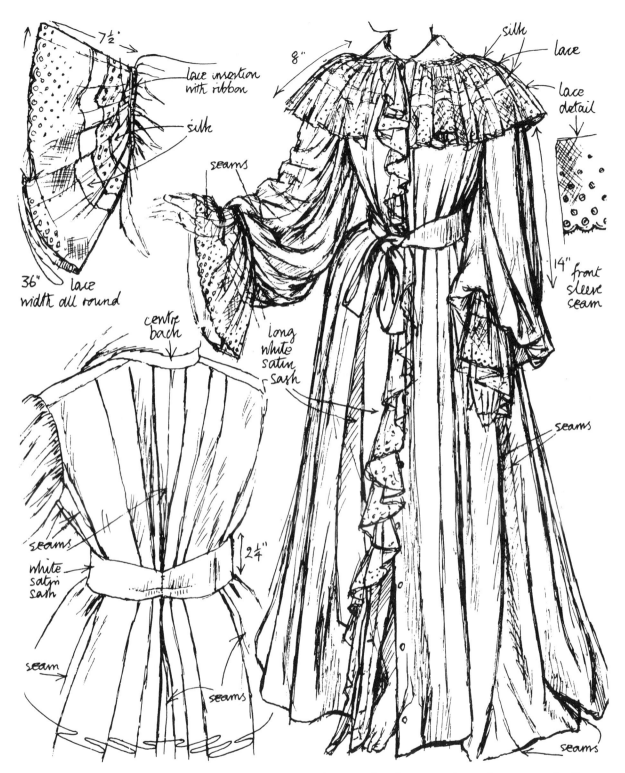

7½"

lace insertion
with ribbon

silk

seams

36"
lace
width all round

silk

lace

lace
detail

14"
front
sleeve
seam

centre
back

long
white
satin
sash

seams

seams

white
satin
sash

2¼"

seam

seams

seams

shoulders. Underwear follows the slim-fitting line to the figure, and combinations of silk, cotton, or wool were popular. In 1885 Jaeger & Co. introduced natural woollen underwear for men and women.

1893–95

White silk négligée, showing cotton lining and details of button-fastening, linings to sleeve, and edging of lace on collar. Matching white silk knickers, fastening with buttons at the sides, with deep wide frills at knee, with tucks, lace and ribbon insertion. Legs long to knee-level. *also given by Mrs Milvane to Snowshill Collection*

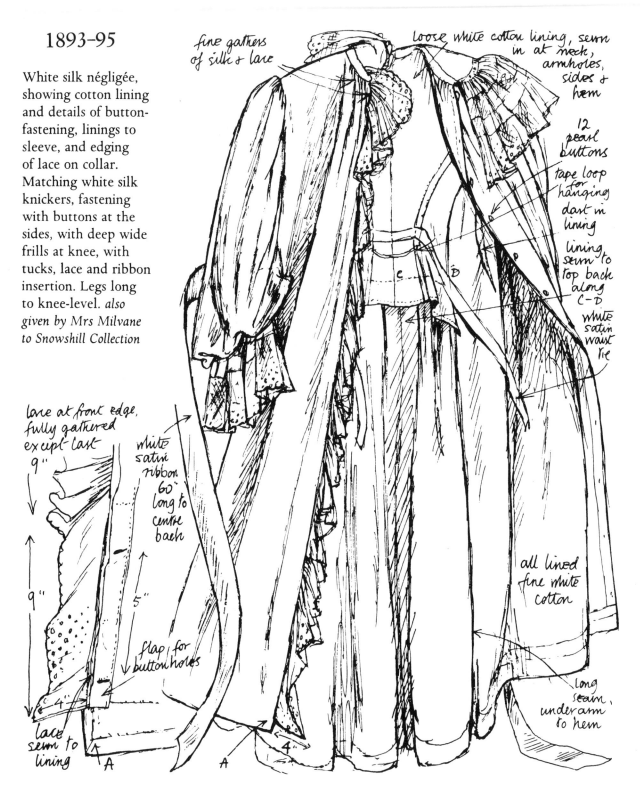

fine gathers of silk & lace

loose white cotton lining, sewn in at neck, armholes, sides & hem

12 pearl buttons

tape loop for hanging

dart in lining

lining sewn to top back along C–D

white satin waist tie

all lined fine white cotton

long seam under arm to hem

lace at front edge, fully gathered except last 9"

white satin ribbon 60" long to centre back

9"

5"

flap for button holes

lace sewn to lining

4"

A

A

4"

The cotton lining is well seamed and darted to fit the figure, with an inner waist-tie as well, giving a neatness and elegance under the soft folds of the silk. Although open-leg drawers continued in use until *c.* 1900, this form of closed knicker, fastening at the side, came into

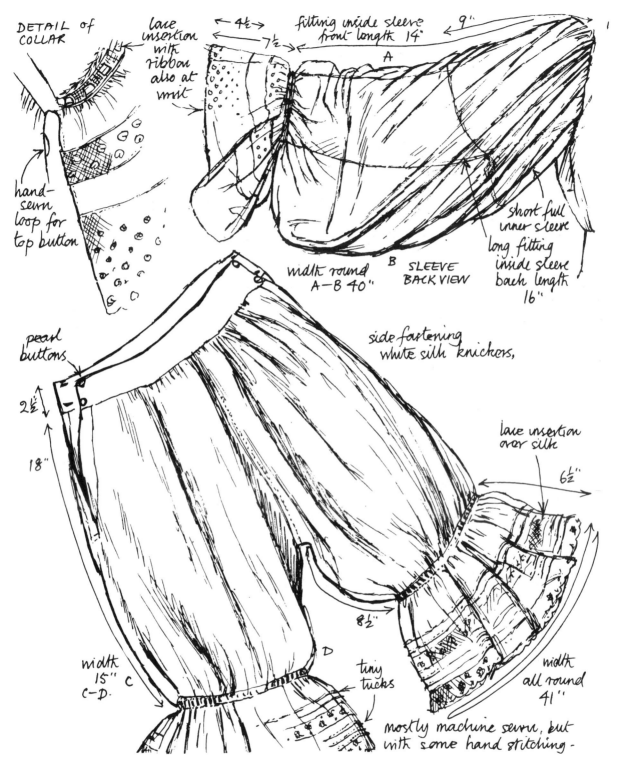

DETAIL of COLLAR

lace insertion with ribbon also at wrist

←4½→
←7½→
fitting inside sleeve front length 14"
9"
A

hand-sewn loop for top button

short full inner sleeve

long fitting inside sleeve back length 16"

width round A–B 40"
B SLEEVE BACK VIEW

pearl buttons

2½"

18"

side fastening white silk knickers,

lace insertion over silk

6½"

width 15" C
C–D.

D

tiny tucks

8½"

width all round 41"

mostly machine sewn, but with some hand stitching –

use by the '80's. They would be worn over the corset and 'cellular' combinations. Suspenders were not yet attached to the corset, but in the late '80's to 1900 were worn on a separate band or belt round the waist.

1894

Pale primrose-yellow spotted muslin, with printed pattern of iris in pink, green, and yellow. Trimmed with lace and lace insertion over under-dress of white silk taffeta. Separate bodice and skirt, both fastening at back. *worn by Lady Evelyn Lindsay before her marriage to James F. Mason in 1895; given by Mrs Wickham Steed to Chastleton House*

showing later stage of full sleeve

from a painting of a Mrs Leonard in The Royal Academy 1898

yellow muslin, cut away under all lace insertion showing white silk lining which is fitting & boned

upper sleeve lined to here

not lined

lace frill

lace insertion on muslin over white silk.

muslin seam

10

yellow muslin blouse front, full & loose, but gathers sewn here

seams

pale yellow muslin over white silk taffeta a fitting & boned underbodice.

Width all round skirt hem 192"

fine net lace with insertion & frills on yellow printed muslin, not sewn to taffeta

Mrs Wickham Steed tells me that this was one of her mother's favourite dresses, and fortunately was preserved by her, with several others of equal interest and beauty. This charming dress has the simplicity of line in the skirt which is typical of these few years, with the

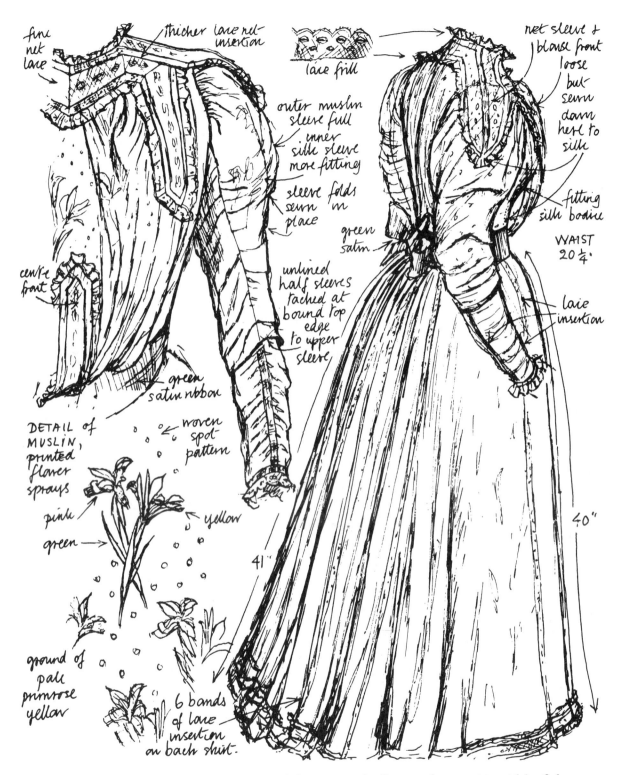

fine net lace

thicker lace net insertion

lace frill

outer muslin sleeve full

inner silk sleeve more fitting

sleeve folds sewn in place

centre front

net sleeve & blouse front loose but sewn down here to silk

fitting silk bodice

WAIST 20¼"

green satin

unlined half sleeves tacked at bound top edge to upper sleeve

lace insertion

green satin ribbon

DETAIL of MUSLIN, printed flower sprays

woven spot pattern

pink

green

yellow

ground of pale primrose yellow

6 bands of lace insertion on back skirt.

41"

40"

elaboration of the bodice with its gathered drapery at the front and increasing width of sleeve at the shoulder. The graceful gathered-up sleeve remained in fashion in slightly varied form for some years.

1894

Pale primrose-yellow spotted muslin with printed pattern of iris. Inside details showing boned bodice and fastenings, with skirt back-fastening and hidden pocket inside under back folds. Inside view of skirt with stiffened muslin lining, and inside satin ribbon tie. Green satin sash, with stitched bow. *Chastleton House*

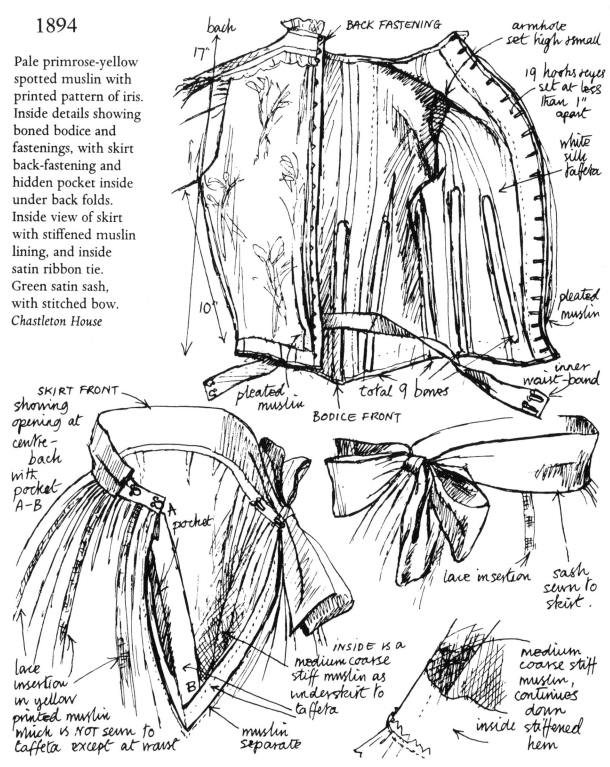

back

BACK FASTENING

armhole set high & small

17"

19 hooks & eyes set at less than 1" apart

white silk taffeta

10"

pleated muslin

inner waist-band

pleated muslin

total 9 bones

BODICE FRONT

SKIRT FRONT showing opening at centre-back with pocket A-B

pocket

lace insertion in yellow printed muslin which is NOT sewn to taffeta except at waist

muslin separate

INSIDE IS A medium coarse stiff muslin as understirt to taffeta

lace insertion

sash sewn to skirt.

medium coarse stiff muslin, continues down inside stiffened hem

The bodice of this period is very deceptive, outwardly appearing loose and simply gathered, but under the filmy surface is a very well-cut and stiffly boned garment, pinching in the waist and keeping the figure well under control. The skirt too is controlled from the inside.

283

NANNY to Lady Evelyn Mason's children in 1898 wearing a bonnet + a dark straw boater in summer

from family photographs

Household Servant fashionably dressed

Bow + sash of soft green satin ribbon sewn to top bound edge of skirt

pocket

FRONT

stiffened white muslin over white Taffeta

SKIRT INSIDE OUT

satin ribbon tie keeping skirt gathers in place.

width of front panel

20"

tuck in stiffened muslin

medium coarse stiffened white muslin

Taffeta centre-back seam

6"

stiffened hem

3" white taffeta

hem of yellow printed muslin

The weight and amount of material in some skirts is considerable. In elegant and wealthy households the domestic staff kept up appearances, and these popular tailor-made costumes were worn by all classes.

1895

'Going-away' outfit, in mulberry-red velvet, fine woollen matching cloth, black satin and jet-bead decoration. Matching hat, muff, and gold muff chain. Jacket with large velvet sleeves, boned bodice. *worn by Lady Evelyn Mason on February 9th, 1895, and given by her daughter, Mrs Wickham Steed, to Chastleton House; at present lent to Snowshill Manor*

max: width across. top of sleeves 26"

centre back 15½"

velvet

from family photograph

Lady Evelyn Mason 1896

cloth over satin

gathers to here

hanging sq: of jet beads

black satin

centre back seam

lead weights

9¼

MATCHING VELVET MUFF with muff chain

tiny pocket lined fawn satin in muff

2 flat round lead weights, the size of halfpence -

fine woollen cloth mulberry red skirt, back length 43"

S

5'

ribbon of black satin, very rich thick quality, with jet buckle

seam

seam

A beautiful Society woman's 'going-away' outfit of the very latest fashion, the huge velvet sleeves and full-skirted jacket showing her tiny 19" waist to great advantage. The upper part of the jacket over the shoulders is almost a tiny bolero joined together under the armpits,

285

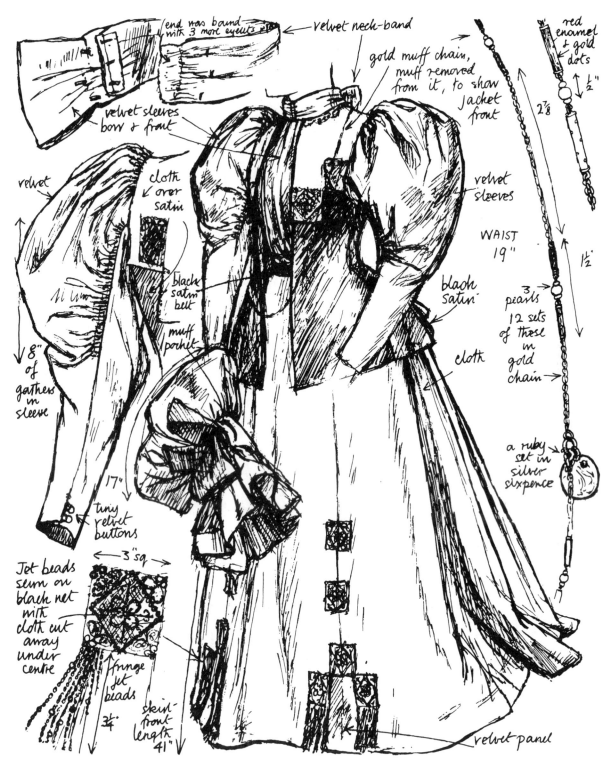

end was bound with 3 more eyelets

velvet neck-band

velvet sleeves bow & front

velvet

cloth over satin

black satin belt

muff pocket

8" of gathers in sleeve

17"

tiny velvet buttons

gold muff chain, muff removed from it, to show jacket front

velvet sleeves

WAIST 19"

black satin

cloth

red enamel & gold dots

½"

2⅞

1½

3 pearls 12 sets of these in gold chain

a ruby set in silver sixpence

Jet beads sewn on black net with cloth cut away under centre

3" sq.

fringe jet beads

3¼"

skirt front length 41"

velvet panel

with the jet-beaded decoration hanging loose from the black satin. The black satin 'skirt' to this jacket is lead-weighted. The fully lined skirt, deeply box-pleated at the back, is very heavy, and is hooked to the boned bodice lining.

1895

'Going-away' outfit of mulberry red and black; detail of skirt and jacket, lining and boning. Matching velvet hat with pale fawn ostrich feathers and black satin ribbon. Silver guinea purse with finger ring, carried by Lady Evelyn Mason with the muff. *purse, photographs, and muff chain lent me by Mrs W. Steed. Dress lent from Chastleton House to Snowshill Collection*

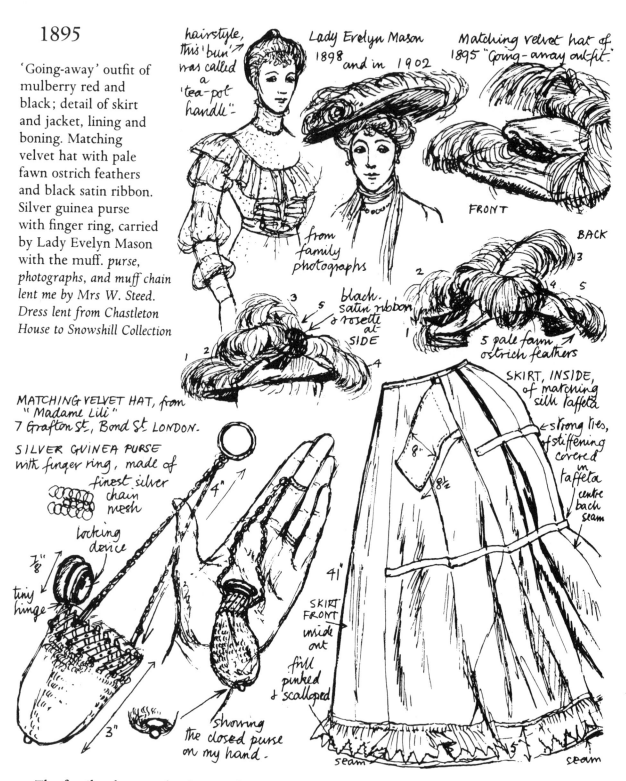

hairstyle, this 'bun' was called a 'tea-pot handle".

Lady Evelyn Mason 1898 and in 1902

Matching velvet hat of 1895 "Going-away outfit."

FRONT

BACK

from family photographs

black satin ribbon & rosette at SIDE

5 pale fawn ostrich feathers

MATCHING VELVET HAT, from "Madame Lili" 7 Grafton St, Bond St. LONDON.

SILVER GUINEA PURSE with finger ring, made of finest silver chain mesh

locking device

tiny hinge

showing the closed purse on my hand.

SKIRT, INSIDE, of matching silk taffeta

strong ties, of stiffening covered in taffeta

centre back seam

SKIRT FRONT inside out

frill pinked & scalloped

seam

seam

The family photographs show Lady Evelyn Mason to have been a woman of great beauty and elegance, with considerable taste in dress and accessories. This outfit is rich in appearance and very well made. The side lacing to the boned silk bodice lining was inserted later for

287

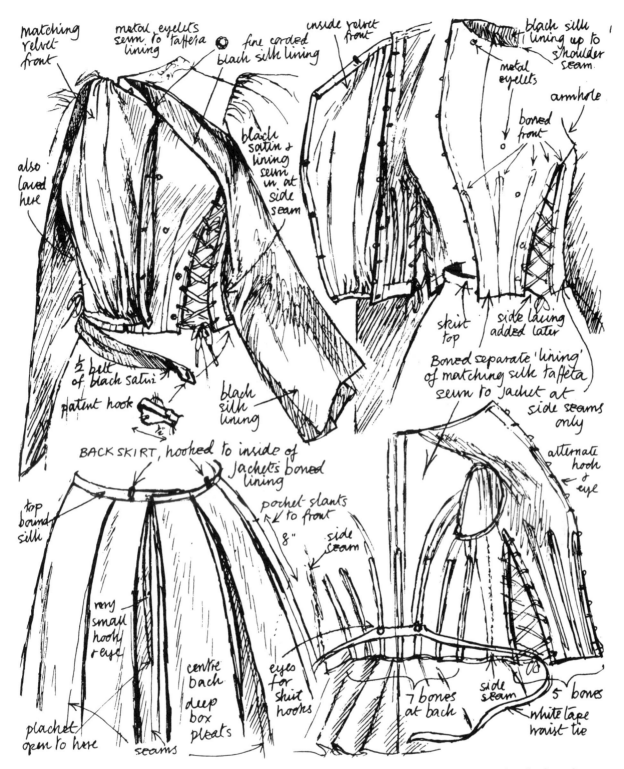

matching
velvet
front

metal eyelets
sewn to taffeta
lining

fine corded
black silk lining

inside velvet
front

black silk
lining up to
shoulder seam

metal
eyelets

also
laced
here

black
satin +
lining
sewn
in at
side
seam

boned
front

armhole

skirt
top

side lacing
added later

½ belt
of black satin

patent hook

black
silk
lining

Boned separate 'lining'
of matching silk taffeta
sewn to jacket at
side seams
only

alternate
hook
+
eye

BACK SKIRT, hooked to inside of
jacket's boned
lining

pocket slants
to front

top
bound
silk

8"

side
seam

very
small
hook
+ eye

centre
back

deep
box
pleats

eyes
for
skirt
hooks

7 bones
at back

side
seam

5 bones
white tape
waist tie

placket
open to here

seams

maternity wear; this is found also in corsets of the period. Her waist measured 27" after the
alteration was made. The velvet hat has a soft crown gathered in to the brim, with a twist
of black satin ribbon under the feathers.

c. 1897

Rich black satin, tiny woven floral pattern in pink and green. Black chiffon over pink on sleeve panels, bolero and skirt, and black chiffon frills at hem sewn to pink taffeta under-skirt. Bodice lined pink silk taffeta, front fastening and fully boned; skirt has back fastening. Guimpe and under-sleeves of cream embroidered net.
Mrs M. J. King

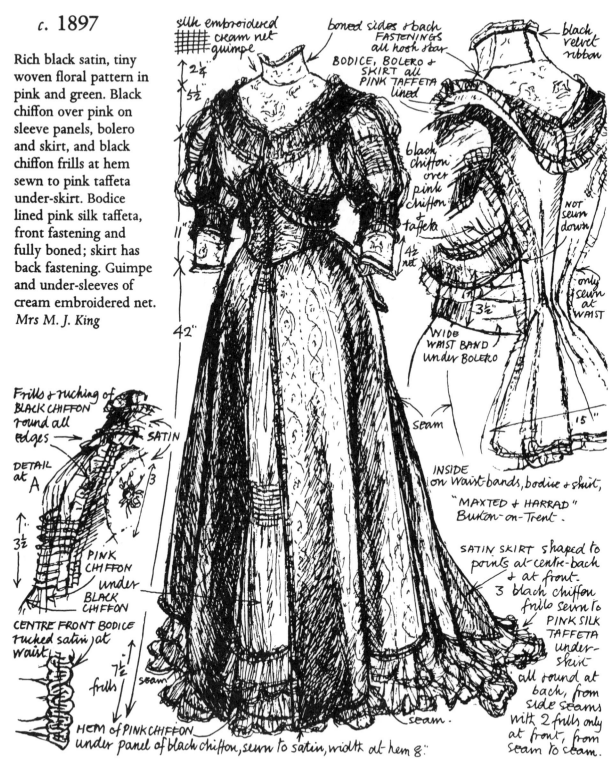

silk embroidered cream net guimpe

boned sides & back FASTENINGS all hook & bar

BODICE, BOLERO & SKIRT all PINK TAFFETA lined

black velvet ribbon

2¼
1½

black chiffon over pink chiffon & taffeta

4½ net

NOT sewn down

only sewn at WAIST

11"

3½"

42"

WIDE WAIST BAND under BOLERO

seam

15"

Frills & ruching of BLACK CHIFFON round all edges →

SATIN

DETAIL at A

3

1"
3½

PINK CHIFFON under BLACK CHIFFON

CENTRE FRONT BODICE tucked satin at waist

7½ frills

seam

HEM of PINK CHIFFON under panel of black chiffon, sewn to satin, width at hem 8"

INSIDE on waist-bands, bodice & skirt, "MAXTED & HARRAD" Burton-on-Trent.

SATIN SKIRT shaped to points at centre-back & at front. 3 black chiffon frills sewn to PINK SILK TAFFETA under-skirt all round at back, from side seams with 2 frills only at front, from seam to seam.

seam.

A most lovely afternoon or evening dress, fully lined in pink silk taffeta. This softly rustling silk is now used a great deal for lining the skirt, which is cut on the cross, fitting smoothly over the hips, the rich folds sweeping out to a wide hemline, all fullness being obtained by

centre back lengths

2½"

4"

A

12½"

WAIST 26"

9½"

44

side 38"

Seams

8'

frills showing

5½"

centre back seam

fine pleating also on cuffs

5½"

2"

10"

½"

3/16"

CENTRE BACK seam sewn in with lining & boned

DETAIL 1"

3 HOOKS on back waist with bars on skirt.

centre BACK

DETAIL 1"

BACK placket hook & bar fastening

cream chiffon lining to all net

PINK CHIFFON undersleeve

BOLERO one hook & eye

10"

all boned Total 11

shaped waist band sewn to lining

WHITE SILK

ALL PINK SILK TAFFETA LINED in skirt, sewn in at top & placket only.

stitched silk tie

DETAIL at B satin hem

2"

pleated black chiffon frills

5

3

5

3½"

5"

5½"

stitched silk Tie

frilled PINK SILK TAFFETA underskirt

the cut of the gores; there are no pleats at the waist, even at centre back. This satin skirt, pointed back and front, is held in position by stitched ties, sewn at intervals to the taffeta under-skirt.

1900–01 From a photograph of a Society woman shortly after her marriage to a rich country gentleman. His Norfolk jacket and her tweed suit and boater are ideal for country wear. There is a 1925 study of her, in a low-waisted Court dress.

1909 From *Country Life*, Dec. 25th. The Marchioness of Donegall, who married the Marquess 1902. She wears full evening dress with coronet. Also from *Country Life*, an advert for 'lightweight all wool Aquascutum coats, suitable for all climates.'

1927 Miss Helen Wills, from *The Illustrated London News*. She was the amateur lawn-tennis champion and engaged to Mr F. S. Moody Jr. He wears a lounge suit and trilby hat; her cloche hat, low-waisted dress, and knee-length hemline are typical of the mid-1920's.

5

1900–1930

The advent of the motor-car brings easier travel, and with it the prospect of week-ends in the country, and wider social activities for the wealthier woman. A greater variety of clothes is needed, not only in the range of 'waterproofs' and 'weatherproofs' as advertised by 1909, but in tailor-mades for 'travelling, racing, sport and country wear, and motor-garments,' also afternoon and evening dresses, exquisite filmy gowns, so typical of the Edwardian period, when fashions are designed for the mature woman.

T. H. Holding in the late 1890's still has something interesting to say about the English tailor-made costumes: 'For nearly twenty years, a considerable proportion of ladies' outer garments have been made by tailors ... but I believe, to the late Mr Morgan of Cowes, is due the credit of having been the first to make dresses for ladies in England, though the renowned Worth, of Paris, has done the same for a great number of years. Worth, however, makes silks, satins, and any other costly and delicate dress material, whilst English tailors, as a rule, merely confine their efforts in this line, to costume cloths.' But Charles Frederick Worth (1825–95) was an Englishman from Lincolnshire, who served as a draper's apprentice in London at Swan & Edgar's. In 1846 he went to Paris, unknown and without capital. Twelve years later he set up a dress-making business in partnership with Dobergh, a Swede, and later won the interest and patronage of the Empress Eugénie and the elegant women of Paris. For thirty years his styles set the tone of Parisian and often English fashions.

In *The Ladies' Field*, June 1911, there is a hint of change: 'Another fascinating dress ... is likely to create a small sensation at Ascot, on account of its following the very favourite fashion in Paris at present, of cutting up the skirt slightly at one side, which allows a certain portion of the ankle to be seen, and gives the beholder hopes of seeing more.' An enormous hat is worn with this creation, and the stockings are of 'rose pink silk with black clocks, and the smartest of black shoes.'

Throughout past centuries women's fashions at times reach a point of excessive extravagance, having gradually evolved or built up to such a pitch that their collapse is inevitable. Vast hooped foundations, huge hats or hair styles, long trailing or clinging skirts —there is a constant movement of fullness, pinching, padding, or drapery, up or down, in or outward. Never before, in recorded English history, have women worn their skirts to knee-level, or cut their hair short, but in the 1920's these two drastic changes occur, and that is not all, for they become bosomless, waistless, and hipless, and at one point the dress, without any form of shaping or fastening, is identical back and front.

1903–04

Fawn silk afternoon dress; trimmed coarse cream lace, and silk and cord tassels. Bodice and skirt are separate, each fastened left-side front. Bodice boned and lined in fawn cotton; skirt is lined grey cotton. Front bodice ruched.
Mr F. Norris, lent to Personal Collection

Black kid strap shoes, jet bead decoration.
Miss Nora Hawker

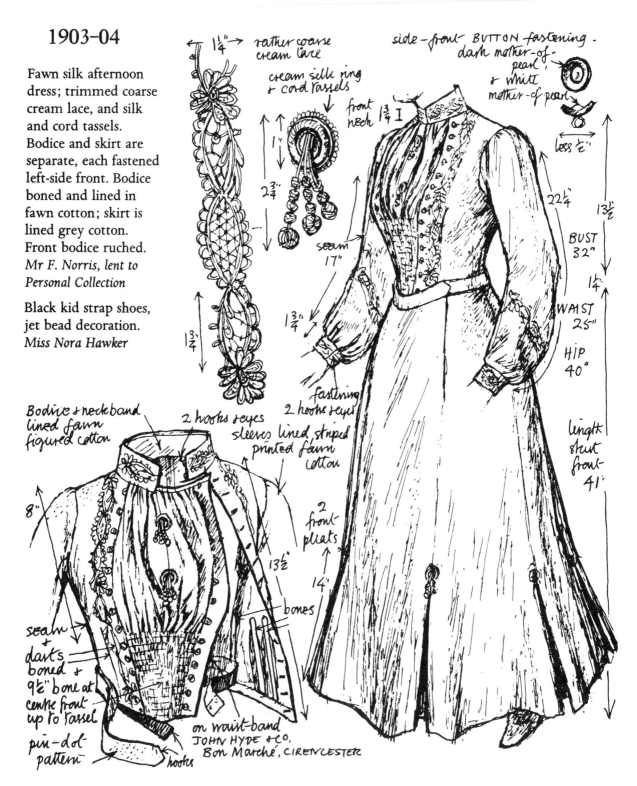

rather coarse cream lace

cream silk ring & cord tassels

1¼"

1"

2¾"

1¾"

side-front BUTTON fastening.
dark mother-of-pearl, & white mother-of-pearl

front neck 1¾" I

less ½"

22¼"

13½"

BUST 32"

1¼"

WAIST 25"

HIP 40"

length skirt front 41"

seam 17"

1¾"

fastening 2 hooks & eyes

Bodice & neckband lined fawn figured cotton

2 hooks & eyes
sleeves lined, striped printed fawn cotton

8"

13½"

2 front pleats

14"

bones

seam + darts boned + 9½" bone at centre front up to tassel

pin-dot pattern

on waist-band
JOHN HYDE & CO.
Bon Marché, CIRENCESTER

hooks

During the first few years of this century there is an increase of decoration and elaboration of both bodice and hemline. Skirts with pleats or frills flare out below the knee, and day dresses, even 'walking costumes,' sweep the ground. The trimness of the bodice front is soon

293

from Illustrated London News March 1907 Tailor-made walking costume

fashion plate. advertisement

from family photograph of Lady Evelyn Mason in 1904

twisted & knotted double row of pearls

Bodice front & sides boned, Total 7

2"

4"

14½"

7½"

1¼"

tape loops

CENTRE BACK

inverted pleat

lined dark grey cotton

SKIRT. SIDE-FRONT OPENING

11"

length skirt back 41½

BLACK KID SHOES

edges bound with corded ribbon

hooks & eyelets

pleats side & back

13½"

large & small Jet bead decoration

1¾

9½

plain round black shoe-buttons

shoes worn by

Miss N. Hawkers' Mother

false hem 1¾" band of black glazed cotton

lost by draperies and frills. During 1903–04 sleeves follow the 'pouched' look, hanging full just above the wrist-band. Hair styles show increasing width, being now dressed over pads, forming a useful foundation for the growing size of the elaborate hats.

1903-07

Creamy white satin afternoon or evening dress, trimmed white spotted net frills edged with baby ribbon. Bodice pouched over wide belt, fastening left-side front and centre front on the boned cotton lining. Separate skirt, placket at left front, trailing frilled hemline, white cotton under-skirt.
Miss Nora Hawker

Two dress-holders.
Snowshill Collection

from Illustrated London News – June 1907 Mrs Robert Goelet.

rows of pleated ribbon

lace

"The Mother of an heir to millions"

tortoiseshell

spring inside

metal

white satin

white spotted net trimmed white baby ribbon

2"

7½"

3¾"

pouched satin front

s

40" skirt front

seam

3 frills at front

2 next frills start on seam

10½"

1½

14"

10"

DRESS-HOLDER (enlarged) clipped to the dress & attached by fine cord or chain to hook at the waist, holding up the skirts to leave both hands free. These are both plain examples.

2½

1½

strong white cotton underskirt

white spotted net frills

fine white cord for lifting skirt

4"

hem of satin

pleated white taffeta frill

A graceful dress made for a small, dainty woman. The satin bodice is well pouched in front over the belt, and is decorated with tiny tucks, back and front and on the sleeves; these, draped, like the shoulder-line, balance the frilled, trailing hemline, leaving the hips smooth

white spotted net with baby ribbon

fine cord tie in hem

9"

tiny tucks in satin

2"

15½"

white satin baby ribbon on net sewn at top edge only

WAIST 24"

hooked

1"
3¾"
2½"

ring for chain or cord

3½"

over belt, of metal with iridescent blue-black finish

2"

DRESS-HOLDER (enlarged).

red velvet tip

side seam

satin

white satin baby ribbon

3¼"

3½"

4½"

extra frills from side seam + here

white satin baby ribbon sewn at top edge only.

7

13 tucks in satin

S

net

boned belt at centre back

seams

A   A

12" fine white cord

full length skirt back 51"

B

B

28" of frills

total 8 frills centre-back

and free from gathers and pleats. An effect even achieved with the 'fan pleated' or 'sun-ray' skirt shown in the small study. The two dress-holders are too plain for such a gown as this, which has its original cord on the back seam, to lift the skirt.

1903–07

Creamy white satin afternoon or evening dress, trimmed with spotted net frills and baby ribbon. Details of pouched bodice, hook-and-eye front fastening, with cord and ribbon ties at neck. Fitting, boned cotton under-bodice. Diagram of hanging drapery on sleeve. Separate skirt with white cotton under-skirt. *Miss Nora Hawker*

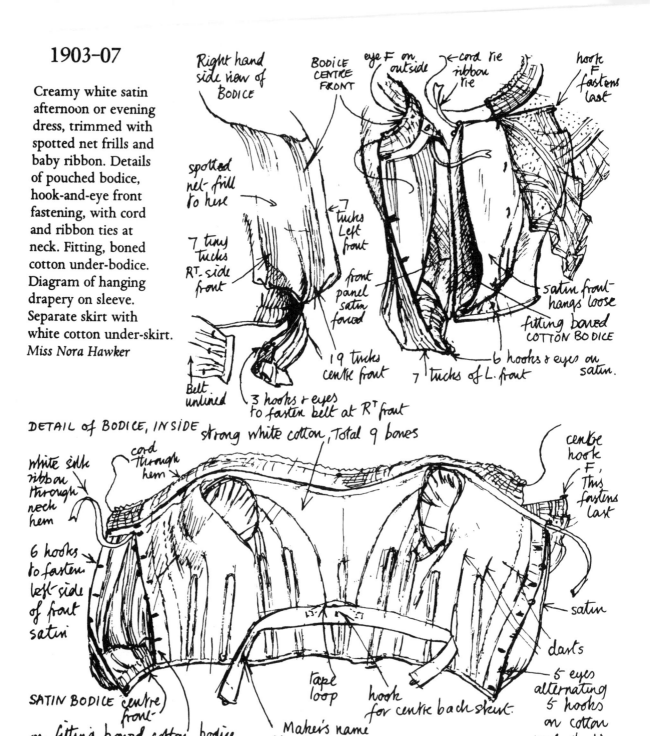

Right hand side view of BODICE

BODICE CENTRE FRONT

eye F on outside

cord tie ribbon tie

hook F fastens last

spotted net frill to here

7 tiny tucks RT. side front

7 tucks Left front

front panel satin forced

satin front hangs loose

fitting boned COTTON BODICE

Belt unlined

19 tucks centre front

3 hooks + eyes to fasten belt at RT front

7 tucks of L. front

6 hooks + eyes on satin.

DETAIL of BODICE, INSIDE   strong white cotton, Total 9 bones

white silk ribbon through neck hem

cord through hem

centre hook F. This fastens last

6 hooks to fasten left side of front satin

satin

darts

5 eyes alternating 5 hooks on cotton underbodice

SATIN BODICE centre front

on fitting boned cotton bodice fastening of 5 eyes alternating with 5 hooks

tape loop

hook for centre back skirt.

Maker's name
Mrs BOCHELL
Dress and Mantle Maker
1, Nursery Road, HOCKLEY
BIRMINGHAM.

So neatly are the hooks and eyes sewn on the draped bodice, it is difficult to see where it is fastened, and so closely fitting is the boned lining, one would have thought corsets were not necessary. But such a vital foundation was worn to control the 'lower' bust, waist, and hips,

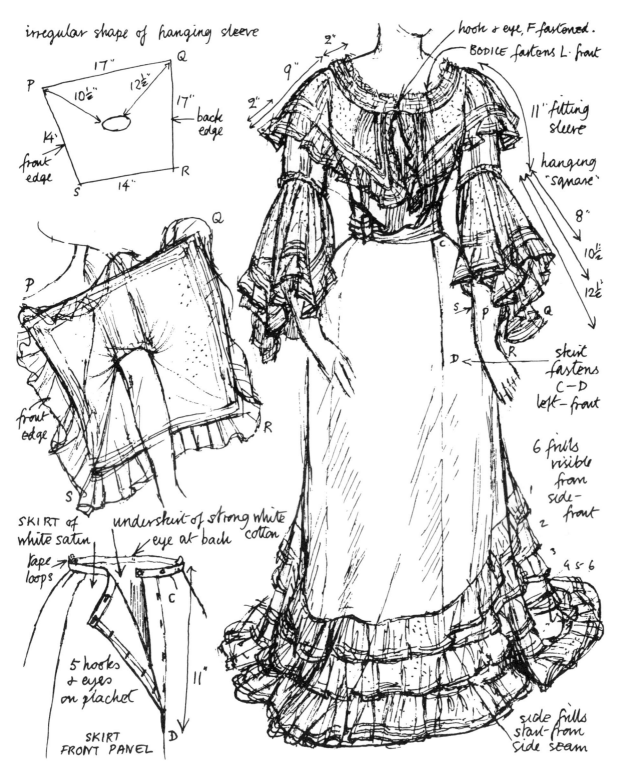

irregular shape of hanging sleeve

17"

P

Q

10½"   12½"

17"

back edge

K"

front edge

S   14"   R

hook & eye, F fastened.
BODICE fastens L. front

9"   2"

2"

11" fitting sleeve

hanging "square"

8"

10½"

12½"

C

S   P   Q

D ←   R

skirt fastens C–D left-front

6 frills visible from side-front

1

2

3

4 5 6

side frills start from side seam

Q

P

R

front edge

S

SKIRT of white satin

undershirt of strong white cotton

eye at back

tape loops

C

5 hooks & eyes on placket

11"

D

SKIRT FRONT PANEL

as the smooth hip-line was one feature of this period. The heavy pleating at the back of the skirt has gone, and, although not now so heavy, the trailing hemline still means that the skirt must be hooked to the bodice.

1903-07

Black lace dress, fine net ground, trimmed black satin ribbon and lace over rich yellow silk taffeta. Separate bodice with pouched front. Centre-front fastening, fully lined white cotton and boned. Separate skirt with taffeta, lined white cotton. Hem padded and with frills. Net skirt is separate.
Chastleton House

net lace over taffeta

net 13"

11"

satin ribbon loops

3/8" wide

very fine lace, open & of 'spider-web' quality, neck & hem

12"

black satin ribbon

DRESS, honeycomb mesh black net is also very fine

net 43"

41'

net 50"

45"

very fine lace frills round sleeve & skirt, different from neck.

enlarged mesh of black net dress.

27"

DETAIL of SKIRT FRILLS
gathered black satin ribbon, edged with lace

5"

lace at hem as round neck

narrow hem on net

5"

An afternoon or evening dress of great delicacy and charm, it has the typical bodice with pouched front and spreading skirt, decorated with ribbon and lace frills, which are cobweb-fine, and are found on the lovely gowns of this period. The taffeta skirt even has a padded

299

front neck hooks & eyes

8"

net sleeve over taffeta

11"

frill of net only 7"

darts on net outside, Total 16 darts on skirt.

front net bodice hooks at side front & hangs very full.

yellow taffeta sleeve only to here, with net seam in at sleeve seam with taffeta

A

hook A

2 front seams in taffeta

18"

S

S

YELLOW TAFFETA BODICE over fitting white cotton BONED lining fastens at CENTRE FRONT.
4 hooks & eyes on Taffeta —
4 on net

A

seam in taffeta

metal eye B
2 hooks & eyes

hook B

boned inside

UNDERSKIRT of YELLOW SILK TAFFETA
lined white cotton

black net frill fold at top edge

3"

3"

3"

on outside + 2" wide padded hem of taffeta, also

INSIDE hem 2 yellow cotton frills

hem in addition to a pleated net frill outside, and cotton frills inside, to ensure the wide, draped, fashionable hemline. The neck and sleeves have richly gathered drapery and deep frills, which, by contrast, accentuate the waist.

300

1903-07

Black lace dress with black satin ribbon and lace trimming over yellow silk taffeta. Back view of dress showing fastening at back skirt of silk and separate net skirt; white cotton lining to silk. Bodice and sleeves lined in white cotton; inside showing bones and fastenings. Studies of hair style and hat. *Chastleton House*

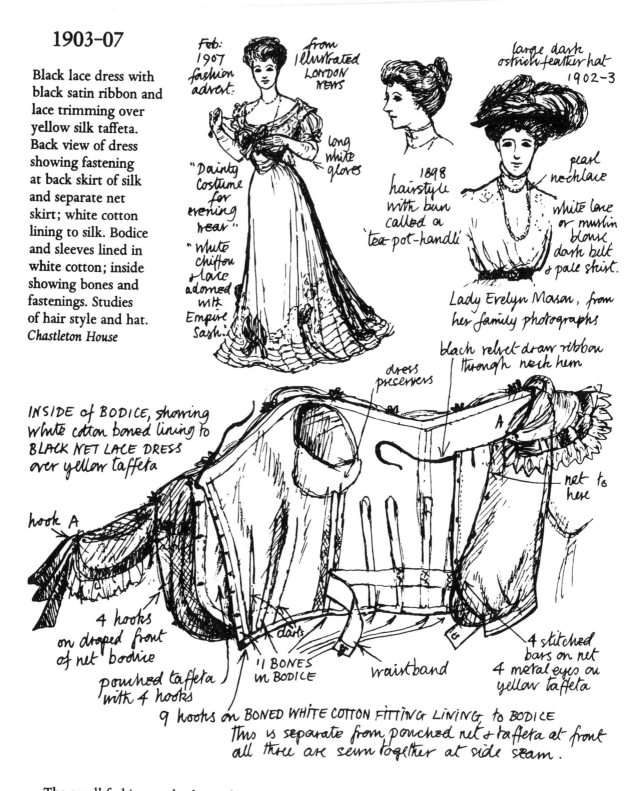

Feb: 1907 fashion advert: from Illustrated LONDON NEWS

"Dainty Costume for evening wear."

"White chiffon & lace adorned with Empire Sash."

long white gloves

1898 hairstyle with bun called a 'tea-pot-handle'

large dark ostrich-feather hat 1902-3

pearl necklace

white lace or muslin blouse

dark belt & pale skirt.

Lady Evelyn Mason, from her family photographs

INSIDE of BODICE, showing white cotton boned lining to BLACK NET LACE DRESS over yellow taffeta

dress preservers

black velvet draw ribbon through neck hem

A

net to here

hook A

4 hooks on draped front of net bodice

pouched taffeta with 4 hooks

darts

'11 BONES in BODICE

waistband

4 stitched bars on net 4 metal eyes on yellow taffeta

9 hooks on BONED WHITE COTTON FITTING LINING to BODICE This is separate from pouched net & taffeta at front all three are sewn together at side seam.

The small fashion study shows the typical Edwardian pose, the straight-fronted corset having a firm control of the figure. The bodices of these dresses are fully boned, and the frothy, transparent lightness of these draperies are merely an illusion. Some of these extremely

black satin ribbon loops

net lace closely fitted at back

taffeta bodice, sleeves & skirt all lined WHITE COTTON

net over taffeta

net over Taffeta

WAIST 24"

back opening in net to here in seam

net only has one seam at centre back skirt →

edges bound taffeta

2 hooks & eyes on separate net & taffeta

skirts

net seam taffeta seams

BOUND BLACK SILK

CENTRE BACK yellow taffeta

net flounce sewn on here & back part slightly gathered

one net seam centre back,

2 seams in taffeta skirt at back

fine lace or net gowns, like those of the previous century, are too frail to survive for long the weight of frills and trimming, however delicate they are, although these lined bodices and skirts, having a strong foundation, last very well.

1905-07

Thin pale green silk afternoon dress, with trimming of dark green velvet, tiny tucks and cream lace over green velvet, on bodice and sleeves. Bodice lined with green cotton and mounted on white cotton boned under-bodice, front fastening. Full sleeves, fitting inner sleeve. Back-fastening skirt with cotton under-skirt.
Miss Nora Hawker

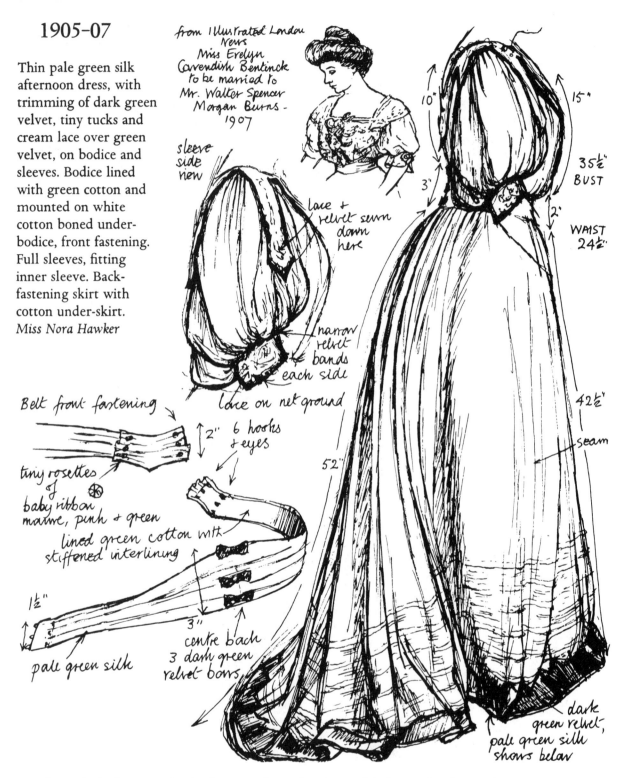

from Illustrated London News
Miss Evelyn Cavendish Bentinck to be married to Mr. Walter Spencer Morgan Burns - 1907

sleeve side view

lace + velvet sewn down here

10"

15"

3"

35½" BUST

2"

WAIST 24½"

narrow velvet bands each side

lace on net ground

42½"

seam

52"

Belt front fastening

2" 6 hooks + eyes

tiny rosettes of baby ribbon mauve, pink + green

lined green cotton with stiffened interlining

1½"

3"
centre back
3 dark green velvet bows

pale green silk

dark green velvet, pale green silk shows below

A particularly attractive back view of a rather beautiful dress; the draped bodice, full rich sleeves, velvet and lace decoration, and the wide, swathed belt accentuating the slightly raised waistline are a perfect foil for the long, sweeping lines of the skirt. The rows of tiny

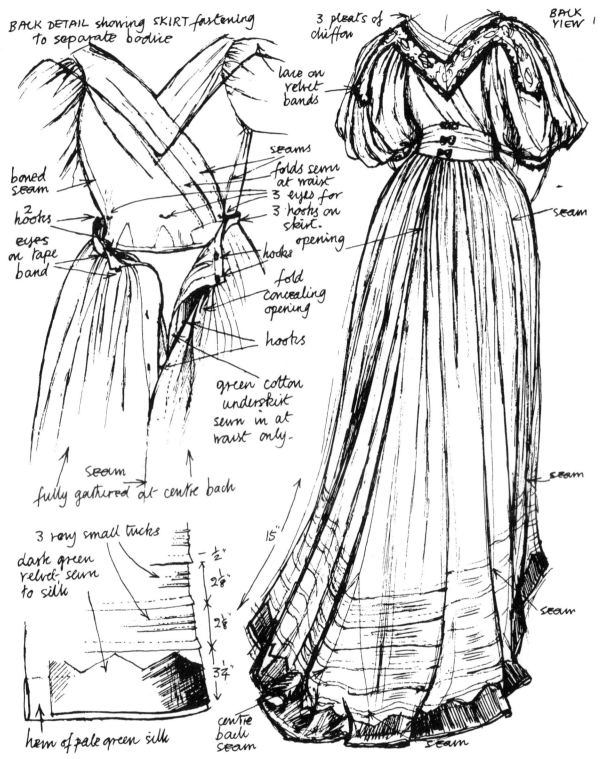

BACK DETAIL showing SKIRT fastening to separate bodice

3 pleats of chiffon

BACK VIEW

lace on velvet bands

boned seam

2 hooks

eyes on tape band

seams

folds sewn at waist

3 eyes for 3 hooks on skirt.

opening

hooks

fold concealing opening

hooks

green cotton underskirt sewn in at waist only.

seam

seam

seam

fully gathered at centre back

3 very small tucks

dark green velvet sewn to silk

— ½"

2⅛"

2⅛"

3¼"

15"

hem of pale green silk

centre back seam

seam

seam

seam

tucks on the skirt, with the band of velvet at the hem, are a fashionable touch, although skirts tend now to have an upward movement, to this higher waist, with the decoration on the bodice having a similar line to the back and front.

304

1905–07

Thin pale green silk afternoon dress with trimming of cream lace over dark green velvet. Front of dress and bodice showing detail of lace, method of fastening, draped front and folded chiffon, and boned cotton under-bodice, patent fasteners for missing guimpe, of net or lace. Maker's name on waistband. *Miss Nora Hawker*

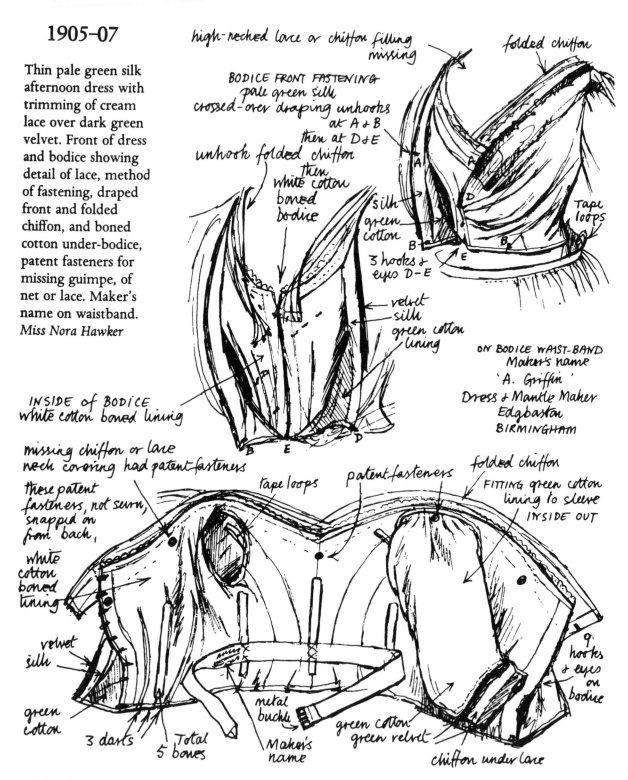

high-necked lace or chiffon filling missing

folded chiffon

BODICE FRONT FASTENING
pale green silk
crossed-over draping unhooks
at A + B
then at D + E

unhook folded chiffon
then
white cotton
boned
bodice

silk
green
cotton

B
E

3 hooks &
eyes D – E

velvet
silk
green cotton
lining

INSIDE of BODICE
white cotton boned lining

B   E   D

Tape
loops

ON BODICE WAIST-BAND
Maker's name
'A. Griffin'
Dress & Mantle Maker
Edgbaston
BIRMINGHAM

missing chiffon or lace
neck covering had patent fasteners

these patent
fasteners, not sewn,
snapped on
from back,

white
cotton
boned
lining

tape loops

patent fasteners

folded chiffon
FITTING green cotton
lining to sleeve
INSIDE OUT

velvet
silk

green
cotton

3 darts

5 Total
bones

metal
buckle

Maker's
name

green cotton
green velvet

chiffon under lace

9
hooks
& eyes
on
bodice

This dress appears so complete that one would not suspect that part was missing, but the patent fasteners round the neckline, inside the bodice, give the secret away. The missing guimpe was probably of cream lace or folded net or chiffon, matching that used on the

305

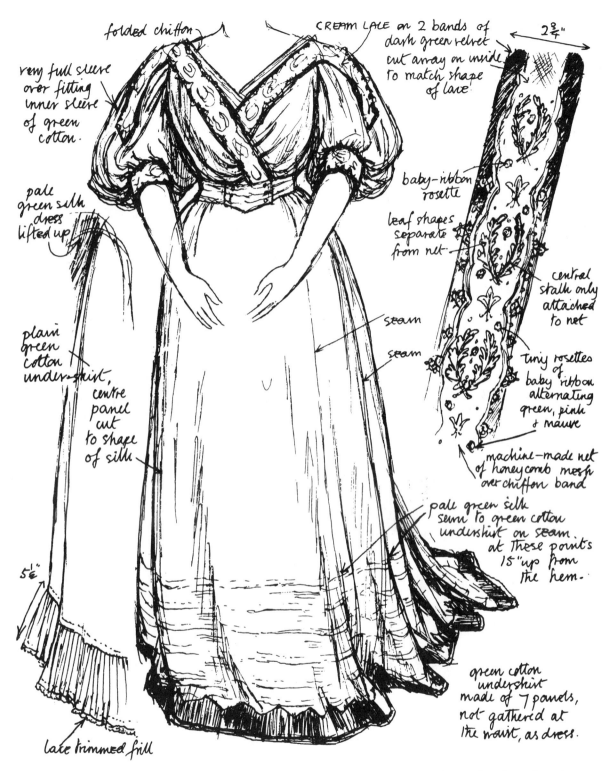

folded chiffon

CREAM LACE on 2 bands of dark green velvet cut away on inside to match shape of lace.

2¾"

very full sleeve over fitting inner sleeve of green cotton.

baby-ribbon rosette

leaf shapes separate from net.

pale green silk dress lifted up

central stalk only attached to net

plain green cotton under-shirt,

centre panel cut to shape of silk

seam

seam

tiny rosettes of baby ribbon alternating green, pink & mauve

machine-made net of honeycomb mesh over chiffon band

pale green silk sewn to green cotton undershirt on seam. at these points 15" up from the hem.

5½"

green cotton undershirt made of 7 panels, not gathered at the waist, as dress.

lace trimmed frill

bodice. An interesting detail in the construction of this dress is that the under-skirt, hanging separately from the waistband, is made in 7 panels, the green silk only caught to it at front and side seams, subtly controlling the folds.

1908

Deep soft pink cotton-sateen, trimmed with black sateen, black braid and decorative embroidered pink buttons. Finely boned guimpe of tucked net over chiffon matching missing under-sleeves. Separate bodice and skirt hooked together. Bodice lined and fully boned, front fastening. Skirt fastening at back. Belt missing.

Miss Nora Hawker

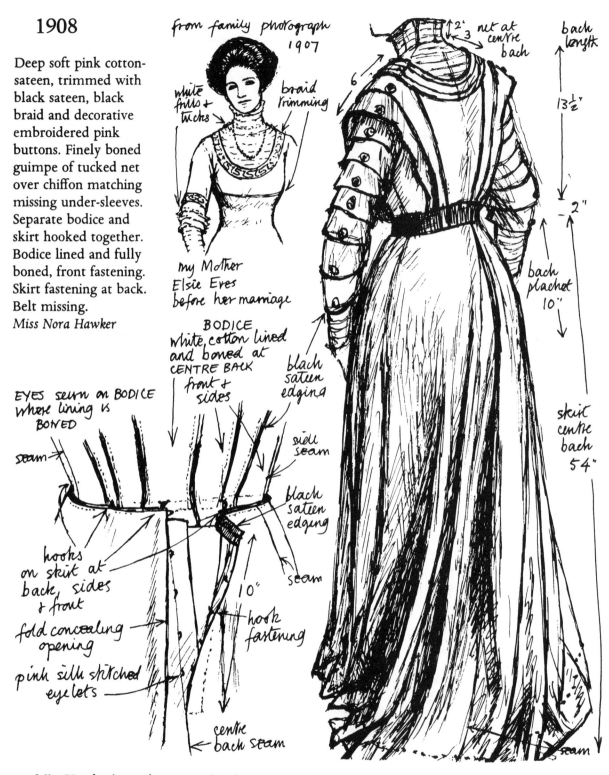

from family photograph 1907

white frills & tucks

braid trimming

my Mother Elsie Eves before her marriage

BODICE white cotton lined and boned at CENTRE BACK front & sides

black sateen edging

EYES sewn on BODICE where lining is BONED

seam

side seam

black sateen edging

hooks on skirt at back, sides & front

fold concealing opening

pink silk stitched eyelets

10"

hook fastening

seam

centre back seam

6

2' 3 net at centre back

back length

13½"

2"

back placket 10"

skirt centre back 54"

seam

Miss Hawker's mother wore this dress at a garden party in July 1908, and on her death later that year it was kept, together with many other things belonging to her. Probably it was also made by 'Fordred' of Birmingham, as it has a similar type of pleating to the skirt-back,

307

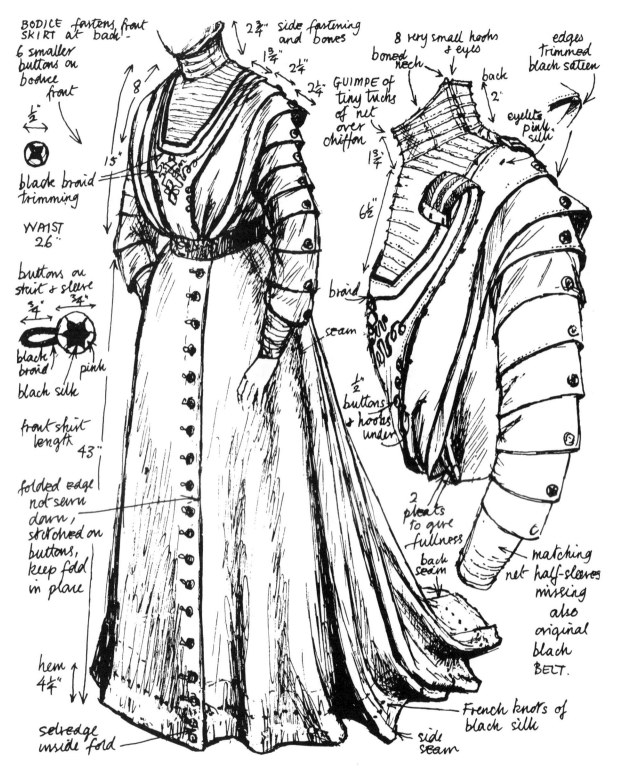

BODICE fastens front
SKIRT at back -
6 smaller
buttons on
bodice
front

2¾" side fastening
and bones

8 very small hooks
& eyes

edges
trimmed
black sateen

½"

black braid
trimming

1¾"

2¼"

2½"

8"

GUIMPE of
tiny tucks
of net
over
chiffon

boned
neck

back

2"

eyelits
pink
silk

15"

1¾"

6½"

WAIST
26"

buttons on
skirt & sleeve

¾"   ¾"

black
braid   pink

black silk

front skirt
length 43"

braid

seam

½"
buttons
+ hooks
under

folded edge
not sewn
down,
stitched on
buttons,
keep fold
in place

2
pleats
to give
fullness

back
seam

matching
net half-sleeves
missing
also
original
black
BELT.

hem
4¼"

selvedge
inside fold

French knots of
black silk

side
seam

with French knots on the hem, as on the blue dinner dress. The slightly off-centre skirt decoration of the front fold and buttons conceals a seam; this use of trimming or embroidery is often found on skirts of dresses at this time.

1908

Bodice of pink sateen garden-party dress, showing construction of sleeve, fastening of net guimpe, and of white cotton boned bodice lining. Fine white cambric chemise and white cambric waist-petticoat, trimmed with lace insertion.
Miss Nora Hawker

White cotton open-leg drawers, *c.* 1908–10.
from Miss A. Eccles to Personal Collection

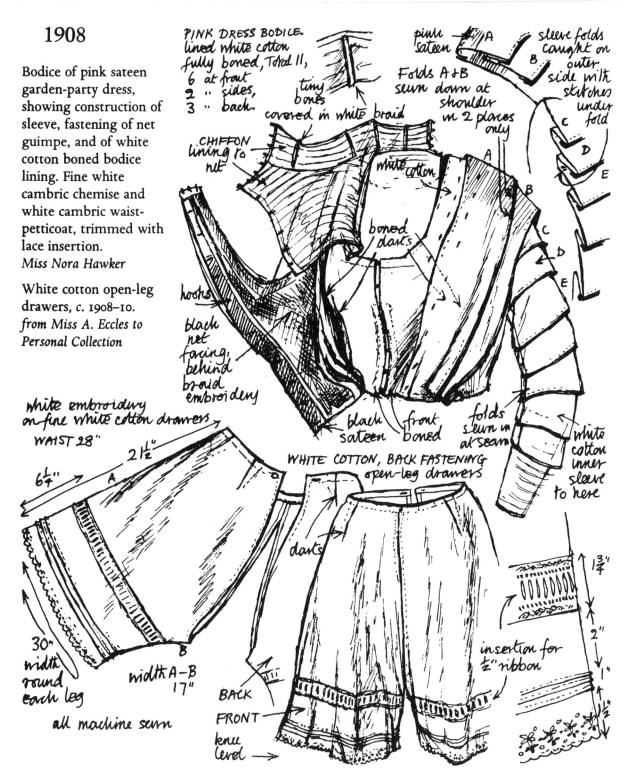

PINK DRESS BODICE.
lined white cotton
fully boned, Total 11,
6 at front
2 " sides,
3 " back.
tiny bones covered in white braid

CHIFFON lining to net

pink sateen

Folds A & B sewn down at shoulder in 2 places only

sleeve folds caught on outer side with stitches under fold

A
B
C
D
E

white cotton

A
B
C
D
E

boned darts

hooks

black net facing behind braid embroidery

black sateen

front boned

folds sewn in at seam

white cotton inner sleeve to here

white embroidery on fine white cotton drawers,
WAIST 28"

6¼"

2½"

A

30" width round each leg

width A–B 17"

B

all machine sewn

WHITE COTTON, BACK FASTENING open-leg drawers

darts

BACK
FRONT
knee level →

1¾"
insertion for ½" ribbon
2"
1"
½"

This is a good example of the type of fastening found on Edwardian dresses. It hooks from the side-back of the neatly boned guimpe, down the left front and the centre front of the bodice, and right round the waist, until the dress is finally unhooked down the centre-back skirt

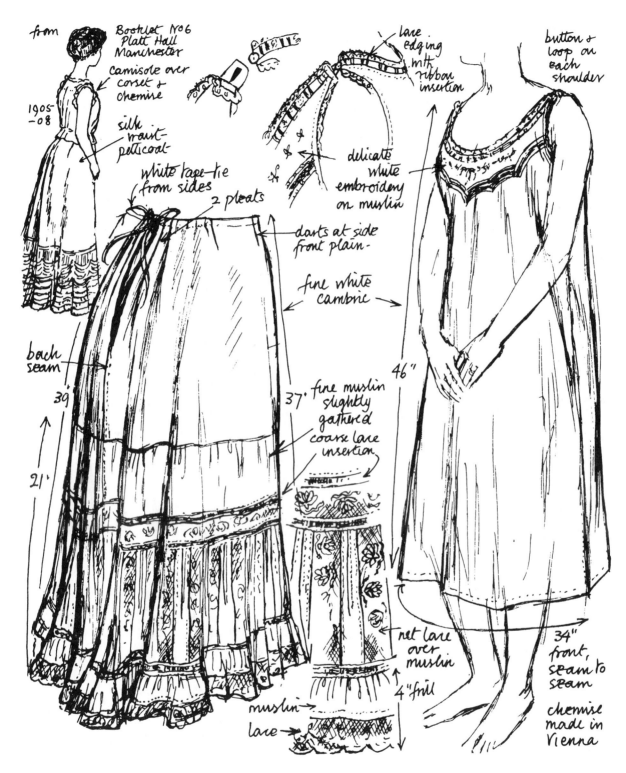

from Booklet No 6
Platt Hall
Manchester

1905 -08

camisole over corset & chemise

silk waist-petticoat

white tape-tie from sides

2 pleats

back seam

39'

21'

lace edging with ribbon insertion

delicate white embroidery on muslin

darts at side front plain.

fine white cambric

fine muslin slightly gathered

coarse lace insertion

37'

net lace over muslin

4" frill

muslin lace

button & loop on each shoulder

46"

34" front, seam to seam

chemise made in Vienna

placket. The white cambric chemise, bought in Vienna by Frank Hawker, was never worn by his wife, owing to her early death. The waist-petticoat with lace insertion, and the open-leg drawers, now at knee-level, go out of use by 1910.

1907-08

Cream satin evening dress, printed with sprays of violets in natural shades and trimmed with rich embroidered panels on skirt, sleeve, and bodice in silvered glass beads. Draped bodice, fastening side-back and centre-back. Long boned lining to bodice in white sateen from neckline to hips.
worn by Mrs H. Maxwell's mother; given by her to Snowshill Collection

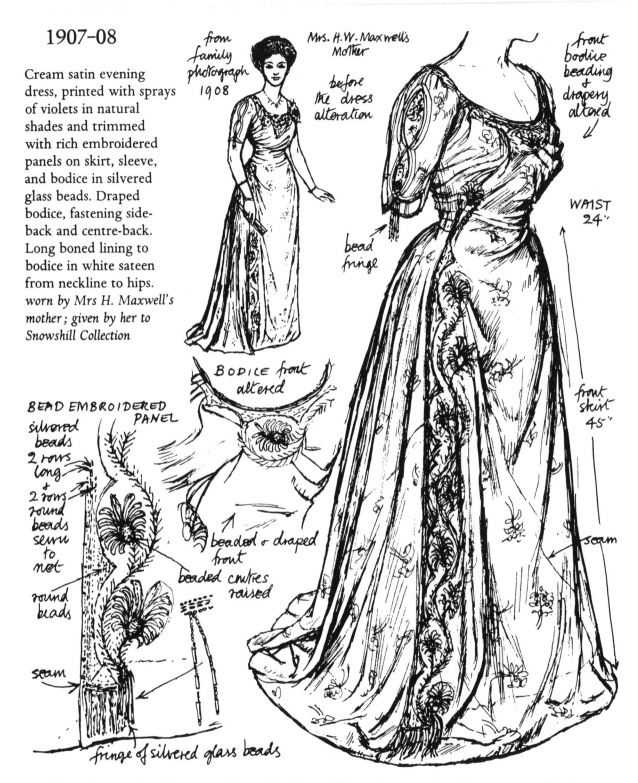

from family photograph 1908

Mrs. H.W. Maxwell's Mother

before the dress alteration

front bodice beading & drapery altered ↓

bead fringe

WAIST 24"

BODICE front altered

front skirt 45"

BEAD EMBROIDERED PANEL

silvered beads 2 rows long + 2 rows round beads sewn to net

round beads

beaded & draped front
beaded centres raised

seam

seam

fringe of silvered glass beads

The photograph, taken 1908, shows Mrs Maxwell's mother wearing this very graceful dress, with the beaded neckline and pouched draped bodice, before it was altered to make it fit the figure more closely. The long, embroidered panel hides a main seam. Lighter and more

311

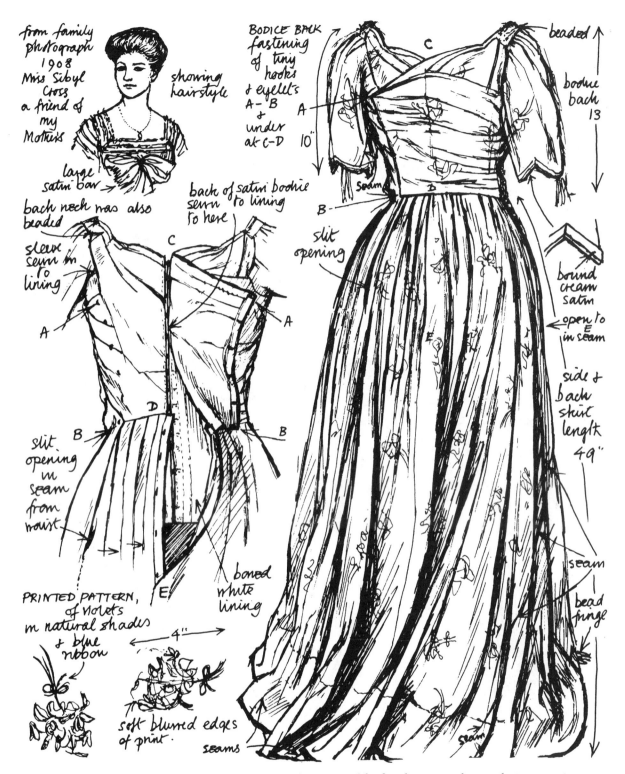

from family photograph 1908 Miss Sibyl Cross a friend of my Mother's

showing hairstyle

large satin bow

back neck was also beaded

sleeve sewn in to lining

BODICE BACK fastening of tiny hooks & eyelets A-B & under at C-D

back of satin bodice sewn to lining to here

slit opening in seam from waist

PRINTED PATTERN, of violets in natural shades & blue ribbon

soft blurred edges of print.

seams

boned white lining

beaded

bodice back 13

10"

Seam

slit opening

bound cream satin

open to E in seam

side & back skirt length 49"

seam

bead fringe

4"

delicate materials in softer colours now make it possible for dresses to be made in one piece, although the bodice, and, in fact, the whole dress, is really now 'hung' from the long, fitting boned lining, which fits almost like a corset, to hip-level.

1907-08

Cream satin evening dress, printed with sprays of violets. Inside of white sateen boned bodice lining, hook-fastening. *Snowshill Collection*

White cambric knickers fastening at sides, legs frilled, embroidery and seams finely sewn. *worn by Mrs N. J. Hawker*

1900-07 fine wool dressing-jacket, pink and white striped. *worn by Mrs A. McKewan; Miss Nora Hawker*

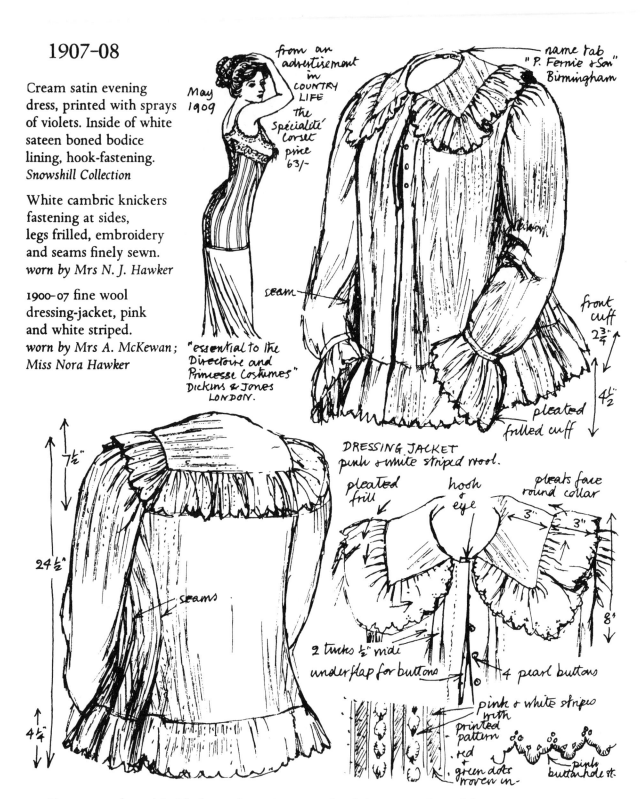

May 1909

from an advertisement in COUNTRY LIFE the *Spécialité* corset price 63/-

"essential to the Directoire and Princesse Costumes" Dickins & Jones LONDON.

name tab "P. Fernie & Son" Birmingham

seam

front cuff 2¾"

4½"

pleated frilled cuff

7½"

24½"

seams

4¼"

DRESSING JACKET pink & white striped wool.

pleated frill

hook & eye

pleats face round collar

3"   3"

8"

2 tucks ½" wide

underflap for buttons

4 pearl buttons

pink & white stripes with printed pattern red & green dots woven in

pink buttonhole st.

Dresses are boned inside from the waist upward, while corsets, boned from below the bust, lengthen to almost mid-thigh between 1909 and 1916 (p. 350), controlling the figure much lower down. How uncomfortable and difficult it must have been to sit and relax. No wonder

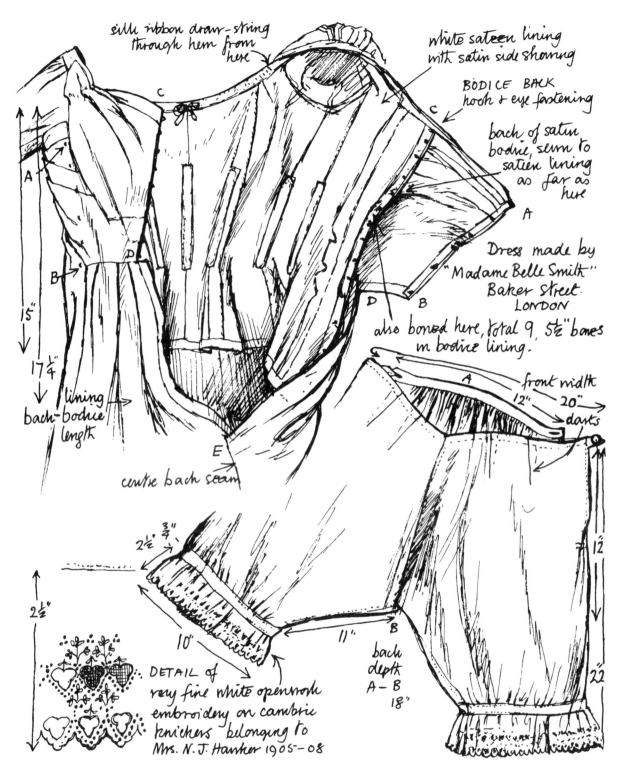

silk ribbon draw-string through hem from here

white sateen lining with satin side showing

BODICE BACK
hook & eye fastening

back of satin bodice, seam to satin lining as far as here

Dress made by "Madame Belle Smith" Baker Street. LONDON

also boned here, total 9, 5½" bones in bodice lining.

A

C

C

A

B

D

B

E

15"

17¼"

lining
back bodice
length

centre back seam

front width

12" — 20"

darts

A

2½" ¾"

2½"

10"

11"

B

back
depth
A - B
18"

12"

22"

DETAIL of very fine white openwork embroidery on cambric knickers belonging to Mrs. N. J. Hawker 1905-08

women enjoyed wearing négligées (p. 319) or wraps and dressing-jackets when they had the opportunity. Knickers such as these, fastening at the sides, are now replacing drawers, giving a smoother line over the hips.

1908

Soft mauve-blue silk crêpe-de-chine dinner dress, high-waisted swathed bodice and fitting sleeves; back fastening. Sewn to longer-waisted boned under-bodice, with mauve satin under-skirt sewn in at the waist. Padded hem. *worn by Mrs Nora Jane Hawker, of Handsworth Wood, Birmingham, and kept by Miss Nora Hawker*

short sleeves of crêpe-de-chine matching dress

bodice front

all sleeve lined finest white transparent silk

long sleeves of transparent thin blue silk gathered on to the white silk undersleeve

5 rows ruching with tucks

14"

8"

8"

8"

WAIST 26"

thin blue silk

crêpe-de-chine

45"

55"

3"

silver-gilt thread

gold thread

1½"

EMBROIDERED BRAID, ground of coarse net

Ball fringe of silver thread blue silk

blue & silver thread

Large French knots of blue silk

padded hem

3"

On December 13th, 1908, Mrs N. J. Hawker wore this charming dress when dining out with her husband, Frank Hawker, M.B.E. It was the last evening dress she was ever to wear, and was kept by her husband and later by her daughter, who kindly lent it to me. This is a very

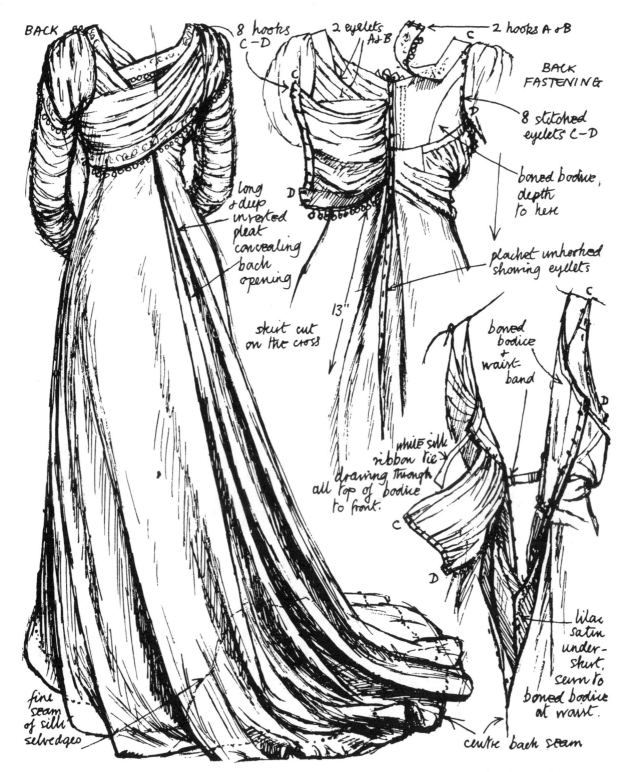

BACK

8 hooks C–D

2 eyelets A & B

2 hooks A & B

BACK FASTENING

8 stitched eyelets C–D

boned bodice, depth to here

long & deep inverted pleat concealing back opening

placket unhooked showing eyelets

skirt cut on the cross

13"

boned bodice + waist-band

white silk ribbon tie drawing through all top of bodice to front.

lilac satin under-skirt, sewn to boned bodice at waist.

fine seam of silk selvedges

centre back seam

good example of the new long, slender, high-waisted 'Empire' line, with the fitting sleeves, embroidered trimming, and ball fringe so much fancied in 1908 and '09. The back pleating and fullness of skirt disappear 1909–10. (See also ball fringe on 1814 dress, p. 375.)

1908

Soft mauve-blue silk crêpe-de-chine dinner dress, worn by Mrs Nora Jane Hawker on December 13th, 1908. Dress made in one, being sewn to boned longer-waisted and fitting under-bodice, with a mauve satin under-skirt sewn to it at normal waist-level.
Miss Nora Hawker

Pink alpaca waist-petticoat, frilled hem.
Mrs M. S. Mallam

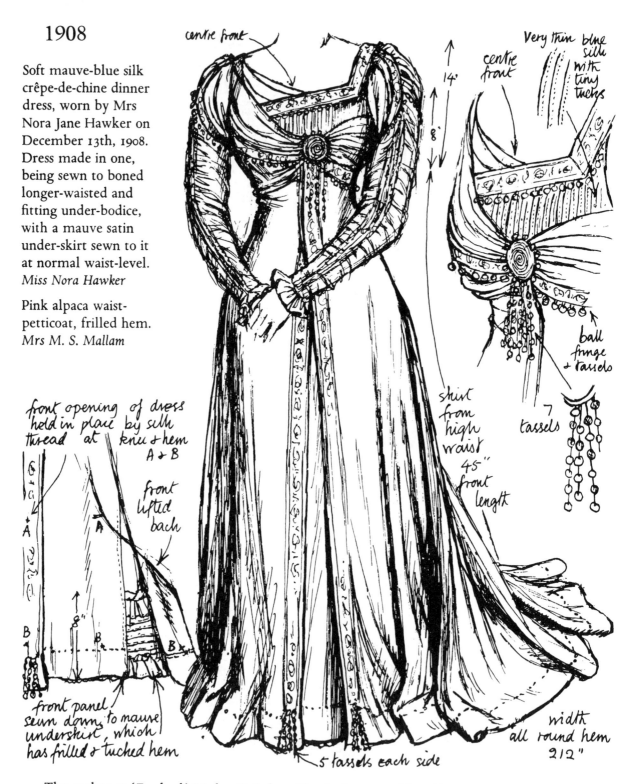

centre front

Very thin blue silk with tiny tucks

centre front

14'

8'

centre front

ball fringe & tassels

7 tassels

skirt from high waist 45" front length

front opening of dress held in place by silk thread at knee & hem A & B

front lifted back

8"

A   B

front panel sewn down to mauve underskirt, which has frilled & tucked hem

5 tassels each side

width all round hem 212"

The maker at 'Fordred' Modes & Robes, Birmingham, could well have been proud of this delightful dress, which is beautifully finished with a considerable amount of fine detailed trimming. The long, slim, ruched and tucked sleeves are of a finer silk, a little more blue

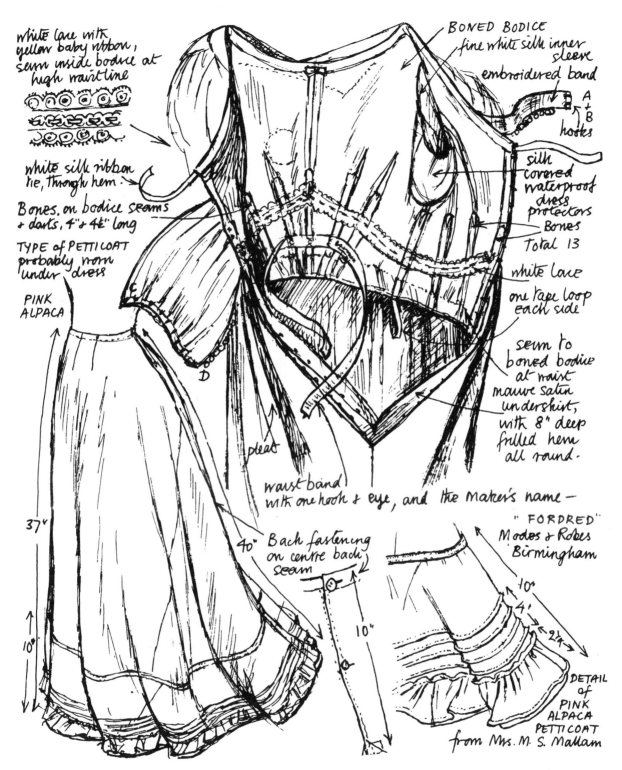

white lace with yellow baby ribbon, sewn inside bodice at high waist line

white silk ribbon tie, through hem.

Bones, on bodice seams + darts, 4" + 4½" long

TYPE of PETTICOAT probably worn under dress

PINK ALPACA

37"

40"

10"

pleat

waist band with one hook & eye, and the Maker's name —

Back fastening on centre back seam

10"

BONED BODICE
fine white silk inner sleeve
embroidered band

A + B hooks

silk covered waterproof dress protectors Bones

Total 13

white lace

one tape loop each side

seam to boned bodice at waist mauve satin undershirt, with 8" deep frilled hem all round.

"FORDRED" Modes & Robes Birmingham

10"
4"
2½"

DETAIL of PINK ALPACA PETTICOAT
from Mrs. M. S. Mallam

and transparent in appearance than the crêpe-de-chine. The very slightly off-centre draping and decoration on the bodice is intriguing. The silk is all cut on the cross. The pink alpaca petticoat is of the style worn at about this time.

c. 1908

Very fine cream net négligée with tiny tucks on bodice and sleeve, with lace insertion & frills; higher waistline. Net fichu, lace-edged, draping the shoulders gathered up front and back. Long, fitting sleeves, fastened at wrist with very small pearl buttons. Insertion and frills of finest Buckinghamshire lace.
Chastleton House; lent to Snowshill

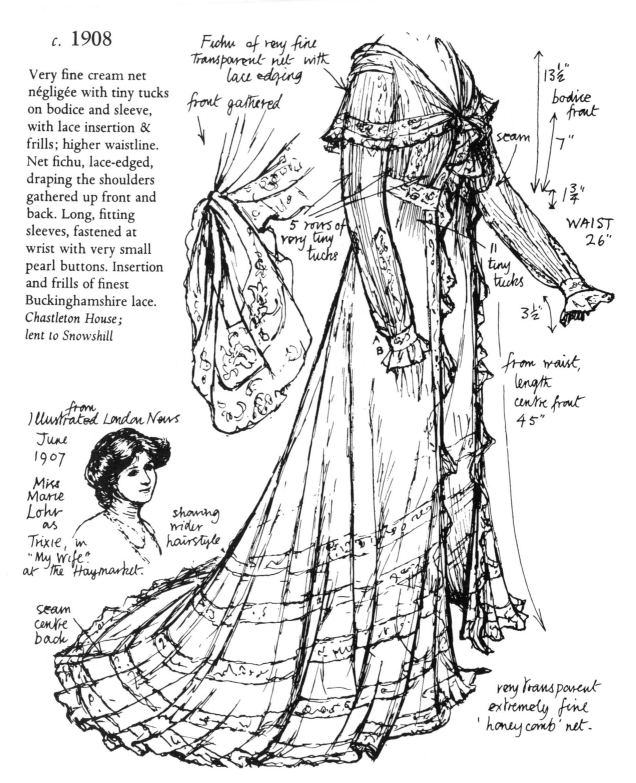

Fichu of very fine transparent net with lace edging

front gathered

13½" bodice front

7"

seam

1¾"

WAIST 26"

5 rows of very tiny tucks

11 tiny tucks

3½"

from waist, length centre front 45"

from *Illustrated London News* June 1907

Miss Marie Lohr as Trixie, in "My Wife" at the Haymarket.

showing wider hairstyle

seam centre back

very transparent extremely fine 'honey comb' net.

An exquisite, transparent, elegant garment, both in material used and in the long slenderness of sleeve and skirt. By 1907 the waistline shows signs of rising, and here, with the delicate tucks on bodice and sleeve, with the addition of the vertical lace insertion, the other new

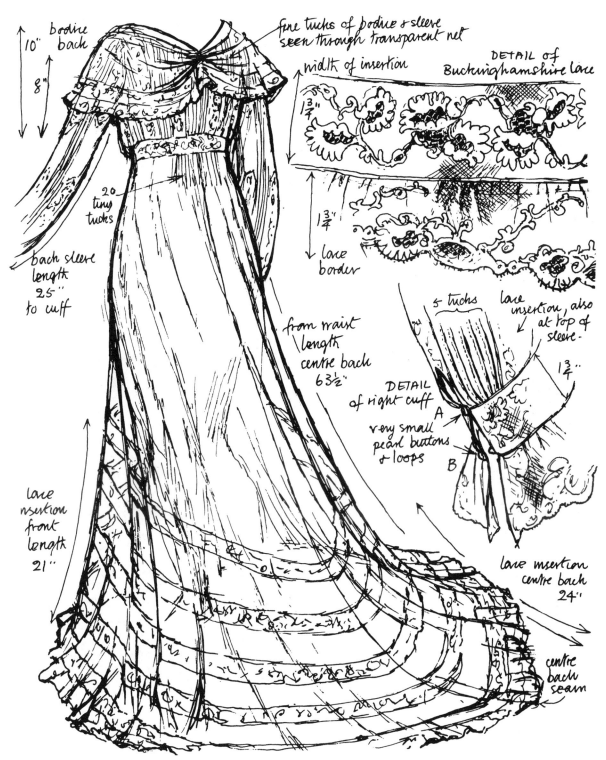

bodice back

10"

8"

fine tucks of bodice & sleeve
seen through transparent net

width of insertion

1¾"

DETAIL of
Buckinghamshire lace

20 tiny tucks

back sleeve length 25" to cuff

1¾"

lace border

from waist length centre back 63½"

5 tucks

lace insertion, also at top of sleeve.

1¾"

DETAIL of right cuff

very small pearl buttons & loops

A

B

lace insertion front length 21"

lace insertion centre back 24"

centre back seam

long slim line is apparent. But this spreading, trailing skirt looks backward to a style soon to become 'old-fashioned.' Some hair styles of this period follow the draped, wide look of this shoulder-line.

1907–09

Small evening bag, cream suède, gilt frame, bronze bead decoration. Long evening gloves of peach-pink kid.
Miss Nora Hawker

Long black lace scarf rich floral motif, silk, finely machine-woven.
from Mrs J. S. Fison to Personal Collection

White satin parasol trimmed gauze frills, ruched white ribbon, long cane handle.
Snowshill Collection

EVENING BAG of cream suède

gilt frame

4½

4½

6½

embroidered very tiny bronze beads, lined white silk

tulle scarf from hat! Undersleeves + guimpe of white net

from COUNTRY LIFE May 1st 1909

afternoon gown with a long "Empire" scarf of embroidered muslin –

very finely machine woven BLACK LACE SCARF length 10 ft.

day dress with long gloves + tiny purse

from a fashion plate in "The Ladies' Tailor" 1907

walking costume

16"

5½

self bound

buttons missing →

5¼

DETAIL

EVENING GLOVES peach-pink kid, stitching to match

width 16½"

Note difference in waist level and skirt fullness from 1907 to 1909 (above).

Both the evening bag and long kid gloves were used by Miss Hawker's mother, 1908, shortly before her death, and they, like the rich lace or filmy gauze scarves and elaborate parasols, important accessories to the Edwardian woman, are soon to disappear from the fashionable

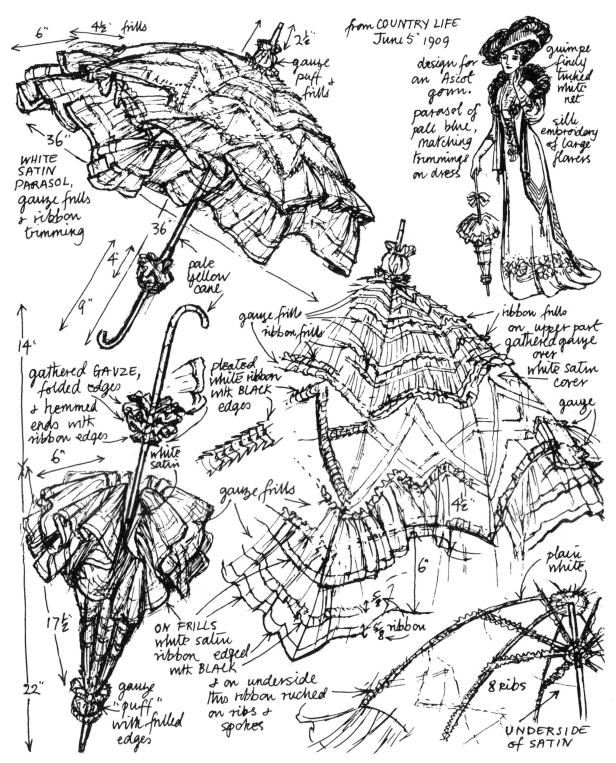

from COUNTRY LIFE
June 5 1909

design for an Ascot gown.
parasol of pale blue, matching trimmings on dress

guimpe finely tucked white net

silk embroidery of large flowers

6" 4½" frills 2½"
gauze puff & frills

36"

36"

WHITE SATIN PARASOL, gauze frills & ribbon trimming

pale yellow cane

4"

9"

14"

gathered GAUZE, folded edges & hemmed ends with ribbon edges

pleated white ribbon with BLACK edges

gauze frill ribbon frill

ribbon frills on upper part gathered gauze over white satin cover

gauze

6"

white satin

gauze frills

4½"

6"

plain white

17½"

ON FRILLS white satin ribbon edged with BLACK

⅝

⅝ ribbon

8 ribs

22"

gauze "puff" with frilled edges

& on underside this ribbon ruched on ribs & spokes

UNDERSIDE of SATIN

scene, together with the huge hats and long, trailing dresses. But *Country Life*, 1909, in commenting on the 'Empire' scarf then worn, says, 'these scarves and others . . . are one of the features of this season's fashions.'

c. 1908

Long cloth and lace combinations, with tucks, broderie anglaise, and insertions. Wide, open-leg style, frilled to mid-calf. Back fastening, tiny pearl buttons, all finely hand-sewn.
Personal Collection

1904-07

Straight-fronted corset, blue and white cotton damask, fully boned.
Miss Nora Hawker

1904 ribbon corset.
Snowshill Collection

delicate white lace
fine faggoting

tiny pearl buttons

⌀ ↕ 3/8

↕ 4"

tiny tucks down back

Maker's name, in fine red lettering "OXFORD underclothing, made of HORROCKSES long cloth." seen inside.

2½"

3½"

2"

8'

BUST 32'

WAIST 28½'

HIP 38'

18"

2"

10½"

1½"

43'

lace panels alternating cambric

2½"

1" wide + tiny tucks fine to centre front

1¼" wide for ribbon

2¼"

detail of central panels of broderie anglaise

fine cambric slightly gathered also 2" band at top.

width round leg 42"

all extremely finely hand sewn

Dresses and underwear of c. 1908 are dainty and elaborate, with lace insertions, frills, and tiny tucks. The waistline is high, but underwear, like the dress, froths out below knee-level. This wide, open-leg style remains in use for about 2 more years. The straight-fronted corset

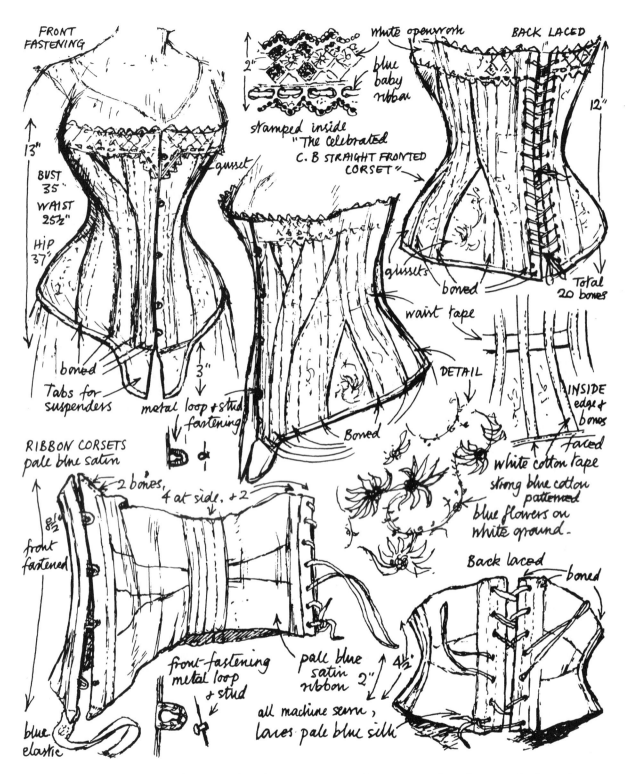

FRONT FASTENING

13"

BUST 35"
WAIST 25½"

HIP 37"

boned

Tabs for suspenders

gusset

metal loop + stud fastening

white openwork

blue baby ribbon

2"

Stamped inside "The Celebrated C.B STRAIGHT FRONTED CORSET"

gussets

Boned

BACK LACED

12"

boned

Total 20 bones

waist tape

DETAIL

INSIDE edge + bones

faced

white cotton tape

strong blue cotton patterned blue flowers on white ground.

RIBBON CORSETS pale blue satin

8½"

front fastened

2 bones, 4 at side, + 2

blue elastic

front fastening metal loop + stud

pale blue satin ribbon 2"

all machine sewn, laces pale blue silk

Back laced

boned

4½"

was worn by Miss Hawker's mother between 1904 and 1907. Boned and gusseted, they give the impression of a tiny waist, allowing the figure to blossom out in rich curves above and below. Ribbon corsets were for sport or worn with négligée.

c. 1909

Crisp fawn silk dress, trimmed with rich blue satin, corded and plain. The guimpe and under-sleeves of tucked cream net and lace, lined with plain net and trimmed with blue satin under machine-made coarse cream lace. Edging on bodice of narrow cream lace. All fully lined fawn cotton, with boned bodice lining.
Miss J. Procter

plain blue satin piped edges

5/8"

back pleated to centre

net & sleeves sewn to lining

1½"

tie stitches from belt to skirt

corded blue satin, & under lace

13"

3/4"

stitched pleat not central

30" WAIST

centre back

dart

lace over net

joining seam of skirt hidden under pleat

back 36"

centre back net

centre front

BACK VIEW INSIDE OUT

lined plain net

Tape covered wire bones machined to lining

7"

FAWN COTTON LINED, sewn in at seams with silk

side seams

SPIRALUXE COLLAR SUPPORT "non silk, no metal no rust, 4 for 4½ᵈ" advert. from the Ladies' Field 1911

Tape loop

centre back seam of lining

seam

stitched pleat, not central

The skirt, although narrower, straighter, and shorter, still has traces of fullness at centre back; it has the fashionable form of decoration below knee-level, to give an illusion of slimness. By 1911 advertisements for dresses for all occasions except sportswear, show them long and

325

June 1911

Smart River Gown 59/6 in Linen

from fashion advertisement in The Ladies' Field

also Raoul's of Paris 21/-

Buckle shoe + button boot 19/6

fawn cotton lining

1¾" 1"

3 patent fasteners on bodice. this seam down to lining at edge for 10"

10"

sleeve seam 7½"

bodice seam here to lining

lining

12½"

blue satin

B

A

B

C

C

10"

D

D

SKIRT has patent fasteners + hooks + eyes

narrow pocket seam to this side

grey cloth & glacé patent.

plain blue satin

narrow lace

tucked net

lined plain net

4½"

sleeve 12"

2½"

6"

front 35½"

self faced

16"

seam

3¾"

buttons self covered + sewn down round outer edge

flat piping plain blue satin ⅛"

5/8"

rich blue corded satin, also under lace on bodice & sleeves

cream machine-made lace rather coarse, but has a rich effect over blue

3½"

width all round hem 65"

tubular, being very narrow, both at hem and hip. As a contrast, hats reach their maximum width. The bodice of this dress has a tunic-top, with the skirt sewn to it just above the waist. Net sleeves and front are sewn to lining.

c. 1909

Detail of fawn silk dress trimmed with blue satin and lace, showing fastening of tunic bodice and guimpe and under-bodice. Inside dress front, showing pocket. *Miss J. Procter*

White combinations, of cotton with broderie anglaise top and leg trimming. Petticoat back with open-leg drawers, worn 1911–17. *from Miss A. Eccles to Personal Collection*

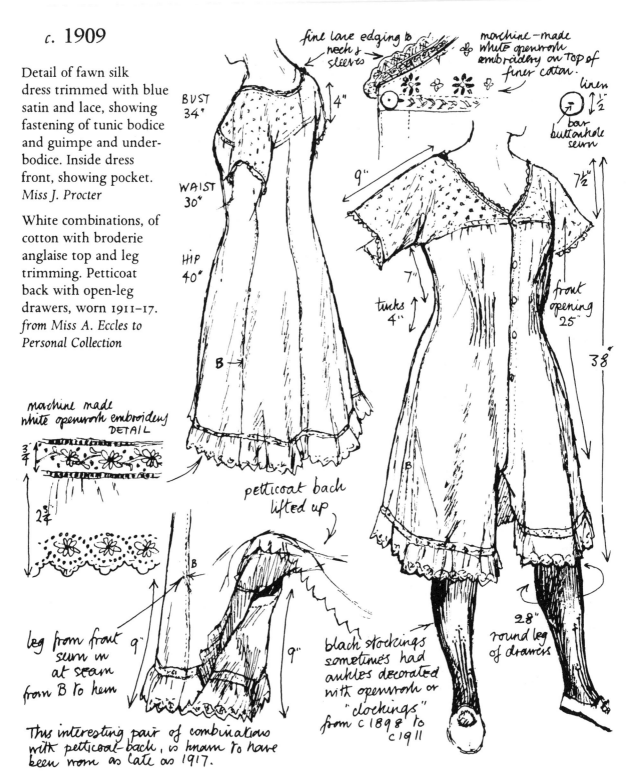

fine lace edging to neck & sleeves

machine-made white openwork embroidery on top of finer cotton.

BUST 34"

WAIST 30"

HIP 40"

4"

linen 1½"

bar buttonhole sewn

9"

7½"

7"

tucks 4"

front opening 25"

38"

B →

machine made white openwork embroidery DETAIL

¾"

2¾"

petticoat back lifted up

B

28" round leg of drawers

leg from front sewn in at seam from B to hem

9"

9"

B

black stockings sometimes had ankles decorated with openwork or "clockings" from c 1898 to c 1911

This interesting pair of combinations with petticoat-back, is known to have been worn as late as 1917.

This practical combined garment seems rather unusual, and it is interesting to know, too, that it was worn as late as this, when the open-leg style of drawers went out of use by about 1911. The sleeve shape is similar to that found on dresses from *c.* 1909 to *c.* 1914. The bodice

327

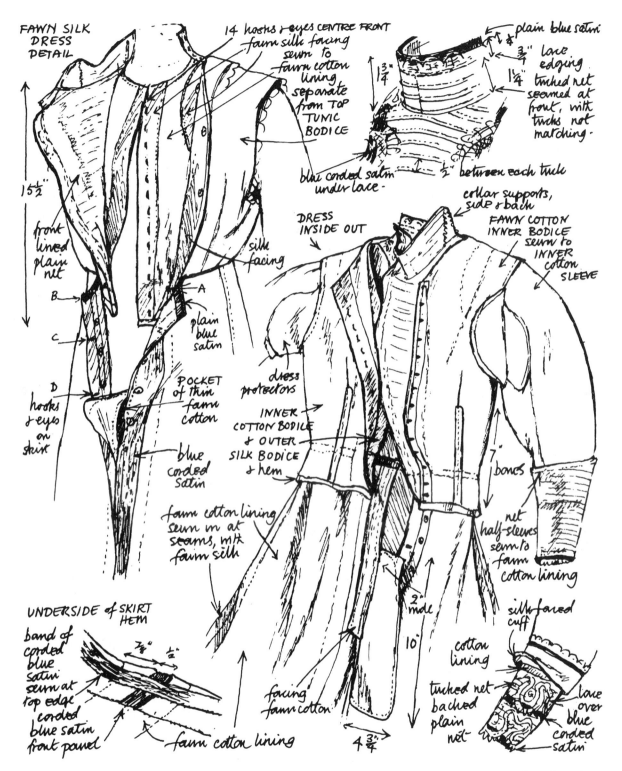

FAWN SILK DRESS DETAIL

14 hooks & eyes CENTRE FRONT
fawn silk facing sewn to fawn cotton lining separate from TOP TUNIC BODICE

15½"

front lined plain net

B.

C.

D.

hooks & eyes on skirt

silk facing

A.

plain blue satin

POCKET of thin fawn cotton

blue corded satin

fawn cotton lining sewn in at seams, with fawn silk

plain blue satin

1¾"

3" lace edging

1¼" tucked net seamed at front, with tucks not matching.

½" between each tuck

blue corded satin under lace.

DRESS INSIDE OUT

dress protectors

INNER COTTON BODICE & OUTER SILK BODICE & hem

collar supports, side & back

FAWN COTTON INNER BODICE sewn to INNER COTTON SLEEVE

7" bones

net half-sleeves sewn to fawn cotton lining

silk faced cuff

cotton lining

tucked net backed plain net

lace over blue corded satin

2" wide

10"

facing fawn cotton

4¾"

UNDERSIDE of SKIRT HEM

band of corded blue satin sewn at top edge

7/8"   ½"

corded blue satin front panel

fawn cotton lining

top of the dress has a similar V-shaped neckline both at front and back; this is often found on dresses 1907–12. The pocket in the front panel of the skirt is a little unusual; it must have been a personal fancy of the wearer.

1909-10

Richly beaded black net evening dress, jet beads and sequins. Black chiffon top under wide beaded net cape, with draped back and front, with tassels. Beige chiffon under-bodice sewn to black satin sheath skirt. Back fastening with hooks on beaded net & on satin under-dress. Bodice lined cream satin, fully boned.
Commander Hart

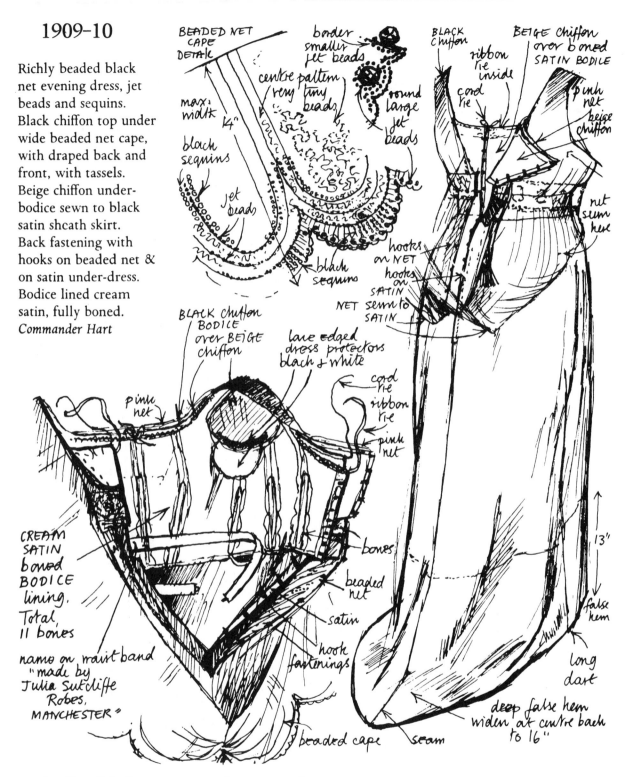

BEADED NET CAPE DETAIL

border smaller jet beads

centre pattern (very tiny beads)

round large jet beads

max. width 14"

black sequins

jet beads

black sequins

BLACK chiffon

ribbon tie inside

cord tie

BEIGE chiffon over boned SATIN BODICE

pink net beige chiffon

net seam here

hooks on NET

hooks on SATIN

NET sewn to SATIN

BLACK chiffon BODICE over BEIGE chiffon

lace edged dress protectors black & white

cord tie

ribbon tie

pink net

pink net

bones

beaded net

satin

hook fastenings

CREAM SATIN boned BODICE lining. Total, 11 bones

name on waistband "made by Julia Sutcliffe Robes, MANCHESTER"

beaded cape

seam

13"

false hem

long dart

deep false hem widen at centre back to 16"

A tall well-built woman must have worn this very expensive beaded dress; the richness of pattern and variety of beads and sequins used, together with the fine workmanship, make one wonder how long this gown was in the making. The heavily beaded border at the hem

BODILE & sleeves
BLACK CHIFFON
sewn to BLACK
beaded net
skirt.
BEIGE CHIFFON
under bodice
sewn to
BLACK SATIN
SKIRT.

from
The
Ladies'
Field.

fashionable
hair-
style
1911

BEADED NET CAPE
black chiffon
bodice & sleeves
over
beige
chiffon
14"

cape

beige
chiffon
Bodice
to here

folded
pink
net

seam
3"

large
flat
beads

tiny jet
beads

beaded
fringed panel
concealing
BACK HOOKED
FASTENINGS.

opening to
here

long
rounded
beads

gathered
back of
BEADED
NET DRESS
over
SHEATH-LIKE
SATIN SKIRT
with
narrow
train.

SKIRT of
BEADED NET
sewn to
SATIN.
keeping
gathers
at back
under cape

Tassels

fringe
of
tiny jet
beads

5"

stripes of beads on net
widen out towards border

12"
heavily
beaded
border

BACK of gown
with BACK FASTENINGS
of hook & eye.

and richly scallop-shaped draped collar give emphasis to the very fine strands of beading on the skirt. The black chiffon top is fine and transparent, and adds a subtle touch of delicacy to this rather fascinating dress.

1909–10

Front and side view of black beaded net evening dress, with chiffon top, over satin under-dress. Beaded dress sewn round at neck and sleeves to under-dress, with net hanging free to hem. Back folds of net held in position by tie-stitches to under-dress detail of beaded net at hemline, and of skirt construction.
Commander Hart

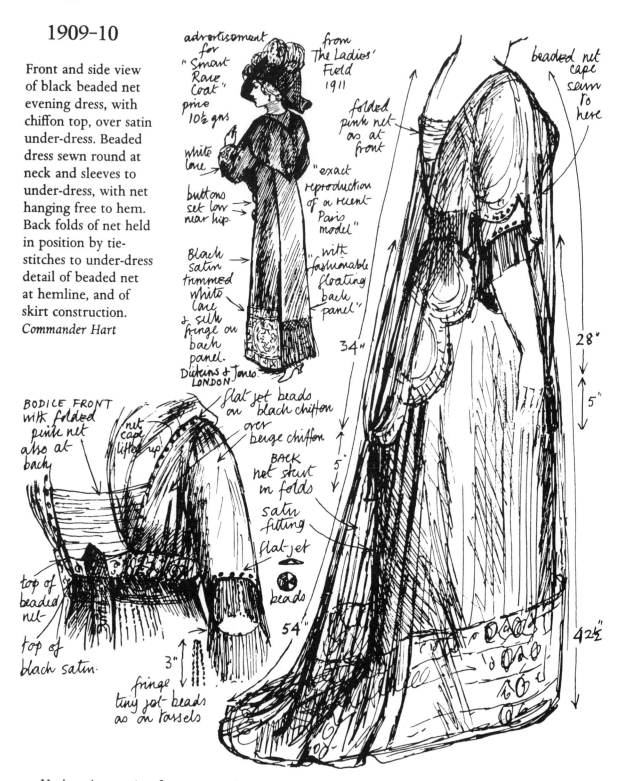

advertisement for "Smart Race Coat" price 10½ gns

from The Ladies' Field 1911

white lace

buttons set low near hip.

Black satin trimmed white lace & silk fringe on back panel. Dickins & Jones. LONDON.

folded pink net as at front

"exact reproduction of a recent Paris model"

"with fashionable floating back panel"

beaded net cape seam to here

34"

5'

28"

5"

BODICE FRONT with folded pink net also at back

net cape lifted up

top of beaded net

top of black satin.

flat-jet beads on black chiffon over beige chiffon

BACK net sewn in folds

satin fitting

flat jet beads

3"

fringe tiny jet beads as on tassels

54"

42½"

Various interesting features are found on this evening dress; it has an elegance and dignity combining both past and present styles. The trailing beaded net does not really hide the sheath-like skirt beneath with its narrow train. And the pink net on the bodice, being almost

flat jet beads under beaded net

beige chiffon

black satin

WAIST 33"

dart

front sleeve 8"

length seam back sleeve 14"

round jet beads

42"

13"

seam

long dart widening at hem to make skirt narrow

deep false hem

seam

pattern on front panel continues up from border

depth beaded border 12"

sequins

+ flat shapes DULL Black

other beads

shiny black

BORDER → very heavily beaded

flesh-colour, gives the impression of a deeply plunging neckline. On both dresses and coats of this period, the eye is frequently taken away from the high waistline, down to hip-level. Hats and hair styles increase in height.

c. 1911

Midnight-blue velvet evening dress. Bodice of Venetian point lace, cream, over cream chiffon. Under-bodice and under-skirt of stiff cream silk taffeta. Bodice lined in white figured cotton, fully boned, fastening at back with hook & bar. Short train with three lead weights, made to button up on inside.
Chastleton House; lent to Snowshill Collection

Underbodice of white taffeta

rich cream lace

fitting chiffon sleeves to fitting chiffon bodice

under draped chiffon with white taffeta under

$13\frac{1}{2}$"

dart

lace

folds of velvet

dart

2 darts

seam

placket to here

Exquisite Venetian point lace, with great variety of "filling in" stitches of flowers etc

DETAIL of cream lace frill on sleeve

the brides being mainly this shape

seams

$14\frac{1}{2}$"

front inset of lace + chiffon over underskirt of stiff cream silk taffeta

$4\frac{1}{2}$"

15"

9"

$11\frac{1}{2}$

2 pairs of tape-ties inside to keep train in position when buttoned up inside skirt.

Straight and slender, with an almost tubular skirt, this rich velvet has quite deep pleating into back panel, to give ease when sitting. The high, wide folded and shaped waistband brings the velvet right up to the bust, making the lace bodice look very dainty and attractive.

lace over chiffon

lace width 3¼"

lace 'sleeve' lightly sewn to chiffon back + front

13"

white taffeta under chiffon, lace over chiffon sewn here

velvet band

lace

WAIST 25"

back fastening hooks & sewn bars

2 folds sewn in at seam

centre seam

back opening to here

seam

40"

3 small flat lead weights in train at A, B or C

B   C

9"

back

4½"

front

7" side

The inset of lace here is a machine-made copy only.

The touch of lace at the skirt-front slit is an imitation. The small lead weights sewn under the tiny trains of these evening dresses, Mrs Wickham Steed tells me, made an amusing sound when going downstairs.

334

c. 1911

Midnight-blue velvet evening dress, bodice of Venetian point lace over chiffon. Skirt with slit front, inset of lace over chiffon. Detail showing back fastening, and inside of bodice with boning, taffeta under-skirt with train, showing buttons, loops and tapes for fastening up on inside.

Chastleton House; lent to Snowshill Collection

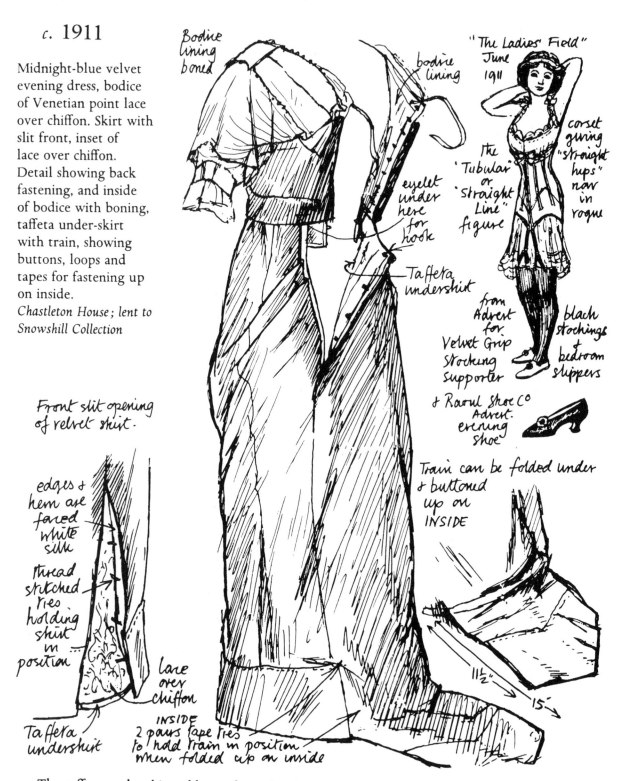

Bodice lining boned

bodice lining

"The Ladies' Field" June 1911

corset giving "straight hips" now in vogue

The 'Tubular' or 'Straight Line' figure

eyelet under here for hook

Taffeta undershirt

from Advert for Velvet Grip Stocking Supporter

black stockings & bedroom slippers

& Raoul Shoe Co Advert. evening shoe

Train can be folded under & buttoned up on INSIDE

Front slit opening of velvet skirt.

edges & hem are faced white silk

thread stitched ties holding skirt in position

lace over chiffon

Taffeta undershirt

INSIDE 2 pairs tape ties to hold train in position when folded up on inside

11½"

15"

The taffeta under-skirt adds a soft rustle of luxury and richness to this very elegant gown. The corsets are now worn under the petticoat and drawers; the advertisements try to convince the feminine world that to be beautiful one must have no hips at all! A difficult thing

evening dress

from *The Ladies' Field* June 1911

cream lace

cream lace

DRESS INSIDE OUT

fitting chiffon undersleeve

white silk ribbon ties from front

white figured cotton lining to white taffeta UNDERBODICE

TAFFETA UNDERBODICE lined white cotton

chiffon

D.P.

1 2 3 4 5

bone at centre front Total 11 bones

TAFFETA UNDER-SKIRT sewn to velvet at waist

Tapes to secure train when fastened up

TAFFETA undertrain white silk lined

VELVET faced white silk

velvet

tie threads

centre back seam

side seam

A

B 2

C

3 LOOPS for BUTTONS to fasten train UP INSIDE

3 small lead weights

1

2

3

14"

white silk faced hem of taffeta under-skirt

Tape sewn through to velvet

Tape sewn to taffeta only

14"

white silk faced hem of velvet

velvet dress Taffeta undershirt

lace over chiffon centre front.

for Edwardian women to reduce their form so suddenly! The other interesting point is the continued use of black stockings, which are preferably of silk for day and evening wear, though white are worn for full-dress.

1911

Trained Court dress of rich gold brocade on cream satin ground, with matching cloak. Worn at Coronation of George V, June 1911, by Lady Evelyn Mason. High-waisted, fitting gown. Lined fine gold tissue. Bodice of net and lace with paste stones. Boned lining of cream silk taffeta.

from Mrs Wickham Steed to Chastleton House; lent to Snowshill Collection

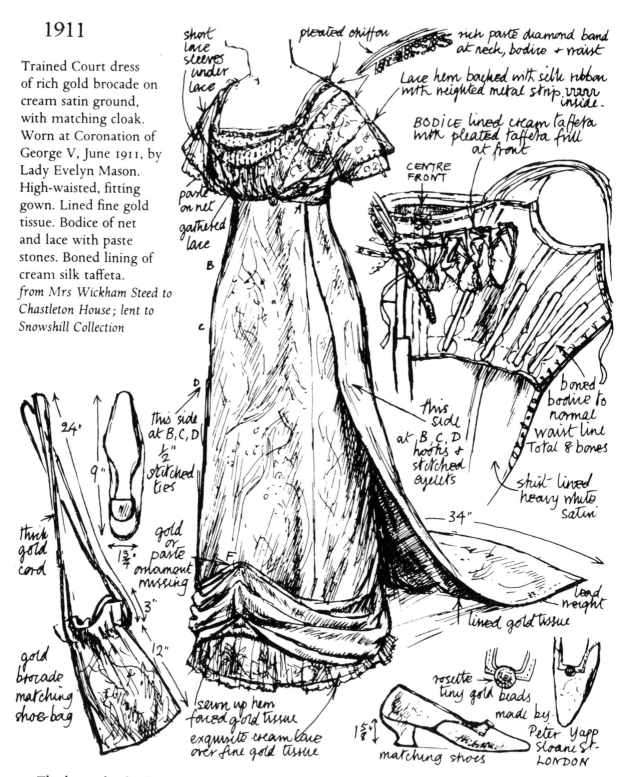

short lace sleeves under lace

pleated chiffon

rich paste diamond band at neck, bodice + waist

Lace hem backed with silk ribbon with weighted metal strip sewn inside.

BODICE lined cream taffeta with pleated taffeta frill at front

CENTRE FRONT

paste on net gathered lace

B

C

D

this side at B,C,D ½" stitched ties

gold or paste ornament missing

this side at B,C,D hooks & stitched eyelets

boned bodice to normal waist line Total 8 bones

skirt lined heavy white satin

F

34"

24"

9"

1¾"

3"

12"

thick gold cord

gold brocade matching shoe-bag

sewn up hem faced gold tissue

exquisite cream lace over fine gold tissue

lead weight

lined gold tissue

rosette tiny gold beads

matching shoes

1⅝"

made by Peter Yapp Sloane St. LONDON

The long, slender line, with narrow skirt and tiny draped bodice of lace and net, is the very height of fashion; even the train is caught to the dress at the sides, so that the slimness of the hips is not hidden. The effect is rich indeed, from the gold tissue lined train, richly draped

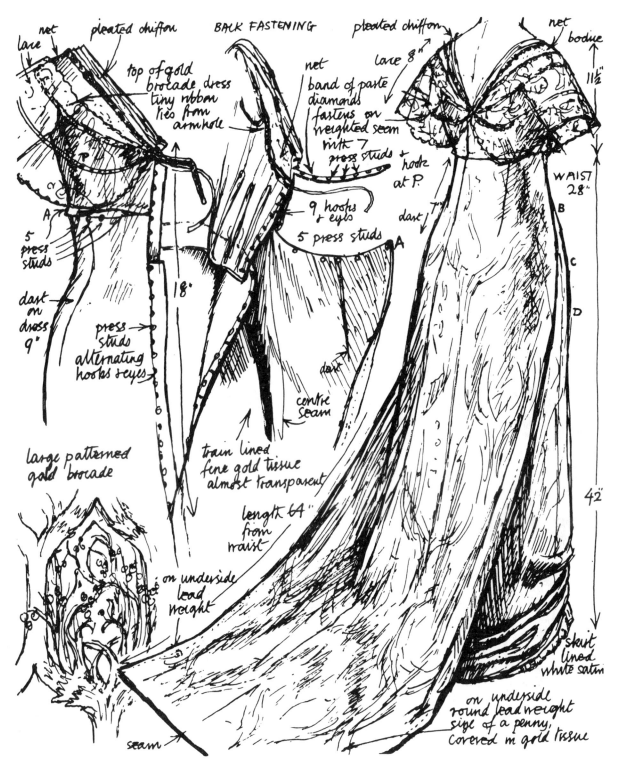

net
lace
pleated chiffon
BACK FASTENING
pleated chiffon
net
bodice

top of gold
brocade dress
tiny ribbon
ties from
armhole

net
band of paste
diamonds
fastens on
weighted seam
with 7
press studs

lace 8"

11½"

hook
at P.

WAIST
28"

9 hooks
+ eyes

dart

5 press studs

A

A

B

5
press
studs

C

dart
on
dress
9"

18"

D

press
studs
alternating
hooks & eyes

dart

centre
seam

42"

large patterned
gold brocade

train lined
fine gold tissue
almost transparent

length 64"
from
waist

on underside
lead
weight

skirt
lined
white satin

on underside
round lead weight
size of a penny,
covered in gold tissue

seam

hemline, with soft touch of lace, to the transparent and tiny, brilliantly sparkling bodice.
One amusing touch, on a note found inside the matching shoes, the words, 'These were made
a size too large'!

1911

Rich gold brocade matching 'cloak' to the Coronation Court dress of Lady Evelyn Mason. Low-waisted cloak, with collar and cuffs of deep blue velvet, lined in white crêpe-de-chine. Pouched back, into corded, low set seam. Fastening at left front with button and loop on hip. *from Mrs Wickham Steed to Chastleton House; lent to Snowshill Collection*

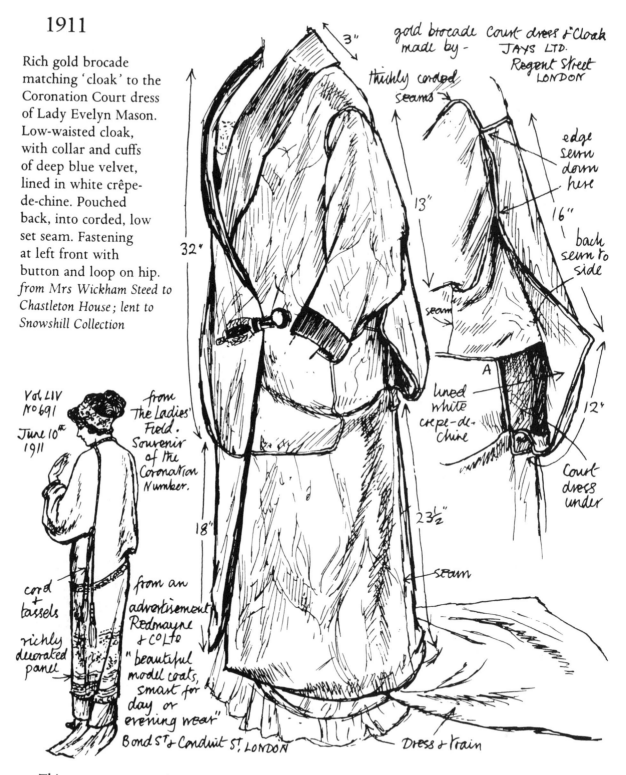

gold brocade made by -

Court dress & Cloak JAYS LTD. Regent Street LONDON

thickly corded seams

edge sewn down here

16"

back seam to side

3"

13"

32"

seam

seam

lined white crepe-de-chine

A

Court dress under

12"

Vol LIV No 691 June 10th 1911

from The Ladies' Field. Souvenir of the Coronation Number.

18"

23½"

seam

cord + tassels

richly decorated panel

from an advertisement Redmayne & Co Ltd "beautiful model coats, smart for day or evening wear" Bond St & Conduit St. LONDON

Dress & train

This coat worn over the Coronation dress was actually called a 'cloak.' It is remarkable that, at a time when dresses were so slim and high-waisted, these coats or outer garments should be so voluminous, and have such emphasis on a very low hip-line, with this pouched back

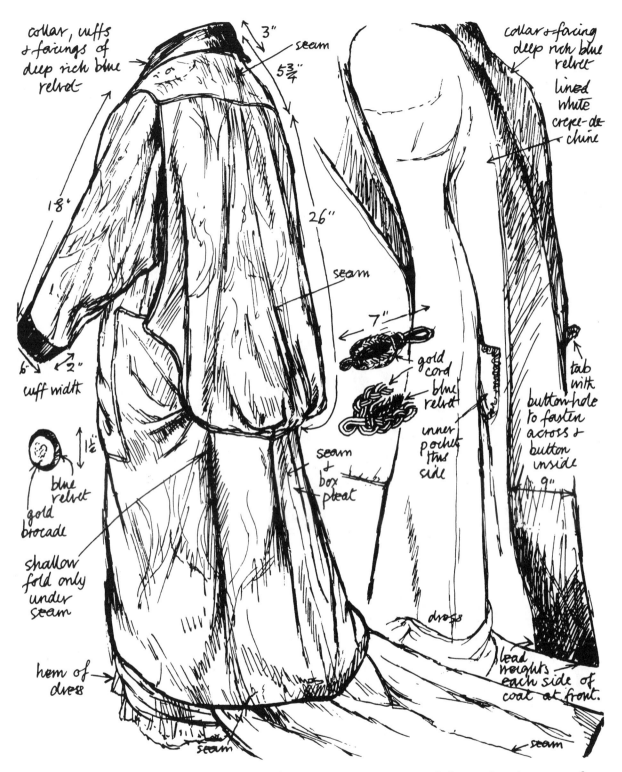

collar, cuffs & facings of deep rich blue velvet

3"

seam

5¾"

collar & facing deep rich blue velvet

lined white crepe-de-chine

18"

26"

seam

7"

gold cord

blue velvet

inner pocket this side

tab with buttonhole to fasten across & button inside

9"

6"

2"

cuff width

1½"

blue velvet

gold brocade

shallow fold only under seam

seam & box pleat

hem of dress

dress

lead weights each side of coat at front.

seam

seam

and almost bat-wing sleeves. But these features are seen in many fashion advertisements of this date, on similar coats, with the front fastening low on the hip. These velvet front facings are lead-weighted at the hem.

1905-12

Olive-green leather handbag, with silver fasteners and initials. Brown suède leather belt with steel buckle. *both belonged to mother of Miss Nora Hawker*

Cotton camisole with lace insertion and tucks, front fastened. *from Miss A. Eccles to Personal Collection*

Cream silk blouse, with lace insertion. *from Mrs A. Cartright to Personal Collection*

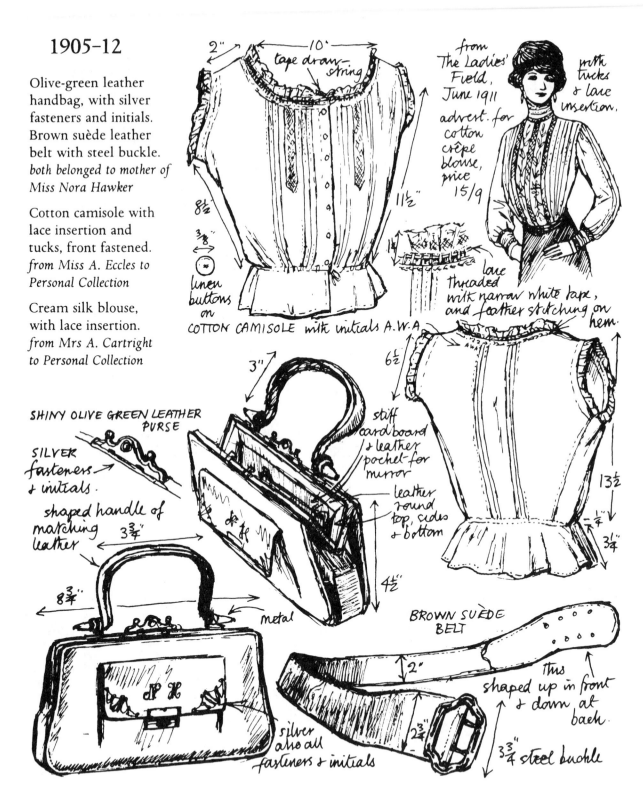

2"
10"
tape draw-string

8½
3/8
linen buttons on
COTTON CAMISOLE with initials A.W.A

11½"

from The Ladies' Field, June 1911 advert. for cotton crêpe blouse, price 15/9

with tucks & lace insertion.

lace threaded with narrow white tape, and feather stitching on hem.

6½

13½

¼

3¾"

SHINY OLIVE GREEN LEATHER PURSE

SILVER fasteners & initials.

shaped handle of matching leather

3"

stiff cardboard & leather pocket for mirror

leather round top, sides & bottom

3¾"

4½"

metal

8¾"

silver also all fasteners & initials

BROWN SUÈDE BELT

2"

2¾

this shaped up in front & down at back.

3¾" steel buckle

Leather handbags, first produced commercially *c.* 1885, were of good quality and usually had a stiff shaped handle similar to this. Leather belts with large metal buckles were worn with the popular blouse and skirt, except during the 'Empire' period of the higher waistline

341

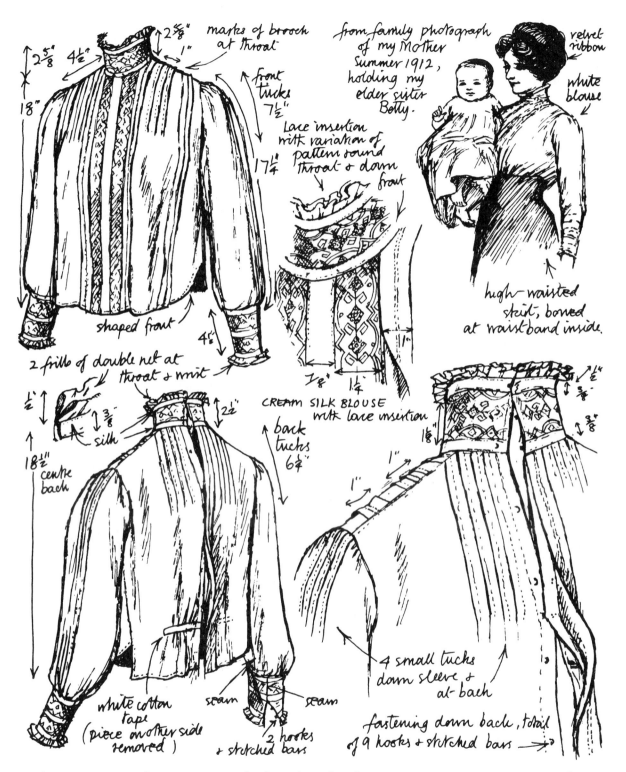

marks of brooch at throat

2⅝"

2⅝" 4½"

1"

18"

front tucks 7½"

17¼"

from family photograph of my Mother Summer 1912, holding my elder sister Betty.

velvet ribbon

white blouse

Lace insertion with variation of pattern round throat & down front

high-waisted skirt, boned at waist-band inside.

shaped front

4½"

2 frills of double net at throat & wrist

1½"

⅜"

silk

18½" centre back

2½"

back tucks 6¾"

CREAM SILK BLOUSE with lace insertion

⅞" 1¼"

1"

1½"

1¼"

⅜"

1⅜"

1⅛"

1"

1"

4 small tucks down sleeve & at back

fastening down back, total of 9 hooks & stitched bars →

white cotton tape (piece on other side removed)

seam

seam

2 hooks & stitched bars

during 1907-14, when sometimes the boned corslet skirt was worn. From *c.* 1820 camisoles were worn over the stays to protect the dress; in the '90's they were called a 'petticoat bodice.' Blouses appeared early in the 1860's.

c. 1913

Finest white lawn afternoon dress, with openwork embroidery, lined throughout with very fine white silk net. Fastening at front, round waist, & down centre back. All dress extremely finely hand-sewn. Folded sash or ribbon belt missing.
worn by Mrs Mary Stuart Dobson; lent by her daughter, Mrs M. J. King

1½"

fine white lace collar + at wrist

14"

BUST 36

WAIST 27½"

HIP 38"

plain lawn

lace

from family photograph, my Mother Mrs A. Bradfield after her marriage.

1910–11

white lawn dress

5"

1¼"

2"

3¾"

4"

BODICE

petersham waistband inside

CENTRE BACK skirt fastens hooks & eyes

silk

2 loops for 2 hooks on silk net undershirt; 7 loops for hooks on skirt all finely sewn

7 hooks at skirt back

seams all faggoted

centre back seam

2"

6"

6'

finest white silk net under dress

with self 5¾ frill

Charming, cool white dresses such as this were popular for afternoon wear for many years, particularly 1910–14. The needlework here is exquisitely fine, and, like the most expensive underwear, is all hand-sewn. The waistline now tends to lower, with increasing emphasis

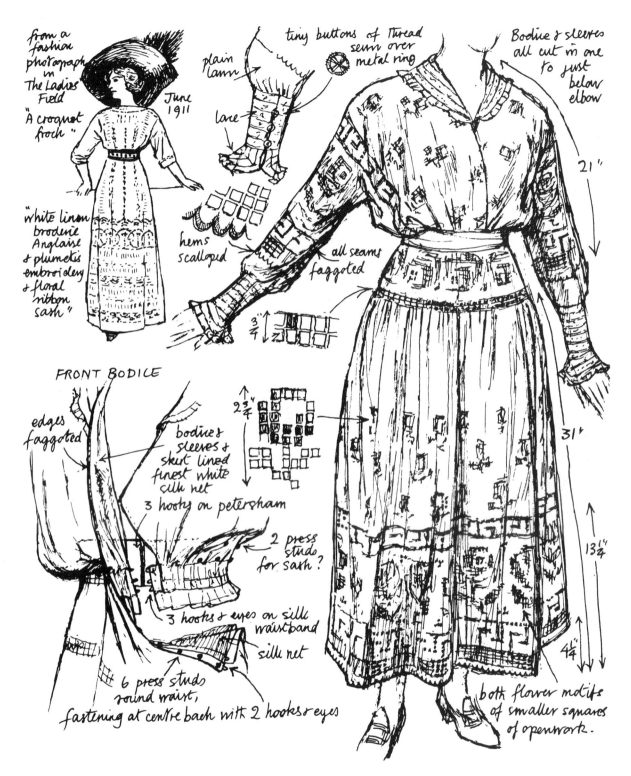

from a fashion photograph in The Ladies Field "A croquet frock"

June 1911

"white linen broderie Anglaise & plumetis embroidery & floral ribbon sash"

plain lawn

lace

tiny buttons of thread sewn over metal ring

hems scalloped

Bodice & sleeves all cut in one to just below elbow

21"

all seams faggoted

$\frac{3}{4}$" z

FRONT BODICE

edges faggoted

bodice & sleeves & skirt lined finest white silk net

3 hooks on petersham

2 press studs for sash ?

3 hooks & eyes on silk waistband

silk net

6 press studs round waist, fastening at centre back with 2 hooks & eyes

$2\frac{3}{4}$"

31"

$13\frac{1}{4}$"

$4\frac{1}{4}$"

both flower motifs of smaller squares of openwork.

at hip and at hem, hinting at changes to come. The 1911 fashion study shows a black slip under the openwork dress, but it would not have been suitable under this one. The large hats of 1910–11 decreased in size towards 1912.

1914

Deep violet satin with silver brocaded floral pattern, dress worn at Court by Lady Evelyn when presenting her daughter Violet. Sleeves of matching silk net, long hanging bands of white paste stones to hip-level. Back fastening hidden under train. Boned & lined in white satin.
from Mrs Wickham Steed to Chastleton House; lent to Snowshill Collection

deep violet silk net sleeves

draped over sleeve of violet silk net with fitting undersleeve of double silk net

train hangs loose from top to D seam here

8½"

WAIST 28"

21"

D

9½"

10½"

D

39½"

fold sewn in place under train

press stud fastening under at D

this side sewn

soft rounded edges to train

skirt lining of white silk hangs only to here

8½"

from her family photographs
1914

Lady Evelyn Mason's daughter, Violet, age 18; later, Mrs. Wickham Steed. Her day-time hair style has a centre parting

seam

21"

The 'hobble' skirt, which appeared in 1910, remained until 1915, restricting movement almost as much as some of the late Victorian dresses, although active women still wore the wider, more practical skirts. Some slender evening dresses such as this often had a gauze or

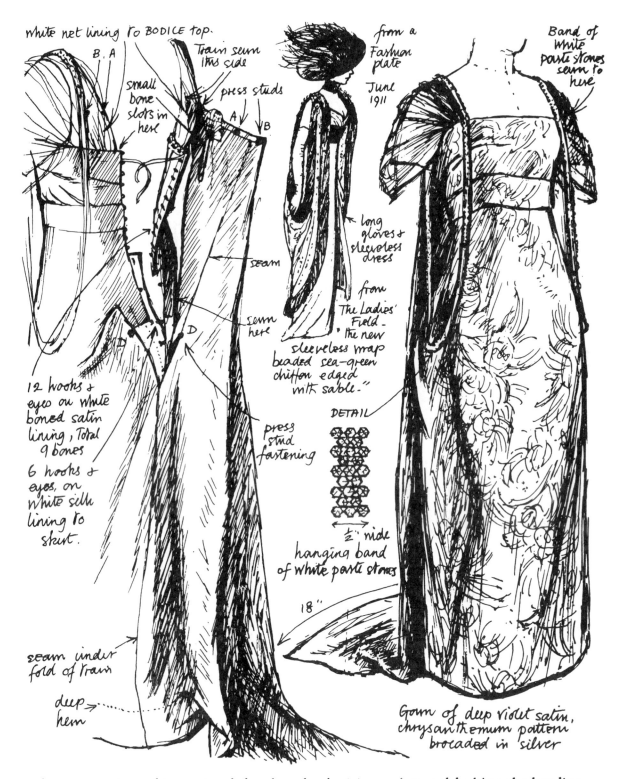

white net lining to BODICE top.

B. A

Train seam this side

small bone slots in here

press studs

A B

from a Fashion plate June 1911

Band of white paste stones sewn to here

12 hooks & eyes on white boned satin lining, Total 9 bones

6 hooks & eyes, on white silk lining to skirt.

seam

seam here

D

D

press stud fastening

long gloves & sleeveless dress

from The Ladies' Field - "the new sleeveless wrap beaded sea-green chiffon edged with sable."

DETAIL

½" wide

hanging band of white paste stones

18"

seam under fold of train

deep hem

Gown of deep violet satin, chrysanthemum pattern brocaded in silver

lace over-tunic reaching to just below knee-level, giving an 'upward look' to the hemline, in the same way as these decorative pendent bands of sparkling stones bring the eye downward, to the hip. A full Court dress of 1925 is shown on p. 359.

1914

Pale blue silk, floral pattern brocaded in gold thread. Evening dress with beaded bodice in pearls, with cream and silvered beads & white paste stones on net over chiffon. Fastening at back, lined white silk. Narrow 'hobble' skirt. *worn by Constance Brown of Oswestry; given by her to Snowshill Collection*

Silver kid evening shoes. *Miss N. Hawker*

BACK DRESS INSIDE OUT & BACK FASTENING

chiffon lined under net

& chiffon inner sleeve

NET

sleeve 13"

white silk

placket 11½"

WAIST 28½"

boned

wide petersham A & B

white paste stones on silver thread on blue georgette

9"

pearls

cream beads on net

rows cream beads on net

28"

white silk lining only to MID-CALF

41"

pearls

darker silver beads for pattern, pearls round edge

¼" corded piping at WAIST

½ lined white kid.

front skirt seam

9½"

shoes worn by Miss Elizabeth Rollason 1¾

1913 evening shoes, silver glacé kid

Artificial jewellery and paste were much used on the tiny bodices of these slim dresses, and this beaded decoration often proves too heavy for the delicate net or gauze to which it is sewn. This particular dress has been beautifully restored by Karen Finch. The cut of these draped

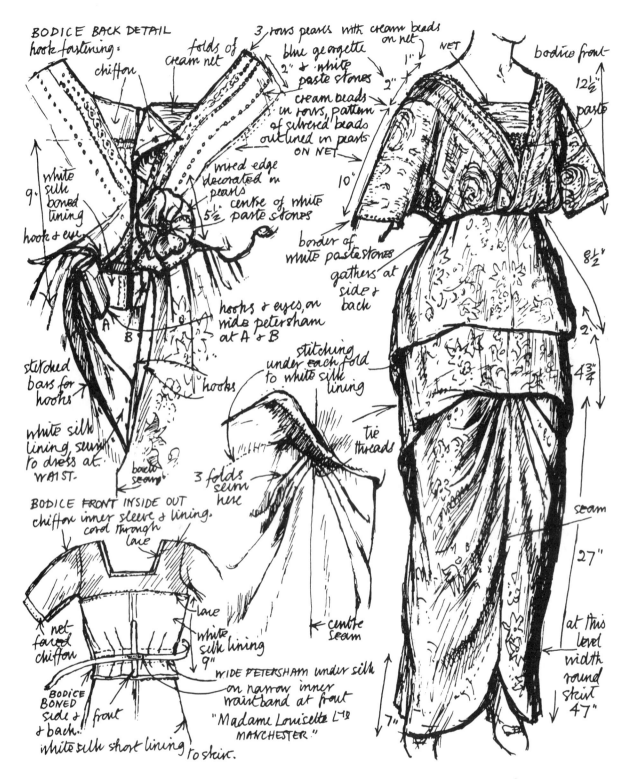

BODICE BACK DETAIL
hook fastening
chiffon
folds of cream net
3 rows pearls with cream beads on net
blue georgette 2" + white paste stones
1"
2"
NET
bodice front
12½"
paste
cream beads in rows, pattern of silvered beads outlined in pearls ON NET
white silk boned lining
9"
hook & eye
wired edge decorated in pearls
1"
5½"
centre of white paste stones
10"
8½"
border of white paste stones
gathers at side & back
A
B
hooks & eyes on wide petersham at A & B
stitching under each fold to white silk lining
2"
4¾"
stitched bars for hooks
hooks
white silk lining, sewn to dress at WAIST
back seam
tie threads
3 folds seam here
seam
27"
BODICE FRONT INSIDE OUT
chiffon inner sleeve & lining
cord through lace
lace
centre seam
net faced chiffon
lace
white silk lining
9"
at this level width round skirt 47"
BODICE BONED side & front & back
white silk short lining to skirt
WIDE PETERSHAM under silk on narrow inner waistband at front
"Madame Louisette Lᵗᵈ MANCHESTER"
7"

bodices lends itself very well to such decoration, although, as in this case, there is often too great a strain on the shoulders. The waist is lightly boned; many women, no longer so stiffly corseted, tend to 'droop,' and they use 'make-up' openly.

1917-18

White muslin dress, hand-embroidered floral motif on front panel, sailor collar, cuffs and hem, with insertion lace at hip-level, and on collar and cuff. Fastening at front. Unlined, wide hemline, above ankle-length. *worn by Mrs J. B. Hooton in India when in her late teens; given by her to Personal Collection*

from The Daily Mail Oct 2nd 1916

advert of serge suit 39/6 in black or navy

at Henry Glave New Oxford St LONDON

+ from Hairdressers' Weekly Journal

London fashion Aug. 1916

BODICE gathered at waist front & back only

14½"

17" front sleeve seam

10"

17"

double muslin

1"

1¼

white lace insertion

White muslin hand embroidered in white cotton

spot pattern enlarged

pattern repeat from A+B round skirt

skirt opens to here

27½

9"

hem faggoted

hem 1½

seam

from SHOE Sale advertisement at Whiteleys, LONDON in Daily Mail, Oct 2 1916

patent or glacé kid, two-bar shoes, Paris toe. Sale price 14/11

Mrs Hooton watched this dress being made by a 'dharzi' as he sat on the verandah, squatting in front of the sewing-machine, using his feet as well as his hands. Always a man made the dresses, never a woman. Hair was now waved and curled, and a wide, flat

349

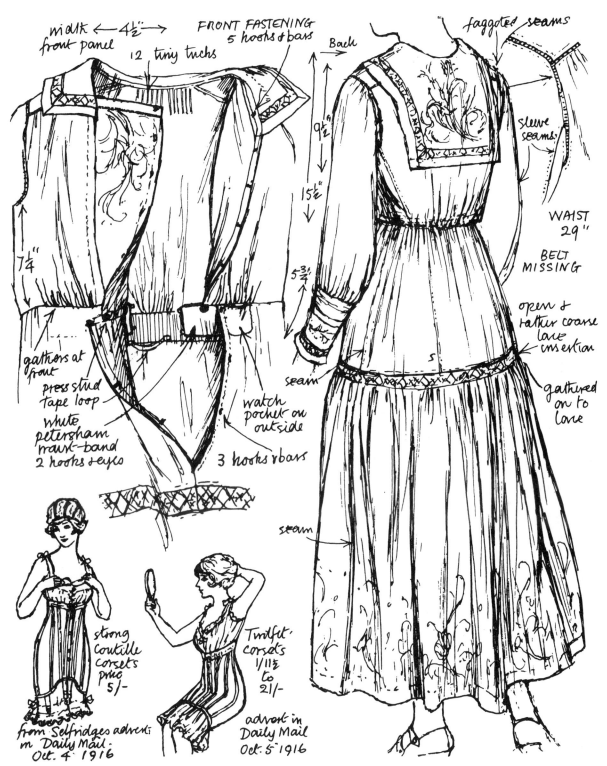

midlk ←—4½"—→
front panel

12 tiny tucks

FRONT FASTENING
5 hooks & bars

Back

faggoted seams

sleeve seams

9½"

15½"

7¼"

5¾"

WAIST
29"

BELT
MISSING

gathers at
front

press stud
tape loop

white
petersham
waist-band
2 hooks & eyes

watch
pocket on
outside

3 hooks & bars

seam

open &
rather coarse
lace
insertion

gathered
on to
lace

seam

strong
Coutille
Corsets
price
5/-

from Selfridges advert
in Daily Mail.
Oct. 4 1916

Twilfit
corsets
1/11½
to
21/-

advert in
Daily Mail
Oct. 5 1916

type of hat as shown in the study was probably worn with this dress. Skirts now reached to above the ankle; and some women still wore corsets which controlled the figure from waist to mid-thigh.

1919

Thick cream lace and heavy cream silk, afternoon or evening dress. Lace, over cream chiffon under-sleeves and top, faggoted to silk under-bodice, sewn to full-length cream satin under-slip. Lace fastens at side back, with under-slip fastening centre back. Ball fringe.

worn by Constance Brown of Oswestry; given to Snowshill Collection

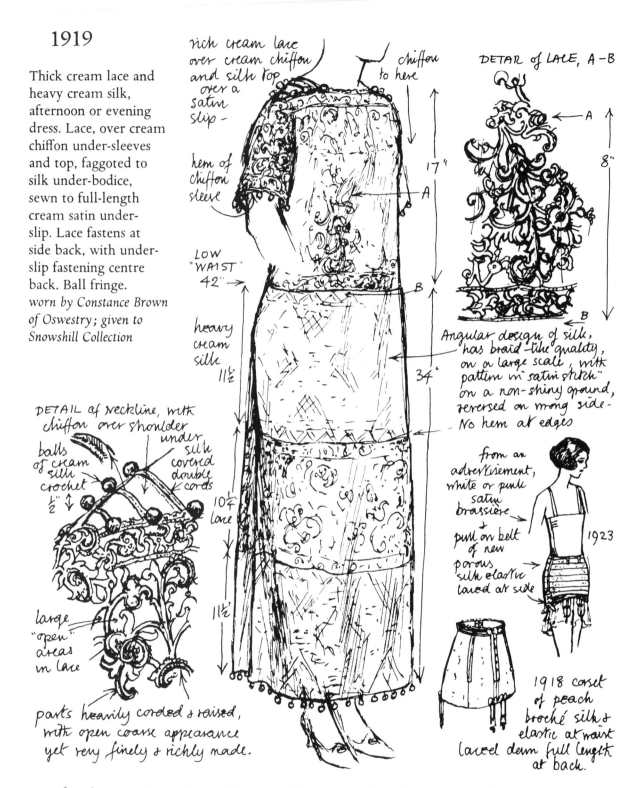

rich cream lace over cream chiffon and silk top over a satin slip –

hem of chiffon sleeve

chiffon to here

DETAIL of LACE, A–B

A

8"

17"

LOW "WAIST" 42"

heavy cream silk 11½

B

34"

Angular design of silk, has braid-like quality, on a large scale, with pattern in "satin stitch" on a non-shiny ground, reversed on wrong side – No hem at edges

DETAIL of Neckline, with chiffon over shoulder

balls of cream silk crochet ½"

under silk covered double cords

large "open" areas in lace

10¼ lace

11½

parts heavily corded & raised, with open coarse appearance yet very finely & richly made.

from an advertisement, white or pink satin brassière + pull on belt of new porous silk elastic laced at side

1923

1918 corset of peach broché silk & elastic at waist laced down full length at back.

After the 1914–18 war, the straight vertical line returns, but this time with a lowered waistline, reaching the hips by 1920, and with slim skirts to ankle-length. Many women, now with their hair cut short and 'bobbed,' have a bosom-less and flat, boyish look, with no bust and no

351

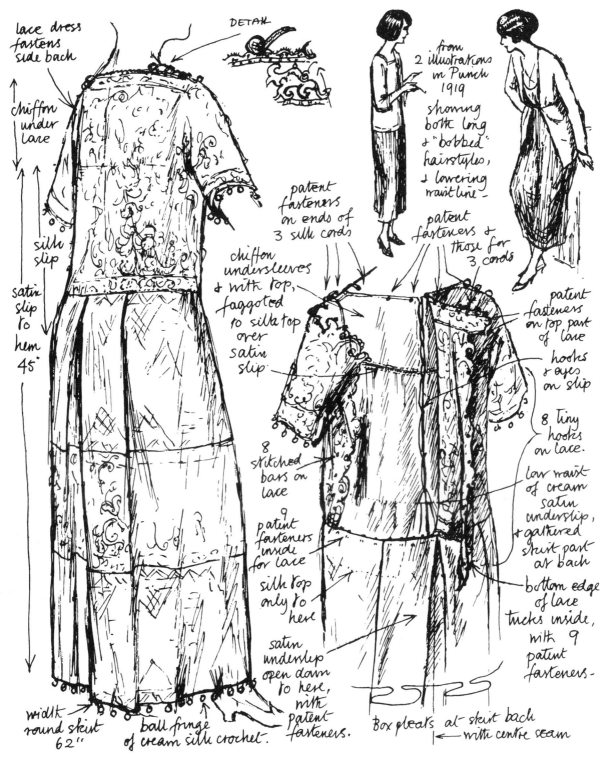

lace dress fastens side back

DETAIL

chiffon under lace

silk slip

satin slip to hem 45"

from 2 illustrations in Punch 1919 showing both long & "bobbed" hairstyles, & lowering waistline.

patent fasteners on ends of 3 silk cords

chiffon undersleeves & with top, faggoted to silk top over satin slip

patent fasteners & those for 3 cords

patent fasteners on top part of lace

hooks & eyes on slip

8 tiny hooks on lace.

low waist of cream satin underslip, & gathered skirt part at back

bottom edge of lace tucks inside, with 9 patent fasteners.

8 stitched bars on lace

9 patent fasteners inside for lace

silk top only to here

satin underslip open down to here, with patent fasteners.

width round skirt 62"

ball fringe of cream silk crochet.

Box pleats at skirt back with centre seam

hips. The 1918 corset and dress are still waisted, but by the '20's dresses, with unrestricted underwear, hang straight from shoulder to ankle, often with back and front exactly alike, and with no fastenings.

1921

Rich orange-red and peach georgette, with silver-embroidered decoration front and back. An evening dress. Matching side-panels on under-slip of peach georgette. Inner petticoat, peach crêpe-de-chine. Long wing panels from shoulders, long tie-ends at hips. *worn by Violet Mason; given to Chastleton House; lent to Snowshill Collection*

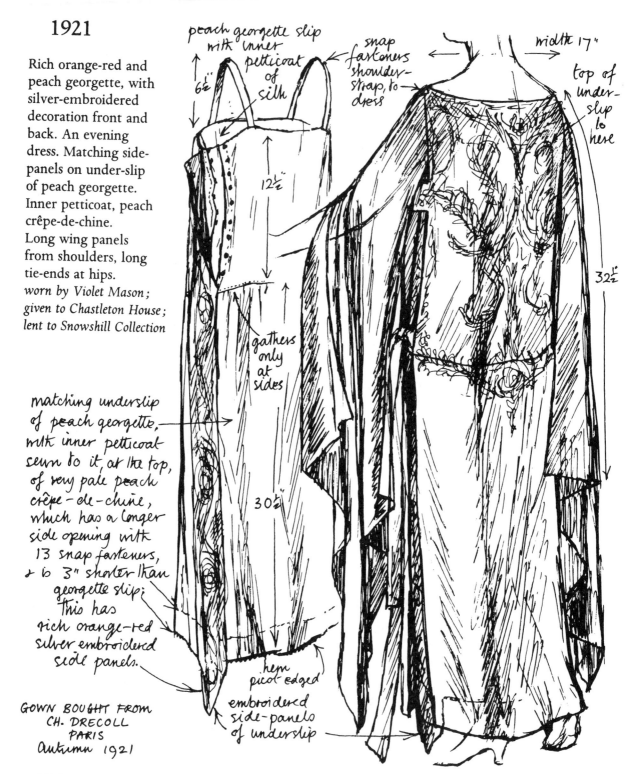

peach georgette slip with inner petticoat of silk

6½"

12½"

gathers only at sides

30½"

matching underslip of peach georgette, with inner petticoat sewn to it, at the top, of very pale peach crêpe-de-chine, which has a longer side opening with 13 snap fasteners, & is 3" shorter than georgette slip; this has rich orange-red silver embroidered side panels.

GOWN BOUGHT FROM CH. DRECOLL PARIS Autumn 1921

hem picot edged embroidered side-panels of underslip

snap fasteners shoulder-strap, to dress

width 17"

top of under-slip to here

32½"

Violet Mason, now Mrs Wickham Steed, was the daughter of Lady Evelyn Mason, and she bought this dress in Paris in autumn 1921. A rich and elegant gown, in the most fashionable colours, and well suited to a tall, graceful Society woman. The very elaborate embroidery

DETAIL of central motif

rich orange-red

rich orange-red georgette with silver thread machine st. embroidery in single flowing continuous line

BACK & FRONT of dress IDENTICAL in every detail

21½"

34"

40" HIP

Two tie ends at sides, orange-red, 41" long, here tied in one loop bow giving short & long ends

rich orange-red

hems picot edged

32"

tie ends

30½"   30"

19"

at sides embroidered panels of peach slip

rich orange-red georgette as on top half of dress

peach georgette double thickness—front & back width 19"

gives the dress an air of distinction. There is no shaping at all from shoulder to hemline; neither is there any difference between front and back; only the left-side fastening on the slip and petticoat betrays that secret to the wearer.

1921

Detail of orange-red and peach evening dress; with long ties at sides undone to show matching slip with side-panels.
lent to Snowshill Collection

1921 lilac silk dress for afternoon wear, with deep flounce. Young girl's dress, worn and lent by *Miss Nora Hawker*

Butterick dress patterns *given by Miss A. Eccles to Personal Collection*

orange-red georgette top embroidered in silver, also under-arm band length A – B 8" and band down side of peach slip.

dress with no sleeves

from Pattern & Deltor Butterick Design No 5080, price 50 cents LADIES' DRAPED ONE PIECE DRESS 1923–24

7½"

2¾"

A
B

with fitting or contrasting sleeves

with bead ornament requiring 1 bunch of beads (500 to a bunch) sleeves sewn to body lining or camisole top. pattern printed in New York, U.S.A.

from paper pattern. 1922 LADIES' DRESS COLLAR

short hair waved

PEACH SLIP gathered only at sides, as also silk petticoat under it.

Pictorial Review Pattern. price 30 cents in U.S.A & Canada & 1/6 in Great Britain. stamped "made in England"

CORSET c1925 of thin pink cotton broché from 'Corsets & Crinolines' by N. Waugh

peach skirt double

peach slip

peach silk under petticoat to here

georgette ties of orange-red, length 41"

width 4½"

A striking evening dress and a perfect example of the line of the latest fashion for the early '20's. Foundation garments flatten and no longer mould or 'improve' the female form. Dress patterns show the sleeveless look, hip emphasis, and the upward movement of the skirt,

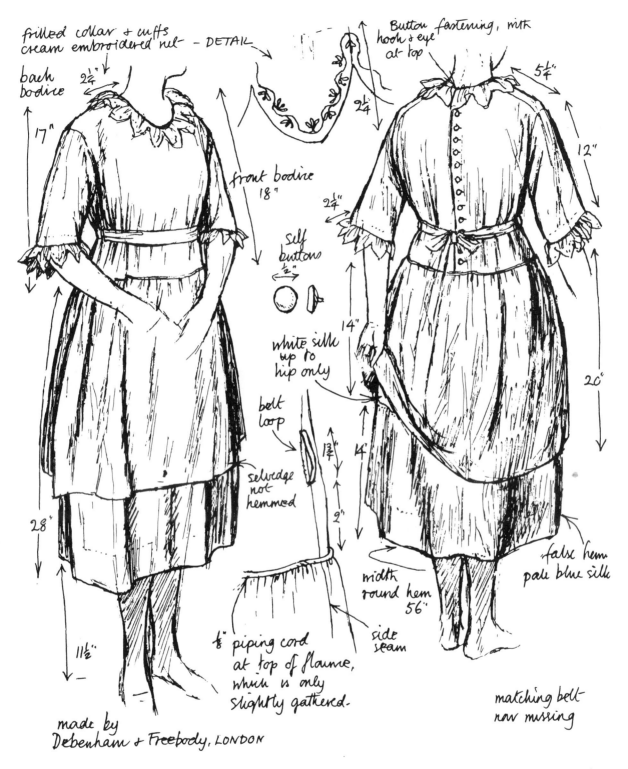

frilled collar & cuffs
cream embroidered net - DETAIL

back
bodice

2¼"

17"

front bodice
18"

Button fastening, with
hook & eye
at top

2¼

5¼"

12"

2¼"

self
buttons
½"

white silk
up to
hip only

14"

belt
loop

13¾"

selvedge
not
hemmed

14"

2"

20"

28"

width
round hem
56"

side
seam

false hem
pale blue silk

11½"

⅛" piping cord
at top of flounce,
which is only
slightly gathered.

matching belt
now missing

made by
Debenham & Freebody, LONDON

taking the accent to knee-level. Although quite a complete contrast in style, this is also found in the young girl's dress with the flounce ending above the knee and the corded seam drawing attention to the hip-line.

356

c. 1922–23

Cream lace and net afternoon dress, with peach crêpe-de-chine sleeveless slip. Low waist, long, fitting sleeves. No fasteners on dress except on sleeves at wrist. Three qualities of net used. 'Limerick' lace on front panel and sleeves, and two top flounces; lower one all in hand-done tambour stitch.

Personal Collection

2½"
outer sleeve 28"

from — 1923 pattern & Deltor Butterick Design, 4332 (price 45 cents)

20

net silk

inside sleeve seam 21"

31"

10½"

LADIES' SLIP-OVER DRESS with plain or wide sleeve

from a set of pattern envelopes given to my collection by Miss A. Eccles

14"

DETAIL of front panel of "Limerick lace"

5"

Appliqué machine-made flowers on net, with embroidery of handmade tambour stitch. Lower flounce all in tambour.

20"

DETAIL of flowers with appliqué petals.

1½"

flowing lines in tambour stitch

petals of large flowers, sewn down round centre and at petal tips.

sewn down at centre only.

A dainty and 'cool'-looking dress, in very good condition. The machine-made lace, though, cannot compete with the exquisite hand-made laces of previous years. The horizontal emphasis of this skirt gives a feeling of uncertainty to the hemline, a warning almost of the remarkable

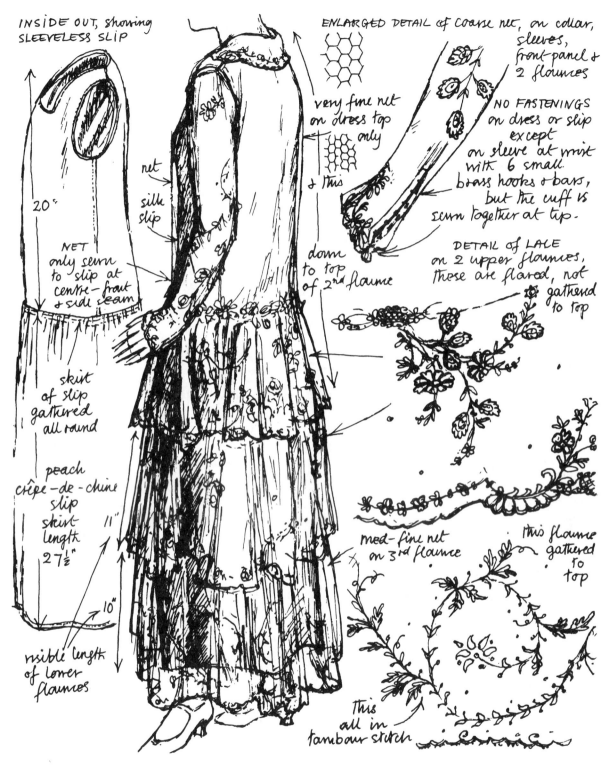

INSIDE OUT, showing
SLEEVELESS SLIP

20°

net

silk
slip

NET
only sewn
to slip at
centre-front
& side seam

skirt
of slip
gathered
all round

peach
crêpe-de-chine
slip
skirt
length
27½"

11"

10"

visible length
of lower
flounces

very fine net
on dress top
only

& this

down
to top
of 2nd flounce

ENLARGED DETAIL of coarse net, on collar,
sleeves,
front-panel &
2 flounces

NO FASTENINGS
on dress or slip
except
on sleeve at wrist
with 6 small
brass hooks & bars,
but the cuff is
sewn together at tip.

DETAIL of LACE
on 2 upper flounces,
these are flared, not
gathered
to top

med-fine net
on 3rd flounce

this flounce
gathered
to
top

this
all in
tambour stitch

changes soon to take place. To use the American term, this is a 'slip-over' dress, with no fastenings. Butterick patterns were patented in the United States Aug. 19th, 1919, and in Great Britain March 23rd, 1916.

358

1923

Medium-pale petunia georgette evening dress, trimmed with silver tissue and silver braid and brilliant beaded embroidery with 3 long tassels, all of tiny coloured beads and some paste stones. Two large squares of drapery as 'sleeves,' side-fastening gown with under-slip of pink crêpe-de-chine. *Chastleton House; lent to Snowshill Collection*

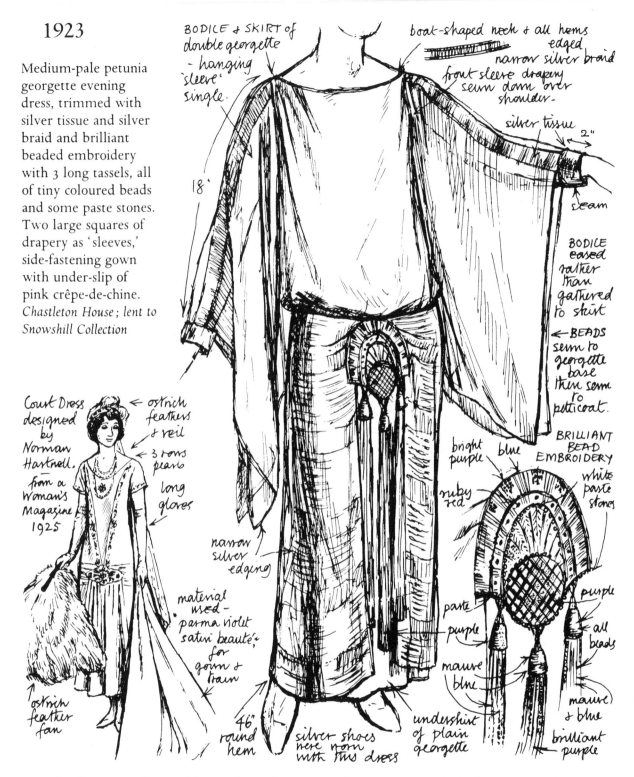

BODICE & SKIRT of double georgette - hanging 'sleeve' single.

18"

boat-shaped neck & all hems edged narrow silver braid

front sleeve drapery seam down over shoulder.

silver tissue

2"

seam

BODICE eased rather than gathered to skirt

← BEADS seem to georgette base then sewn to petticoat.

Court Dress designed by Norman Hartnell. from a Woman's Magazine 1925

← ostrich feathers & veil

← 3 rows pearls

long gloves

ostrich feather fan

narrow silver edging

material used - parma violet satin beauté for gown & train

46" round hem

silver shoes here worn with this dress

undershirt of plain georgette

BRILLIANT BEAD EMBROIDERY

bright purple

blue

ruby red

white paste stones

paste

purple

purple

mauve blue

all beads

mauve & blue

brilliant purple

The discovery of Tutankhamen's tomb in November 1922 certainly had quite an effect on women's dress, and this Egyptian influence remained for some years. The colours of the bead embroidery and tassels are intensely brilliant, and the weight is astonishing. Inside are tape

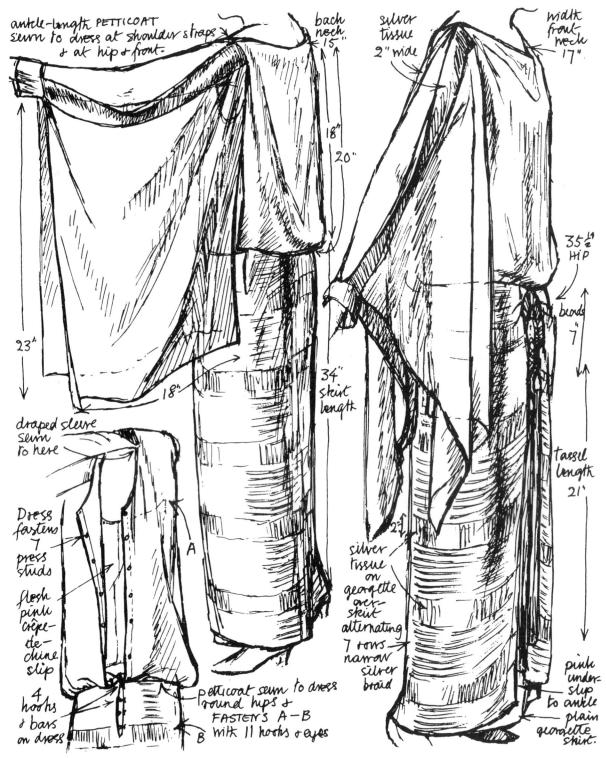

ankle-length PETTICOAT
sewn to dress at shoulder straps
& at hip & front.

back
neck
15"

silver
tissue
2" wide

width
front
neck
17"

18"

20"

35½"
HIP

beads
7"

23"

18"

34"
skirt
length

tassel
length
21"

draped sleeve
sewn
to here

Dress
fastens
7
press
studs

flesh
pink
crêpe-
de-
chine
slip

4
hooks
& bars
on dress

A

B

petticoat sewn to dress
round hips &
FASTENS A–B
with 11 hooks & eyes

2"

silver
tissue
on
georgette
over-
skirt
alternating

7 rows
narrow
silver
braid

pink
under-
slip
to ankle
plain
georgette
skirt.

loops which support this, when the dress is hung up, or even perhaps when worn. The silver braid and tissue give a subtle, soft shimmering effect to this dress, which belonged to Violet Mason, later Mrs Wickham Steed.

1920's

Lawn combinations, white, early open-leg style, button down front to waist only.
from Miss A. Eccles to Personal Collection

c. 1924

Coarse black net tunic dress, with all-over-pattern in silver-foil strip. Low hip-line. Short skirt to below the knee. Two pairs of strap shoes.
from Miss A. Chatwin to Personal Collection

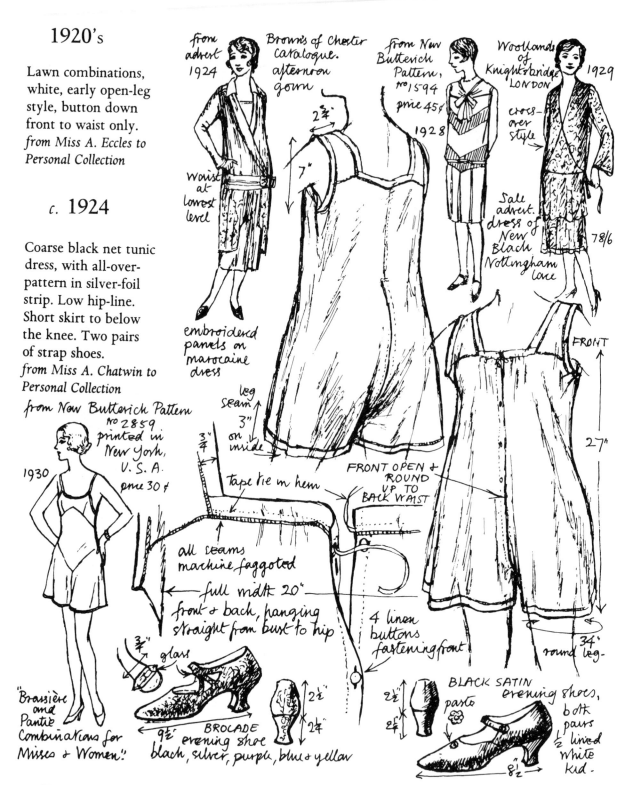

from advert 1924

Brown's of Chester catalogue. afternoon gown

from New Butterick Pattern, n° 1594 price 45¢ 1928

Woodlands of Knightsbridge LONDON 1929

cross-over style

2¾"

7"

waist at lowest level

Sale advert. dress of New Black Nottingham lace

78/6

embroidered panels on marocaine dress

FRONT

leg seam 3" on inside

27"

3¾"

tape tie in hem

FRONT OPEN & ROUND UP TO BACK WAIST

from New Butterick Pattern n° 2859 printed in New York, U.S.A. price 30¢

1930

all seams machine faggoted

full width 20" front & back, hanging straight from bust to hip

4 linen buttons fastening front

34" round leg.

3¾" glass

"Brassière and Pantie Combinations for Misses & Women".

9½" BROCADE evening shoe black, silver, purple, blue & yellow

2½"
2¾"

2½"
2½" paste

BLACK SATIN evening shoes, both pairs ½ lined white kid.

8½"

Women now show their legs up to the knees, and dresses hang loose, with little shaping, from shoulder to hem, until waists return by the '30's; this also applies to underwear. These combinations have the open-leg style, rare after 1911. Usually leg seams fasten with three or

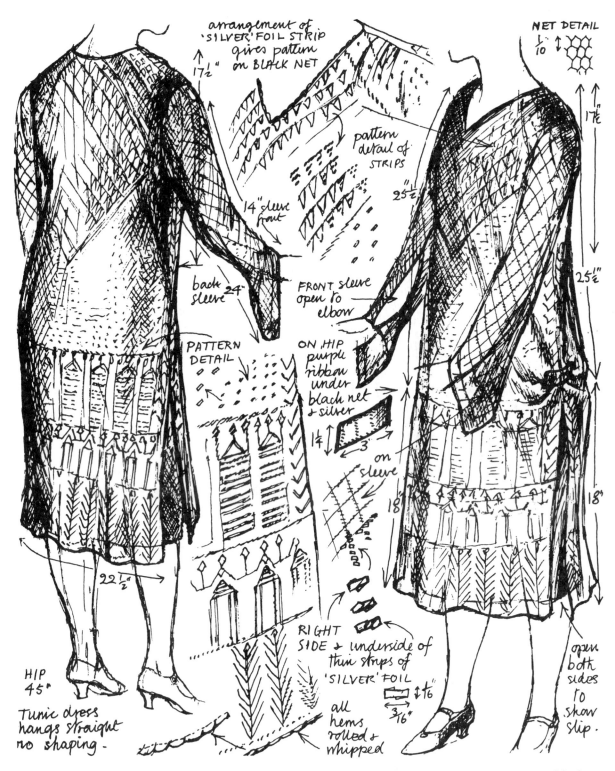

arrangement of 'SILVER' FOIL STRIP gives pattern on BLACK NET

NET DETAIL ↓↑ 1/10

↑ 17½"

pattern detail of STRIPS

25½"

↑ 17½"

25½"

14" sleeve front

back sleeve 24"

FRONT sleeve open to elbow

PATTERN DETAIL

ON HIP purple ribbon under black net & silver

1¼"
3"

on sleeve

18"

18"

open both sides to show slip.

22½"

HIP 45"

Tunic dress hangs straight no shaping.

RIGHT SIDE & underside of thin strips of 'SILVER' FOIL

↕ 1/16"
3/16"

all hems rolled & whipped

four buttons. The missing under-slip from this silvery gleaming dress, must have been black as the sleeve lining is double black chiffon. Although the whole dress is decorated, it is quite light compared with a beaded one, weighing only 16 oz.

1926

Mid-blue georgette evening dress with 'handkerchief' skirt from low hip-line. Points hanging below calf-level, with tunic dress straight from shoulder to knee. Short sleeves, with silk lining sleeveless. Silver beadwork at neckline. Pink evening shoes. This dress was worn on February 6th for her 21st birthday party by *Miss Nora Hawker*.

neckline width 10"

2½"

4"

18"

from PUNCH 1926

and in 1930 evening dresses

21"

20"

24"

17"

4" 4"

each stitched & slightly overlapping the next.

Total 11 "handkerchiefs"

13"

Most seams finished by hand & these edges finely oversewn rather than a rolled hem

Rose embroidered in shades of pink

2½"

silver tissue appliqué

silver bead embroidery, but beads now missing), traces of stitching remain.

bound edge in blue georgette & blue silk embroidered band

dress made by Madame Robinson, BIRMINGHAM.

a white slip was worn under this dress.

Silver ribbon belt, with flat bow on left side, now missing

A good example of a dress of the 1920's, though sleeveless ones were more usual for evening wear. With waistline firmly established at hip-level for some years, skirts waver from above the knee, 1925–26, down to ankle-length by the '30's. Uneven hemlines help the transition

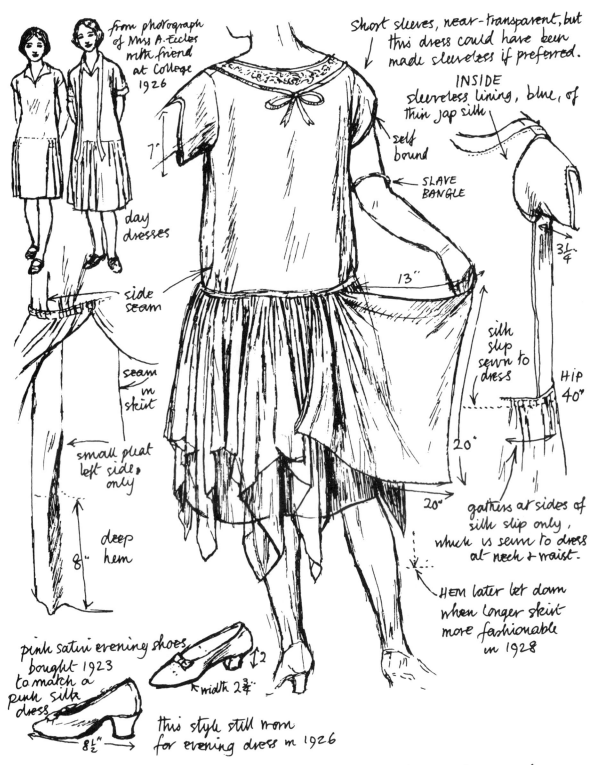

from photograph
of Miss A. Eccles
with friend
at College
1926

day
dresses

side
seam

seam
in
skirt

small pleat
left side
only

deep
hem
8"

pink satin evening shoes,
bought 1923
to match a
pink silk
dress

width 2¾"

8½"

this style still worn
for evening dress in 1926

Short sleeves, near-transparent, but
this dress could have been
made sleeveless if preferred.

INSIDE
sleeveless lining, blue, of
thin Jap silk

self
bound

SLAVE
BANGLE

7"

13"

3¼

silk
slip
sewn to
dress

HIP
40"

20"

20"

gathers at sides of
silk slip only,
which is sewn to dress
at neck & waist.

HEM later let down
when longer skirt
more fashionable
in 1928

up or down. Day dresses remain short for some years, after long evening gowns become
fashionable. Flesh-coloured stockings of 1921–22 become an even brighter and more shiny
pink with these short skirts.

1926-27

Three evening dresses. Pale yellow-green beaded georgette, same back and front, decorated silver beads. Delicate salmon-pink beaded georgette, straight back, front skirt gathered, silver and white beads.
Mrs M. J. King

Powder-blue muslin heavily beaded over all surface in silver.
from Miss A. Chatwin to Personal Collection

BACK of PINK DRESS one length neck to hem

BACK of GREEN DRESS identical to front

hems self bound

$6\frac{1}{2}$"

9" $2\frac{3}{4}$"

$17\frac{1}{2}$"

HIP 38"

4"

silver beads 10"

$7\frac{1}{2}$

42"

seam

$17\frac{1}{2}$"

from 1927 Butterick Pattern no 6809 printed N.Y. U.S.A

24'

18'

price 40 cents

Ladies' & Misses' BATHING COSTUME, slip-over blouse & shorts.

OPEN FRONT to beaded skirt, 55" round HEM. front gathers of SKIRT whipped at top, under beads.

silvered glass round beads, in groups of 3. also

opaque white glass

PATTERN of glass silvered beads.

$6\frac{1}{2}$

$\frac{1}{2}$

1"

hem under beading & gathers hand sewn

5 rows of silvered glass beads

$\frac{1}{4}$"

$\frac{1}{8}$"

hem

width round hem 78"

The two delicately beaded dresses were both worn by Mrs King's sister, the late Miss E. M. Dobson. They are probably earlier than the heavily beaded blue one with the deeply plunging 'neckline,' which hints at a change in both waist and hem level, as do the pointed or scallop-

INSIDE of gathering

tiny press stud on loop end to keep shoulder straps in place

longer beads

7 STRANDS of longer silvered beads on blue thread – added later? –

edges bound

rows of med size silvered glass beads

9½"

22"

HIP 42" →
silvered glass beads at edges & for pattern

4"

19½"

9¼"

seams

round silver balls for flower centres

sequins in centres of pattern

3 TYPES BEADS USED
1. silvered glass for all-over pattern
2. "silver" metal stamped sequins in pattern centres
3. tiny silver balls in flower centres only –

all edges self bound in blue muslin.

width round hem 66"

shaped hems on all three dresses. The flat boyish figure too will soon be on the way out when waists return. The 1927 bathing-costume pattern, printed in the U.S.A., has a surprisingly modern 'mini-skirt.'

1927–28

Sun-tan georgette, very heavily beaded evening dress, with hemline dropped at the back very slightly. *from Miss A. Chatwin to Personal Collection*

Gold lace ball dress, waisted bodice with hip-line and full skirt dropped at side and back. Peach georgette lining now missing. Worn in 1928, when aged 23 years, by *Miss Nora Hawker*

burnt orange beading round borders

8"

2"

43"

one length with one seam

FRONT

DETAIL of BORDER

3 rows

4 rows + more

all closely + heavily beaded

all-over pattern on dress "indefinite" of silvered beads + burnt orange glass beads

side seam

understirt sewn to front here

one zig-zag seam here

entire underside covered in stitching

plain hem

seams

3"

21" plain front under "apron"
sides beaded to here — up to side seams

BORDER DETAIL at A

BORDER AT 2" FRONT HEM

evening dress

from 1927 photograph

side panels hang from hip

all bead embroidered

Separate apron front hangs from hip

A

For such a heavily beaded dress, this one is in a wonderful condition, particularly as it weighs $3\frac{1}{2}$ lb. The beads are closely sewn over the entire surface, and the pattern is given by the arrangement and colouring of the beads. This may date from autumn '27, when the first

BACK

46"

19"

2"

17"

22"

9"

SKIRT
46"
all round

from 1927 photograph.
with hair
shingled:

+ artificial flower
at shoulder

Velvet
flower
in pink
+ flame
9"

6½"

10½"

2"

25"

bound
gold
Braid

LENGTHS
down
CENTRE
BACK

17"

waist
seam
drops
at back

6"

24"

MAX:
skirt
length
side & back
24"

Artificial flowers
were fashionable from
c.1924
pinned to shoulder
of dress or coat.

Velvet flowers
pink & flame
edged
in gold thread
& embroidered
in silver & gold
thread

GOLD TISSUE
LACE - DETAIL

signs appeared on evening dresses of the 'dropped' hemline. Longer skirts for 'afternoon'
and evening wear, were returning by 1928, and some were ankle-length. Waists too returned
to normal level, as seen in the gold lace dress.

368

1930

Pale green georgette evening dress, rich embroidery in silver and gold thread, the flower motif in peach silk openwork. No fastenings on dress or pale yellow-green satin under-slip. Flared panels and dress, cut on cross. My own evening purse of gold sequins and beads, and gold kid evening shoes.
Personal Collection

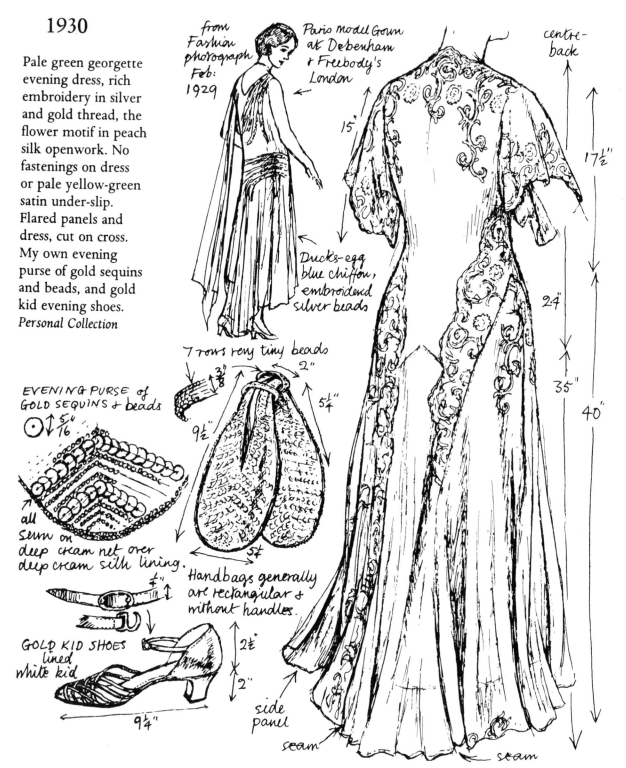

from Fashion photograph Feb: 1929

Paris model Gown at Debenham + Freebody's London

centre-back

15"

17½"

Ducks-egg blue chiffon, embroidered silver beads

24"

35"

40"

7 rows very tiny beads

3/8"

2"

5¼"

EVENING PURSE of GOLD SEQUINS + beads

↕5/16"

9½"

all sewn on deep cream net over deep cream silk lining.

5¼"

Handbags generally are rectangular + without handles.

¼"

GOLD KID SHOES lined white kid

2½"

2"

side panel

seam

seam

9¼"

By the '30's long skirts return for formal occasions; fitting the hips, they flare out below the knee; slight shaping only at first, hints at a normal waistline. Day dresses lengthen, reaching to between calf and ankle, until c. 1938. The hair, after being so short in the mid '20's, matching

369

pale yellow-green satin slip, all edges bound in chiffon

6"

No fastening on Gown or slip.

3½"

9½"

from the New Butterick Patterns. 1930 afternoon & evening wear

No 3113

No 3460

slip-over frock in sheer crêpes, chiffon cotton voile, or rayons.

printed in New York U.S.A.

7½"

8"

only slight shaping at waist

HIP 38-40"

pattern inside of cobweb of fine silver thread

OUTLINES of PATTERN

thick gold or silver machine sewn on.

picot edging in green silk.

side panel seam only at top

9"

10"

length of under-slip 55"

gold & silver borders

seam

2"

centre of openwork embroidery in peach silk.

33" side panel length

32" panel width at hem

WIDTH all round hem 150"

seam

the very short skirts, now shows signs of lengthening, and is softly waved and curled. Strapless court shoes are by far the most popular; dainty sandal styles are more usual for summer or **evening wear.**

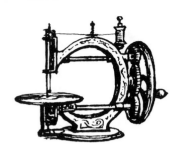

The Lady's Own Paper, 1868, advertises the 'Little Wanzer' hand lock-stitch shuttle machine, price £4 4s. This is one of over a dozen makes in use at this time, including the 'Singer' machine, also the 'Howe,' established in 1845 by Elias Howe Jr, inventor and maker, New York, U.S.A.

APPENDIX

This comprises detailed studies and text on two Regency dresses, a wedding pelisse and its matching bonnet, and a fascinating evening dress of 1913, all of which are in my private collection. Also included here is an article which throws new light on the true origins of the practical attire called the 'reform' dress or 'bloomerism', later known as 'Rational dress'.

This series of drawings and articles first appeared in the *Journal of the Costume Society* in 1972, 1973, 1974 and 1975.

Grey silk Quaker dress 1806-10 and black silk bonnet
Made in a fine soft twilled silk, this is a charmingly simple dress; its fascination lies perhaps in the subtle quality of its colour, the grey having a hint of olive green.

This dress, together with the other items here illustrated, belonged to Mrs Fayle, a Quaker and great-great-grandmother to Lady Corfield, who has very kindly presented them to my collection.

It is interesting to compare the cut of this silk dress, made with a wrap-over front to the bodice, a style which appears in many fashion plates and actual dresses early in the 19th century,

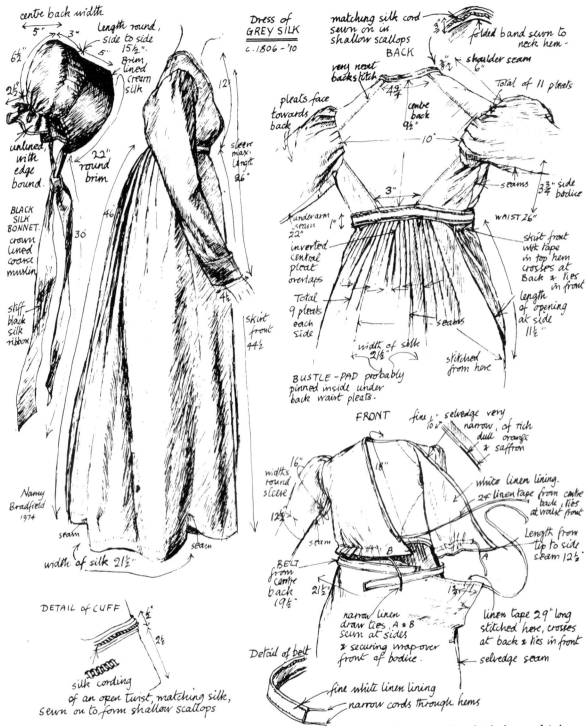

centre back width

5" → ← 3"

6½"

2½"

Length round, side to side 15½". 5" Brim lined cream silk

unlined, with edge bound.

BLACK SILK BONNET. crown lined coarse muslin

22" round brim

stiff black silk ribbon

30

46

Nancy Bradfield 1974

seam

width of silk 21½"

12"

sleeve max. length 26"

4½"

skirt front 44½

seam

Dress of GREY SILK c. 1806 - '10

matching silk cord sewn on in shallow scallops BACK

¾"

folded band sewn to neck hem.

⅜" shoulder seam 6"

very neat backstitch

pleats face towards back

4¾"

centre back 9½"

10"

Total of 11 pleats

seams 3¾" side bodice

3"

underarm seam 22"

1"

inverted central pleat overlaps

Total 9 pleats each side

width of silk 2½"

seams

WAIST 26"

skirt front with tape in top hem crosses at Back & ties in front

length of opening at side 11½"

stitched from here

BUSTLE-PAD probably pinned inside under back waist pleats.

FRONT

fine ½" selvedge very narrow, of rich dull orange & saffron

16"

18"

widths round sleeve

12½"

seam

white linen lining.

24" linen tape from centre back, ties at waist front

Length from tip to side seam 12½"

B

A

BELT from centre back 19½"

21½"

narrow linen draw ties, A & B seam at sides & securing wrap-over front of bodice.

linen tape 29" long stitched here, crosses at back & lies in front

selvedge seam

Detail of belt

fine white linen lining

narrow cords through hems

DETAIL of CUFF

½"

2½"

silk cording of an open twist, matching silk, sewn on to form shallow scallops

with that of its companion, the fine white muslin dress (See illus. p. 373), which has a high stomacher front, giving a straight line across the bosom, the apron front of the bodice being joined to the skirt front, a fashion which is commonly found 1800–10. With this type of front, the back is usually cut extremely narrow, giving the illusion of a tiny waist, due to the sleeves being set in deeply at the back and over the shoulder.

The width across the back of this muslin dress is only 5¾″, almost half that of the silk, which

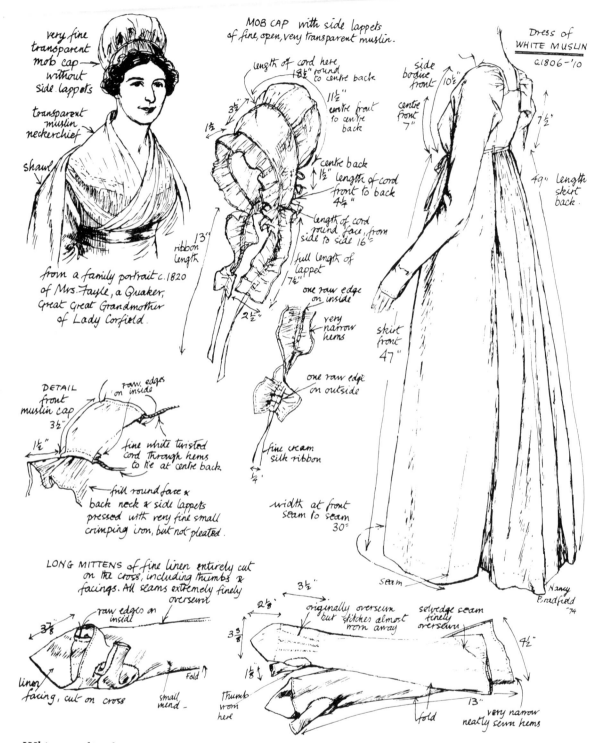

very fine transparent mob cap without side lappets

transparent muslin neckerchief

shawl

from a family portrait c.1820 of Mrs. Fayle, a Quaker, Great Great Grandmother of Lady Corfield.

13" ribbon length

MOB CAP with side lappets of fine, open, very transparent muslin.

length of cord here 18½" round to centre back

11½" centre front to centre back

3½"

1½"

centre back 1½" length of cord front to back 4¼"

length of cord round face from side to side 16"

full length of lappet 7½"

2½"

one raw edge on inside

very narrow hems

one raw edge on outside

fine cream silk ribbon ¼"

Dress of WHITE MUSLIN c.1806-'10

side bodice front 10½"

centre front 7"

7½"

49" length skirt back

skirt front 47"

width at front seam to seam 30=

seam

Nancy Bradfield '74

DETAIL front muslin cap 3½"

raw edges on inside

1½"

fine white twisted cord through hems to tie at centre back.

frill round face & back neck & side lappets pressed with very fine small crimping iron, but not pleated.

LONG MITTENS of fine linen entirely cut on the cross, including thumbs & facings. All seams extremely finely oversewn

raw edges on inside

3⅜"

linen facing, cut on cross

small mend

Fold

3½"

2⅛"

3⅝"

1⅛"

Thumb worn here

originally oversewn but stitches almost worn away

selvedge seam finely oversewn

4½"

13"

fold

very narrow neatly sewn hems

White muslin dress 1806–1810, mob cap and long linen mittens
has a low stomacher front, the bodice not being joined to the skirt front.

The grey silk is in very good condition, but the white muslin dress shows considerable wear, particularly on the sleeves, the ends of the muslin waist ties and the tiny buttons on the bodice front. The muslin itself is fine and soft, but it is not transparent.

On the other hand the mob cap is very transparent, retaining its crispness well, the delicate

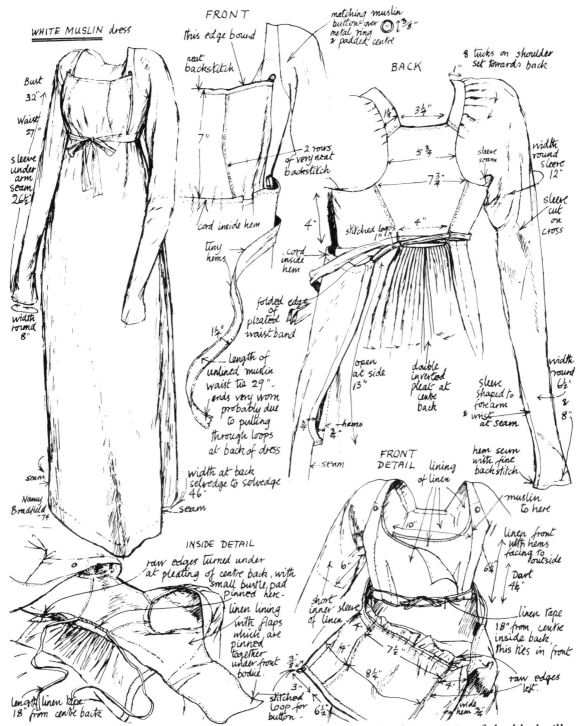

WHITE MUSLIN dress

FRONT
this edge bound

matching muslin
button over
metal ring
x padded centre ⊙ 1⅜"

neat
backstitch

BACK

8 tucks on shoulder
set towards back
1"

Bust
32"

Waist
27"

sleeve
under
arm
seam
26½"

7"

1⅜"   3¾"

5¾"

7¾"

sleeve
seam

width
round
sleeve
12"

sleeve
cut
on
cross

width
round
8"

2 rows
of very neat
backstitch

cord inside hem

tiny
hems

4"

stitched loops
1"

cord
inside
hem

double
inverted
pleat at
centre
back

open
at side
13"

sleeve
shaped to
forearm
x wrist
at seam

folded edge
of
pleated
waistband

1½"

length of
unlined muslin
waist tie 29".
ends very worn
probably due
to pulling
through loops
at back of dress

3¾"   hems
½"

seam

width
round
6½"
&
8"

hem seam
with fine
backstitch

FRONT
DETAIL   lining
of linen

muslin
to here

width at back
selvedge to selvedge
46"

seam

Nancy
Bradfield
'74

seam

10"

6½"

linen front
with hems
facing to
outside

Dart
4½"

INSIDE DETAIL
raw edges turned under
at pleating of centre back, with
small bustle pad
pinned here.

linen lining
with flaps
which are
pinned
together
under front
bodice.

short
inner sleeve
of linen

6"

4"   7½"

8¼"

3⅜"

3"

stitched
loop for
button

6½"

Length linen tape
18" from centre back

linen tape
18" from centre
inside back,
this ties in front

raw edges
left

wide
hem ¾"

crimping on the frills round the face being clearly visible. The plain severity of the black silk bonnet is enclosing and demure.

Of particular interest are the long linen mittens, kept with the dresses, mob cap and bonnet: they appear very similar to those worn by the young woman of 1806 on p. 85. They are also of a style frequently seen in the mid 18th century; these though are plain without any coloured silk on the facings or any embroidery. They have been worn a very great deal, so much so that the fine stitching on the back has been almost worn away.

374

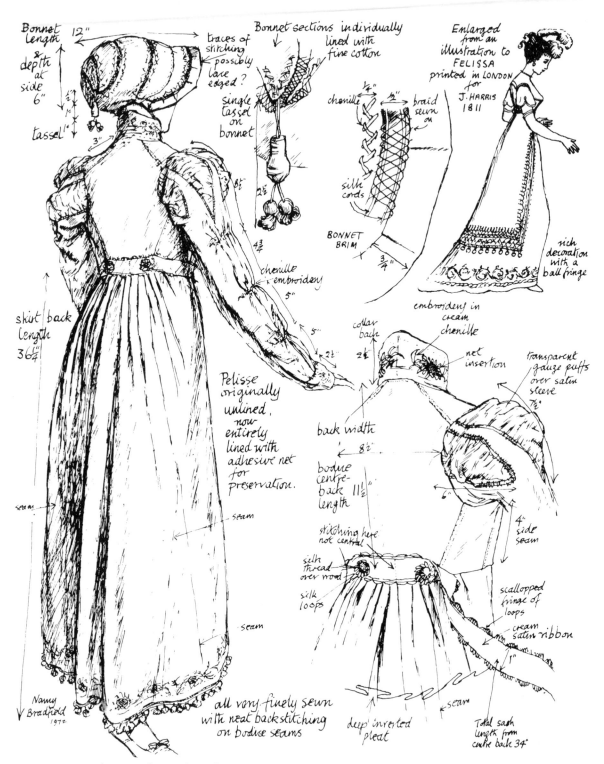

Bonnet Length 12"
& depth at side 6"

tassel 1"

3"

traces of stitching possibly lace edged?

single tassel on bonnet

2½"

4¾"

Bonnet sections individually lined with fine cotton

chenille ¼" ½" braid sewn on

silk cords

BONNET BRIM

¾"

Enlarged from an illustration to FELISSA printed in LONDON for J. HARRIS 1811

rich decoration with a ball fringe

embroidery in cream chenille

skirt back length 36¼"

8½"

chenille embroidery

5"

5"

2½"

Pelisse originally unlined, now entirely lined with adhesive net for preservation.

seam

seam

seam

Nancy Bradfield 1972

Pelisse originally unlined, now entirely lined with adhesive net for preservation.

collar back

2½"

net insertion

transparent gauze puffs over satin sleeve 7½"

back width 8½"

bodice centre-back length 11½"

6"

4" side seam

stitching here not central

silk thread over wood

silk loops

scallopped fringe of loops

cream satin ribbon

1"

deep inverted pleat

seam

Total sash length from centre back 34"

all very finely sewn with neat back stitching on bodice seams

An 1814 pelisse and matching bonnet
This delicate cream satin pelisse and bonnet were worn by Mary Dunham in 1814, when she married John Anthony at Chalfont St Giles, Bucks.

The high waistline with fine silk ribbon sash, the charming sleeves with the petal-shaped gauze puffs, and the gathered bands of embroidery down the arm, together with the delight-

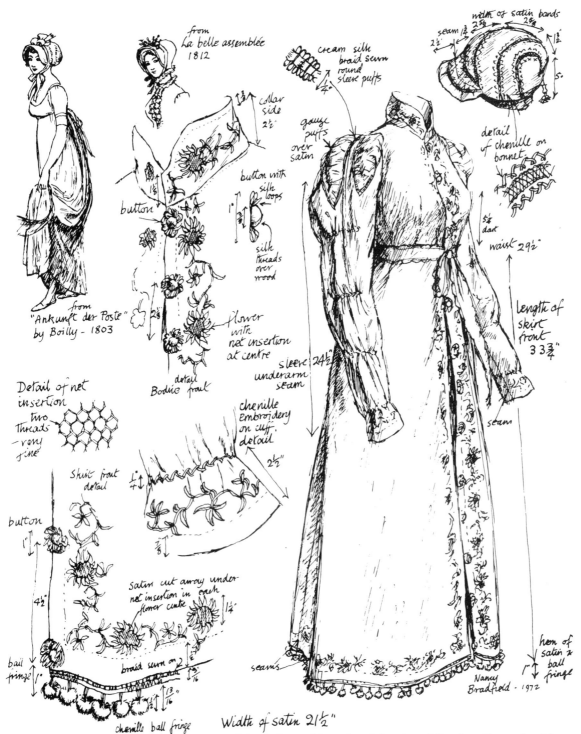

from
La belle assemblée
1812

from
"Ankunft der Poste"
by Boilly - 1803

cream silk
braid sewn
round
sleeve puffs

width of satin bands
2¾ 2¾
seam 1½
2½
1½
5.
detail of chenille on bonnet

collar
side
2½
1¾

1⅜

button

button with
silk
loops
1"
¾
2½
silk
threads
over
wood

gauze
puffs
over
satin

flower
with
net insertion
at centre

detail
Bodice front

Detail of net
insertion
two
threads
- very
fine

Skirt front
detail

button
1"

4½

chenille
embroidery
on cuff
detail
4¼
2½"
⅞

satin cut away under
net insertion in each
flower centre
1¼

braid sewn on 2
⅜
3/16
13/16"
⅜

ball
fringe 1"

chenille ball fringe

Width of satin 21½"

5¼
dart
waist 29½"

length of
skirt
front
33¾"

sleeve 24½
underarm
seam

seam

seams

hem of
satin &
ball
fringe
1"

Nancy
Bradfield - 1972

fully shaped bonnet, are all typical of the fashionable style of the time. The chenille embroidery and ball fringe are also in matching cream colour; so too is the net insertion in each flower centre. Net was manufactured at Nottingham from 1810. Ball fringes recur later, 1908, 1909 and 1919. The bonnet was held in place by ribbons and decorated with flowers or feathers.

The dress which was worn under the pelisse was probably used on many other occasions; it has not survived. Mrs Mary Anthony's great-great-niece Mrs Betty Birks has very kindly given pelisse and bonnet to my collection.

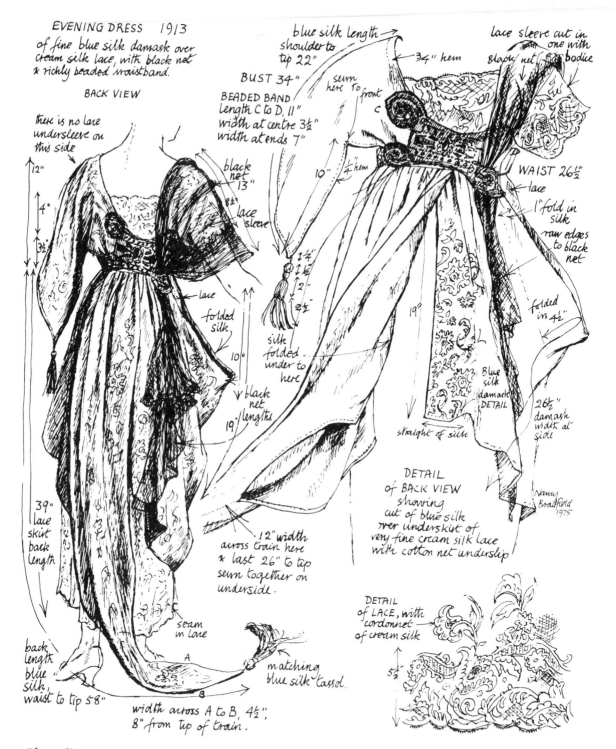

Blue silk and cream lace evening dress of 1913

The designer, in the creation of this gown, has exploited the nature of the materials, draping the feminine form to enhance the curves and drawing attention to the face and neck, the waist, and long line of leg from hip to ankle.

All this is so soon to change within the next decade, when dresses will hang straight from shoulder to hem, with back and front of the garment often identical, without any shaping or

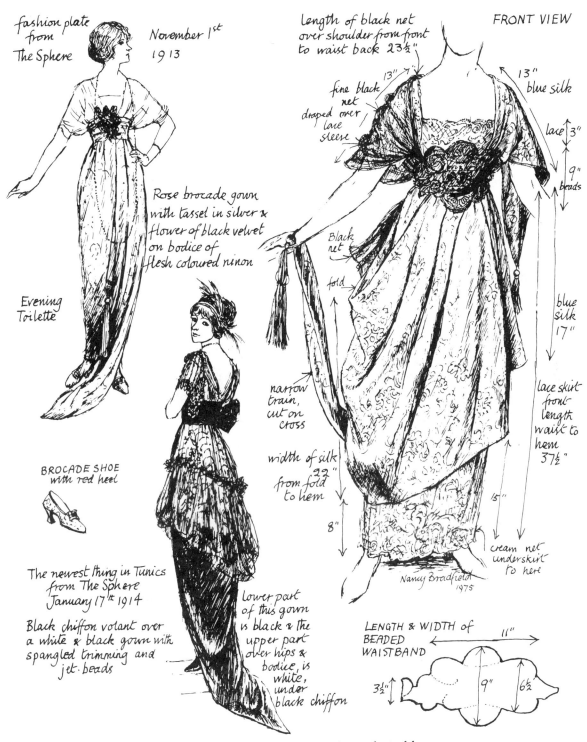

fashion plate from The Sphere

November 1st 1913

Rose brocade gown with tassel in silver & flower of black velvet on bodice of flesh coloured ninon

Evening Toilette

BROCADE SHOE with red heel

The newest thing in Tunics from The Sphere January 17th 1914

Black chiffon volant over a white & black gown with spangled trimming and jet beads

Lower part of this gown is black & the upper part over hips & bodice, is white, under black chiffon

Length of black net over shoulder from front to waist back 23½"

FRONT VIEW

fine black net draped over lace sleeve

13" 7"

13" blue silk

lace 3"

9" beads

Black net

fold

narrow train, cut on cross

width of silk 22" from fold to hem

8"

blue silk 17"

lace skirt front length waist to hem 37½"

15"

cream net underskirt to here

Nancy Bradfield 1975

LENGTH & WIDTH of BEADED WAISTBAND

11"

3½"

9"

6½"

fastenings, ignoring all the features previously thought so desirable.

But now, by 1913, designers turn to the East for their inspiration, following the dramatic effect Léon Bakst's costumes for *Schéhérazade* had on the world of fashion, although before Diaghilev's ballet appeared in Paris in 1909 and London in 1910, another designer, Paul Poiret, had already moved away from the then orthodox styles. This dress is typical of these few pre-war years. Tassels were very much in fashion by 1910 and gave added movement to the dress.

An advertisement for Cyclax Beauty preparations in the *Lady's Pictorial* of October 25th 1913 shows a couple dancing the new sensational Tango; the young woman's dress has a small pointed train, not quite so long as the one shown here, but she allows hers, complete with tassel, to swing out freely behind her as she dances.

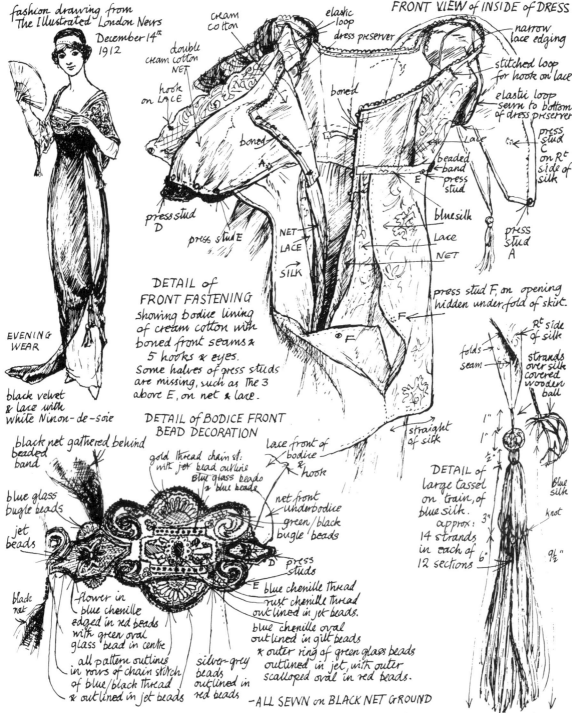

The complicated hidden fastenings on dresses at this time show that many women still employ a maid; no one could have got in or out of such a gown as this without assistance.

So before Europe was plunged into World War I, fashions were set on the brink of change; even the long ropes of beads or pearls, as well as the tunic tops or drapery, for daytime or evening wear, were taking the eye downward, away from the waist and towards hip level.

This charming dress was given to Mrs Margaret Bodley by Mrs L. Carpenter, who, as a child, remembers it being made for her mother. It has now been presented to my collection.

CYCLING IN THE 1890s

All the information in this article is based on letters and papers from the Buckman files of the late 1890s, which because of their considerable interest were recently lent to me for examination.

While research was being carried out recently into the life of S. S. Buckman, the geologist, by Dr Hugh Torrens of the University of Keele, some fascinating papers were found. These letters, cuttings, and photographs were kindly lent to me to examine, as they related to certain aspects of women's dress, and some of them threw new light on various features. I therefore feel that a brief outline of their contents would be of value to others interested in Victorian dress.

Sydney Savory Buckman became involved in the Rational Dress League during the late 1890's. As a geologist, he welcomed the advent of the bicycle to help him in his field of work, 'making long forays into the Cotswolds from his home in Cheltenham.' He encouraged his wife and four daughters to take up cycling, and they often accompanied him on his excursions. It was thus inevitable that he should become involved in the question of what was practical and fitting for a lady to wear when riding a cycle. Were bloomers suitable?

The *Rational Dress Gazette* No. 16, January 1900, in the Buckman files proved extremely interesting on the historical aspect of this garment, and an article by Edward M. Richards entitled 'Bloomerism' (reprinted from the *Wexford Independent*) drew attention to the true origin of this practical attire.

In America in 1848 two ladies, Mary Crayin and Mrs Noyes, were the first to appear in public wearing trousers under short frocks, which was a costume on the same general lines as that worn among the North American Indian women since the first settlement of the country, and one that had certainly existed from time immemorial in the East.

Mrs Amelia Bloomer '(as she herself often declared) so far from having invented the reform dress, was neither the first to advocate it, nor the first to wear it.'. . . 'Her part was simply this. After the idea had been started by others, she saw the merit of it and favoured the movement in her

journal *The Lily*. Of course, she was amongst the first early wearers. . . .' 'It was the Press of the time that coined the name "Bloomerism", the public at once adopted it, and gave the editress of *The Lily* the credit of the new style, and with her it will probably ever (wrongfully) remain.'

Owing to the ridicule and open opposition from all sides, the wearing of bloomers was abandoned in 1851, and they were not revived again for over forty years.

By 1895 a tailored outfit comprising jacket and knickerbockers was gaining considerable popularity among the cycling ladies of America, France and Germany. The Italians were less enthusiastic, as a notice displayed in 1897 in some of their buses in Florence indicates; translated, it reads 'Female cyclists wearing the rational costume, or being otherwise indecently dressed, are not allowed to use these omnibuses.'

In Cheltenham, in February 1897, the Western Rational Dress Club was formed, the President being Viscountess Harberton. S. S. Buckman was Secretary, and his wife Captain. The leaflet issued setting down the objects of the club is well worth reading:

The objects of the Club are the following:—

1. To promote a dress-reform whereby Ladies may enjoy outdoor exercise with greater comfort and less fatigue.

2. To advocate the wearing (particularly for Cycling) of the Zouave or Knickerbocker Costume, as adopted by the ladies of France, Germany and America.

3. To take all necessary steps, in connection with kindred Associations in London, to encourage this desirable reform.

The disadvantages of the skirt for cycling are numerous. Under ordinary circumstances it adds so greatly to the labour that it makes 30 miles more tiring than 50 would be. It makes riding against a headwind almost impossible. It adds greatly to the danger, and has been the cause of several serious accidents. Its flopping with every movement of the rider is very unbecoming. It necessitates the employment of a weaker and 8lbs. heavier machine. The disadvantages of the skirt for any outdoor exercise are obvious. Even by holding it up, which is a fatigue, the wearer cannot prevent it from becoming wet and draggled with mud. Its use for sweeping the steps of buildings and vehicles cannot be commended.

None of these disadvantages belong to the new style of costume, which is to be commended from the point of view of health, comfort and safety.

The Club consists of (1) Members, (2) Associate-Members, (3) Associates. Those who always wear Rational Dress for cycling

re eligible as Members; those who wear it occasionally, as Associate-
Members; those who do not wear it, but who sympathise with the
objects of the Club, are eligible as Associates.

The Annual Subscription of Members is 2/6, of Associate-
Members 2/-, of Associates 1/6; but only Members have the right to
vote.

Both Ladies and Gentlemen may belong to the Club.

(MRS.) M. BUCKMAN,
Captain.

Those who advocated this practical and comfortable form of dress for the active woman saw to
it that as much as possible was done to draw attention to the value of this style. Reports of accidents
involving lady cyclists wearing skirts appeared frequently in the Press; one of them, which is typical,
appeared in *The Citizen* for Friday April 23rd 1897:

THE DANGERS OF SKIRTS.

A CHELTENHAM LADY'S EXPERIENCE.

On Good Friday (says a correspondent) a Cheltenham lady set out
for Gloucester. She was not a novice at cycling as she had ridden
for three years; but she was riding a strange machine. In about two
miles her skirt caught in the gearing, so that she became tightly
fixed, and could only dismount with difficulty. Her companions
tried in vain to extricate her. Several male cyclists stopped to offer
assistance. They took the machine more or less to pieces, but it was
useless. The skirt had to be cut away, and then got out of the cog-
wheel in pieces. Then the journey was resumed, but still the now
dilapidated skirt would not behave; and several dismounts were
necessary to relieve entanglements. Finally the apprehension of
catching made her so nervous that when the road became a bit
tricky in Gloucester she lost her presence of mind and fell on the
tramlines, cut her face badly, and had to be carried into a chemist's
shop. She returned home by rail. *Moral:*—The only safe dress for
cycling is knickerbockers, whether the machine be familiar or
strange, bar frame or open framed, whether it be guarded or
unguarded, whether the garments be wide or narrow—the lady
clad in knickerbockers has not to think at all of these matters. She
is perfectly free from any apprehension of catching, with its
attendant dangers.

By the autumn of 1897 seven cycling clubs had
banded together, and had arranged that members
wearing rational dress should, in order to publicize
the movement, cycle from London to Oxford. The
day chosen, however, September 4th, was showery
and windy, and made progress extremely difficult.
The bifurcated attire caused much ridicule from
the crowd, and some ladies at first wore skirts over
their knickerbockers. But although many members never reached Oxford, some fifty cyclists
eventually arrived, and dinner at the Clarendon
Hotel took place as planned. The following morning a competition was held to choose the three
most approved costumes; one worn by Miss Maude
Gatliff was very similar to the outfit seen on Miss
M. Coole in the cycle advertisement.

MISS M. COOLE on the "ROYAL SPITFIRE" Cycle

In 1898 various incidents occurred which, although they gave considerable publicity to rational
dress, did not really help the movement to any
great extent, and must certainly have given the
ladies concerned some unpleasant moments.

Landlords of some hotels refused to serve
women wearing knickerbockers; in fact, they were
often surprisingly rude. One, Richard S. Cook of
the White Horse Hotel, Dorking, wrote to the edi-
tor of the *Daily Mail* on May 11th, saying:

I have given orders that women in that dis-
gusting dress called rationals are not to be
admitted into my coffee-room, as they are
objectionable to ladies and gentlemen staying
there, and should be very pleased if any one
aggrieved would take out a summons against
me and let the magistrate decide the matter.

This in fact is exactly what Viscountess Harberton
did, and the court case that followed in 1899 was
reported in all the papers. She had hoped to make
a test case of a visit to the Hautboy Hotel, Ockham,
but the result was disappointing. The *Daily Mail*
reported the whole matter very fairly:

DAILY MAIL.
LADY HARBERTON'S BLOOMERS.

The case of Viscountess Harberton against Mrs. Sprague, the landlady of the Hautboy Hotel at Ockham, heard yesterday at the Surrey Quarter Sessions, leaves the rational dress question exactly where it was. Bloomers have been neither banned nor vindicated.

The fact is that the Cyclists' Touring Club, who took up Lady Harberton's complaint, made a mistake in tactics by selecting for championship a very weak case, from their point of view. There have been earlier cases in which publicans have courted formidable indictment by adopting towards the bifurcated feminine costume a hostility much less reasoning than that of the discreet Mrs. Sprague. The club which hesitated to prosecute in those cases was lost when it tackled the resourceful dame of the Hautboy, at Ockham, though her conduct may not have approximated to a model of astuteness.

Publicans will be making a great mistake if they infer that yesterday's decision gives them any right to determine what clothes their guests shall wear. The jury has not given them a mandate to dictate to women bicyclists whether they shall come in skirts or in bloomers, any more than it has authorised them to insist upon linen shirts and birdseye ties for every man who orders a chop. Mrs. Sprague did her duty to frequenters of her coffee-room by closing its doors against Lady Harberton's bloomers; for some customers object to sitting down with the "rationally" attired woman, and it is not for the landlady to inquire into the academic question of whether such objections are well or ill founded. But having done her duty to her customers Mrs. Sprague might well have offered an adequate substitute in the way of accommodation to Lady Harberton. The bar parlour of an inn is not a very pleasant place for a lady to lunch in. Still, it seems to be the law that guests cannot choose their refreshment room, and the jury was obviously of opinion that the bar parlour was good enough for the bifurcated woman. This is not very satisfactory, but the only thing for the bifurcated is to change the law.

In spite of the obvious benefits of rational dress, the ordinary woman remained generally unconvinced, and the men, it seems, of over seventy years ago preferred to see their womenfolk in long skirts and petticoats, with only an occasional glimpse of a well-turned ankle.

A personal letter written by Viscountess Harberton to Sydney Buckman gives an intimate account of the situation as she saw it on February 5th, 1899. Writing from 108 Cromwell Road, S.W., she says:

Dear Mr Buckman

So many thanks for the papers you lent me. I had not seen some of them at all as I only began to take the "Lady's Own" last year, and even then I did not keep all the extracts as I should have done. I have now copied all the skirt accidents in cycling, as they may as well be given to our Counsel to work up into his speech. By the way I saw in the James' Gazette of Friday that "The Road" has taken up the Landlady's case and is starting a subscription for her Legal expenses, "as it has a great dislike to this latest fad of lady cyclists!" I have no idea what "The Road" may be, but remembering all the tales about the Gaiety Coach, I daresay it has something to do with coaching. It is rather a good thing for us, as it will prevent any maudlin talk about a wealthy Association backing one side up against a woman with her living to make etc. That sort of thing is apt to influence a jury.

I can quite well undertake to make 25 copies of the circular when it is wanted. I am afraid you are very busy, but in the end this will

give you less work. Unless indeed Rational Dress makes a sudden start, of which I grieve to say I see no beginning at present.

I fear this Society will accomplish nothing more than the old one did. People join, and write, and talk, but until they wear the dress no progress has been made. Quite between ourselves I am sure there are less wearing it than there were a year ago, and very many less than there were two years ago. But this is only for the elect, as its no use telling the enemies that sort of thing. Except myself I don't think I have seen one this winter! And the Club runs have nearly ceased. It is not very encouraging!

Ever, Your's very truly

F. W. HARBERTON

But although the champion of rational dress was despondent, knickerbockers did continue in use, and some were still to be seen during the first few years of the twentieth century.

T. H. Holding, in his third edition of *The Direct System of Ladies' Cutting*, published in 1897, clearly agrees with the Viscountess:

Bloomers, fortunately or unfortunately, are not popular in England. Many efforts have been made during the past three years to bring them into use as on the Continent, but English ladies insist on cycling in skirts, and not only taboo the wideness, but almost boycott the ladies who wear these garments.

Now, after a lapse of more than half a century, Englishwomen of all ages, shapes and sizes have been wearing the trouser suit since 1964—and consider themselves very fashionable. . . .

383

BOOKS CONSULTED

Alison Adburgham: *A Punch History of Manners and Modes, 1841–1940* (1961).

Max von Boehn: *Die Mode, Menschen und Moden im achtzehnten Jahrhundert* (1909).
Die Mode, Menschen und Moden im neunzehnten Jahrhundert, 1790–1817 (1908).
(English translation) *Modes and Manners,* vols. iv & v (1927).

Alan Bott: *Our Fathers, 1870–1900* (1931).

Alan Bott & Irene Clephane: *Our Mothers, 1870–1900* (1932).

Anne Buck: *Victorian Costume & Costume Accessories* (1961).

C. W. & P. Cunnington and Charles Beard: *A Dictionary of English Costume* (1960).

C. W. Cunnington: *Englishwomen's Clothing in the Nineteenth Century* (1937).
Englishwomen's Clothing in the Present Century (1952).

C. W. & P. Cunnington: *Handbook of English Costume in the Nineteenth Century* (1959).
History of Underclothes (1951).
A Picture History of English Costume (1960).

P. Cunnington & Anne Buck: *Children's Costume in England, 1300–1900* (1965).

John W. Dodds: *The Age of Paradox, 1841–1851* (1953).

Joan Edwards: *Bead Embroidery* (1966).

Alison Gernsheim: *Fashion and Reality, 1840–1914* (1963).

Charles Gibbs-Smith: *The Fashionable Lady in the Nineteenth Century* (1960).

T. H. Holding: *The Direct System of Ladies' Cutting,* 3rd edition (1897).

Vyvyan Holland: *Handcoloured Fashion Plates, 1770–1899* (1955).

John Irwen: *Shawls* (1955).

R. Brimley Johnson: *Mrs Delany* (1925).

Francis M. Kelly & Randolph Schwabe: *Historic Costume, 1490–1790* (1925).

Carl Köhler: *A History of Costume* (1928).

James Laver: *Taste and Fashion, from the French Revolution to the Present Day* (1945).

Lady Victoria Manners & G. C. Williamson: *John Zoffany, R.A., His Life and Works, 1735–1810* (1920).

Mrs Bury Palliser: *History of Lace* (1865).

Samuel Pepys: *Diary and Correspondence,* deciphered by the Rev. J. Smith from the original shorthand MS. in the Pepysian Library, published by George Bell & Sons (1898).

Jacques Ruppert: *Le Costume, l'antiquité et le moyen âge* (1930).

Mary Sharp: *Point and Pillow Lace* (1913).

Lawrence E. Tanner & J. L. Nevinson: *Archaeologia,* vol. lxxxv, an article on 'Some later Funeral Effigies in Westminster Abbey' (1936).

Andrew W. Tuck: *Forgotten Children's Books* (1898–99).

Norah Waugh: *Corsets and Crinolines* (1954).

MUSEUM PUBLICATIONS

London Museum: Catalogue No. 5, *Costume.*

Manchester City Art Galleries: *Gallery of English Costume,* women's costume booklets, vols. 1 to 6.

Victoria and Albert Museum: *English Printed Textiles, 1720–1836* (1960).
17th and 18th Century Costume (1959).

PERIODICALS

The Beau Monde.
La Belle Assemblée.
Country Life.
The Englishwoman's Domestic Magazine.
The Illustrated London News.
Le Journal des Demoiselles.
The Ladies' Cabinet.
The Ladies' Field.
The Lady's Magazine.
The Ladies' Mirror.
The Lady's Monthly Museum.
The Lady's Own Paper.
The Ladies' Pocket Magazine.
The Ladies' Treasury.
Petit Courrier des Dames.
Punch, or the London Charivari.

INDEX